printmakers' secrets

anthony dyson

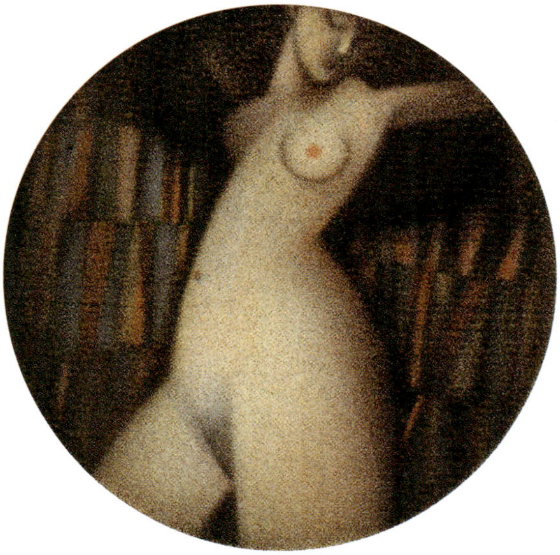

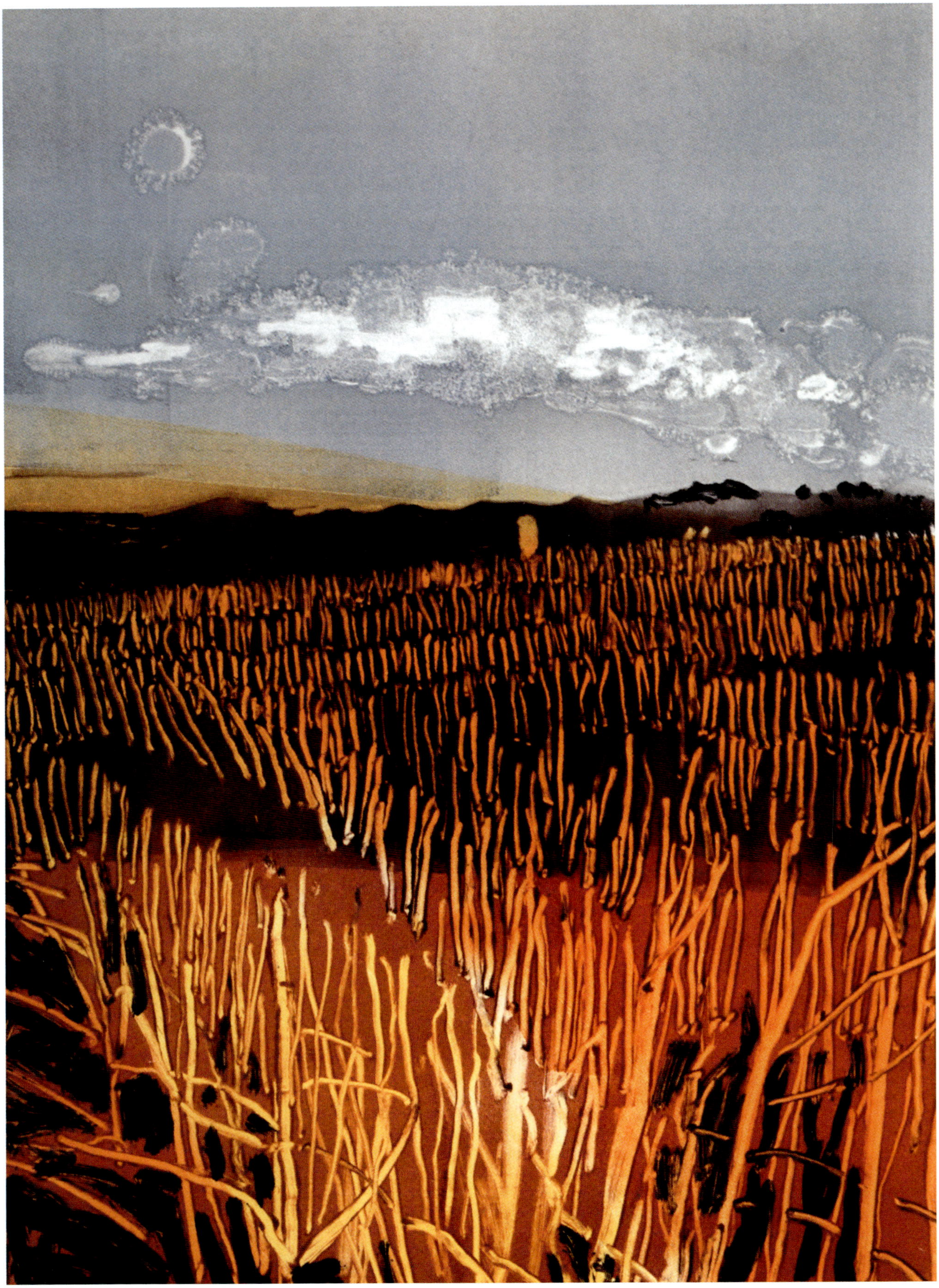

printmakers' secrets

anthony dyson

Bloomsbury Visual Arts
An imprint of Bloomsbury Publishing Plc

BLOOMSBURY
LONDON • OXFORD • NEW YORK • NEW DELHI • SYDNEY

Bloomsbury Visual Arts
An imprint of Bloomsbury Publishing Plc

Imprint previously known as A&C Black Visual Arts

50 Bedford Square
London
WC1B 3DP
UK

1385 Broadway
New York
NY 10018
USA

www.bloomsbury.com

BLOOMSBURY and the Diana logo are trademarks of Bloomsbury Publishing Plc

First published in 2009 by A&C Black
Reprinted 2011
Reprinted by Bloomsbury Visual Arts 2016

British Library Cataloguing-in-Publication Data
A catalogue record for this book is available from the British Library.

ISBN: 978-0-7136-8911-2

Library of Congress Cataloging-in-Publication Data
A catalog record for this book is available from the Library of Congress

Book design by Sutchinda Thompson and Jo Tapper
Cover design by Sutchinda Thompson
Commissioning Editor: Susan James
Managing Editor: Sophie Page
Copy Editor: Julian Beecroft
Proofreader: Julian Beecroft
Editorial Consultant: Anne Desmet

Name page:
Etude III, Roger Harris, 1999. Mezzotint, 6.8 cm (2¾ in.) diameter.
Frontispiece:
Landscape with White Tower, Howard Jeffs, 2004. Monotype, 38 × 28 cm (15 × 11 in.).

Printed and bound in India

Contents

Foreword

This is a most exciting time for printmaking. I might be spending months cutting a woodblock, or even years on a portfolio of etchings (such as the Betjeman's Women *I am currently working on). On the other hand, I can go to the Coriander Studios in Perivale with a packet of images in my pocket and, working on a computer with Brad Faine or his son Dan, I could by the end of the day have made ten images measuring up to ten feet by thirty on an inkjet machine.*

These extremes embrace original printmaking of many kinds; it is clear that the artists contributing their first-hand accounts to this book are, between them, exploring to the full this wide range of possibilities from the traditional to the new.

Sir Peter Blake, CBE, RDI, RE, RA (resigned)

Acknowledgements

My debts of gratitude are many: to all the colleagues who have with such openness contributed accounts of their working procedures; to Nana Shiomi RE, a visit to whose studio set me thinking about a project of this kind; to Jonathan Parker for valued advice at an early stage of planning it; to Susan James, Commissioning Editor at A&C Black, for her belief in the book's feasibility and for her constant encouragement during its evolution; to her colleague, Sophie Page, for efficiently seeing it through to press; to Sutchinda Thompson and Jo Tapper for their sensitive approach to its design; to Denise Dyson and Tamra Cave for invaluable help with typing and photography respectively; to Hilary Paynter PRE for her support and her shrewd observations on many of the scripts; to Professor David Ferry ARE for advice on glossary items relating to computer-generated prints; to Gerry Baptist ARE for giving me an appreciation of the role of computers in printmaking and for allowing me to illustrate my introduction with one of his prints, as did Flora McLachlan ARE and Glynn Thomas RE, to both of whom I am also indebted; to Hannah Hawksworth of the Bankside Gallery, who compiled the list of contributors and their contact details; and, above all, to Anne Desmet RE who, as Editorial Consultant, thoroughly scrutinised all the scripts, making many valuable suggestions and saving me from many an error. Needless to add, any extant mistakes and omissions are attributable only to me.

A.D.

Introduction

Although I studied printmaking at art school it was some years later, whilst doing art-historical research, that I stumbled across an experience that was to implant in me an enduring fascination for the many ingenious and ever-changing ways in which prints are made. Quite by chance, I was invited to visit what was simply described to me as 'a printer's workshop'; I was totally unprepared for what I found. I entered the shabby building in south-west London to be greeted by a remarkable scene that transported me back to the 19th century: before me was a row of half a dozen rolling presses, some of them with enormous flywheels six feet in diameter and each operated by a printer with hands blackened to the wrist. I was to discover that the firm (at that time named Thomas Ross & Sons) had an unbroken record of transactions dating back to 1833, the year of its foundation, and that among the several thousand plates in its possession were some of the finest examples of the work of once-celebrated engravers, produced in close collaboration with George Stubbs, Thomas Gainsborough, John Constable, J.M.W. Turner and many other prominent artists. I was hooked. I changed my field of study and, inspired by the rich resources at Ross's, I spent the next nine years researching the history and techniques of reproductive intaglio prints in 19th-century Britain (1).

Having until then thought of printmaking as a mainly autographic process, I began to appreciate the different degrees to which skilled engravers and master printers also had a creative role. The search led me in many different directions. An early discovery was the renowned studio in Paris that had been founded in 1929 by Roger Lacourière but is now, sadly, dismantled (2). When I first visited in 1979 Lacourière had died, but his assistants, Robert and Jacques Frélaut, showed me plates by Chagall, Picasso, Henry Moore and other modern masters with whom they had been collaborating (3); and in the last year or two visits to London studios – notably Advanced Graphics London – have given me deepened insights into the ever-evolving collaboration of artist and master printer (4).

The studios of individual artists, often with restricted space and equipment, have also been of great interest to me. The beautiful reproductive mezzotint plates of

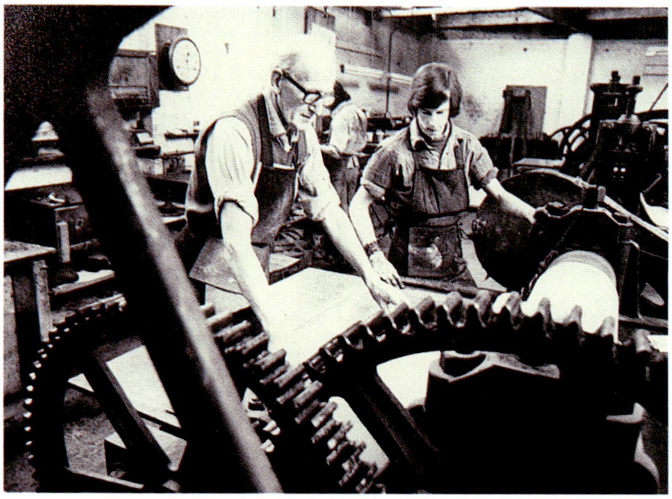

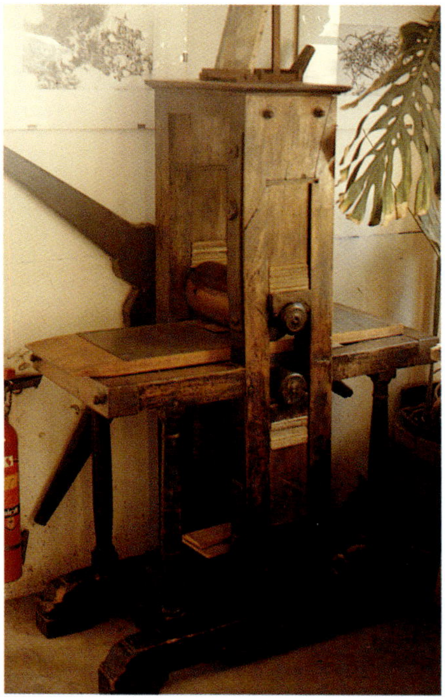

Above: Philip McQueen, master printer at Thomas Ross & Sons, working with an apprentice in the 1970s

Left: A wooden press (probably 18th-c) at Lacourière's, a forerunner of the later iron presses and symbolic of the studio's commitment to fine intaglio printing.
Photograph: the author

Laurence Josset RE (1910–95) were worked on with infinite patience at his dining table and were proofed at intervals on his 150-year-old rolling press in an adjoining lean-to shed (5); and I have had the privilege of visiting the studios of many printmakers of a younger generation – some of them contributors to this book – who often work in cramped conditions with an enterprising range of materials

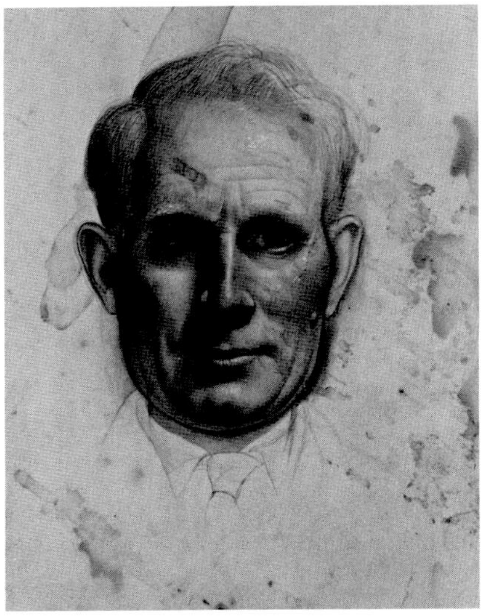

Lawrence Josset, self-portrait c.1970, pencil and watercolour heightened with gouache, 12 x 10 cm (4 ¾ x 4 in.). Collection: the author.

and equipment, new and traditional, achieving wonderful work. It is the generally unsuspected ingenuity – the 'secrets' – of such people that has brought me to the decision to ask artist colleagues metaphorically to open their studios, reveal their sources of inspiration and describe their working methods. This book is the result.

All the contributors are members of London's Royal Society of Painter-Printmakers (RE). The title is significant: when the Society was founded in 1880 it was named The Royal Society of Painter-Etchers by artists (mainly painters) who had become impatient with the disinclination of London's Royal Academy of Arts to take seriously the printmaking aspect of their professional work. Happily, this situation no longer obtains, and in more recent years the Society's name has been modified to cater for artists working across the whole spectrum of printmaking techniques (6). The point is that these are all first and foremost artists; some of them work almost exclusively in print, but, for many, print is just one aspect of their creative output.

When the book's title was proposed, it was greeted with some misgiving even by several of the prospective contributors, who protested that they had no secrets. Whilst confident that most of my colleagues have in the literal sense no closely guarded secrets relating to their art, I was equally sure that they would have much of great interest to reveal to fellow artists and print enthusiasts alike. For many people there is a mystery (and I use the word in the 'tricks of the trade' sense in which it was applied to medieval European craftsmen) about printmaking procedures. The aim of this book is to give the reader an intimate glimpse of the relatively solitary process of pictorial invention that is the daily preoccupation of the artist who makes prints: the creative germ, the thinking that nurtures it and the technical means by which it is finally given printed form. The fascinating thing about this process is that it rarely takes place in the ordered way I have just proposed. It is a process that defies tidy analysis. The flashes of creative insight may occur at any point in the development of the work, not least whilst the technical solutions are being devised. It might justifiably be argued that it is hardly relevant to the artist to enter into this kind of self-examination; his or her business is the inventing of images. It may be thought that the study of the artistic process may be left to the art historian and the philosopher; but this is so only up to a point. The struggles of the artist-printmaker can be described with more vivid immediacy by those whose hands have been stained with ink and calloused by the press handle.

There is widespread misunderstanding of the term 'print'. One of the difficulties is that the word covers such a broad range of printing activity, so it would be just as well to establish at the outset the meaning of the term as used throughout this book. I wish to make a clear distinction between images which are conceived from the outset as prints – artists' original prints – and those which simply reproduce images first created in another medium. My concern and that of my artist colleagues is with the former. Artists' prints may come about in many different ways. Sometimes, as we have seen, an artist will independently undertake the whole process from idea to completion; sometimes he or she may enlist the collaboration of a master printer who may to a greater or lesser extent contribute to the cutting of a block or the etching of a plate; but always, even though the work may not be entirely autographic, the concept is the artist's and the essential control remains with the artist from the beginning of the process to the signing of the edition – and this, incidentally, was largely true of the artist-reproductive engraver collaboration of former times (7).

The techniques used by artist-printmakers today are many. Often, they are not easy to classify because different techniques may be used in combination and individual artists often devise their own unorthodox ways of achieving their creative ends. Furthermore, the field has become even more varied with the increasing use of computer-generated images and, often, the combining of these with hand-drawn imagery, screen-printing and other methods. Whilst, taken together, there is a rich store of technical information in the texts that follow, it may be useful at the outset to give a brief 'bare bones' account of the main groups into which these various approaches fall.

Glynn Thomas RE, **Whitby**, 2007. Etching, 36 x 60 cm (14¼ x 23 ⅝ in.)

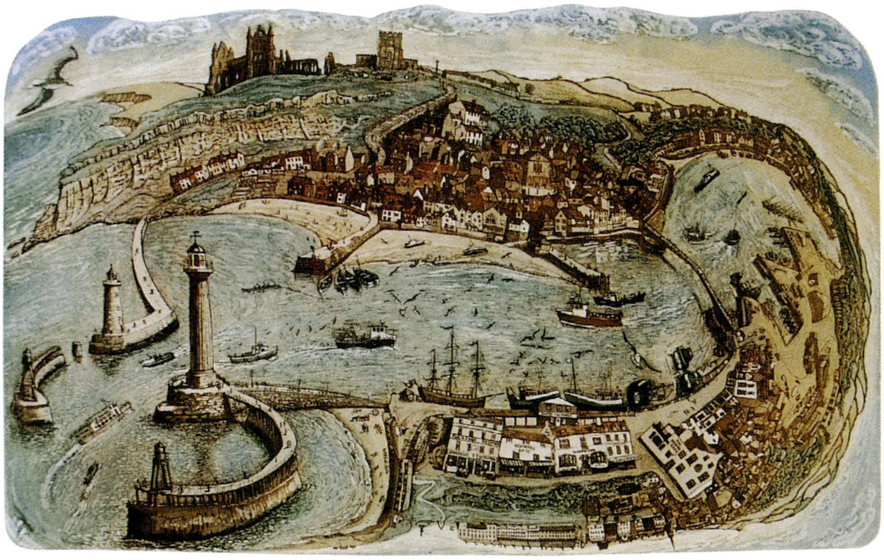

Relief prints, such as woodcuts, wood engravings and linocuts, are impressions taken from inked surfaces. In a woodcut, knives and gouges (and sometimes, these days, electric routers) are used to make incisions into the side grain of a woodblock; such prints are usually bold in character. Wood engraving differs in that the cuts are made with fine engraving tools into the end grain of a block of hardwood (such as boxwood) that has a smoothed surface that makes great delicacy possible. Artificial substitutes for the traditional boxwood are often used. Linocut, used with dramatic power by Picasso and Michael Rothenstein, for example, is a 20th-century descendant of the woodcut.

Intaglio prints are taken from ink wiped into the pits and grooves of a metal plate or other suitable matrix with a pad of stiff scrim (tarlatan). Etchings, aquatints, engravings, drypoints and mezzotints are all inked in this way and printed on damp paper by being run through a rolling press under blankets of felt. In etching, a plate of copper (or zinc or steel) is covered with a thin wax ground through which the line work is lightly drawn with a needle (properly called an etching point) to expose the metal. The back of the plate having been protected with an acid-resistant varnish, the plate is placed in a shallow tray of mordant and given a series of carefully-timed bites to create different depths of crevice, which will hold varying amounts of ink and will print as lines of different strength. Tone is sometimes added with aquatint, a way of creating in the plate a fine, pitted texture which will hold ink. Some artists colour their etchings with watercolour; others work different colours of ink into the plate's aquatint texture and run it through the press to obtain a fully chromatic image in a single impression; sometimes several plates are used, once for each different colour, and printed in superimposition to achieve a polychrome image.

Line engraving is the oldest and purest form of intaglio work. There is no mordant involved: the line is simply engraved into the bare metal. Drypoint is similar in that grooves are ploughed into a plate with a hardened point that in displacing the metal raises a burr, or irregular crest, alongside each scar. The burr, as well as its companion groove, will hold ink and give the eventual print a characteristically velvety quality. Though in line engraving and in drypoint the means may seem limited, both methods are capable of great beauty and subtlety. Mezzotint works on the same principle as drypoint in that the surface of the copperplate is displaced to create an overall burr which retains ink when the plate is wiped. The plate is systematically textured with a mezzotint rocker, a tool resembling a short, broad chisel with a curved, toothed cutting edge. The toothed edge is rocked firmly over the surface of the plate, making densely textured strips across it from edge to edge. These strips are carefully criss-crossed in as many as thirty directions until a beautifully regular surface of tiny pits and crests is formed. Even a relatively small plate can take days to prepare before work on the image begins. This is done by scraping the plate's texture to varying degrees of smoothness to create the full tonal range, unscraped parts retaining most ink, smoothest parts holding hardly any and thus giving highlights.

A collagraph is a print taken from a collaged surface; materials of all kinds, as long as they are in low-enough relief to be printed, may be glued to any flat surface such as a metal plate, plywood or hardboard. Collagraphy is a

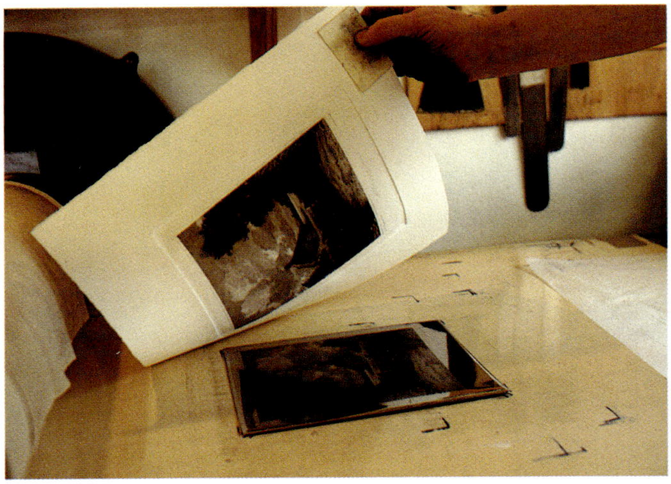

The author lifting a proof of a mezzotint plate engraved by David Lucas (1802–81) after a landscape by John Constable. Photograph: Jo Dyson

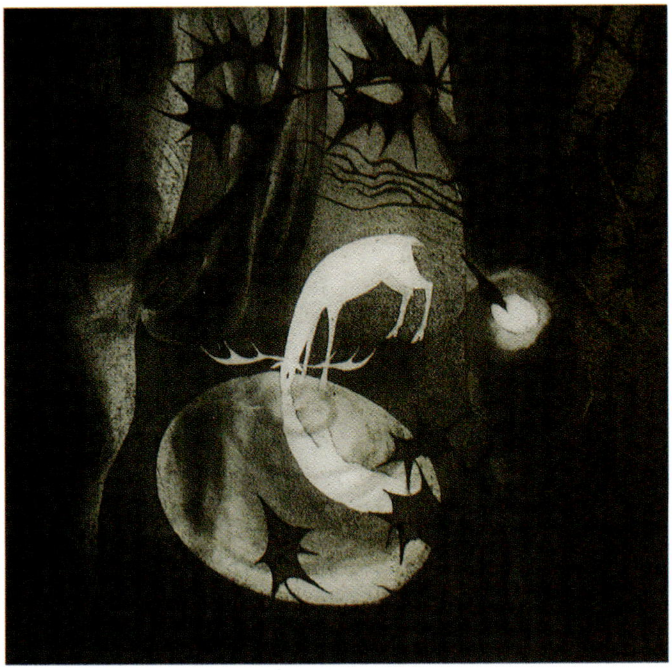

Flora McLachlan ARE, **The Wood Pool**, 2007. Etching and collagraph, 27 x 24 cm (10⅝ x 9½ in.)

hybrid technique in that the matrix may be inked in relief, intaglio or in both simultaneously. The possibilities are many: for example, a conventionally prepared etching plate may be printed over a collagraph to great effect (8).

The lithographic printing from tablets of stone that so captivated the imagination of artists as its secret spread rapidly through Europe from the turn of the 18th and 19th centuries has, since the end of the Second World War, largely been supplanted by new, lighter printing surfaces and machinery infinitely more sophisticated than the former hand-presses. The principle of making an image in greasy pigment on the absorbent surface of a smoothed slab of limestone – which when wetted will accept oil-based ink on the drawn or painted areas and not on the damped parts of the stone – enables crayon, brush and even pen drawings to be printed with great directness and faithfulness. Artists making lithographic prints today tend to collaborate with a master printer, but there are still some using stone and hand-presses with impressive results.

Screenprints are made with stencils supported on fine mesh (originally of silk but now more usually of a finely woven synthetic fabric) stretched tightly over a frame. The possibilities range widely, from simple paper stencils and brushed-on solutions to the high degree of precision attainable through the use of photographically transferred images.

A monotype is a single impression that cannot be exactly repeated, usually achieved by forming an image in printers' ink (or some other suitable medium) on an unengraved metal plate or similar surface and transferring the image to paper, either in a press or by hand pressure. From about 1874, Edgar Degas was a prominent exponent, bringing to the medium a painter's sensibility: he simply covered a blank plate with greasy ink and worked into it with fingers, rag and brush from dark to light to produce his composition; or he worked directly, applying pigment so that the result was a dark image on a paler ground. In other words, his approach was sometimes subtractive, sometimes additive (9). Monotype and monoprint are sometimes confused: the latter is an impression uniquely different from others taken from the same printing matrix.

Many artists are now making creative use of computers in producing their prints. Whilst some traditionalists may regret the apparent absence of the textural surface that is characteristic of hand-wrought prints, computer-generated images may often incorporate significant elements of traditional origin. For instance, images may be taken from different sources and 'collaged' to give a similar effect to that achieved with scissors and paste by Picasso and other innovators nearly a century ago; painted marks by the artist may be scanned electronically and transformed digitally into any one of an unlimited range of colours to add a new layer to a developing image in much the same way as each of the several blocks of a linocut image can be inked in its own colour and superimposed on the evolving image to contribute to the final effect; screenprinted layers are also often added.

All these categories of print are well represented in this book and, in addition, examples of photo-etching, as

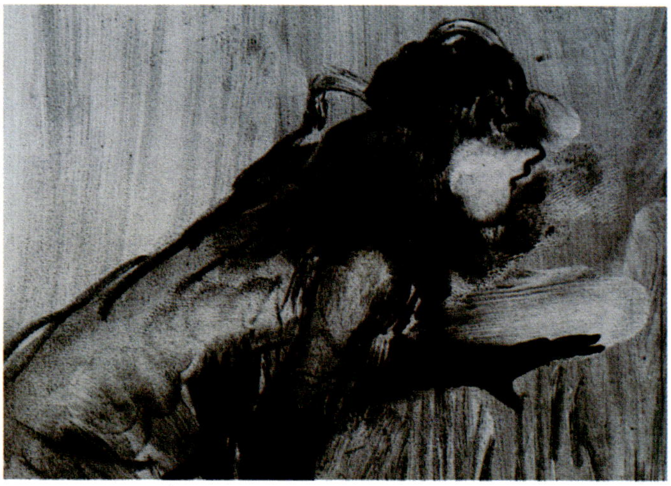

Edgar Degas, monotype

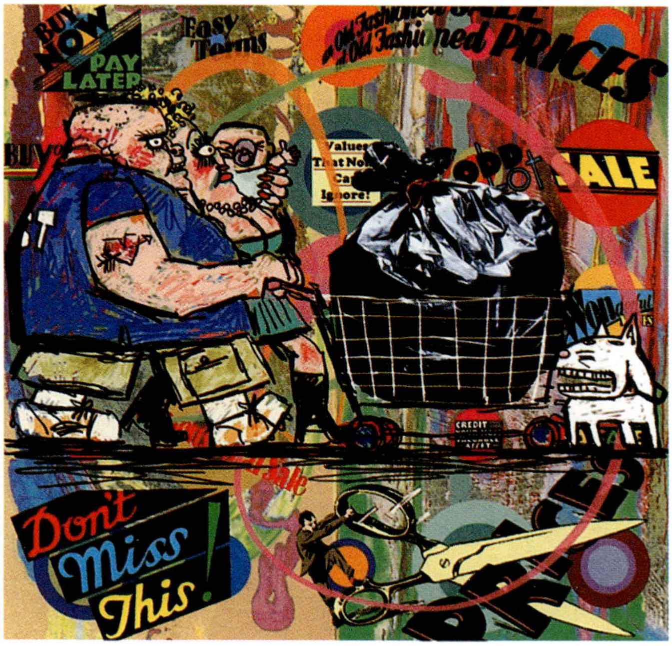

Gerald Baptist ARE, **Supermarket Man**, 2007. Digital print with screenprint, 70 x 70 cm (27½ x 27½in.)

well as print on garments and other textiles and on sculpture are discussed.

I had originally imagined that the major part of each artist's writing would focus on technical solutions. However, I have been helpfully reminded that idea and technique are always inextricably linked in the work of any dedicated artist. In their writing, many colleagues have modulated naturally from one to the other. Some have concentrated almost exclusively on the practicalities, but always with an implication of the motivating idea; others have dwelt to a large extent on sources of inspiration, but have demonstrated in their images the success with which their ideas have been given form. None of this, of course, is to overlook the role of spontaneity, of the deliberate suspension of conscious control on occasion, or of an acceptance of the happy accident.

It was decided at the outset that each artist would, in his or her own style and in the first person, give a frank and intimate account of an aspect of their work. In editing, I have tried to interfere as little as possible with the artist's individual 'voice'. Also, since this is not intended to be (except incidentally) a manual of technical instruction, I have tried to dissuade colleagues from engaging in unduly detailed discussion of generally well-understood methods. Instead, this aspect has been catered for in the brief account above and in a glossary. Due to the difficulty of classification, contributions are not grouped according to printmaking method but are simply arranged in alphabetical order of writers' names; a list of the participating artists with contact and other details can be found at the end of the book. A.D.

NOTES

1. Dyson, A., *Pictures to Print*, Farrand Press, 1984
2. Dyson, A., 'The End of an Era – Atelier Lacourière-Frélaut, Paris', p. 29, *Printmaking Today*, Vol.17 No.2, summer 2008
3. For details of Lacourière's collaboration with Picasso, see Norman Ackroyd, pp. 12–13.
4. Dyson, A., 'Perfect Partners', pp. 10–11, *Printmaking Today*, Vol.16 No.2, summer 2007
5. Dyson, A., 'Reproductive Mezzotint Engraving: the Epilogue', pp. 69–86, *Journal of the Printing Historical Society*, No. 25, 1996. For further mention of Josset see Holly Downing, p 51.
6. For a brief history of the Society, see Winkelman, J., pp. vii–xiii, *Printmakers: the Directory*, A&C Black, 2006
7. Although such engravers were reproducers of original paintings, it may be argued that their work, since it consisted of translating the visual language of paint into that of bitten and graven line, was essentially interpretative and therefore qualitatively different from that of photographic reproduction
8. For a full discussion see Hartill, B., *Collagraphs and Mixed Media Printmaking*, A&C Black, 2005
9. Janis, E.P., *Degas Monotypes*, Fogg Art Museum, Harvard, 1968

Norman Ackroyd

Etching, like swimming, depends so much on the first immersion. I was extremely fortunate over fifty years ago to be 'immersed' in etching at Leeds College of Art by Norman Webster, a consummate craftsman and enthusiast. I was immediately addicted. The scope and potential of the medium seemed unending; I instinctively realised that its limits were its freedoms.

I naturally became inquisitive about who had gone before; Dürer, Rembrandt, Goya and many others showed me that they had had the same addiction, but the one who really excited me was Picasso, and especially his collaboration with the great master printer Lacourière in the 1930s and 1940s.

High Island, Connemara, 2006. Sugar-lift aquatint, 16 x 25 cm (6⅝ x 9⅞ in.)

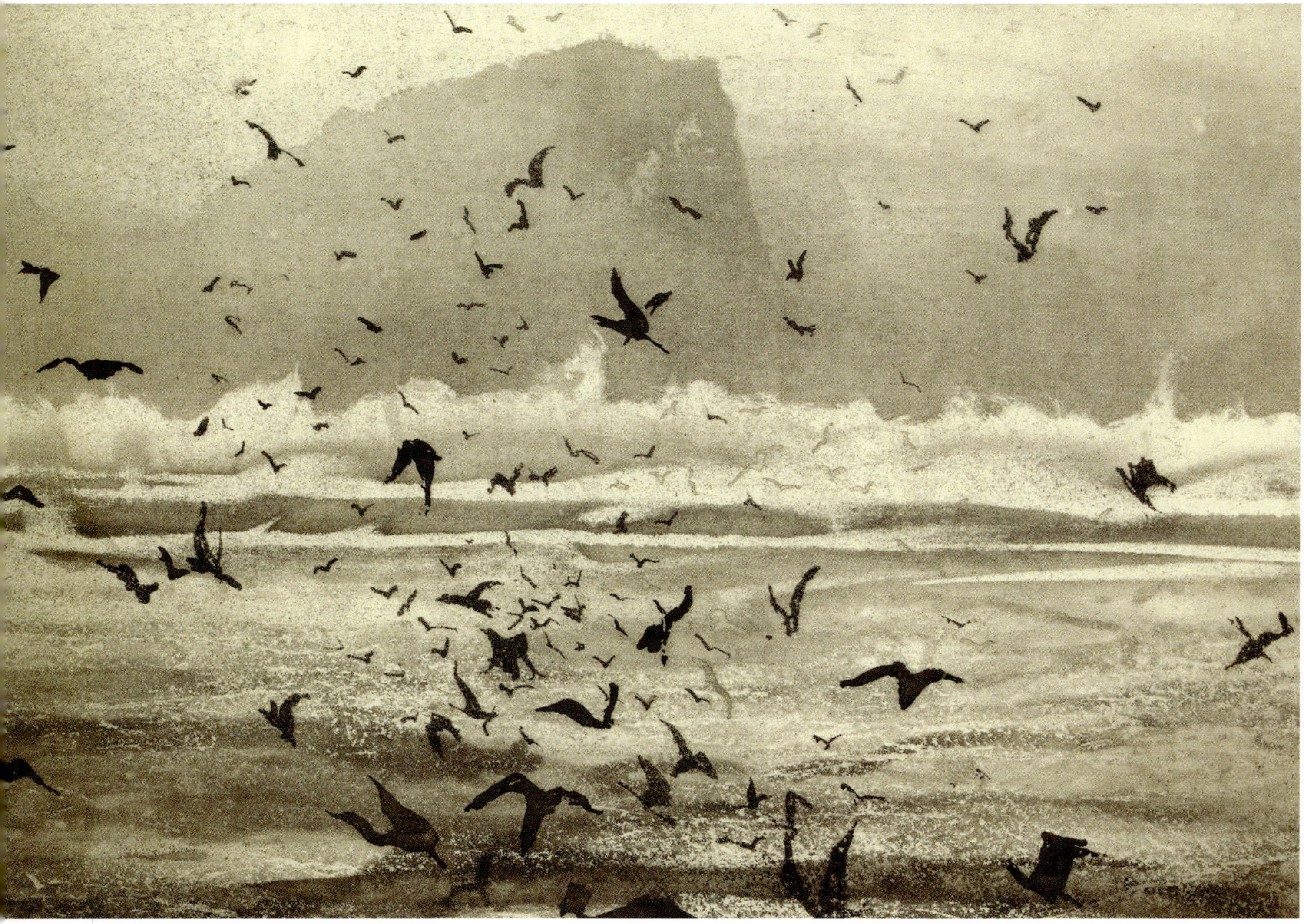

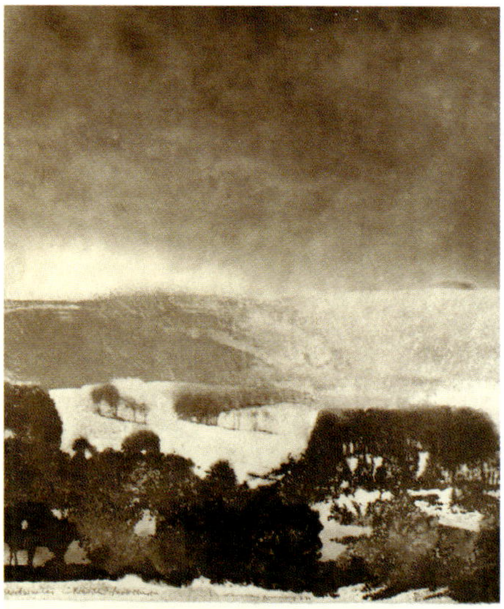

Midwinter, North Yorkshire, 1999. Sugar-lift aquatint, 59 x 52 cm (23¾ x 20½ in.)

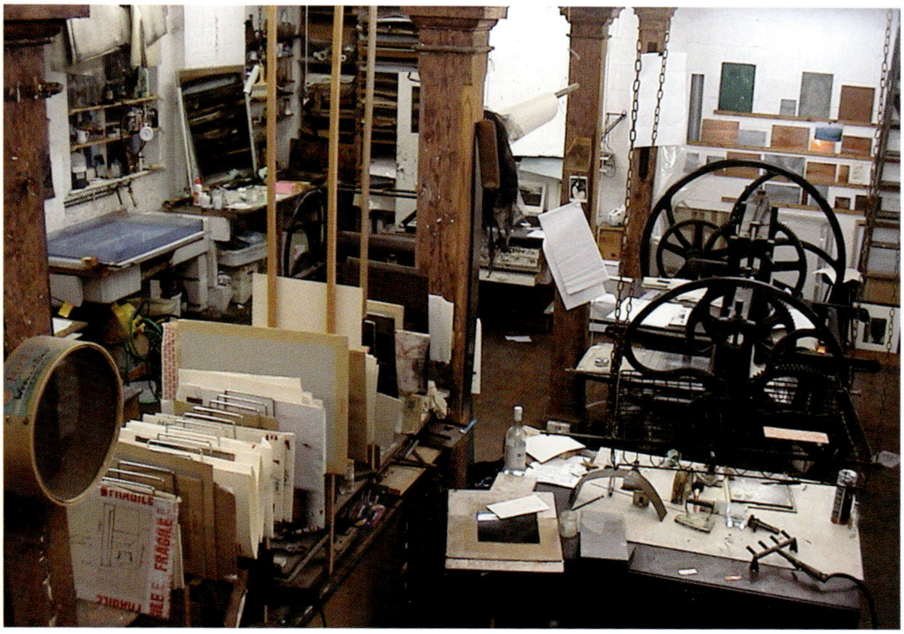

Norman Ackroyd's Bermondsey studio in Morocco Street, London SE1

One great series that came out of the collaboration was the 36 animals illustrating Buffon's *Histoire Naturelle* in 1942. The etching of *The Bull* is, I think, one of the great etchings of the 20th century. I studied it in depth and became convinced that Picasso was using sugar lift with a pen nib as well as with a brush. I simply had to visit the great studio where all this had been produced. A few years later I presented myself at the door of the Montmartre workshop. It was an Aladdin's cave of many fabulous presses, cast-iron hotplates, paper racks and all the accoutrements of an etching studio. Framed etchings by Picasso, Braque and others adorned the walls. Two of the presses were in use, but the energy and freedom implied in Picasso's plates seemed lacking. A wonderful smell of coffee emanated from a small room off the main studio and, hopefully, I wandered in.

I was confronted by an old but handsome woman with a mass of beautiful hair piled high. She was very friendly and we talked about etching, Picasso, minotaurs and the sugar-lift process. She went to a wall cupboard where there was a stack of boxes containing tubes of real gamboge watercolour. She took my coffee cup out of the saucer and put three or four lumps of white sugar in the saucer. She added hot water until the sugar dissolved and then added about half the tube of gum gamboge. She spat into the saucer to break the surface tension and mixed thoroughly. Finally, she decanted about half the mixture into another saucer and added water until it ran off a pen.

'There,' she said, 'that is the mixture Picasso used for his sugar-lift etchings.'

'How do you know?' I asked.

'Because I used to mix it for him every morning,' she replied.

My hair stood on end; as I left the workshop I realised I had been talking with Madame Lacourière.

I had a marvellous vision of a whole line of glowing copperplates covered with the gamboge-yellow drawings of 36 animals. Picasso, who was over sixty at this time, was obviously drawing freely with pen and brush on the bare, un-aquatinted copper. The advantage of this approach was that an unsuccessful drawing could simply be washed off and a fresh start made. It was also obvious that a thin but perfect hard ground was the only way to get the finest pen lines to lift. I have, of course, developed my own mixture and process based on the revelatory experience of that morning. Gum gamboge, a naturally occurring pith, is toxic and *dangereux*. One does need a perfect roller and a perfect hotplate to lay the hard ground (which I make myself) evenly and thinly; one also needs a good aquatint box in order to lay the finest aquatints. Once you have these, the possibilities and freedoms are limitless.

Hilary Adair

Some imagery stays with me; it is in my mind's eye and will haunt me until I find a way of expressing it in visual form. As a printmaker, I work with several different media, but I have most experience with etching, which I use for its beauty of line and its textural and tonal qualities. My ideas start with sketches, which develop into a more fully resolved working drawing, which in turn becomes the basis for my print. I know that I must work with the medium, which means being flexible at each stage of the proofing process; indeed, part of the excitement of printmaking lies in going with the changes and mood of an image that evolves during the creative journey. I do a lot of experimenting with colour as I progress towards the eureka moment, when I know that the print is how I want it.

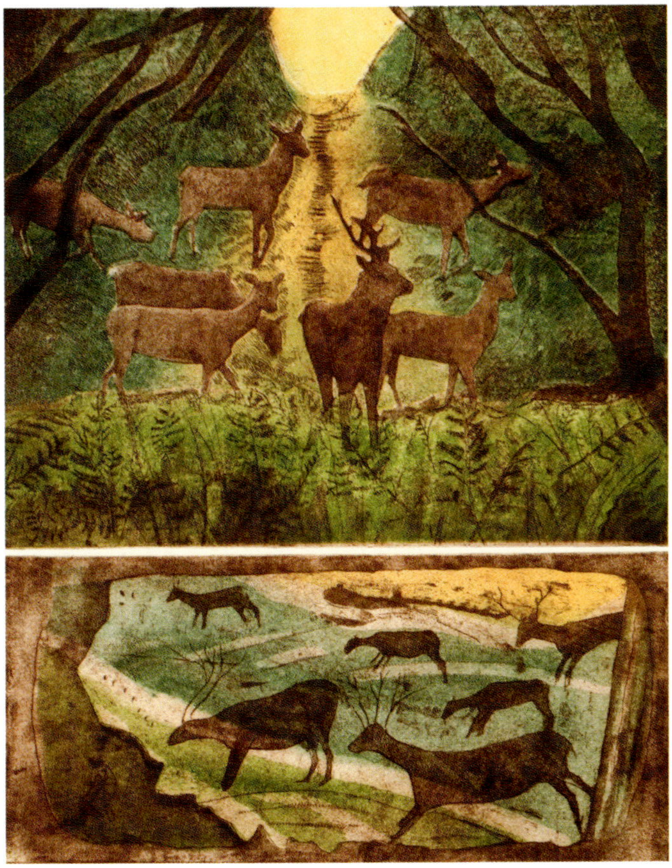

Red Deer Crossing, 2003. Etching and aquatint, 32 x 25 cm (12⅝ x 9⅞ in.)

Flight Shadow came about after I flew over Exmoor in a small plane. It was an exciting experience to see a familiar area from above, and I have used the imagery in both paintings and prints. Etching is a medium of great subtlety, which I felt was appropriate for the rendering of *Flight Shadow.* To create the quality of a palimpsest of the landscape, I used two superimposed plates, making the map-like imagery by using wax ground and aquatint; however, after much struggle and staring at the image and wondering why it didn't work, I thought of adding the small landscape plate at the top. This depicts Dunkery Beacon from a ground-level view, which helps to lead the eye up and out, as well as giving a sense of space. The plane's shadow is also crucial to the print, evoking the fleeting nature of my journey in both a literal and a metaphysical way, as it passes over my home. *Flight Shadow* is printed from four plates (that is, two for the larger and two for the smaller image) using four colours, in an edition of 20, on Somerset etching paper.

Exmoor, where I live, has been the habitat of red deer for many centuries. They are elusive creatures, sometimes seen at evening, moving quietly through the trees. One evening, when a hind jumped on and over the bonnet of my car, my reaction was to notice how much it resembled a cave painting of a deer, with outstretched legs and body silhouetted briefly against the car headlights. These two images of deer, one contemporary and one thousands of years old, are linked in the etching *Red Deer Crossing.* Again, I have used juxtaposed plates, which allows for a dialogue between the two images. *Red Deer Crossing* is printed from four plates using four colours, in an edition of 50, on Somerset paper.

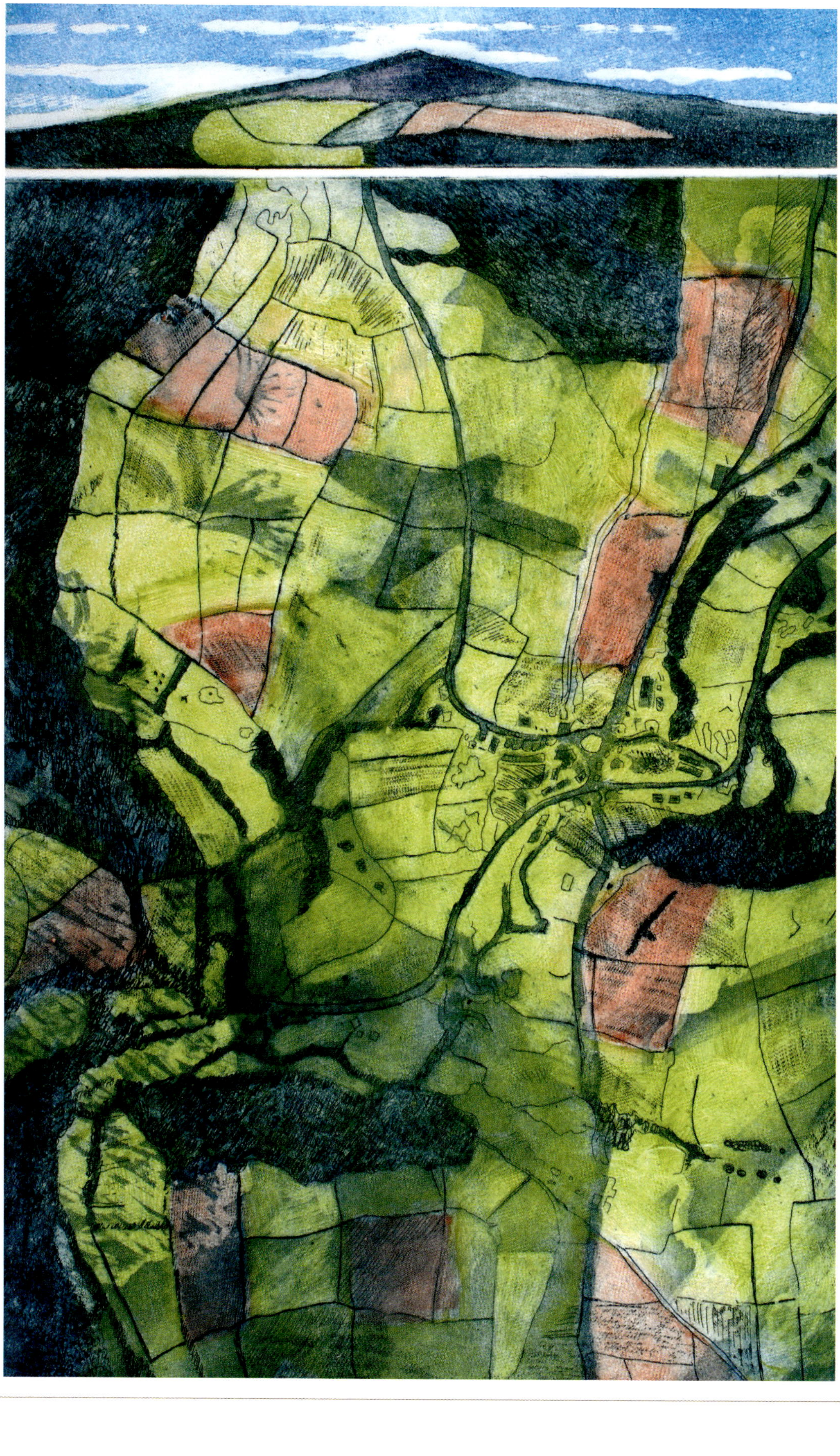

Flight Shadow, 2005. Etching and aquatint, 44 x 28 cm (17¼ x 11 in.)

Jim Anderson

When I was in my teens, I had the good fortune to have an art teacher whose mantra was the delightful phrase 'the only rule is: there are no rules', a splendid piece of wisdom that has served me well ever since.

I frequently employ four or five different print techniques in one image and the results of these wayward combinations often surprise me as much as anyone else. I try to work quickly and cheaply. Because of the low or non-existent costs of my materials, I feel able to work fast and freely on a large scale, without the inhibiting fear of wasting expensive ingredients if I go wrong – which I frequently do. The emphasis in my work is on recycling; most of my basic printmaking materials come out of skips. It is said that, in the early 1960s, Robert Rauschenberg created his assemblages and 'combine paintings' almost entirely out of the garbage he found littering the streets around his New York studio. Although my work has almost nothing in common with his, I find this attitude extremely inspiring. I like the alchemical aspect of transforming banal materials and the idea of giving the abandoned debris of everyday life a second chance. I usually start with collagraph plates – these can be constructed from old hardboard, cardboard, string, sand, glue, sawdust and other abandoned materials, stuck together and sealed with waterproof carpenters' glue – from which I then intaglio-print the major elements of the image onto pieces of my own handmade paper.

The paper onto which I print is an important element of the process. I was taught to make handmade paper by a kind South African artist named Susan Rothenberg, whom I met at Oxford Printmakers' Cooperative in 1984. It was a craft I was eager to learn because, considering the major part the paper plays in creating the particular character of a print, it seemed to me perverse to leave the job to a faceless manufacturer in a paper mill. Also, in those Cold War days there was a pervasive sense that shortly we would all have to be relearning basic crafts. My paper is cooked up from soft rags, scraps of reclaimed paper and card, and occasionally organic matter such as onion skins or even human hair. (A decade ago, a student of mine – who was aware of some of my working methods – had a particularly severe haircut and posted me her shorn locks in a Toblerone box; I'm still using her hair in my paper today.) These ingredients are torn into pieces about the size of a thumbnail, soaked in water for a night, then mixed with more water and pulped in a Kenwood soup blender (not the one I use in the kitchen!) until the mixture is roughly the consistency of porridge. The paper pulp can be coloured by stirring into it acrylic paints or fabric dyes. I then spread the multicoloured porridge onto large pieces of cotton sheet stretched over boards, and leave the water to run away and the paper to dry. When dry it can be peeled off. It has the texture and appearance of soft, pastel-hued crispbread – though perhaps it's not as tasty. Thus the paper, even before it has been printed on at all, is already a highly textured, coloured and integral part of the image. It is also extremely thick, sometimes up to 5 mm (⅕ in.), and it is rarely flat. I welcome working on this unpredictable, spongy, rough-hewn material as I feel it makes the resulting print into more of a thing, more of an object, as opposed to a flat image impressed onto an even-surfaced industrial product.

After the initial collagraph structure of the image has been printed, I will usually work over it and embellish it with a cocktail of linocut, stencil, drypoint and hand-colouring. The leaves and shoes in *Genetic Modification 1 (Grow Your Own Lady)* are linocuts, as is the wild hairdo of the woman in *Bath.* Linoleum can still occasionally be found in skips, so it is worth having a look amongst the debris when an old house is having a makeover.

I am much addicted to the many and various applications of stencilling – another way of enriching a print. The pattern on the figure's skirt in

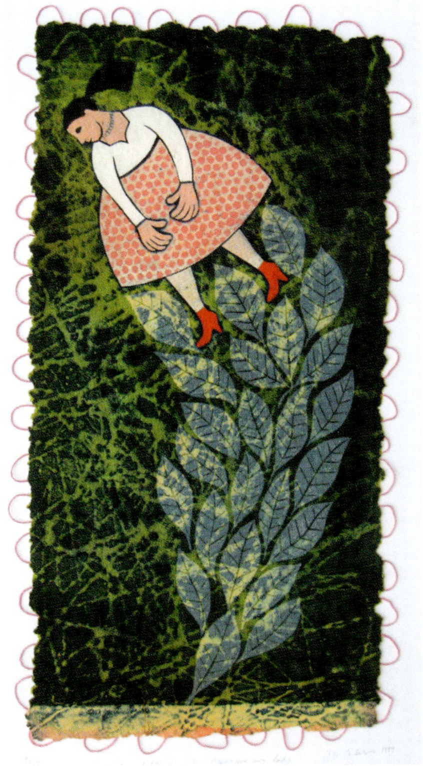

Above: **Genetic Modification 1 (Grow Your Own Lady)**, 1999. Collagraph, linocut and stencil on handmade paper, 72 x 45 cm (28³⁄₈ x 17³⁄₄ in.)

Right: **Bath**, 1998. Collagraph, linocut and stencil on handmade paper, 72 x 45 cm (28³⁄₈ x 17³⁄₄ in.)

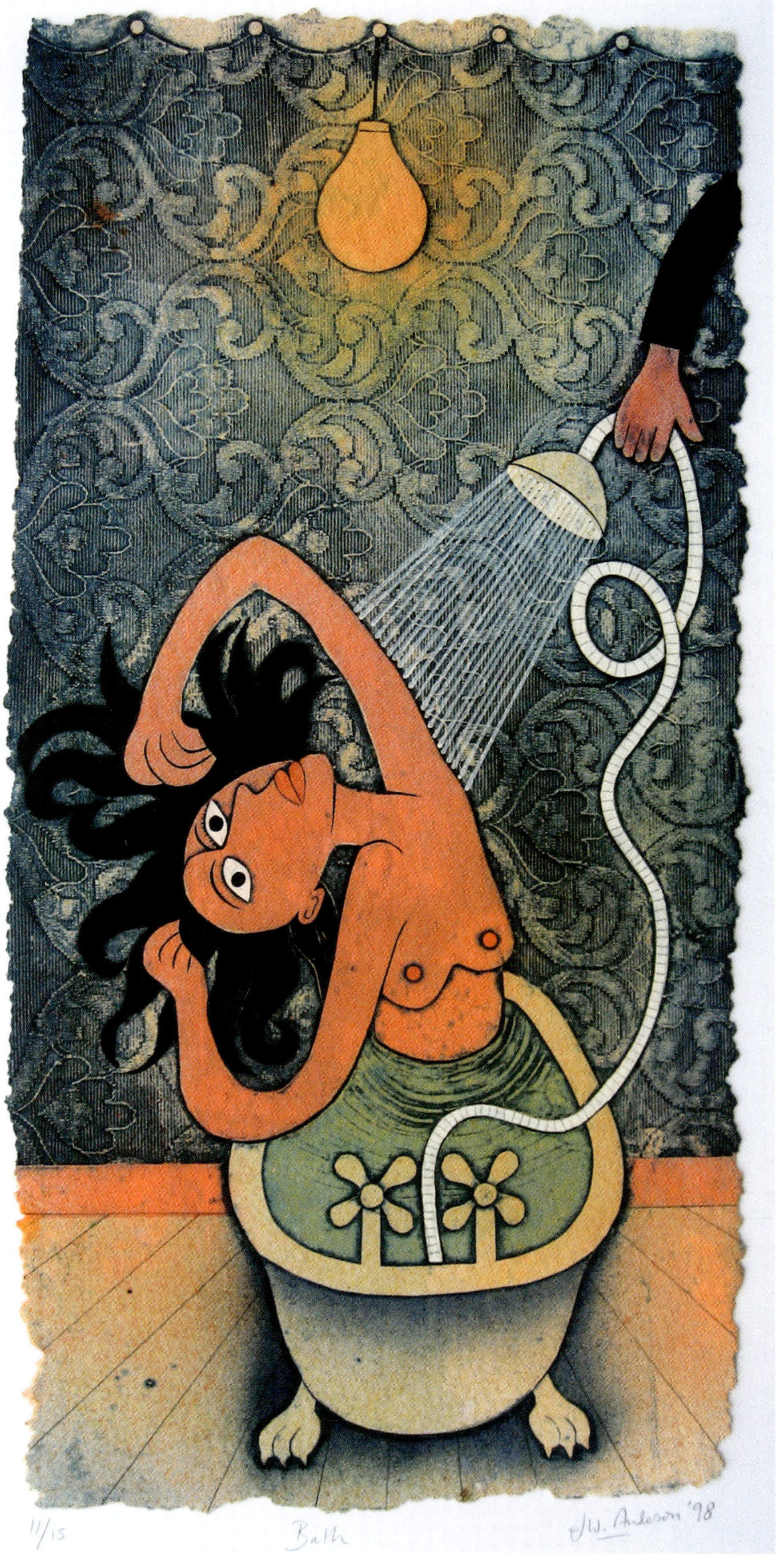

Genetic Modification 1 is achieved this way, by dabbing acrylic paint with a sponge through a thin piece of perforated metal. Spraying with an atomiser, or with pigment flicked from an old toothbrush, can also be effective, as can be seen in the gentle colour gradations and areas of soft tone in *Bath*.

Due to the highly varied textures and colours of the paper and the sometimes unpredictable results of mixing several different media, most of the finished prints have small variations. It is rare for me to produce an edition of identical prints, and even when I do so the editions are very small – rarely more than ten and never more than fifteen. My aim is not to produce identical images but to achieve surprisingly painterly effects.

Andrew Antoniou

I am intrigued by the workings of the subconscious in our dreams and in everyday life, by the mercurial nature of remembered experience and by the true poetic nature of the imagination. The influences in my work are many and varied, and often the purpose in trying to realise an image is to bring together the many strands of what are seemingly unrelated thoughts, feelings and experiences. This results in what could be termed 'absurdism', in which the imagery has a cryptic nature, creating a narrative that is layered with elusive meaning and references. I work almost exclusively from the imagination (as distinct from observation), drawing on my memory as a source for recreating images from the subconscious. I have taken elements from the theatre, pantomime, song and film. I often find that a line from a song or a passage from a film or play inspires my own narrative and provides a starting point for a reworking of the idea through my own experiences.

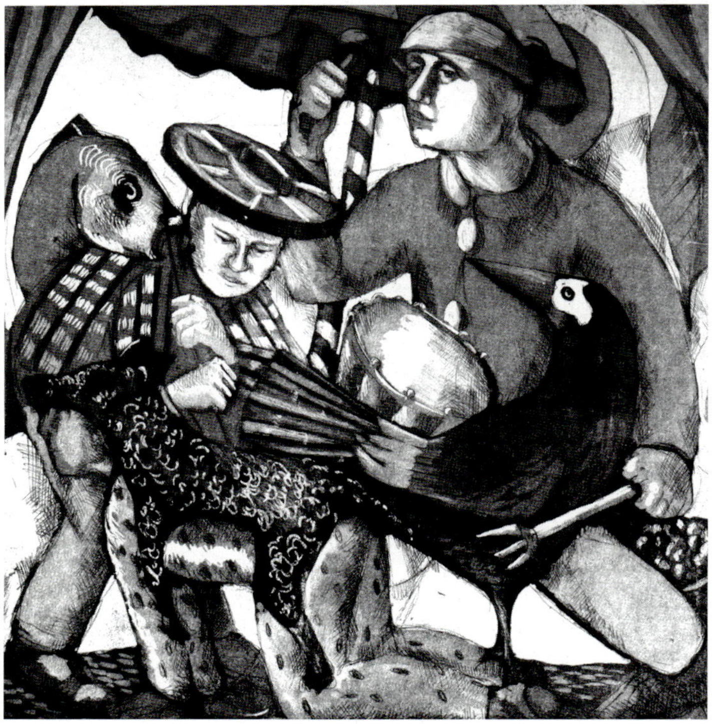

Twilight Creeping, 2005. Etching, 32 x 34 cm (12⅝ x 13⅜ in.)

Throughout my working life I have looked to and been influenced by figurative artists of the past whose work embodies a strong vision of the inner story. My first great influences were William Blake, Goya and Picasso and, more recently and most importantly, Max Beckmann. It is no coincidence that these artists were great printmakers, and it has been their work in print that has inspired me most.

I have developed a method of collaging compositions together that enables me to direct the narrative. I make several drawings of individual characters in different poses and costumes, as well as settings that are made up of collaged pieces of landscapes and interiors. The next stage is to try to bring together these elements into a meaningful composition. Often I won't even know the nature of the narrative until the separate elements are arranged on the page. From here, there is the consideration of translating the drawing into print. Sometimes I make a drawing in graphite, based on the final collage piece, then damp it and transfer it onto a smoked hard ground by running it through the press. Otherwise, I run the collage piece itself through the press onto a soft wax ground and, after one bite in the mordant, use the impression as a template for further work. Generally I work with a combination of hard ground and aquatint, building the image through many bitings. Etching allows me to think and work in layers, and the scraping and burnishing back to expose underlying work and create subtleties of tone brings about the effect I seek. The diverse qualities of line that can be achieved in etching, whether broad and daring, light and nimble, or scratchy and edgy, are essential to expressing the mood of the piece; for me, no other medium does it better.

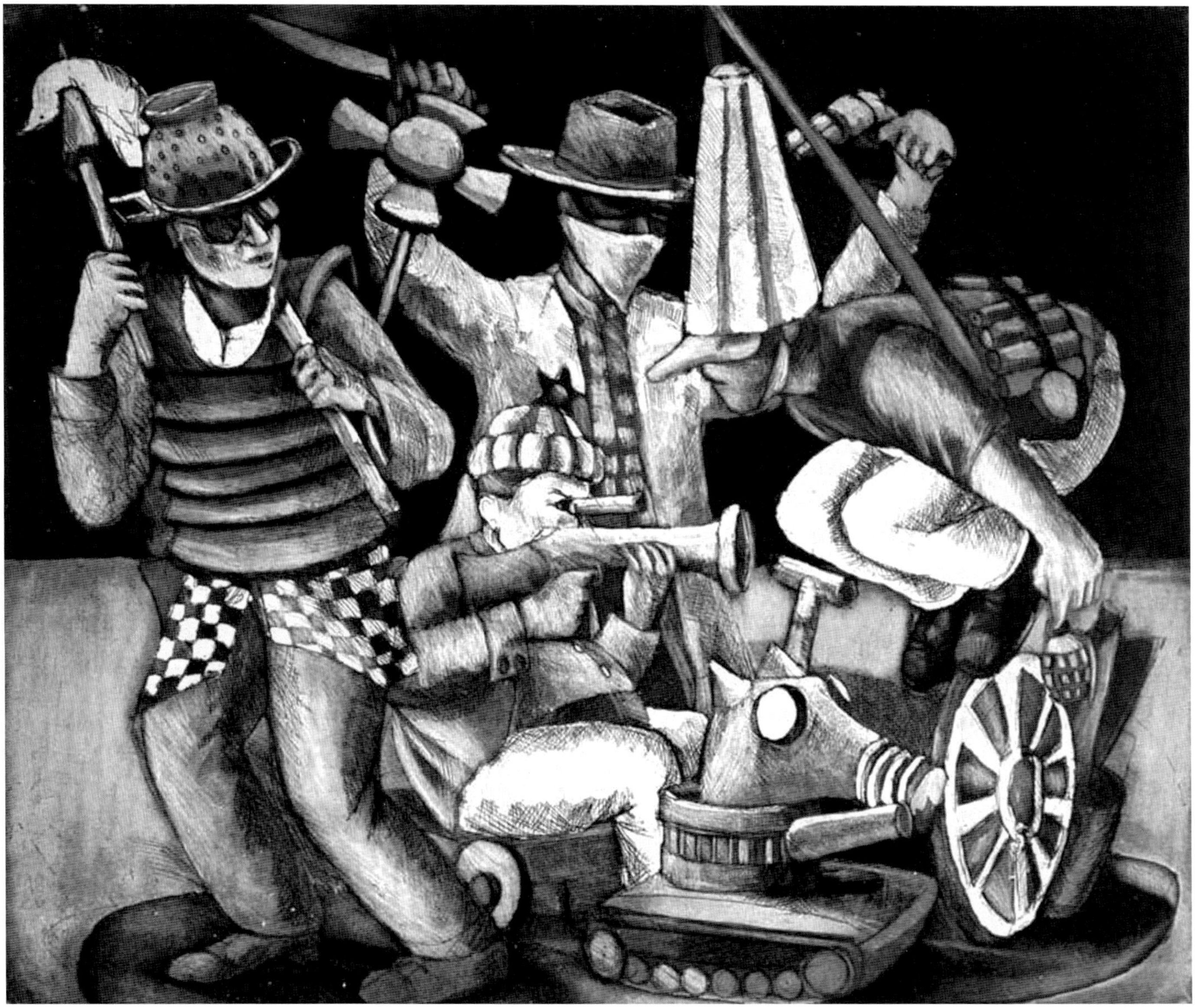

Act of Surrender, 2007. Etching, 49 x 59 cm (19¼ x 23¼ in.)

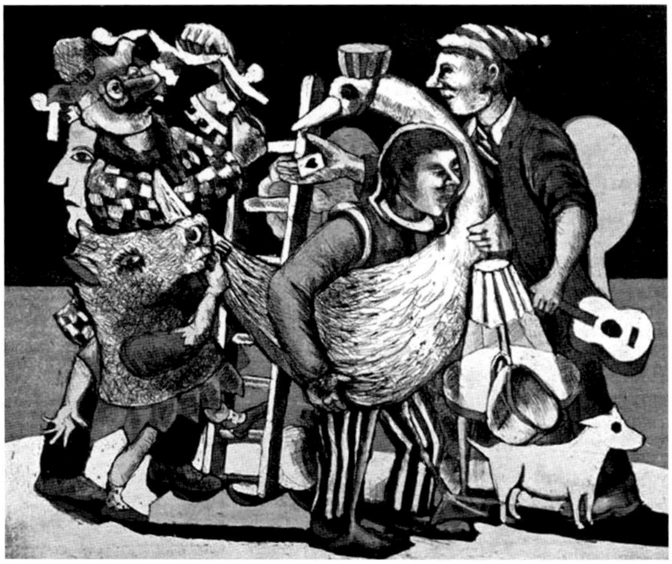

Costume Drama, 2006. Etching, 40 x 50 cm (15¾ x 19¾ in.)

Margaret Ashman

One of the major influences on my practice is the work of video artist Bill Viola. We have never met but we seem to share a concern for spiritual subjects and for the notion of time. We also, perhaps, have a mutual interest in the portrayal of emotion and the provocation of an emotional response in the viewer, through the presentation of facial expression and gesture. Viola does this through video; I do it through print. One of Viola's methods is to slow down his films of people expressing emotion until they reveal micro-expressions, fleeting gestures of intense concealed emotion. I capture micro-expressions with video stills or digital photography, which I use as sources for my photo-etchings.

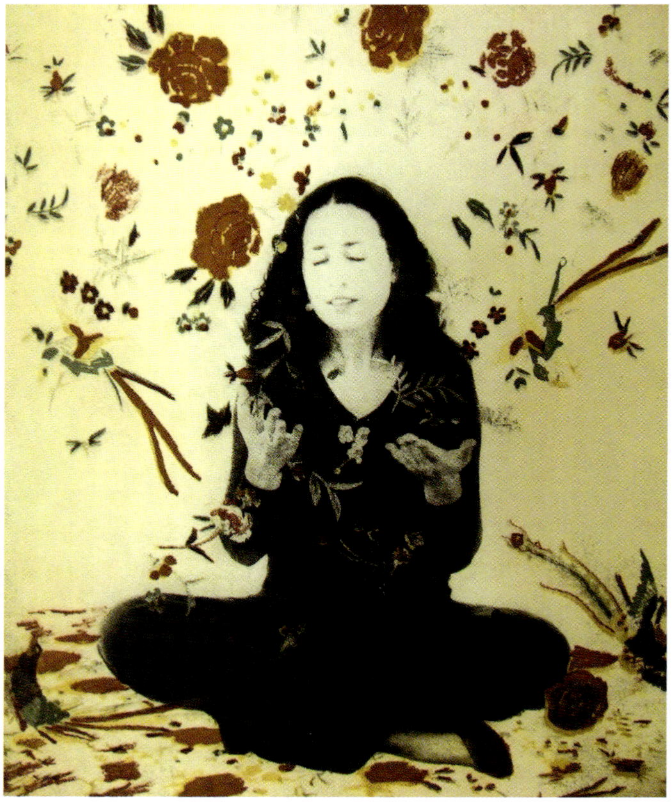

Falling Flowers, 2006. Photo-etching, 57 x 47 cm (22½ x 18½ in.)

Another feature of my work, which may not be apparent, is that I photograph people communicating in sign language. The texts to be signed are chosen with care, and hiding the text in sign language parallels the way that different layers of life, namely the spiritual and emotional realms, exist below the surface. I favour central, symmetrical compositions that have iconic religious associations. I like the image to remain slightly mysterious, to have a level of ambiguity or a lack of clarity. The very process of etching can produce a blurring of the image. Some of my prints are made by superimposing two photographs separated by a short time difference. This has the effect of introducing uncertainty or ambiguity. Other works are combinations of photographs of people signing and images of oriental paintings and embroideries of flowers or birds.

Printmakers often work in layers, producing the final image by overprinting with different plates or combining techniques such as etching and screenprint. I combine photographs with digital layering techniques in Adobe Photoshop, producing a single digital colour image. I then split up the image into layers, using channels and bitmap mode, to produce the artwork to make a set of printing plates. I then ink these in different colours to recombine them in a single print. When I bitmap my images I use diffusion dither, the most random bitmapping option available. I set the dots per inch between 100 and 220. Sometimes I print the bitmaps on my A3 home printer and enlarge them up to A0 size by photocopy; these photocopies have to be oiled to turn them into transparencies for

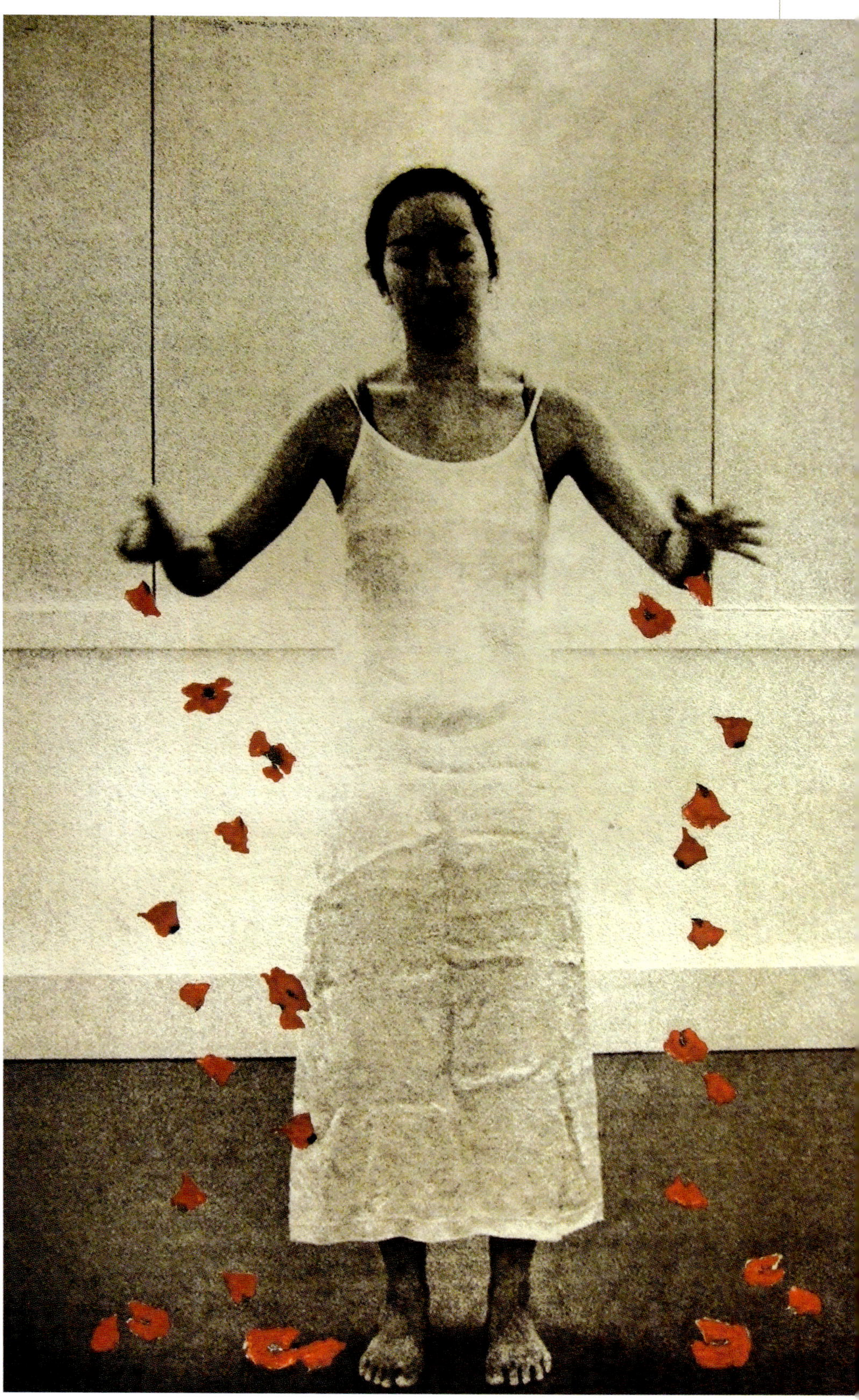

Torn, 2007. Photo-etching, 75 x 49 cm (29½ x 19¼ in.)

photo-etchings. Sometimes I have them printed from CD at the correct size onto acetate; this is necessary if I am making a multiplate image, because enlarging by photocopying is too inaccurate. Printing from CD also allows for finer detail in the finished print.

I have encountered problems when processing large photo-etching plates using Photrak, a roll-on photo-etching emulsion. One problem that is magnified when working with high-resolution images is that part of the image is faint or missing, usually in bands near the edge of the plate. This is caused by the transparency sticking in one area, preventing the air between the transparency and the plate from escaping in a uniform manner. This can be rectified by two measures. The first is to allow the coated plates to dry for longer than usual before using them. They should be very shiny and very smooth to the touch. This is especially important if the Photrak has been mixed with reducer (E 12) before being applied. The second measure is to apply a liberal dusting of talcum powder between the transparency and the plate. This does not seem to affect the image, but the small talc particles act as a buffer, allowing air to escape between the plate and transparency when the vacuum pump is switched on. When all is working correctly I am able to generate the large areas of uniform grainy tone which are characteristic of my etchings.

Ted Atkinson

I came to printmaking late (via sculpture). On the whole, my work still tends to be about manipulating solid forms in space and, hopefully, some of the three-dimensional qualities are still apparent in the finished print. I don't see myself as an innovator, more a coloniser. I hone and polish, repeat thoughts, reprocess ideas, make decisions again and again and, for all the speed of the medium I am currently using, the work comes together very slowly.

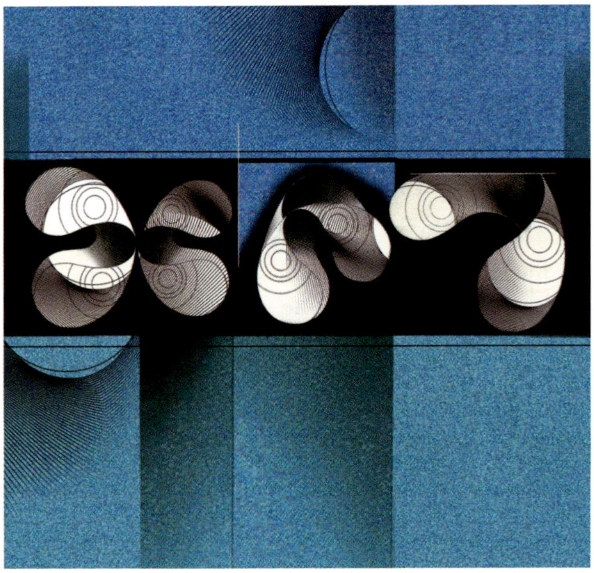

Right: **Bone Collection,** 2008. Digital print, 21 x 23 cm (8¼ x 9in.)

Below: **The Bone Collection 4,** 2007. Digital print, 14 x 21 cm (5½ x 8¼ in.)

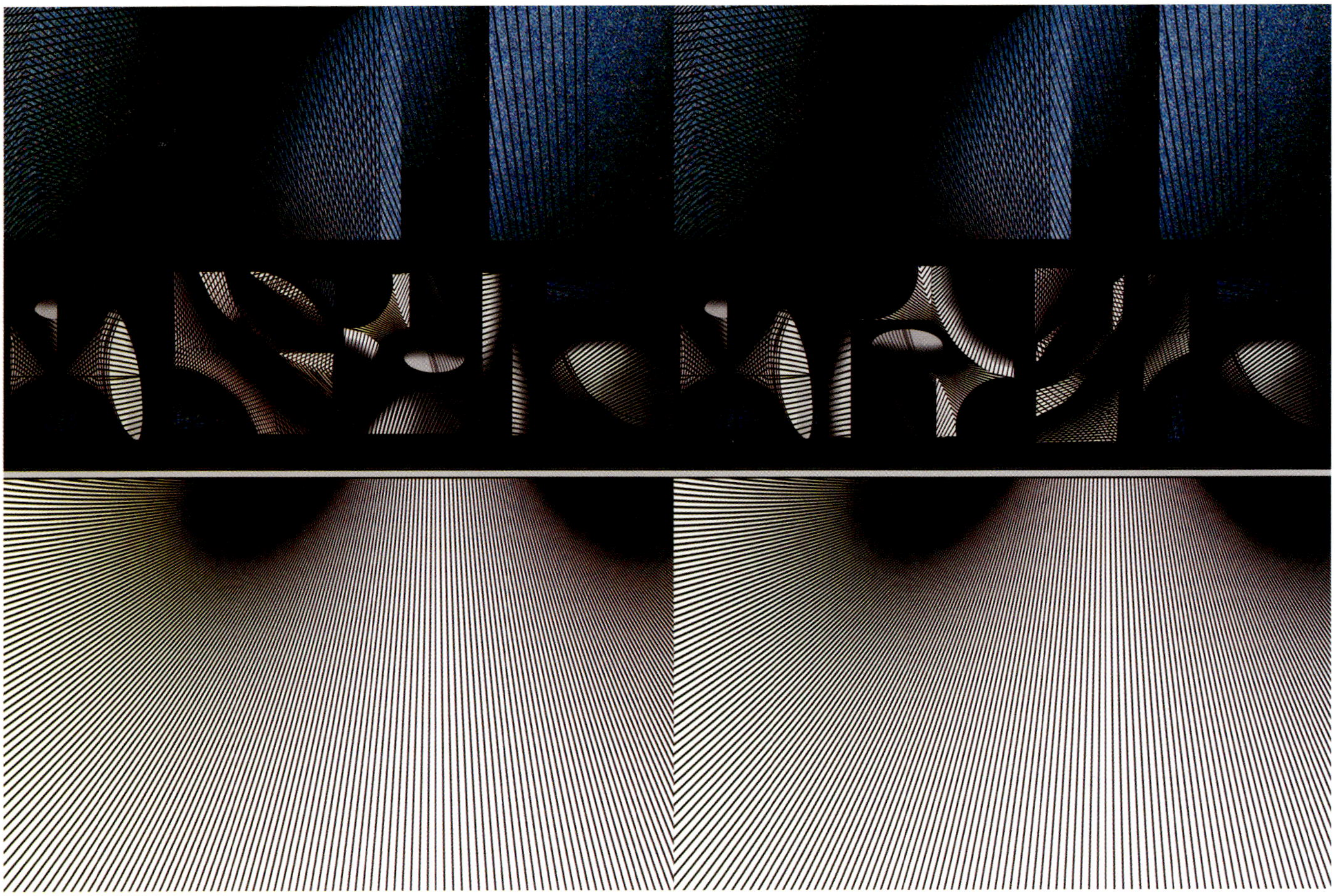

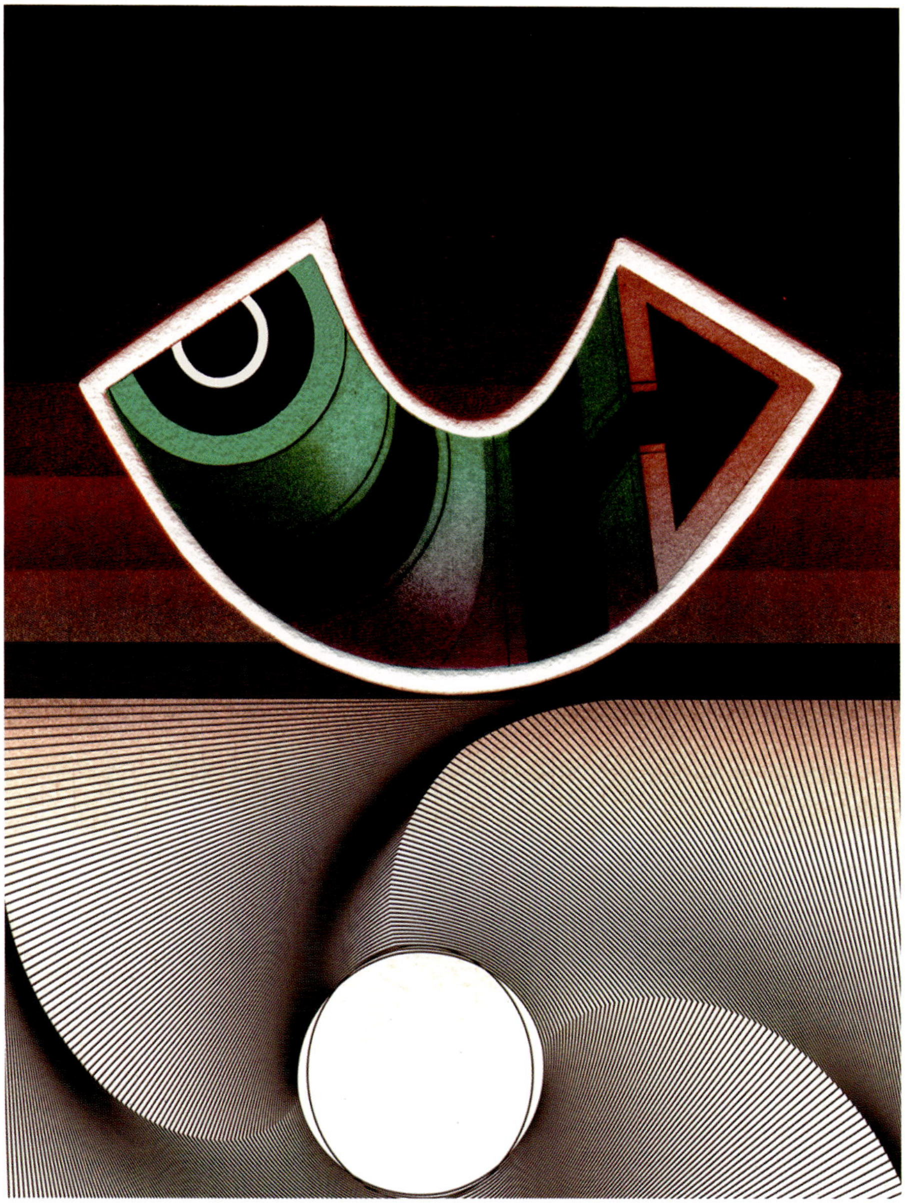

Geometrix 4, 2005. Digital print, 18 x 13 cm (7⅛ x 5⅛ in.)

Although I am now doing all my art work on the computer, I am far from being an expert and am only capable of using small parts of two programs: Photoshop and Coreldraw. The great advantage to both these programs is the facility they offer of working in layers (imagine layers as sheets of glass stacked one above the other). As an example, one could 'paint' a blue rectangle on one layer and a yellow circle on the second, which, being opaque, would block out layer one. However, the layers can be reversed, with layer one now blocking layer two. The top layer could then be gradually made transparent, allowing the lower layer to emerge, in this case no doubt producing an infinite number of greens. Then, consider that the colour on both layers can be changed, as can the image, size, shape, texture, brightness, contrast and so on; and then consider that it's not unusual to work with fifty or more layers! Technically simple, but aesthetically mind-boggling.

In the past I have worked on one or two mezzotints but didn't enjoy the experience, firstly because I found it singularly difficult to see what I was doing, and secondly because I couldn't work in my normal way, which is to take lots of progress proofs of my etchings. Mezzotint proofs need to be kept to a minimum as, each time the plate goes through the press, some crispness is lost from its textured surface. However, all these mezzotint prints resulted in a richness and subtlety far beyond my expectation; and here lies the downside of working digitally: it's rather like working on a slide where the backlight brings out the brilliance of the colour. Unfortunately, there's no way a printer can do justice to this onscreen image; the print is invariably a disappointment. This doesn't mean the work is without merit, but it does give rise to much thought about the not insignificant question of whether the destination is paramount or whether the journey can in itself be fulfilling.

Adrian Bartlett

Among the earliest visual images to influence me were the Italian films I watched between the ages of 8 and 12 at the Saturday morning cinema. I remember Visconti's 1948 La Terra Trema. *I loved the flickering light and shade and also what I now recognise as the director's sense of spatial impartiality, which was echoed in the reproduction of Breughel's* Hunters in the Snow *that hung on my bedroom wall.*

Evening Run. Woodcut, 28 x 36 cm (11 x 14⅛ in.)

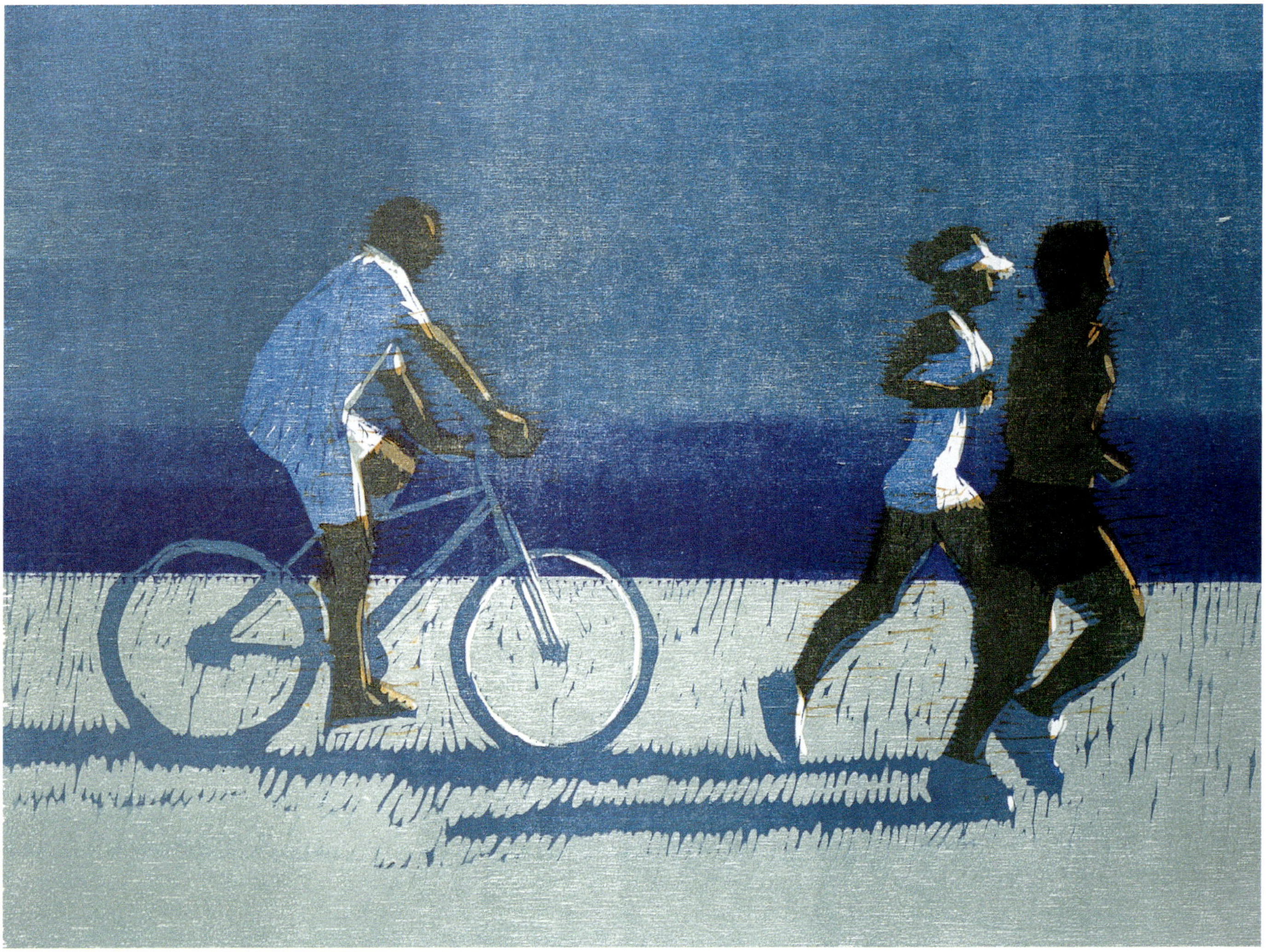

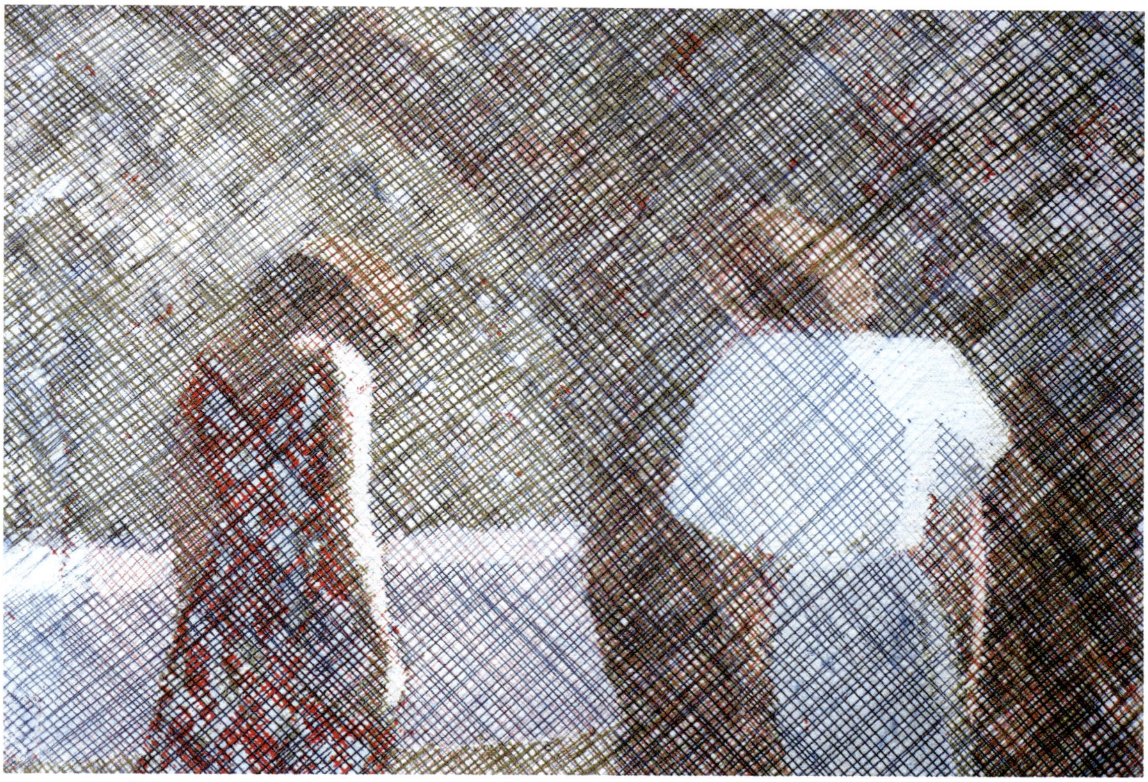

Sisters, 19 x 30 cm (7½ x 11¾ in.) (detail). Etching, 30 x 40 cm (11¾ x 15¾ in.)

As a painter turning to etching, I have tried to give myself a wide tonal range in black and white, and as large a palette of colour as possible. With my black and white etchings this means biting the plate in many different stages. With colour the same is true, but there are of course further complications. I am most frequently asked how I make my colour etchings. I will try to explain the technique and how I came to work in this way.

After some experiments with aquatint I evolved a version of one of Jacques Villon's methods. Villon was employed for a while to make etched copies of paintings in the Louvre. For these he used many different plates and also added extra colours, both *à la poupée* and by hand, but for his own prints he settled on a three-plate system with a plate for each of the primary colours. He did some of these with drypoint and some with hard-ground etching, in the latter case ruling lines in different directions across each plate. This ensures that there will be a little speck of white showing between the lines, which gives the surface a bright sparkle. However, I did not like the rather mechanical appearance of this method, so I decided to draw all the lines freehand, which I find gives a much more vibrant surface. I also found that having just one direction of lines on each plate is not sufficient to give the maximum variety of colour intensity. I have ended up by cross-hatching each of the three plates in four directions.

As these marks on the plate already cover the whole surface and the biting is to be done in many different stages, it is clear that the actual drawing must be done with the stop-out varnish. In order to have a bright-red area in the etching, this will be stopped out on the blue and yellow plates at the beginning, and the red plate will be bitten strongly in that area. Other parts of the red plate will of course be stopped out in order to give blues or yellows or greens, all in different stages so as to achieve the greatest degree of subtlety, once all the plates are inked and printed in superimposition. If any colour becomes too strong the plate can of course be scraped or burnished so that it retains less ink. As a result of drawing with stop-out varnish and a brush rather than with a needle for the colour etchings, I now make my black and white ones in the same way.

When an image seems better expressed in flatter shapes I sometimes turn to woodcut, which is a wonderfully direct medium. However, just as the element of white paper showing through the network of lines in my etchings gives the transparency I prize, I use transparent inks with the woodcut to create pictorial space.

Richard Bawden

Excited by what I see, I am driven by a compulsion to draw and paint. Sometimes I am inspired by the sheer grandeur of a location and sometimes by its details, by the richness and depth of colour and texture. I am not ashamed to admit that I love decoration. Yet I am also enraptured by monumental geometric simplicity and the satisfying tension of a straight line. As an artist, my starting points are many: people, places, open landscape, intricate interiors, things which are odd or, at first glance, even completely boring (though inviting transformation). For me, making a print is a way of extending an idea a stage further than drawing or painting. A spontaneous drawing is often the starting point for a considered design, frequently lurking in my mind in several forms.

Crag Path, Aldeburgh, 2006. Linocut, 22 x 34.5 cm (8⅝ x 13⅝ in.)

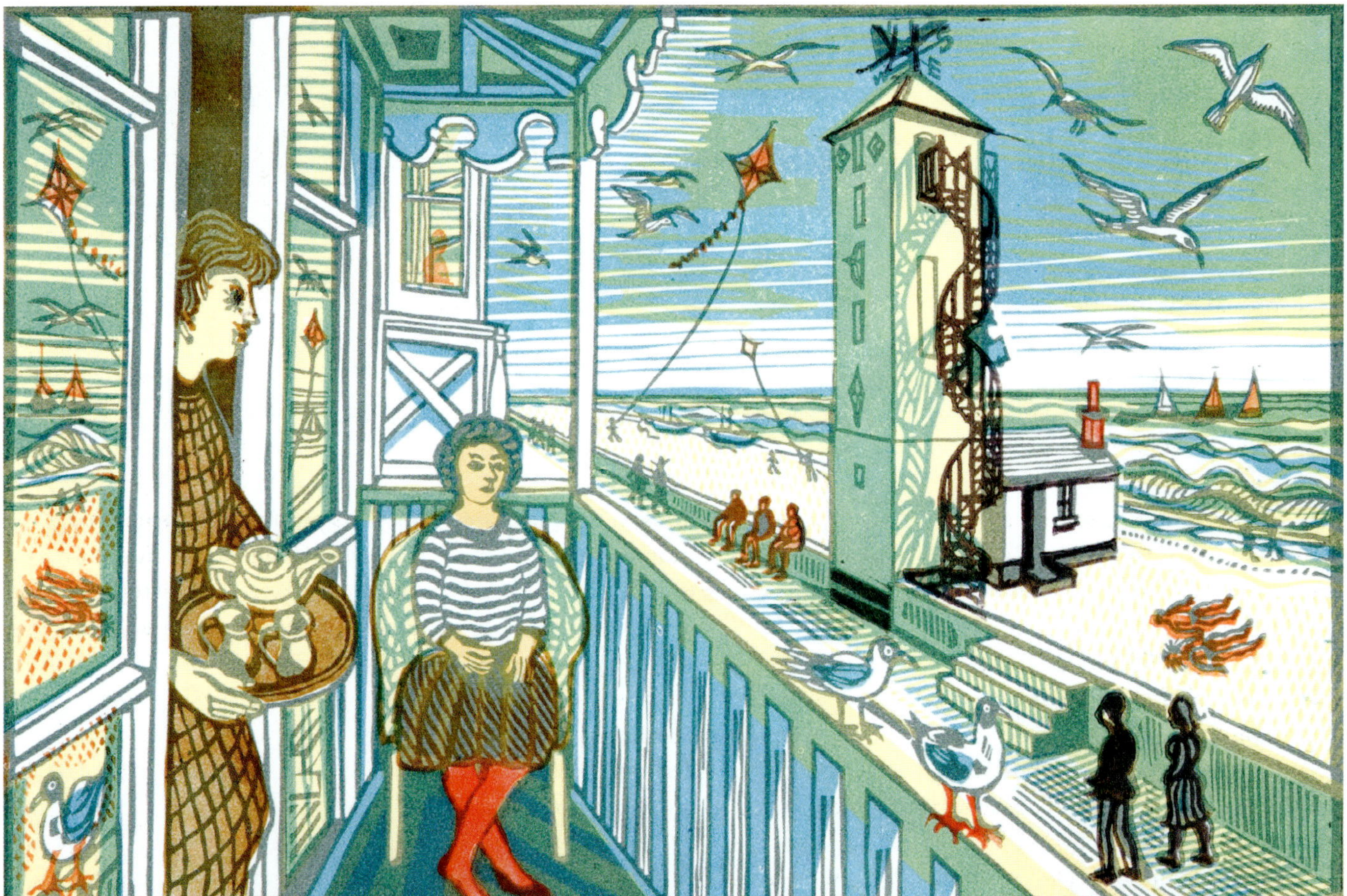

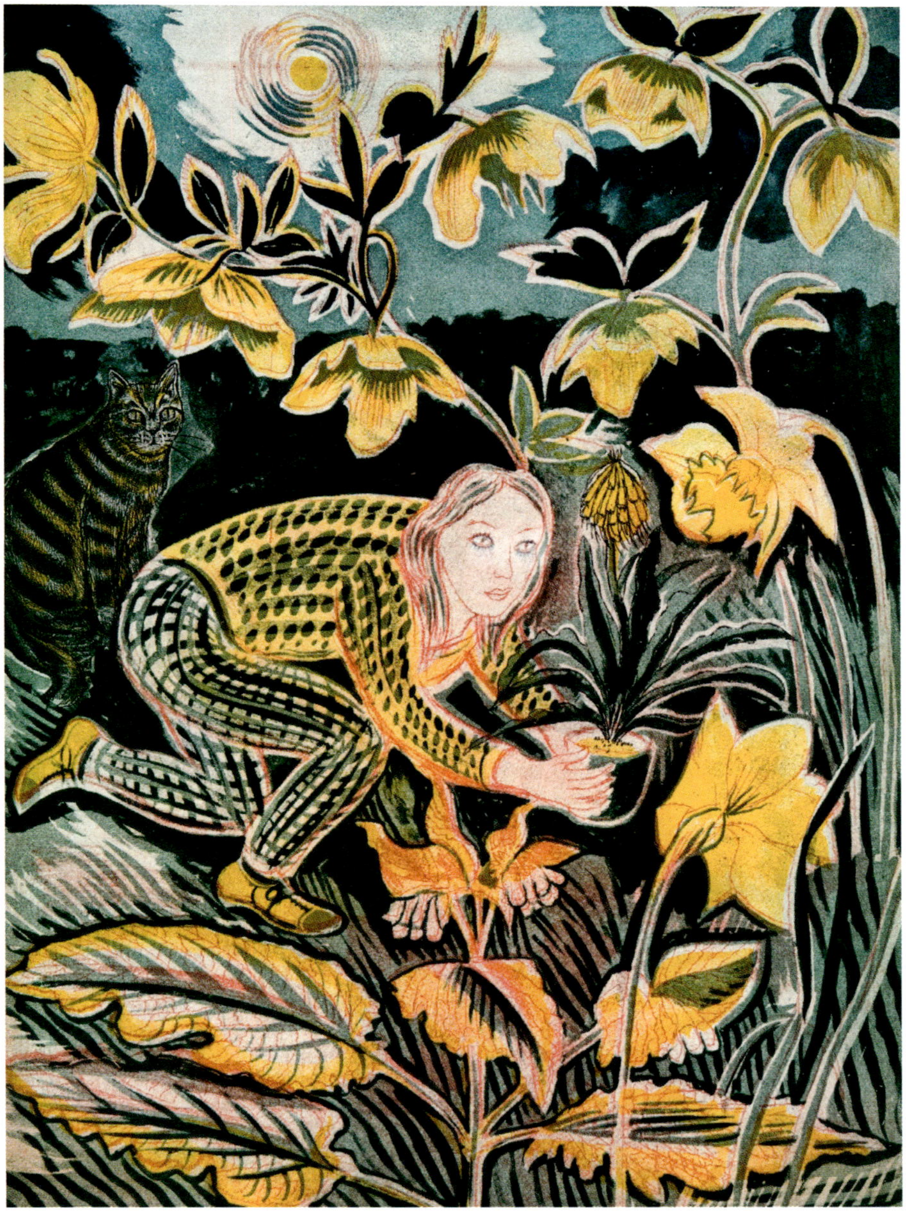

The Ardent Gardener, 2007. Sugar aquatint, 41 x 31 cm (16⅛ x 12¼ in.)

I work both in linocut and in etching; these are very different mediums, each with its own character and potential. I cut lino with a Stanley knife, producing crisp lines and contrasting flat, solid shapes. This leaves nothing to chance; everything is carefully considered and thought out.

Etching, by contrast, can be free and painterly. A plate, which in my case might be copper or steel, can be etched with a great variety of textures and tones: sugar-lift aquatint will produce a direct brushstroke effect; soft-ground etching has the quality of a chalk or crayon drawing; and a hard wax ground invites a virtually limitless range of incised line. I normally start by establishing the composition with an etched line. Next, I make a proof on which I work with watercolour or crayon to help me make further decisions; and tone and texture are added using aquatint or cross-hatching. If the print is to be in colour, I etch a separate plate for each colour; when these plates are overprinted, surprises often result. I take several proofs in different combinations of colour with inks I prepare myself, using pure powder pigment and linseed oil, grinding the mixture to the correct smoothness and consistency with a muller on a slab of plate glass.

At this stage, adjusting colour and intensity to achieve a satisfactory working proof is an important part of the creative process. Once the colour is as it should be, any necessary corrections to the plates are made using scrapers and burnishers; or some areas might be subjected to open bite, which involves protecting the surface of the plate (and, of course, its reverse side) with an acid-resistant varnish, leaving unprotected the areas to be bitten further. Scraping, burnishing and open bite each have their own characteristic effect. Slowly, the print evolves and eventually an artist's proof is pinned up. It sometimes accords with my vision but at times the outcome is unexpected, in which case the proof might lead me in an unforeseen direction.

James Beale

Having been used to working in large studios during my art-school teaching career, I now find that I must adapt my working procedures to a much smaller personal studio space. I used to work on several zinc etching plates at the same time, developing the images by drawing directly on each plate with diluted stop-out varnish using rags, brushes and anything else at hand to build up the effect I was seeking.

Tuscany, 2007. Monotype, 61 x 76 cm (24 x 30 in.)

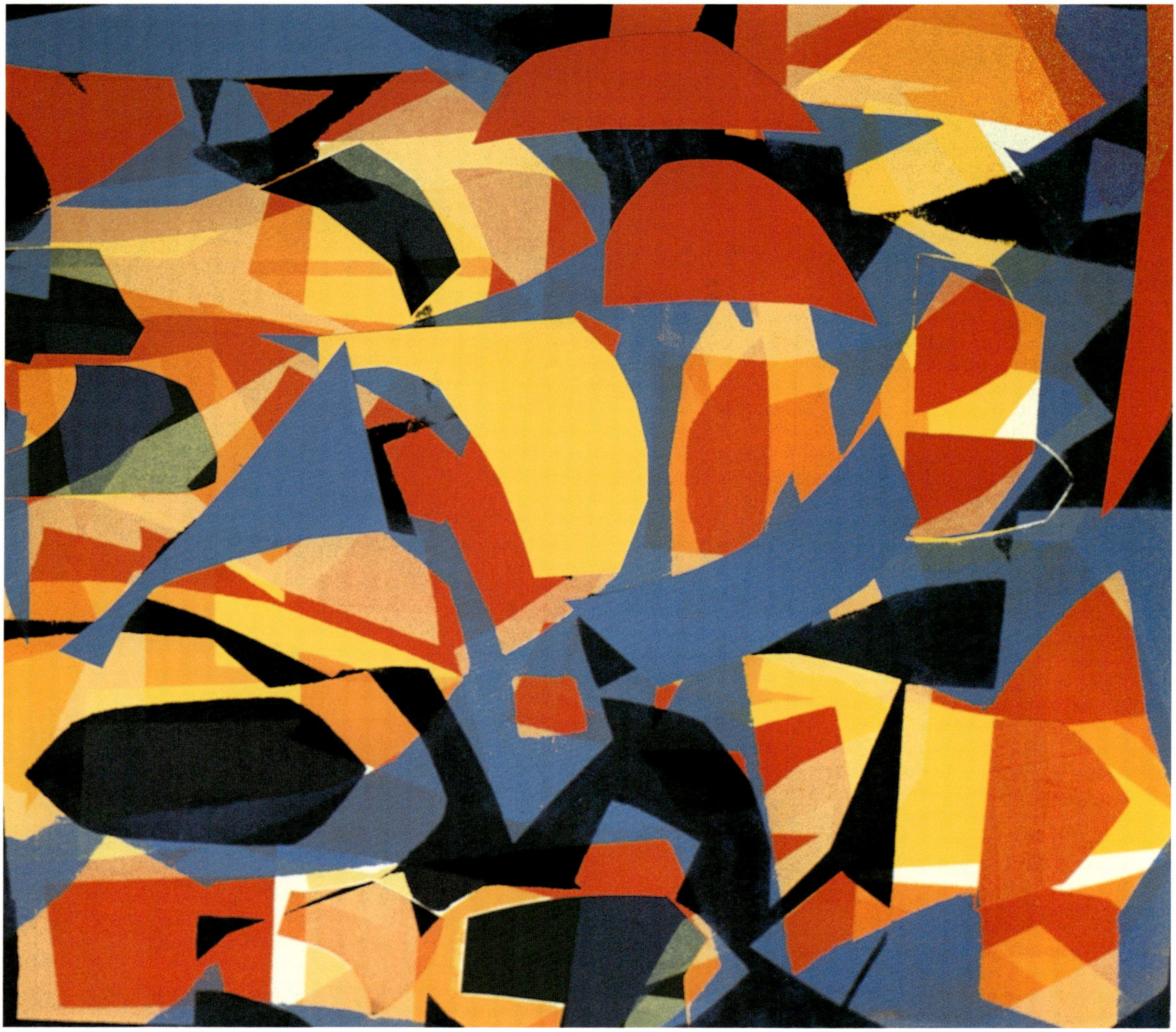

Venice, 2007. Monotype, 26 x 46 cm (10¼ x 18⅛ in.)

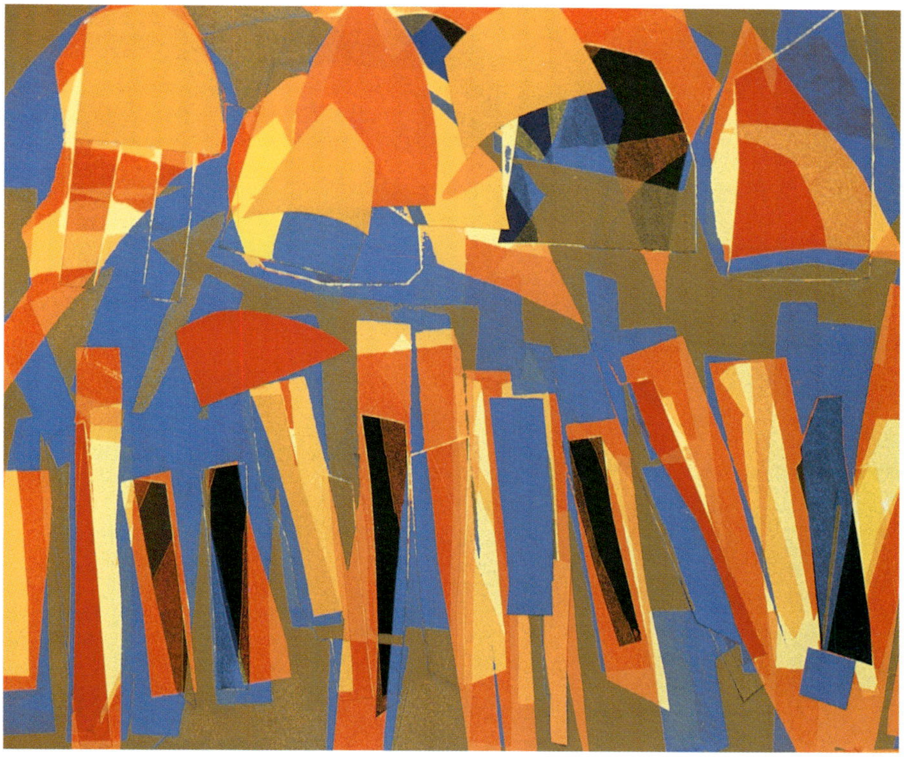

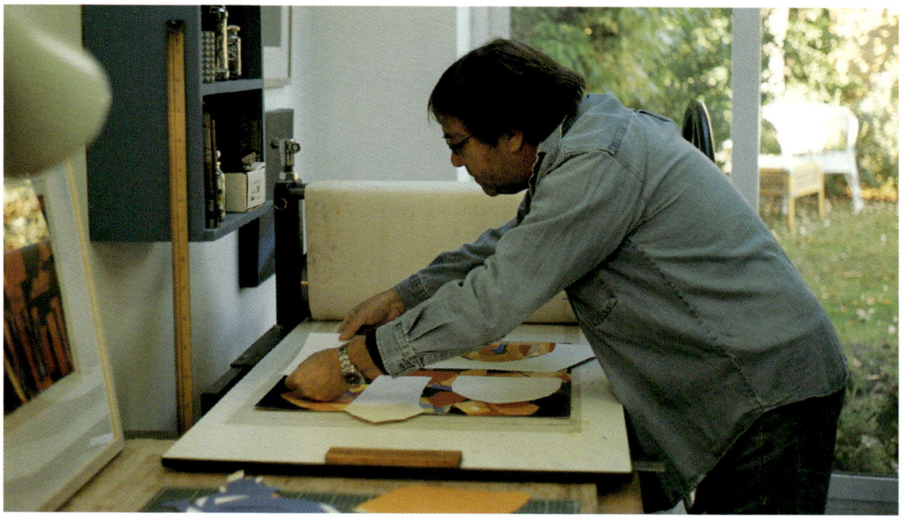

The artist in his studio

The plates would then be left to dry before being worked on again, as the image gradually resolved itself. At some point I would lay an aquatint ground and etch the plate; after the plate was cleaned, more drawing, sometimes with strong acid, would then be superimposed, followed perhaps by further aquatinting. After proofing I would often rework the plate using glass paper, scrapers or drypoint needles.

In my new studio, working simultaneously in this way with a large number of plates would take up all my available space, so I now limit myself to working on only two etchings at a time, giving myself room to make monotypes and collagraphs whilst varnish is drying and plates are being etched.

These new images, abstract and in strong colour, are inspired by Mediterranean experiences. I begin by rolling a layer of relief or lithographic printing ink onto a zinc or copper plate and printing with dry paper on the etching press (since this is purely surface printing there is no need for the paper to be damped, as for an etching). The plate is removed from the press and the print is laid face up on the bed. Using good-quality paper, I will then cut or tear shapes and arrange them on the printed surface. The plate, having been cleaned and inked in a different colour, is laid inked surface down on the print, with edges carefully registered.

This is again run through the press, the plate lifted and the paper shapes peeled off and laid aside to be used as collage. The process is repeated with further shapes and colours until the image is judged complete.

My last two series are based on Tuscany and Venice. I don't make finished drawings as research for these images. I prefer to collect as much varied information as possible, using a digital camera as well as a sketchbook, noting perhaps the colour of a particular building or its shape against the horizon.

Back in the studio an evaluation of all this collected material forms the basis for transforming rich visual experiences into the metaphor of an abstract image.

Jeremy Blighton

I am always observing and making mental notes in my daily life or when travelling, as there is much to see. I will build up a bank of information which will be further developed in my head long before I put pencil to paper. With landscapes, which I will concentrate on here, I find there is no substitute for the experience gained by working outdoors at a location that inspires me; I can immerse myself in its atmosphere and get a real feel for the place. I will sketch in watercolour, graphite or charcoal the elements that fascinate me. Sometimes I exaggerate these elements, taking the study to a point bordering on abstraction. This can be suggested to me whilst in the act of sketching, or later, when developing the composition for the eventual etching.

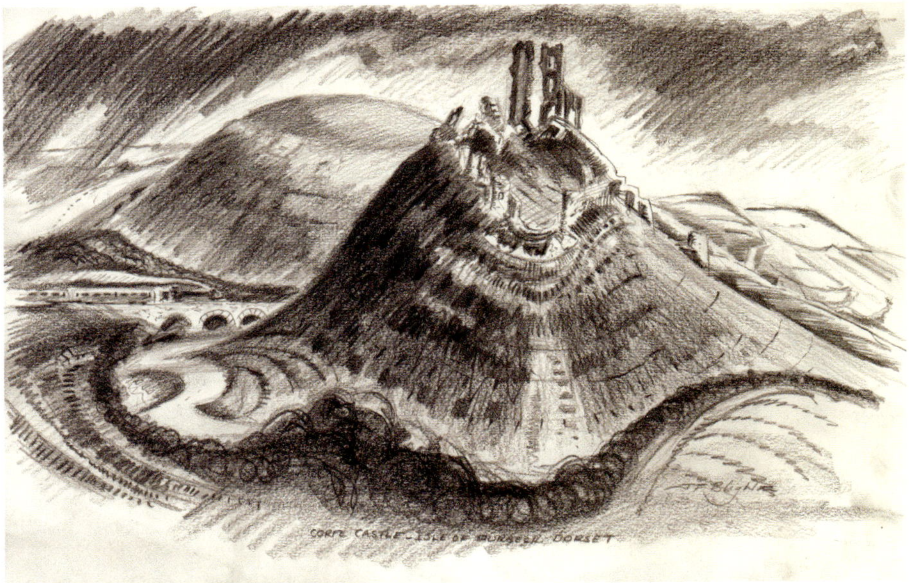

Corfe Castle and the Purbeck Ridge, 2007. Sketch made on the spot, graphite, 25 x 40 cm (9⅞ x 15¾ in.)

The sketch is only the beginning. When viewed back in the studio it can help focus the mind and reignite the emotional response to the recorded place. This I can draw on when working on the final composition. I start with a tonal drawing in graphite. By this time I will usually have a fairly clear idea of what I want to do with the subject, due to the experience of the sketching day and having normally worked on it mentally for a few days too. I build and change the composition until I am happy with it, shaping it into an image that satisfies me, but one that is also a clear reflection of a time and place.

Then on to the etching stage. After the main lines are bitten I apply the aquatint. It is during the stopping-out phase that most of the invention of surfaces takes place. I will experiment with brushstrokes and invent shapes and patterning. The working drawing is only an indication of the effects I want to achieve: I may discover different ways of interpreting them during this process. It's a bit like painting freely, inventing things on the canvas, but in etching you can only attempt to predict the outcome of your brushstrokes because you cannot see the result until the whole operation is finished and the first print is pulled. The creative process continues throughout the printing procedure as I continue to build the effect I am seeking with varying degrees of tone, gently dragging up ink from the plate's crevices with soft muslin, and hand-wiping selectively.

Each part of the journey, from sketching in the landscape to pulling the final print, enables me to add in a different way to the development of the piece. It is very satisfying when the result turns out well, a fitting reward for all those hours invested: one glance at the finished work will instantly take me back to the day spent on the spot where it all began.

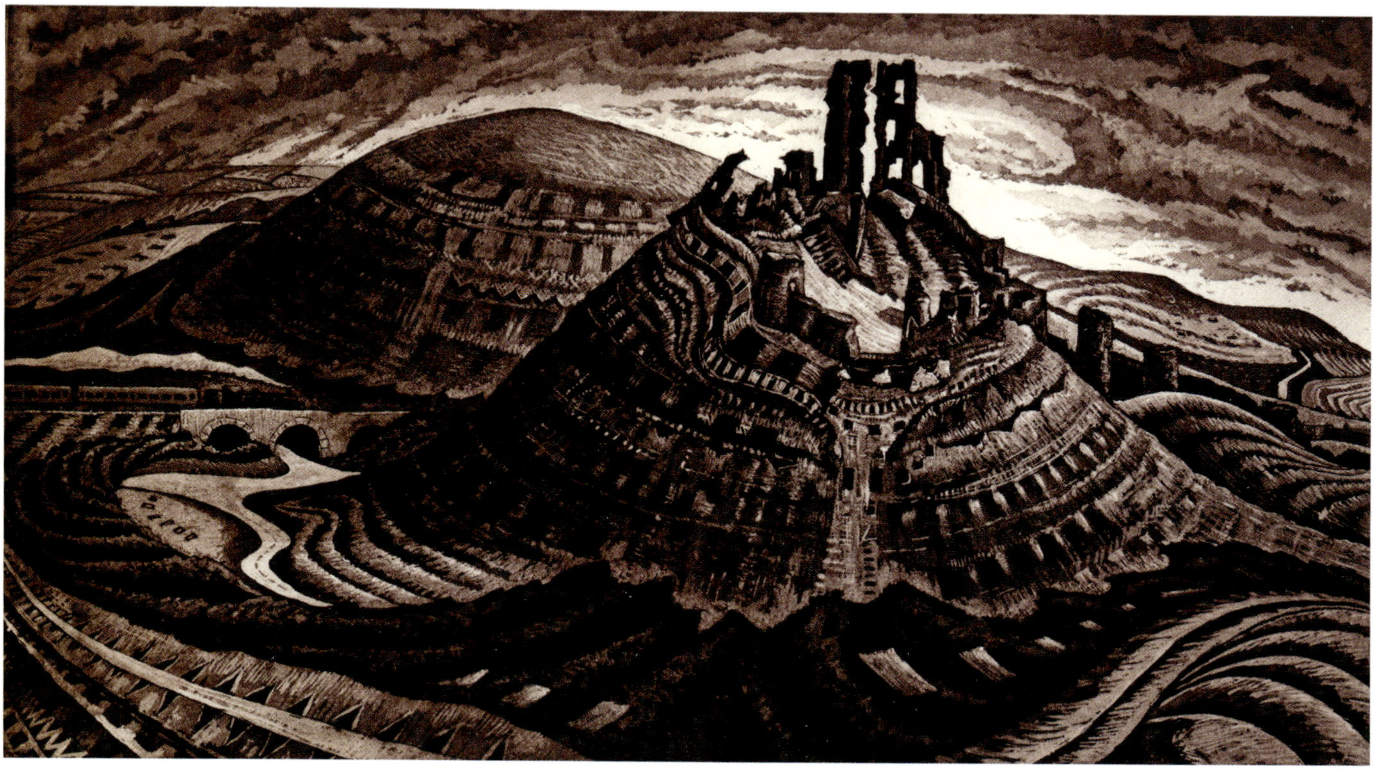

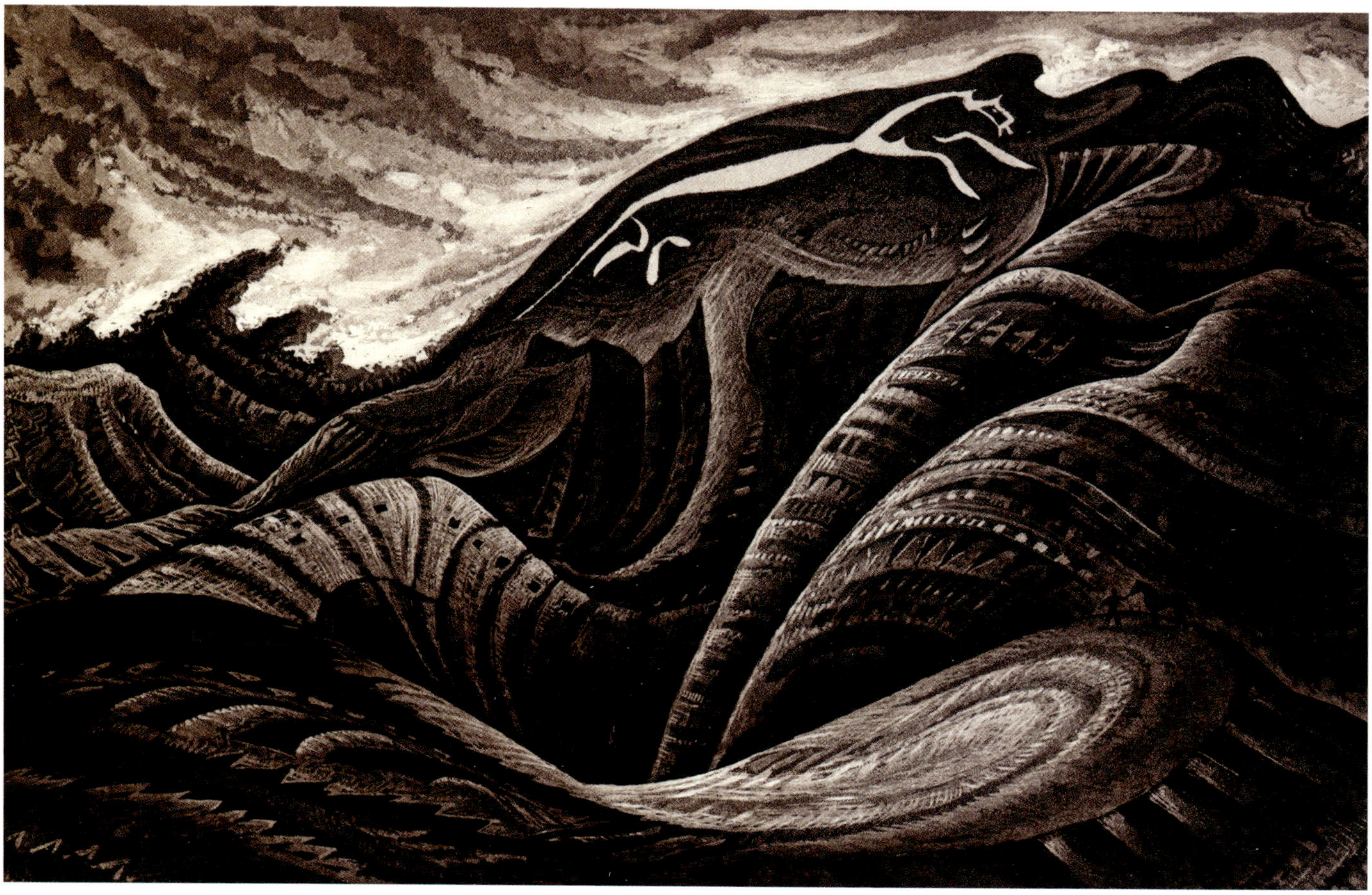

Top: **Corfe Castle and the Purbeck Ridge**, 2007. Etching and aquatint, 16.5 x 30 cm (6½ x 11¾ in.)
Above: **White Horse Hill**, 2006. Etching and aquatint, 21.5 x 34 cm (8½ x 13⅜ in.)

Gail Brodholt

I am interested in the effects of light, especially in an urban setting, and I try to achieve a richness of surface in my work to express the intensity and depth of the long shadows at the end of the day, or the city lights at night. As a painter, I can portray these qualities in various ways, but as a printmaker I have to work much more within the constraints of the medium.

To my mind, lino does not lend itself particularly well to a linear approach; it has no intrinsic texture and I find it is generally more effective at portraying broad sweeps of flat area and colour. I have tried various ways of overcoming these challenges, pushing at the boundaries of whatever detail and texture I can achieve. There is a limit to how much detail I can attain by cutting into a lino block. Careful calculations have to be made as to which details are essential and how much can be achieved with a few structural lines. I like to print the first block with a very dark tone and then print the second with a paler colour, the incisions in the second block revealing the dark layer of ink underneath. This can produce some very fine dark lines, providing a good framework for the finished print. This approach contrasts with the more usual method of printing the lightest colour first and then progressing through to the darkest in order to get those very strong, flat blocks of colour that are so characteristic of the medium.

Another challenge for me is in

Snow in the Suburbs, 2007. Linocut, 40 x 70 cm (15¾ x 27½ in.)

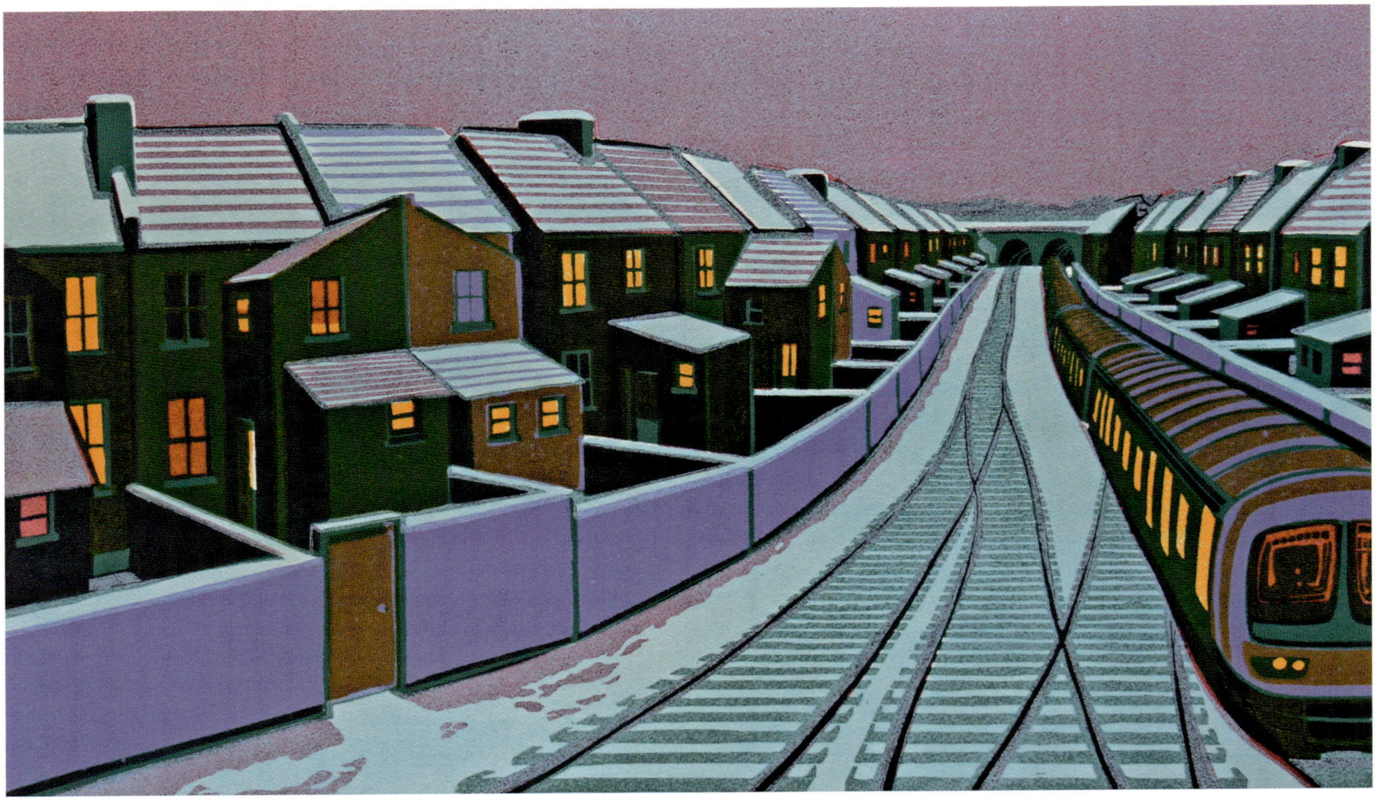

trying to create an interesting surface. I have developed several ways of extending the range of textures by experimenting with the sequence of printing. By beginning with a dark colour and overlaying with a paler tone, as described above, a texture can be created (mottled, pitted or highly glazed, to give three examples) depending on how thickly the subsequent inks are applied. By printing the first block with an opaque ink, a flat surface is created, and by printing the second colour very thinly over the top, the base colour shows through and creates a grainy effect. Adding reducing medium to the ink creates an even thinner layer and results in a smooth shiny glaze, often giving rise to another colour in the process. For example, using a crimson glaze over a matt turquoise produces a wonderful purple-black. This technique is especially effective if parts of the first block are cut away and the glaze used on the second is printed not only over the first colour but also directly onto the bare paper, as the white shows through the glaze to create a luminous quality, contrasting well with the mottled and grainy areas.

As printing progresses, more pronounced peaks and troughs are formed on the surface, and every subsequent layer of ink becomes harder to cover evenly. This in itself creates an interesting surface, the pitted and thickly inked parts of the image contrasting sharply with the vibrantly glazed areas. In this way I build up the various layers of transparent and opaque ink to create an atmospheric, painterly effect, although the finished result can be hard to predict. It can be a time-consuming and laborious process, as I often have to make numerous proofs before I get the result I want; but the often unexpected results can take me in new and rewarding directions.

Shadows in the City, 2007. Linocut, 40 x 70 cm (15¾ x 27½ in.)

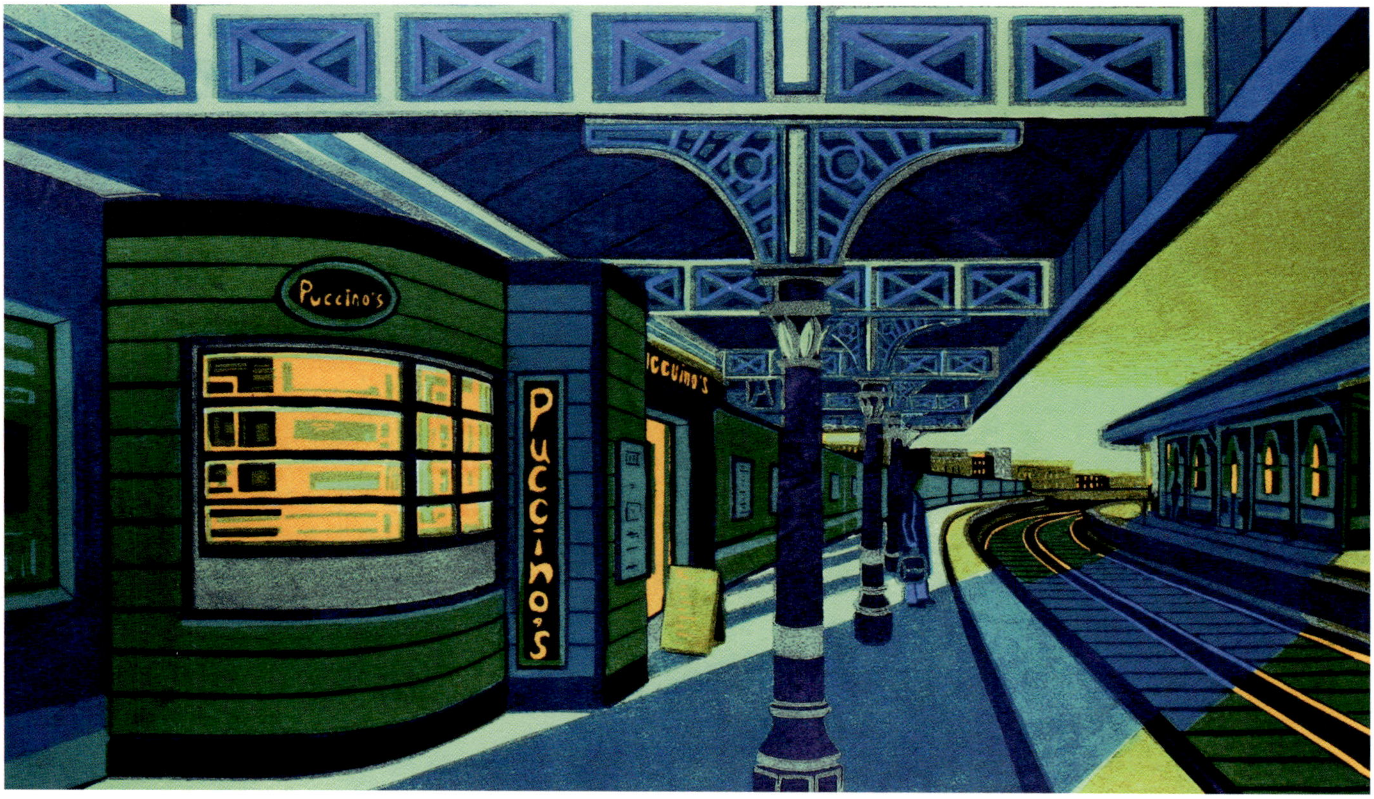

John Bryce

My first introduction to wood engraving was in the sixth form at school. My art master, J. Harvey Bloom, an accomplished wood engraver, took me under his wing. He was a wonderful teacher who inspired me in my later printmaking work.

Testing the Trent, John Bryce, 1995. Wood engraving, 12.5 x 10 cm (5 x 4 in.)

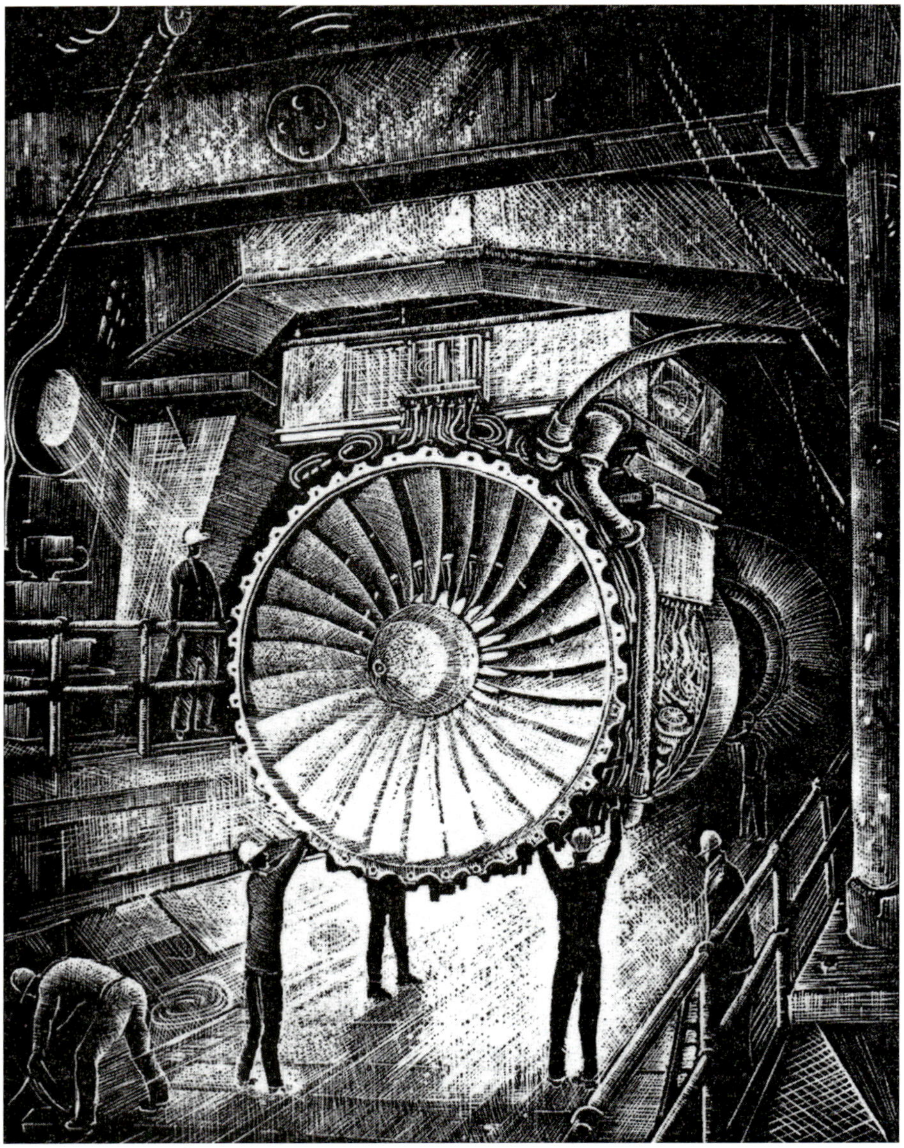

After graduating in mechanical engineering from King's College London, I entered the Royal Aerospace Establishment, Farnborough, to work on aero engine research. This challenging and absorbing technical work had one big and unexpected influence on my art, because it gave me access to the magnificent aero engines being installed in the test cells. During the ten years or so before retirement I was granted permission to sketch these engines. Being very interested in the dramatic contrasts of light and shadow in the enclosed, artificially lit environment of a cavernous test cell, I used my drawings as the basis for the wood engraving *Testing the Trent* in which these striking effects of lighting were further heightened.

I attach great importance to personal experience and to drawing directly from the subject. Therefore, I obtain most of my material for engraving by painting on the spot as a member of two inspiring groups of painters. The first, the Guild of Aviation Artists, represents a natural extension of my previous experience as an aviation researcher. On one of my painting days, I came across a brace of propellers in a hangar at Duxford. This inspired the wood engraving *Props*, with its interplay of light on the blades and background fuselage and with the distant figure emphasising the scale of the aircraft and hangar.

The second group is The Wapping Group of Artists. Limited to 25 members, it meets every Wednesday

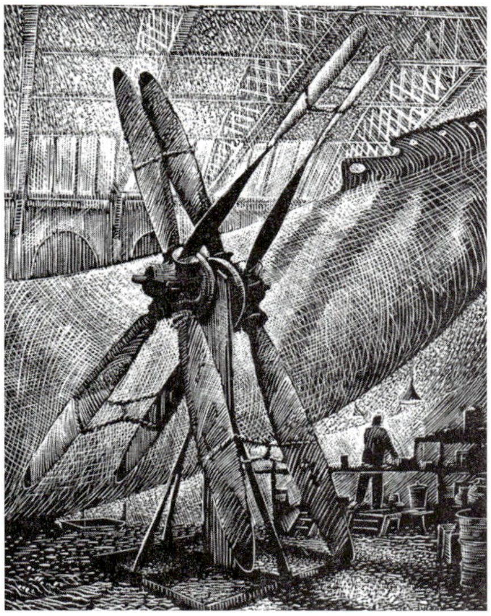

Props, 2002. Wood engraving, 10 x 7.5 cm (4 x 3 in.)

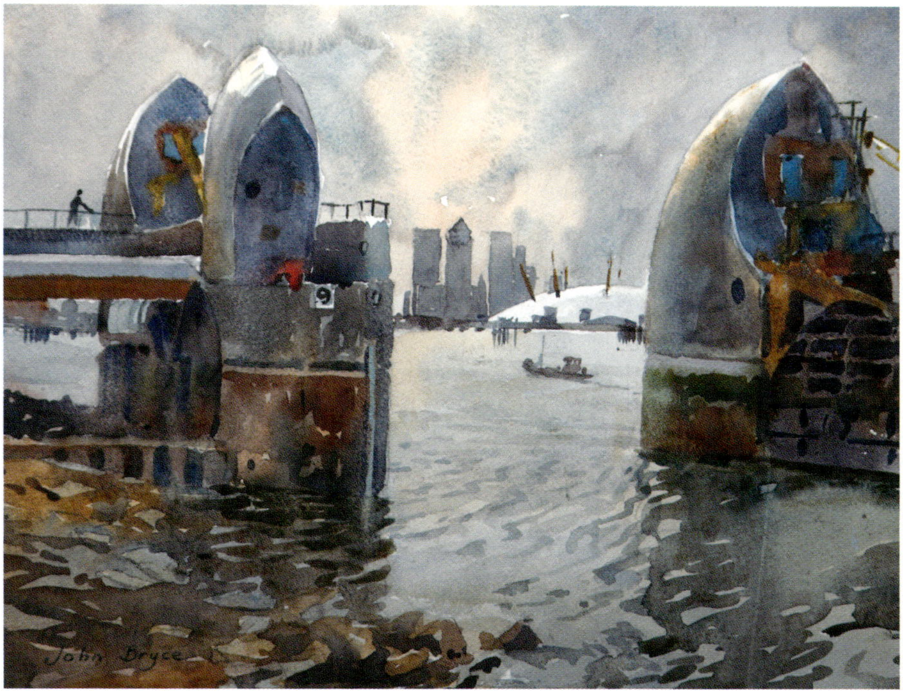

Thames Barrier, 2007. Watercolour, 24 x 34 cm (9½ x 13⅜ in.)

throughout the summer to paint at different spots along the River Thames, from Henley to the Estuary. These expeditions have spawned many wood engravings; one of which I am particularly proud is *Thames Barrier*, a prize winner at the Royal Academy Summer Exhibition in 2007. Using my watercolour painting as inspiration, my objectives for the wood engraving were threefold: firstly, to depict the view through the Barrier to the Millennium Dome and Canary Wharf in the distance; then to show the machinery and cabins in stark contrast; and lastly, to introduce a metaphysical atmosphere with dramatic light in the sky and turbulence in the water.

In my latest wood engravings I have been greatly influenced by the work of Gertrude Hermes RA RE, who so skilfully applied her engraving tools to cut a multiplicity of varying marks to depict mood. I tried to emulate these ideas in *Thames Barrier* by using scorpers, gravers and spitstickers to produce marks suggesting violence and fantasy in the sky and water.

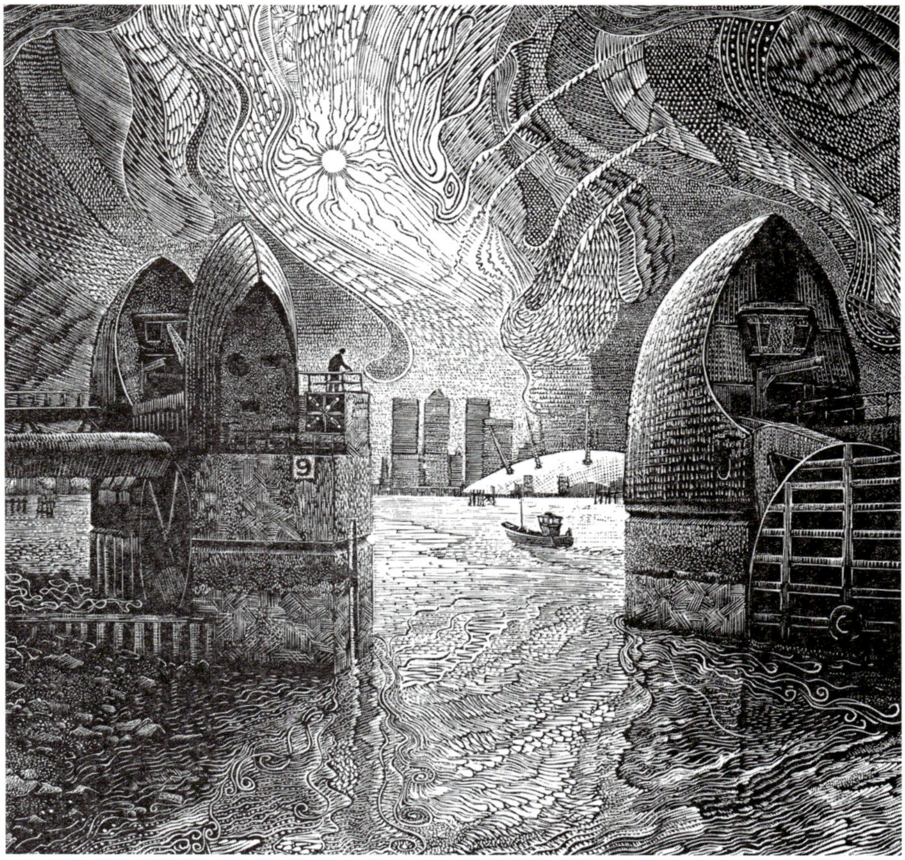

Thames Barrier, 2007. Wood engraving, 16.5 x 18 cm (6½ x 7 in.)

Corinna Button

For me, painting and printmaking are very closely linked; they seem somehow fused, cross-referenced, with shared textural qualities. Starting with the intention of making a print, I sometimes end up with something more like a painting. I often begin with the surface of the paper, perhaps by spraying or brushing on a layer of emulsion paint for textural effect and rubbing in ink or superimposing a wash of thinner paint; I then continue by printing in monotype on this prepared surface. I am constantly in search of freshness, spontaneity, immediacy of line. I don't like images that look rehearsed. To reach this goal I sometimes attack the built-up surface, scraping and carving through layers of dried paint and ink to bring to light, with a new richness, the layers beneath. This can also give surfaces an intriguing ambiguity. It also means that I don't always make a print suitable for editioning in the conventional way, though my process does often lead to interesting monotype images, unique and unrepeatable.

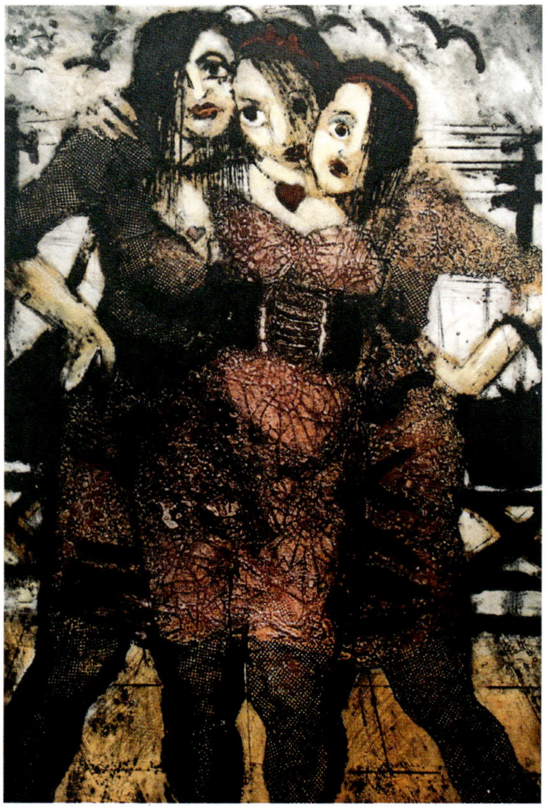

On the Pull, 2007. Collagraph with carborundum, etching and drypoint, 85 x 60 cm (33½ x 23⅝ in.)

It is evident that accident can play a very important part in this procedure and that the result can often be positive. An account of the evolution of the collagraph *Moonlighting* explains the benefits of the unpredictable. My plate was a sheet of white-coated hardboard and all the stages of printing were made from this. First, I glued card and carborundum grit to the surface and added layers of enamel paint. When all this was firmly set, I used gouges and a drypoint tool to define the shapes of the figure and the vase of flowers. Next, I loosely painted the surface with thinned acrylic paint and blotted it with tissue paper to achieve a mottled effect. My printing paper, already trapped and laid back on the upper roller of the etching press, was very quickly lowered onto the painted surface, and I rubbed the back of it, gently transferring the colour. The damped paper, still trapped to ensure accurate registration, was laid back over the roller.

I rolled black etching ink on the textured surface of the plate and wiped with a pad of scrim, as for an etching, leaving ink in the crevices. I also ground red oil pastel and worked it into some of the gouged-out flower shapes. The plate was put back on its marked-out place on the bed and run through the press; this established the key image.

Next, the plate having been thoroughly cleaned, a layer of Prussian-blue etching ink, mixed with extender to reduce its strength, was rolled on; selected areas were blotted with tissue paper and others wiped with muslin to create highlights, and the print was taken.

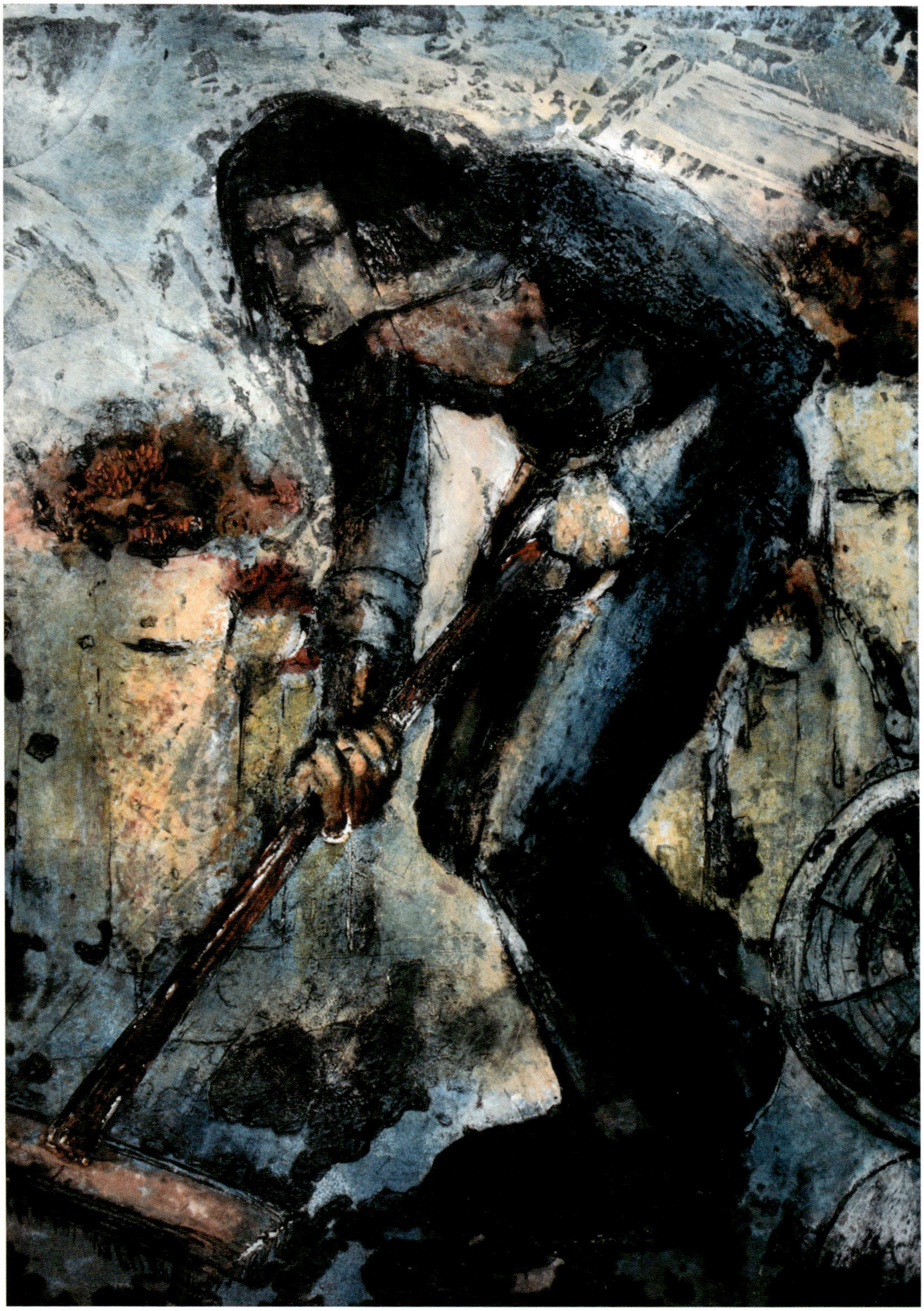

Moonlighting, 2001. Collagraph with carborundum and monotype, 81 x 61 cm (31⅞ x 24 in.)

Finally, I had planned to overprint the thin residue left on the surface after the previous printing; but the sudden interruption of my daughter bursting into the room made me lie the plate the wrong way on the press bed and so, of course, it printed upside down – and it worked! The ghostly traces of the foreground had appeared in the sky, enhancing to good effect the turbulence of the image!

David L. Carpanini

The term painter-printmaker is, in my case, absolutely correct. There is no order of importance; each method of pictorial resolution allows me to explore different aspects of my personal vision, which is almost exclusively concerned with the Afan Valley, the place of my birth in South Wales.

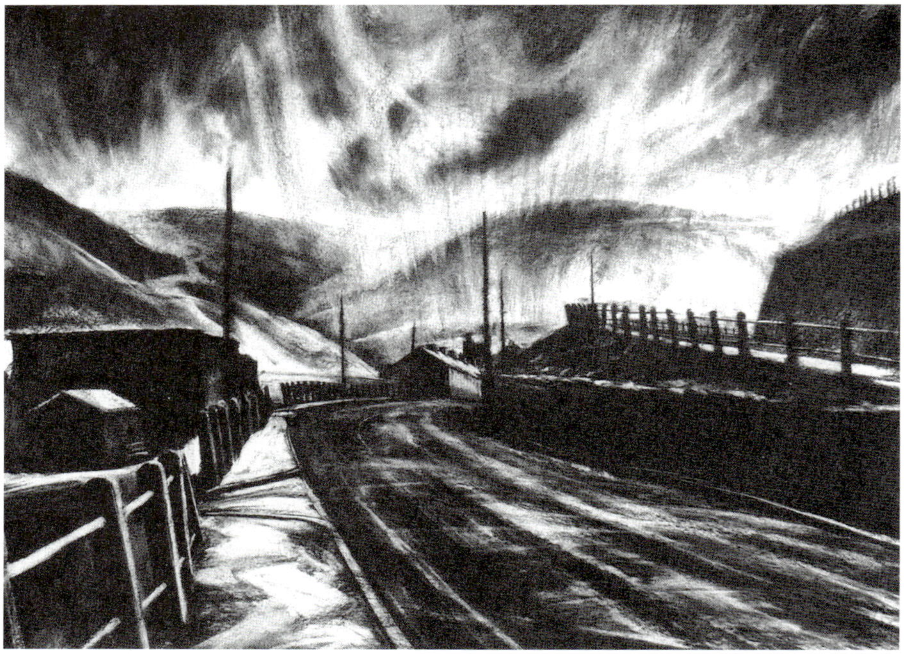

Storm over the Bwlch. Etching 33.3 x 46.5 cm (13⅛ x 18¼ in.)

Storm over the Avon. Etching, 48 x 58.5 cm (18⅞ x 23 in.)

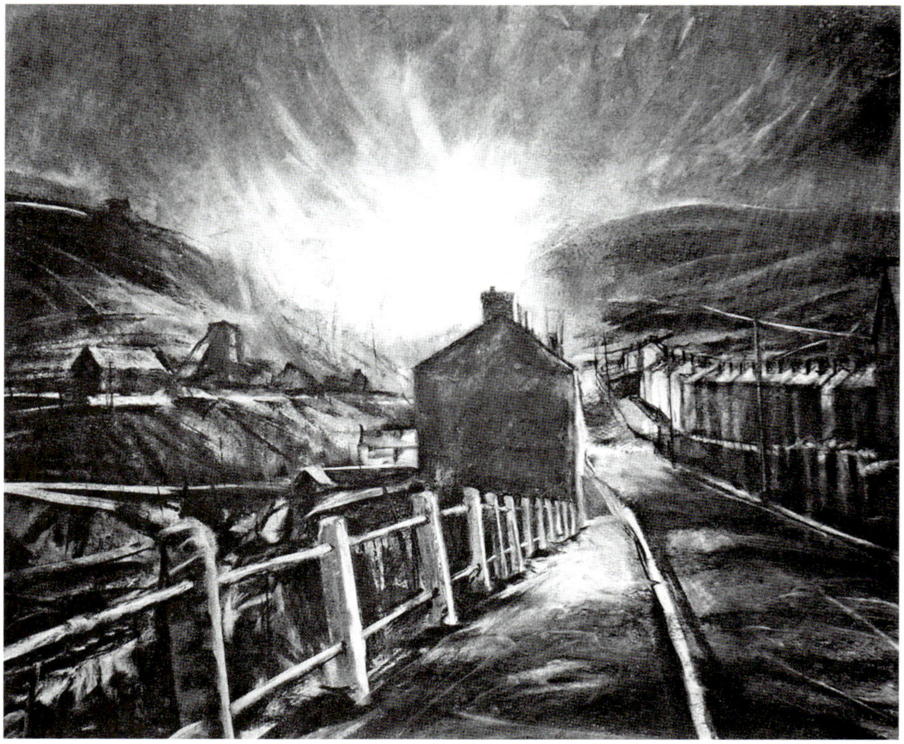

Wales is a land of enormous contrasts and variety of scenery. However, my inspiration lies in the contemplation of the familiar. I believe that man has a special bond, a special relationship with that part of Earth which nourished his boyhood and it is in the valleys and former mining communities of South Wales, scarred by industrialisation but home to a resolute people, that I found the trigger for my creative imagination. I remain grateful for having been born there at a particular time in the history of those valleys and with a modest facility for recording my reactions.

The stark landscape and the close-knit and often claustrophobic social infrastructure are a fundamental part of my own background. I have attempted to use the natural drama of this location to explore aspects of the human condition such as fear, isolation, loneliness, brutality, dignity, pride and hope – concepts with which we can all identify regardless of personal circumstances or background. My imagery is drawn

Thunder Mountain. Etching, 47.5 x 34 cm (18¼ x 13⅜ in.)

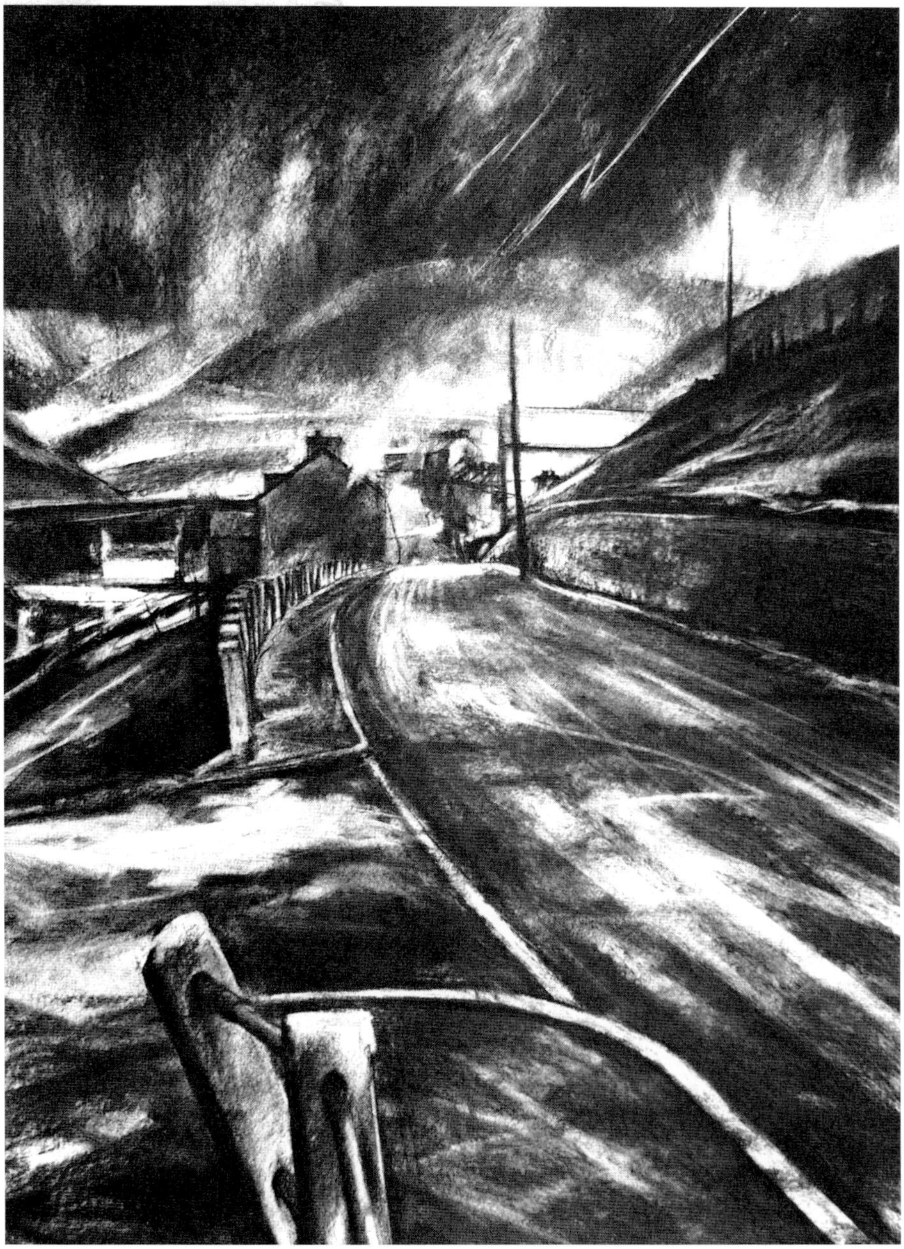

from my background and experience because it is what I know best. Inevitably, there is the danger of nostalgic insularity, but with a measure of critical awareness it is possible to go beyond time and place and touch a universal chord of human understanding.

All my paintings and prints are studio assemblages; unhurried distillations of sketchbook observations and visual memories. I have always made extensive use of small notebooks. These are working tools in which I make records of both a graphic and literary nature of figures, clouds, buildings; of whatever fleeting impression or group of forms captures my attention. These observations are not always put to immediate use; indeed months, even years, may elapse before a particular theme is explored further. It is an accumulative and assimilative procedure that in Graham Sutherland's words makes the artist 'as absorbent as blotting paper and as watchful as a cat'. For me, it is also the kind of remorseless practice that I find essential to representation at the deepest level.

It is from this reservoir of material that my pictures grow. Serial drawings are developed, compositional studies, searching for the right grouping of figures and their correct relationship to an appropriate setting, anticipating that the eventual combination of forms will prove emotionally expressive and decoratively striking. For me, the design and manner of any work arises as a natural process of growth and evolution, as an extension of object and purpose, not imposed in a preconceived way.

Quite naturally, every artist's work varies considerably in approach. Style and method develop in accordance with personality and temperament. Indeed many psychological and physical factors enter into each person's view of their world. My love of etching, for instance, is closely related to my instinctive delight in 'black and white', and a natural inclination to see and compose in terms of tonal masses. There can be no hard and fast rules, and I am far from being a technical purist in any aspect of the visual arts, but I do believe that we should try to equip ourselves with a knowledge and understanding of the conventions of our craft in order that we can express our vision in a coherent and visually articulate manner.

Eileen Cooper

I still feel new to printmaking. I hope this means that I am always keen to learn from printmaking colleagues and never too proud to ask 'how'. I love the authority of print, the integrated surface, the relationship with paper and the collaborations and workshop banter, so different from working alone as a painter. I find lithography the most difficult process, and here I need maximum support from the printer. The subtlety throws me. In etching I take more control and, as I am confident in drawing, this has begun to work for me. I long to make black etchings, but this eludes me and I inevitably use colour.

Full House, 2007. Screenprint, 69.5 x 89 cm (27 3/8 x 35 in.)

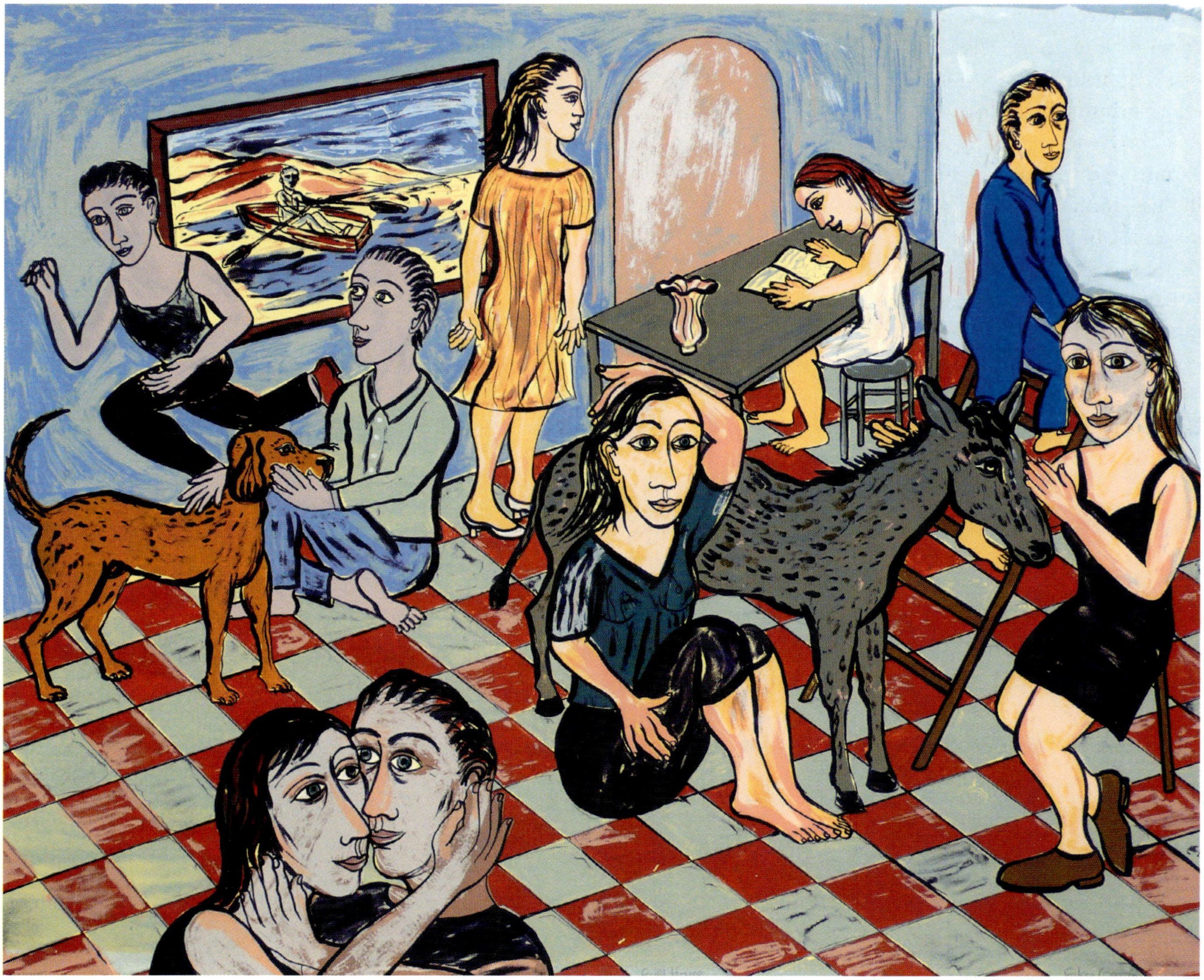

Little Dramas, Scene II, 2008. Linocut, 45 x 61.5 cm (17 3/4 x 24 1/8 in.)

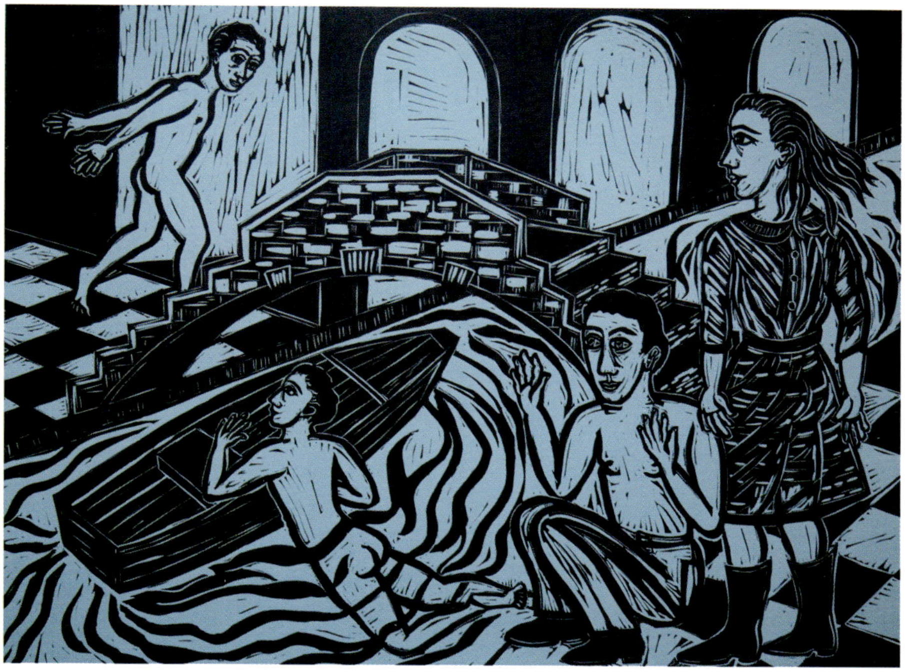

My screenprints have all been made at Glasgow Print Studios with water-based inks and working with master printers. I work intensively on the colour separations in my studio, using film and sending it on to the printers. When I arrive, the screens have been made and the pressure to produce the image is on. It is very exciting.

The process that I have made my own, however, is block-printing. I adore its immediacy and, in hand-printing, its low-tech availability. Hand-printing gives freedom and flexibility: there is huge potential for exploring different effects through the use of a wooden spoon and a baren for burnishing. When establishing an image on a block, I begin working with charcoal and then gouache to define the image until I am ready for cutting. After proofing, I clean off the ink with a little turps, which leaves the gouache drawing in place, for reference, in case I want to do more cutting. Finally, when the cutting is complete, I clean off the block with water, and the charcoal and gouache disappear to leave the block pristine and ready for editioning. Recently, I have been using water-washable inks. I respond to both wood and lino, but in particular it is the flat, bland and forgiving qualities of lino that I hope will help me to do my best work.

The print world has embraced me and has extended my practice. I have worked with wonderful, generous artist-printmakers and have been incredibly fortunate both to be able to teach the subject and to be involved with the new challenges of print. I also believe my painting has been nourished by engaging with printmaking.

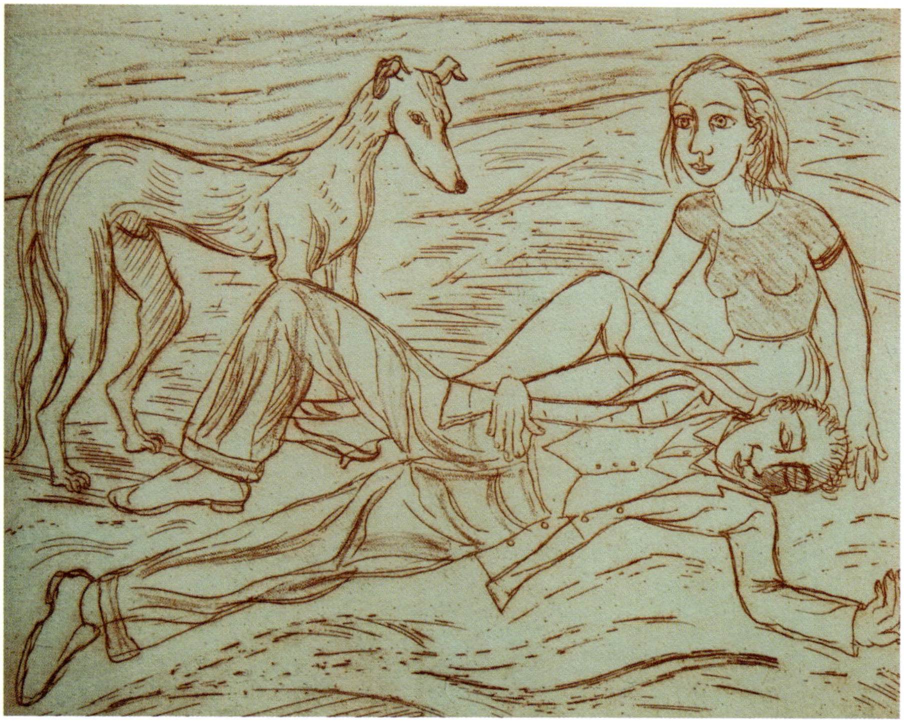

Journey, 2008. Etching with chine collé, 20 x 25 cm (7 7/8 x 9 7/8 in.)

Paul Croft

In hindsight there have been two formative experiences that have had a significant role in the development of my career as an artist. In 1992 I was fortunate to receive an award from the Canadian Elizabeth Greenshields Foundation that enabled me to travel to Japan, where I was to visit Tokyo and Kyoto. In 1994 a further grant from the same foundation allowed me to take up a place on the Master Printer Training Programme at the world-renowned Tamarind Institute in Albuquerque. Whereas the visit to Japan was to awaken within me an almost spiritual and aesthetic approach to conceiving graphic art, it was the rigorous training at the Tamarind Institute that equipped me with the technical dexterity and self-discipline needed to execute images in lithography.

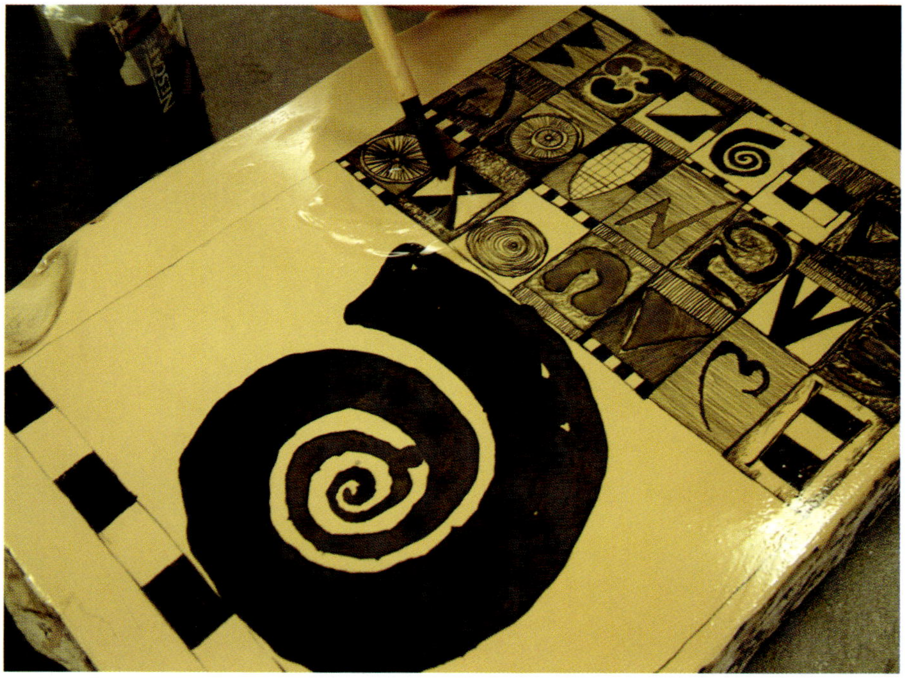

Spot-etching a lithographic stone

In printmaking, it is the practicality of method and material that I find so appealing: the physicality of cutting wood, gouging into lino, etching and engraving metal plate. As for lithography, it is the smell of freshly grained limestone and the alchemy of gum arabic and acid that is so enticing, together with the fascination for tusche – which as it dries upon the polished stone surface reticulates into a tracery of myriad weblike lines. The versatility of lithography is such that all manner of drawn marks can be printed and layered, from the subtlest grey to the densest black and from the slightest tint to full, saturated colour.

Drawing on paper is for me a vital means of expression, though I often employ mixed media – collage, acrylic paint, gouache and graphite. In sketchbooks, drawing is also a means of recording, collating and developing ideas for understanding how an image should be put together. Prior to working on stones and on plates, I endeavour to plan a series of compositional ideas: sets of images that may be executed as lithographs, etchings or screenprints. Important for reference purposes, such drawings are then put aside as the print develops independently and in response to technical factors, mistakes and unexpected outcomes.

Underpinning much of my work there has always been interest in language and the development of visual vocabulary, an obsession confirmed by exposure to the calligraphic nature of Japanese culture. Impressed as I was by the sheer graphic quality of signs, banners, scrolls, packaging, advertising and the language of Hiragana, Katakana and Kanji, I have since discovered that I am fascinated by the etymological development of language and the pictographic origins of symbols, letters, alphabets, characters and words. By the same token I find I am also intrigued by systems of classification and how information is presented by charts, diagrams, lists, lexicons, dictionaries and as thesauri. What appears to be developing in my work is a pictorial language derived from a wide variety of sources, including symbols and characters borrowed and adapted from languages both contemporary and ancient. Inspiration has also come from rock-carved spirals, dots and chevrons found at sites like Newgrange in Ireland and similarly from the petroglyphs of the American South-west. Of course, material both observed and found as flotsam and jetsam from the beach has potential and is capable of synthesis into a new, defined vocabulary.

Recently, with the aid of a computer, I have begun attempting to catalogue and categorise the great many symbols, letters and characters that I have used during the last twenty years. Developing a lexicon of visual characters, a thesaurus of shapes, signs and marks, this dictionary is like no other. As well as incorporating alphabetical letters it also seems to include categories for triangles, circles, stripes, stars, chevrons, dots, crosses and so on. This continuing research seems to be necessary and is leading to new drawings and prints that inevitably will exploit systems for cataloguing such as charts, tables and flow diagrams.

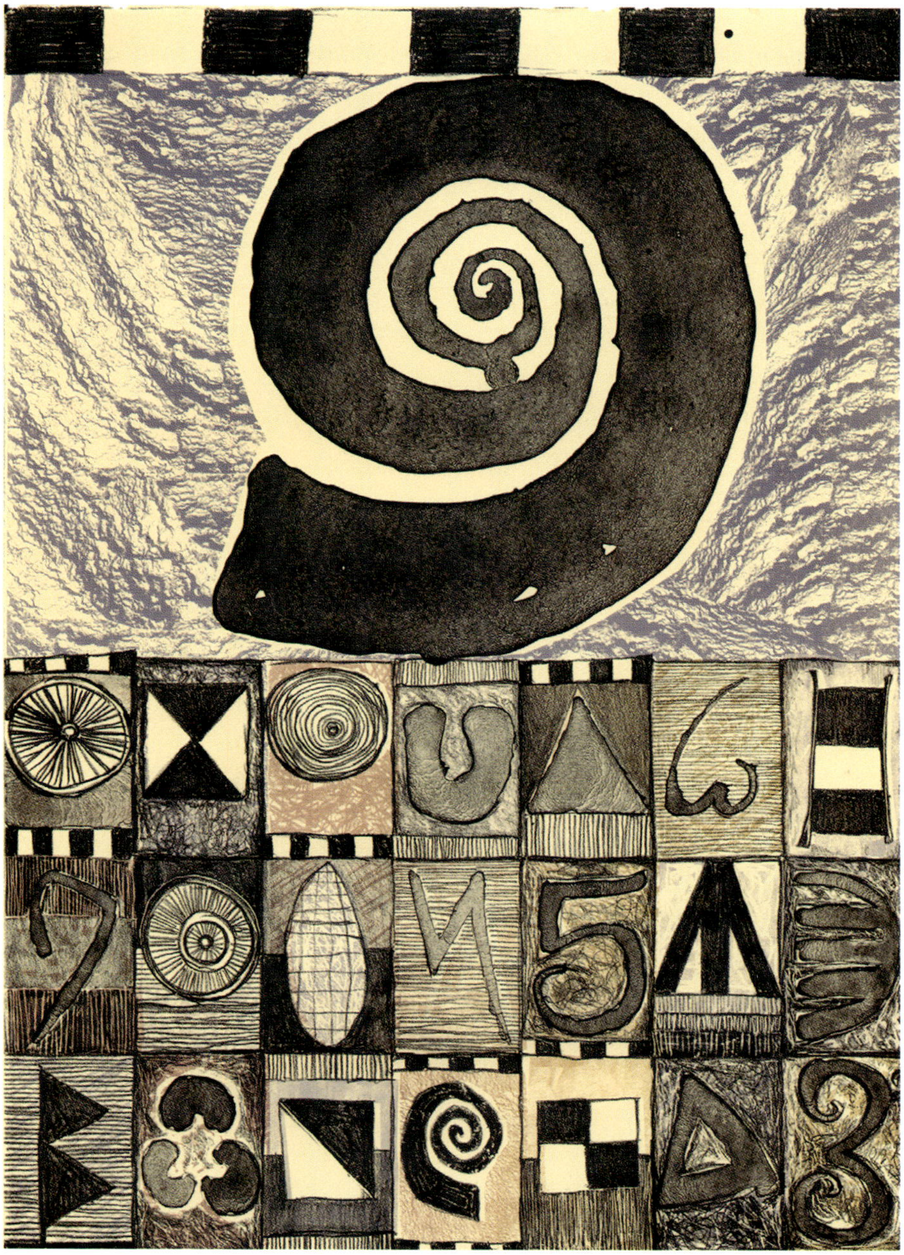

Alphabet D, Lexicon Series: Duong, 2008, Lithograph, 38 x 28 cm (15 x 11 in.)

Claire Dalby

In the uncompromisingly black and white medium of wood engraving my preoccupation is with trying to achieve a wide range of subtly graded tones. I do this by careful planning, cutting and finally printing, to ensure that each part of the block receives just enough pressure to transfer ink to dampened paper. It is a perverse property of physics that a new, uncut woodblock placed in the press will receive more pressure around the edges than in the centre; similarly, an isolated peak of uncut wood will print heavily while a large black area will appear pale and speckly. Light areas, especially near the edges of the block, will need special treatment (lowering) before engraving, while dark areas will also need attention (make-ready) before printing.

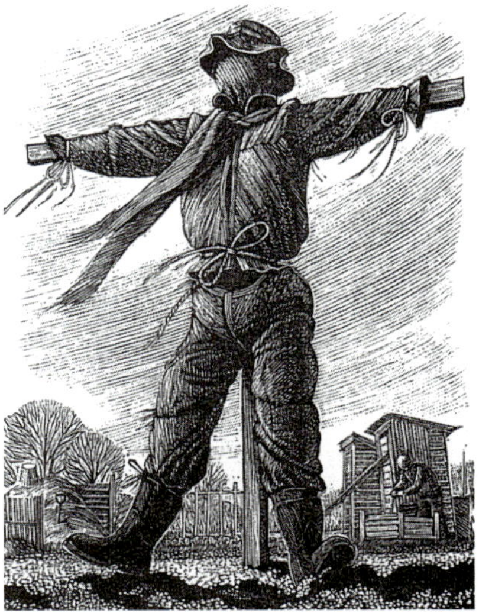

Scarecrow, 1995. Wood engraving, 7.2 x 5.5 cm ($2^7/_8$ x $2^1/_8$ in.)

Below: **Byre at Fladdabister**, 1991. Wood engraving, enlarged from 10.5 x 12.5 cm ($4^1/_8$ x $4^7/_8$ in.)

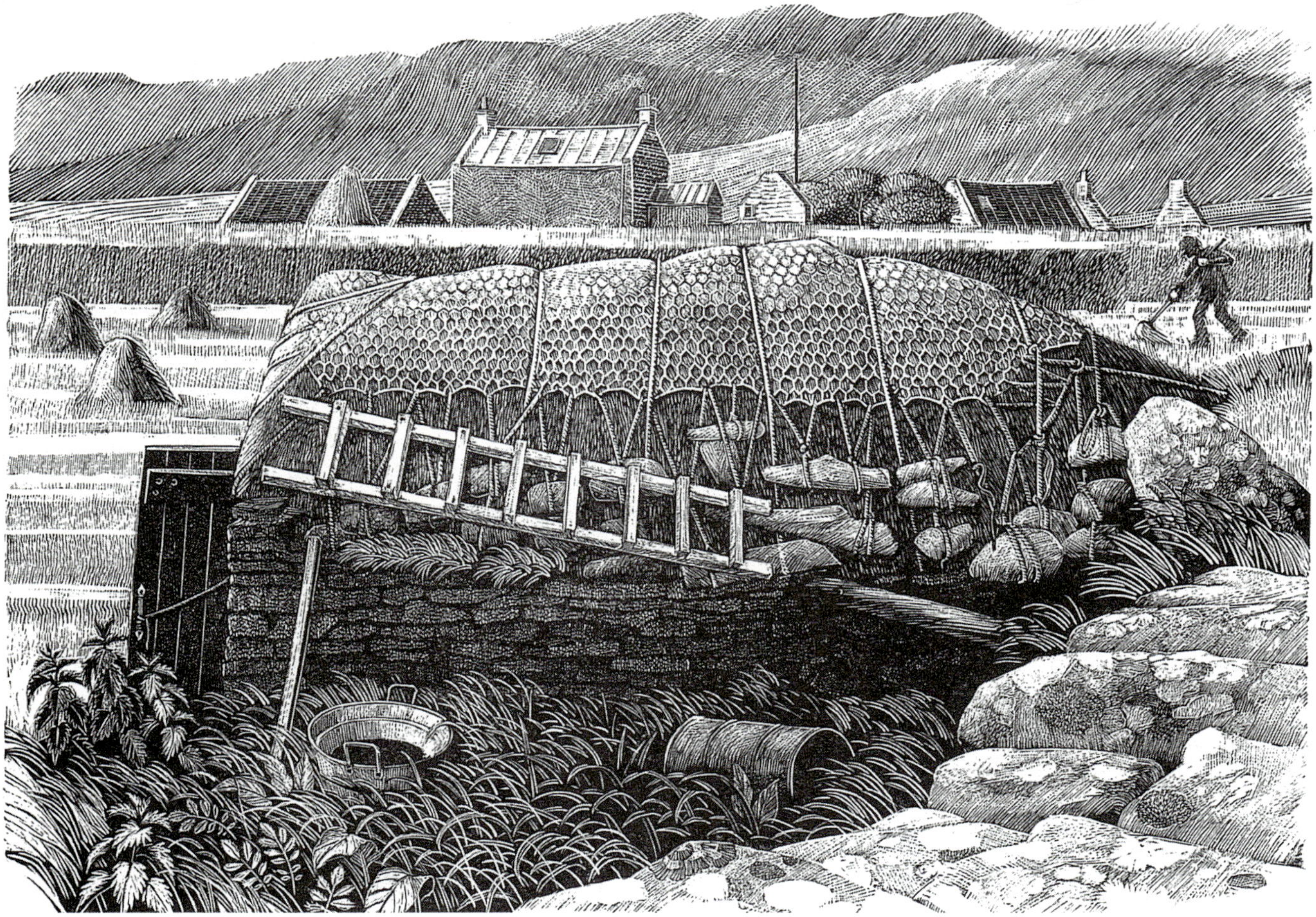

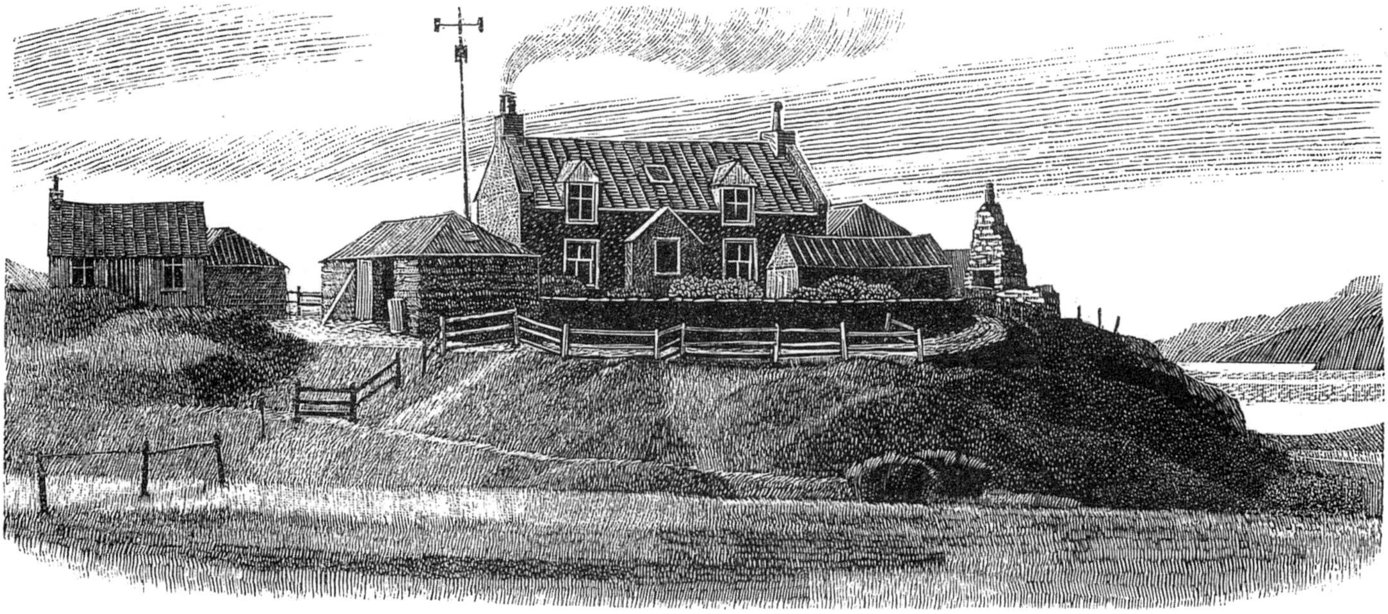

The Croft at Gunnister, 1990. Wood engraving, enlarged from 5.6 x 13 cm (2¼ x 5⅛ in.)

I start by planning an engraving in considerable detail on paper before transferring the drawing (via red chalk-filled grooves scratched in clear acetate) to the slightly whitened (with gouache) boxwood block and going over it in pencil, then ink. This is followed by an extremely thin layer of rubbed-on printing ink so that both the pen drawing (black) and the cut wood (pale) will show up as I work. At this point I borrow a technique from Thomas Bewick (1753–1828), who achieved wonderfully subtle tonal gradations and pale silvery greys by lowering (scraping down) the block's surface extensively to various depths before engraving. This practice is hardly used now, but it ensures that the lowered areas receive both less ink and less pressure. My own lowering, using an etcher's three-sided scraper, is in selected areas: the larger the area and the paler the grey desired, the deeper I excavate, though I rarely exceed 0.75 mm – except towards the edge of a block, where I may want a sky to fade out gradually. While wishing that my pen lines could have penetrated the wood grain and remained visible, I now have to reinstate the parts eliminated by the lowering.

Engraving is a slow process with me, but with the linear and tonal structure of the image clearly drawn, I am free to choose the tools and the marks to make with them to represent textures (foliage, masonry, etc.), and to calculate how many superimposed workings may be needed to achieve a particular tone. I check progress with mini-rubbings, using pencil on tissue paper. Eventually, it is time to take a print; this first impression is invariably miserably dark and patchy and reveals where more work is needed. Now I work with the block in and out of its fixed place in the bed of my Albion press, using a print made directly onto paper stuck to the underside of the tympan and therefore situated precisely over the block. By turns, I engrave to improve the lighter areas, and paste intricately torn layers of tissue paper (make-ready) onto the tympan print to build up pressure on the darker areas.

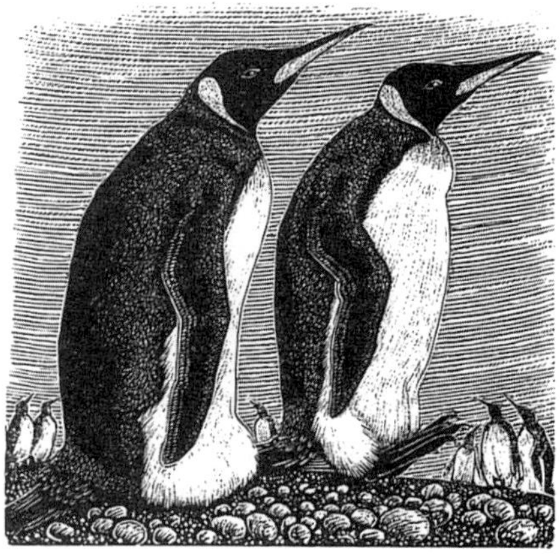

King Penguins, 2002. Wood engraving, enlarged from 4.8 x 4.9 cm (*c.* 2 x 2 in.)

Finally, after some twelve states, the results are acceptable, and then printing the whole edition is, by contrast, a very speedy procedure.

Anne Desmet

My starting point is in drawings in pocket-sized sketchbooks. Here I get to grips with the way light creates sculptural illusions and highlights unexpected shapes – such as the ovoid splash of sunlight cast through the oculus of Rome's Pantheon. I draw in pencil or pen, adding a monochrome wash of black fountain-pen ink heavily diluted with water. This grey-blue liquid isn't lightfast but it is an invaluable instant formula for recording dramatic shadows. I never copy slavishly from a drawing: engraved/cut lines are so different from those generated by drawing tools and so diverse that, to me, the excitement of creating a print comes in the spontaneous mark-making that happens on the block.

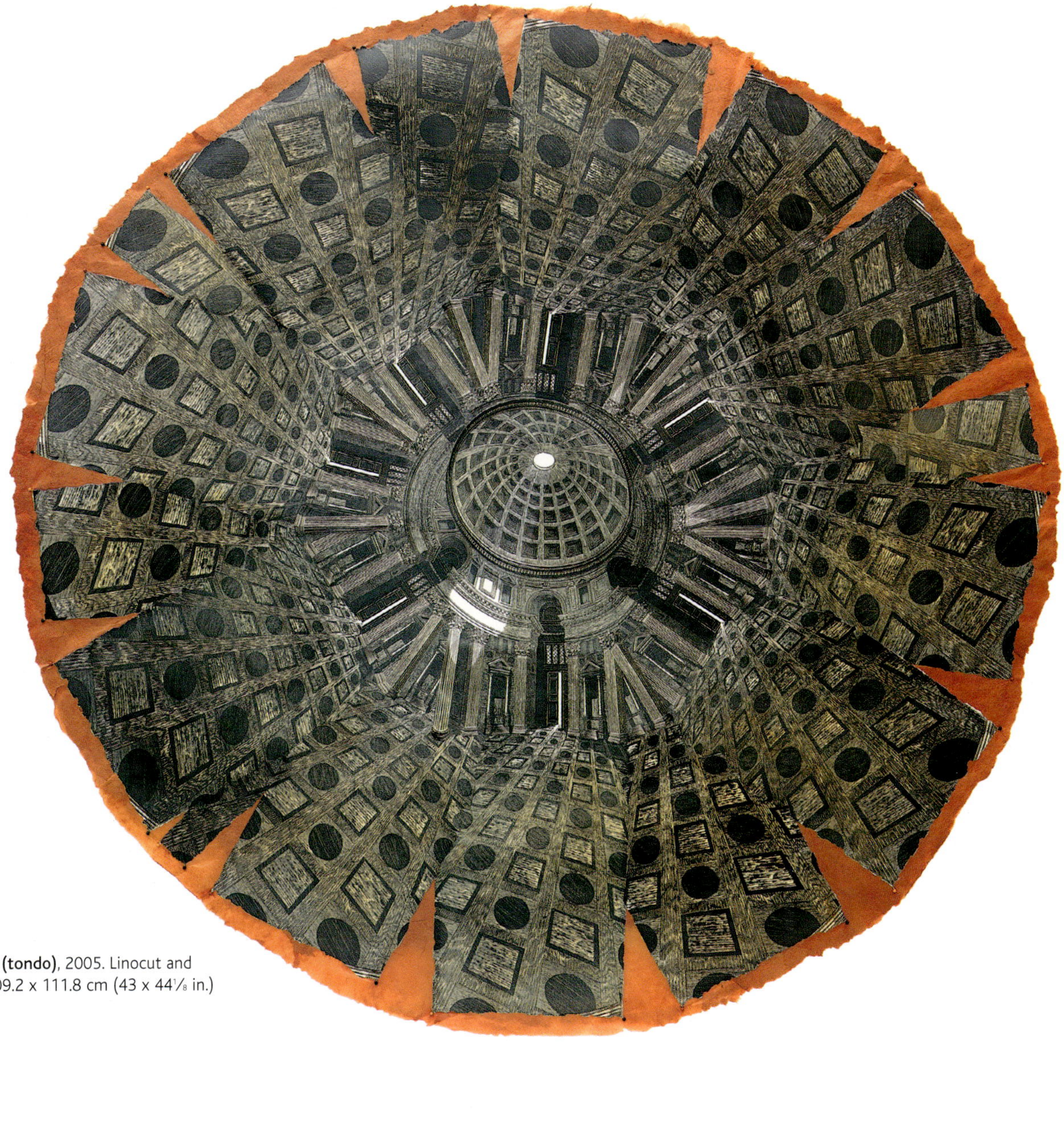

Pantheon (tondo), 2005. Linocut and collage, 109.2 x 111.8 cm (43 x 44⅛ in.)

Right: **Pantheon**, 1992. Pencil and ink wash, 28.5 x 9.6 cm (11¼ x 3⅞ in.)

Far right: **Pantheon**, 2000. Two-block linocut, 61 x 20.3 cm (24 x 8 in.)

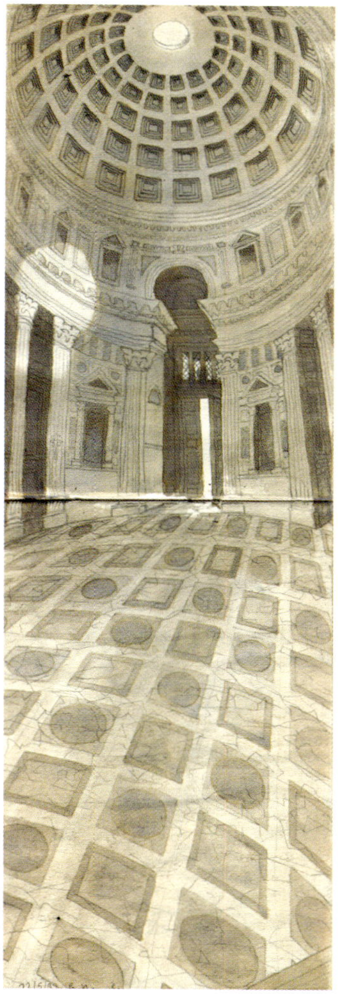

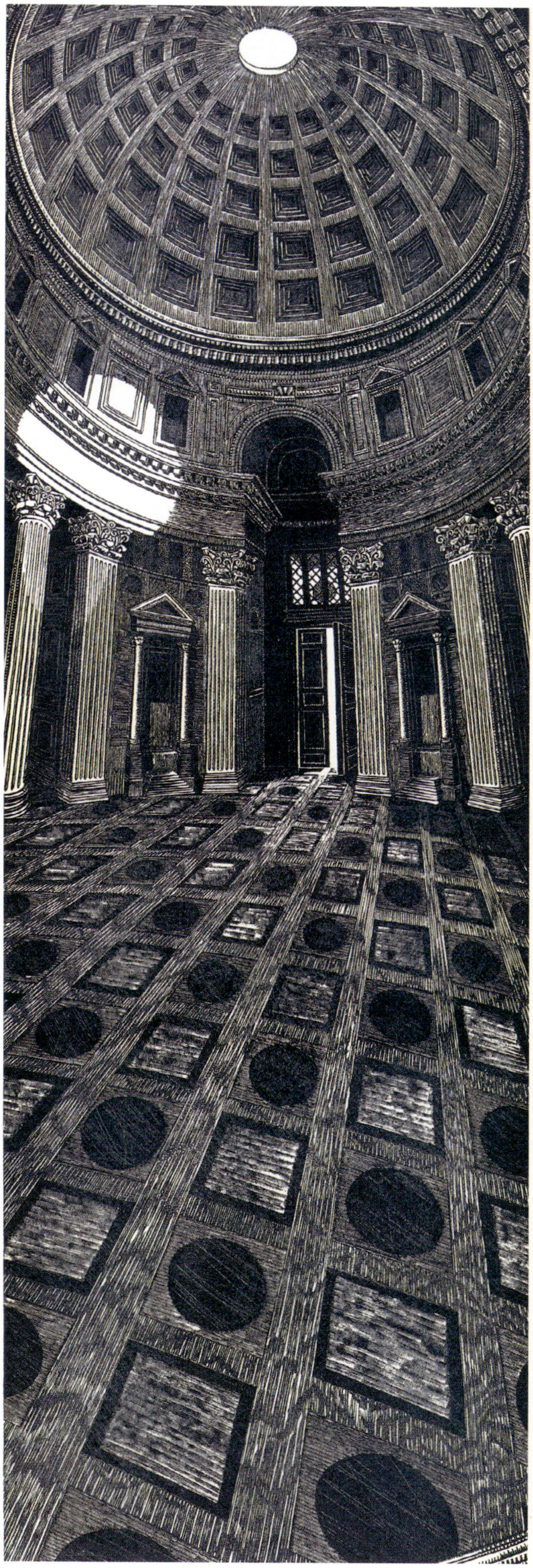

To develop a drawing into a print, I start by polishing the lino with wet & dry sandpaper – applied wet – to rub its surface to a glassy smoothness that will print much more crisply than if left untreated. I make two black and white photocopies of my drawing, enlarged or reduced to the selected block's size. One copy is a mirror image of the original, which I find a handy reference whilst cutting. I use acetone to transfer the toner from the non-reversed copy onto the lino.

Scaling up revealed perspectival oddities that I remedied by drawing on the block with a Chinagraph (waxy) pencil; this can be rubbed off with a rag and redrawn, as necessary, before fixing final outlines in indelible pen.

I cut lino with V and U-gouges – my favourites (and many of my wood-engraving tools) once belonged to the fine painter-etcher Paul Drury PPRE (1903-87). On this block, too, I used a wood-engraving 'multiple tool' – a fine blade with about five teeth for cutting ultra-fine parallel lines; just skimming the surface, it engraves lino surprisingly well. I also used a roulette wheel to indent lines of dots on the block.

When printing from lino or wood, I apply finely rolled, stiff, oil-based ink and print on Japanese papers: Gampi Vellum or Kozu shi; or European: Somerset Satin (as in this print) or Zerkall. My Albion press is too small for a block of this size, so I placed block and paper (in registration 'L' slots) on a long thin board and slid this 'sandwich' onto the press bed, with half sticking out. I printed the half on the bed, then turned the 'sandwich' around to print the other half. I then offset a print from the key block onto a second block, out of which I cut a few highlights before overprinting a cream tone.

My prints also provide the raw material for collages, such as *Pantheon (tondo)*. This comprises some fifteen torn coloured strips from proofs of the Pantheon linocut, assembled in a rough circle, radiating from a central point on the building's oculus and collaged against a red-hued Nepalese paper. The aim of the work was to convey a sense of being within, and enveloped by, this dizzying elliptical structure.

Kate Dicker

The Toy Cupboard *was produced in collaboration with Tom Martin, studio manager at The Curwen Studio. It took two days to transform my toy-soldier line drawing into an expressive colour print.*

We made four lithographic photo-sensitive plates. It was intended that the first one would be experimental, and it was made by manipulating a mixture of chemicals over its surface to bring unpredictable and exciting results. Once the plate was brought from the darkroom Tom gave me two minutes, in daylight, to create an 'explosive' background! I carefully, but randomly, poured, dribbled and mixed equal amounts of motor oil and photographic developer over the plate's emulsion. Immediately, the emulsion was dissolved, before finally reconstituting itself with a dappled effect. Again, with the mixture I made a few sweeping strokes with a little rag and watched as these completely wiped away the green emulsion. These areas left no base for the printing ink at all and therefore would read white (the paper colour) on the final print. Quickly, the chemicals were rinsed off and the 'image' established. As it was intended to provide the background, this plate

Toy Cupboard, 1994. Offset lithograph, 44 x 66 cm ($17\frac{3}{8}$ x 26 in.)

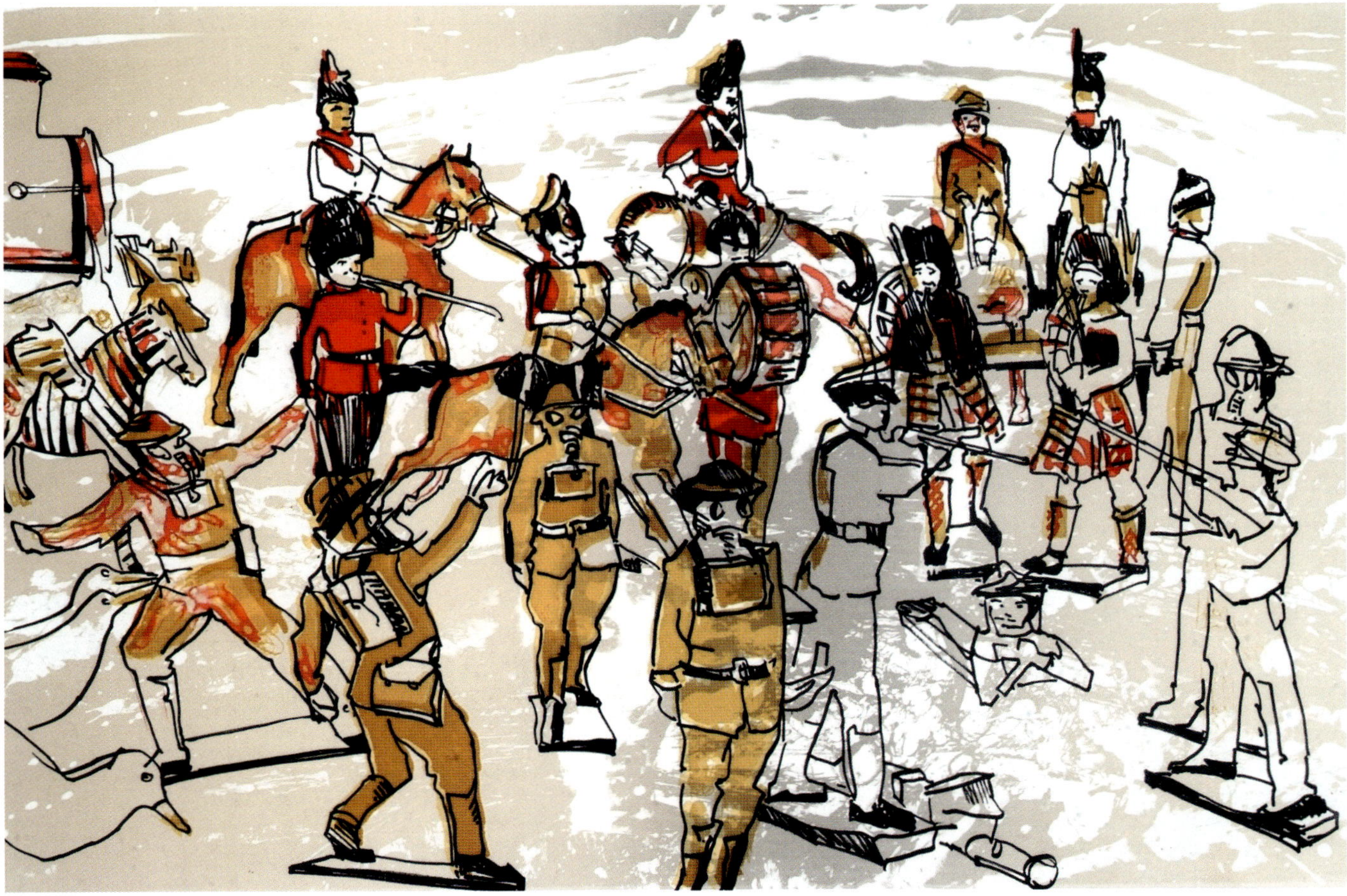

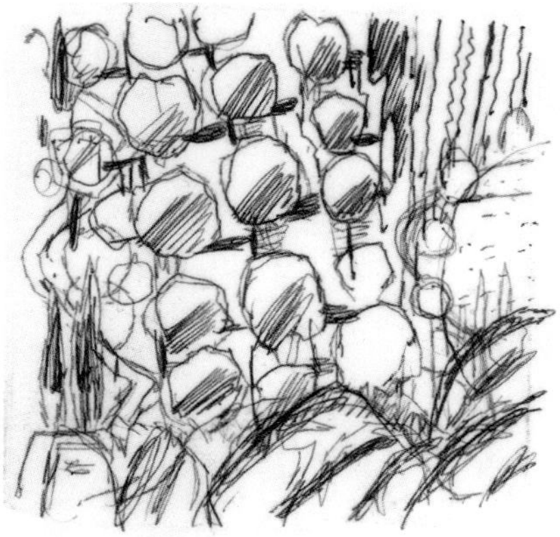

Above: **Tuscan Trees,** 2002. Sketch, 10 x 10 cm (4 x 4 in.)

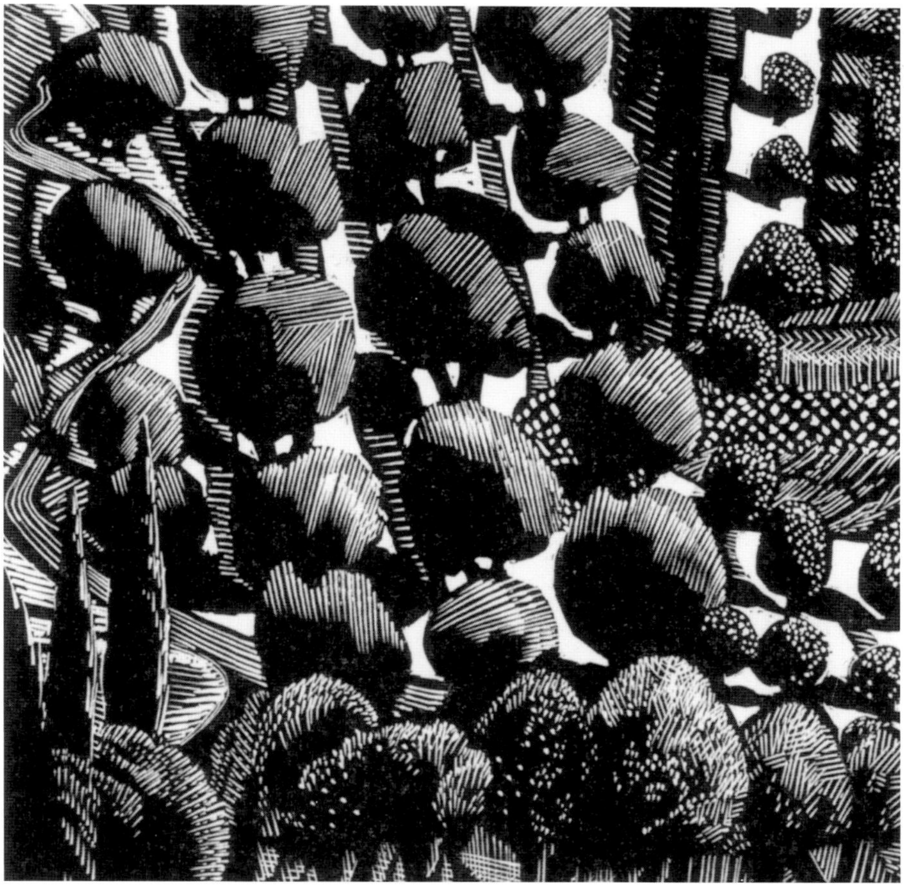

Right: **Tuscan trees,** 2002. Wood engraving, 10 x 10 cm (4 x 4 in.)

was the first to be printed, using a blend of warm and cool browns.

The second plate carried my felt-tip, A2 line drawing, which was copied onto acetate and enlarged slightly to fit the plate size. It was exposed onto an aluminium photosensitive plate in the studio's ultraviolet-light unit. The third and fourth plates carried the two 'spot' colours, red and khaki, which we added to give strength to the toy figures. These two plates were made from two colour separations that I prepared at the studio by painting, with ink, onto True-Grain textured drafting film. These two plates were also exposed in the UV unit.

Consistent with the studio's high standards, I was taught to sieve the inks before printing to ensure that no trace of skin would make an appearance during the print run. Working on the offset press took on a rhythm of its own as, for each print, I hand-loaded the paper into the grippers, as Tom pressed the starting button for the heavy rollers to transport the ink over the paper and return.

Tuscan Trees represents the contradiction in my approach. This wood engraving shows the movement of shadows that are cast by olive trees. Using scraperboard for a preliminary sketch allowed me the freedom to draw unselfconsciously. It made a valuable contribution to the final image because the drawn lines are white, as are the incised lines in a wood engraving.

I hoped I would engrave the block in the same free way as I had drawn on the scraperboard. However, the procedure I adopt in preparing any drawing for a block always becomes very deliberate. Partly this is driven by the intention to avoid expensive mistakes, but mostly it is because I need a clear map of where white can be cleared and black can be held, and where specific areas are either tones or textures. With *Tuscan Trees*, I redrew the scraperboard image onto layout paper and then made successive alterations until I hit upon the right composition that fitted the block exactly. Once the drawing was transferred onto the block, I started clearing the white areas between the terraces with a square scorper and with the same tool created the dots in the sunflower field. I continued with the tones of the terrace shadows and the road, before finally using the spitsticker to engrave the mid-tone light on the trees. The cutting entailed some ten hours of precise working, and preparing the drawing had taken even longer, though the scraperboard took a mere 25 minutes! I still hope I will one day make an engraving with something of the same spontaneity that I had achieved with scraperboard, but I tend to inhibit myself by wanting to engrave extremely well!

Holly Downing

A year of studying Romanesque architecture in France gave me an appreciation of a connection to a rich historic past that was absent in my Californian upbringing. I was reminded of its austere beauty when, as a university student, I discovered the mezzotints of Mario Avati Hon.RE, reproduced in printmaking books. These, along with the etchings of Rembrandt and Giorgio Morandi, were important sources of inspiration when I made my own attempts at the mezzotint technique. After graduation I sought a postgraduate place at the Royal College of Art in London, the city where mezzotint had flourished two centuries before. To my disappointment, there was little interest in mezzotint at the Royal College in the mid-1970s.

Ashes to Dust, 2005. Mezzotint, 28 x 32.5 cm (11 x 12¾ in.)

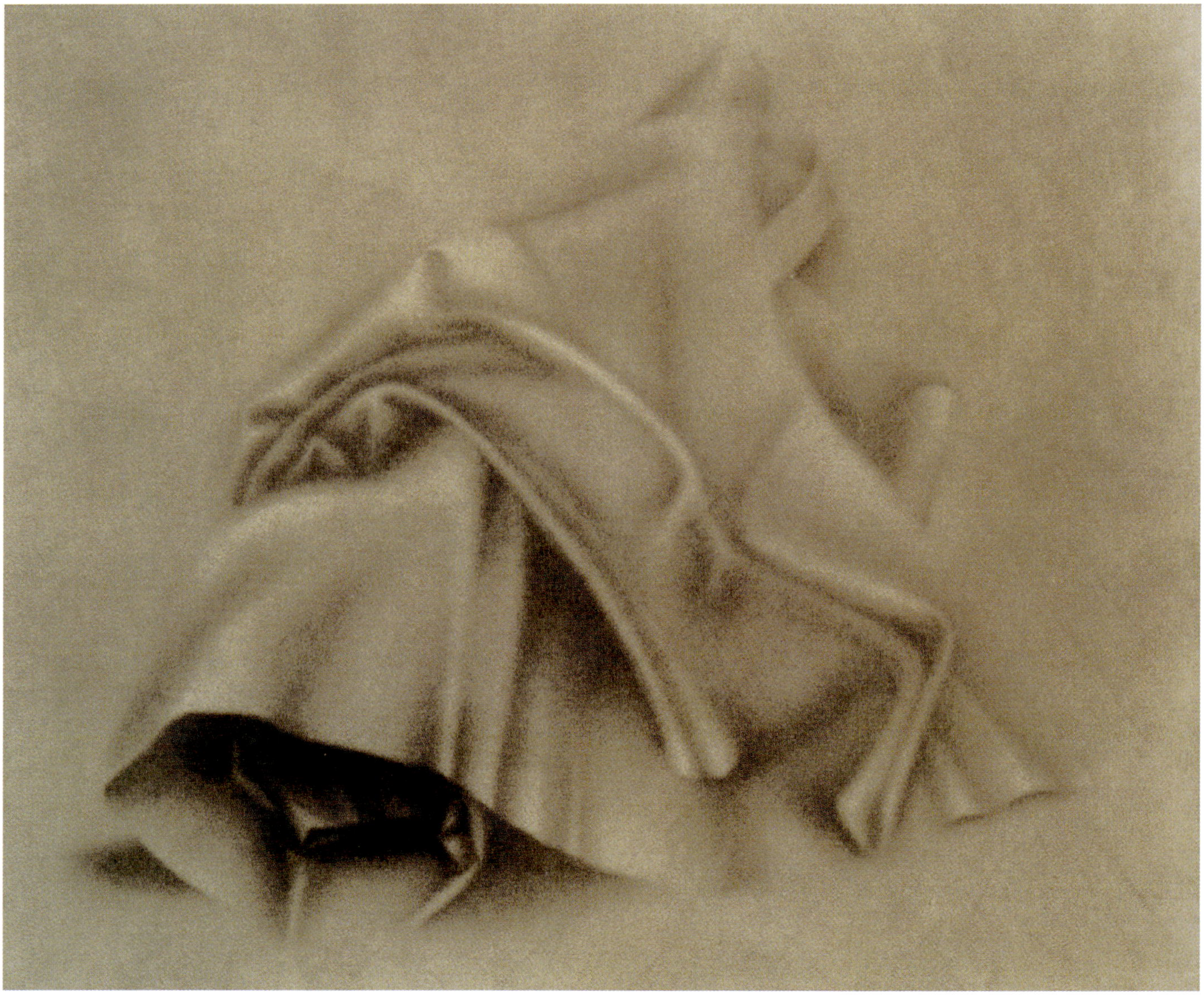

Right, above: **Elegy**, 2000. Mezzotint, 33 x 47 cm (13 x 18½ in.)

Below: **Elegy** (enlarged detail showing rocker and scraper marks)

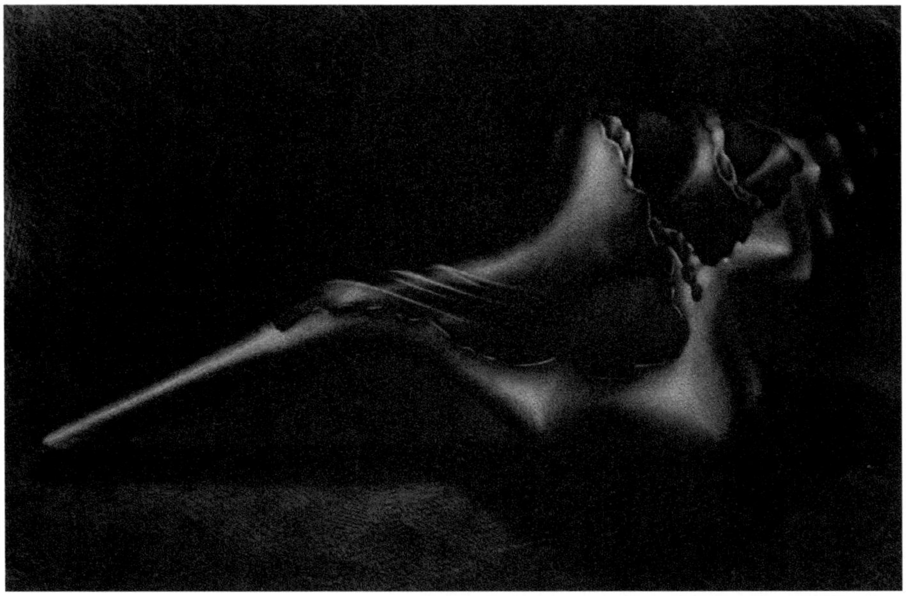

However, the mezzotint tools of Sir Frank Short PRE, RA on display at the V&A Museum reminded me of an earlier British mastery of the craft. Eventually, with the support of a US fellowship from the National Endowment for the Arts, I found my way to the studio of the reproductive mezzotint engraver Lawrence Josset RE. Josset inherited Frank Short's method of systematically rocking the plate along a grid of parallel lines, and he generously passed on his mezzotint secrets to me, suspecting that there was no future in reproductive mezzotint engraving. I appreciated his foolproof method of ensuring that the roughened plate would produce the velvety blacks I loved and would provide an utterly dependable surface for scraping to produce the subtle range of greys. His system of rocking served me so well that I have followed it for over thirty years.

I complete a detailed tonal pencil drawing before deciding if an image warrants the painstaking work required in making a mezzotint. Over a period of months, I contemplate and distil. Then, using an 85-teeth-to-the-inch mezzotint rocker and a pole and apparatus (as a pivotal arm), I start the rocking process. I zigzag the rocker, held at approximately a 75° acute angle from the table surface, down parallel lines one inch apart. I rock four 'ways' (or directions) for each of thirteen angles (from 90° to 50°) drawn in pencil from the centre bottom edge of the plate. After completing 52 ways, the mirror surface of the copper is totally matt. I keep track of each rocked 'way' with a protractor diagram.

Working from my drawing and proofs, I delicately scrape the burred surface with an old penknife, and the lights of the image gradually emerge. After steel-facing, printing is done on a Rochat etching press, shipped by me from Britain in 1979 to my studio in the USA. This traditional iron press, based on 19th-century antecedents, provides the firm pressure required for printing mezzotints. Furthermore, it represents another connection to the tools and methods of the past, to an age when things moved more slowly, when craft and handiwork were respected. As I work, light and shadow transform the immutable, the sanctity of everyday life is acknowledged, psychological states of mind reveal themselves, and my outer and inner worlds connect, as the past and present meet.

John Duffin

I was born in Barrow-in-Furness and left school at 16 to be apprenticed in the shipyard there as a draughtsman and naval architect. This entailed four years of intense training during which I worked on my own paintings and drawings in the evenings and at weekends. Several days after qualifying as a ship draughtsman I went to London to study Fine Art at Goldsmiths College. I was 20 years old, probably no more than a year older than my fellow students who had arrived at the college by the traditional route of A-levels and foundation course, but my training in industry made me feel very different to them, and my artistic beliefs had been founded in the Marvel comic books that had inspired me as a boy and in the superb public galleries of Manchester, Liverpool, Leeds and Edinburgh.

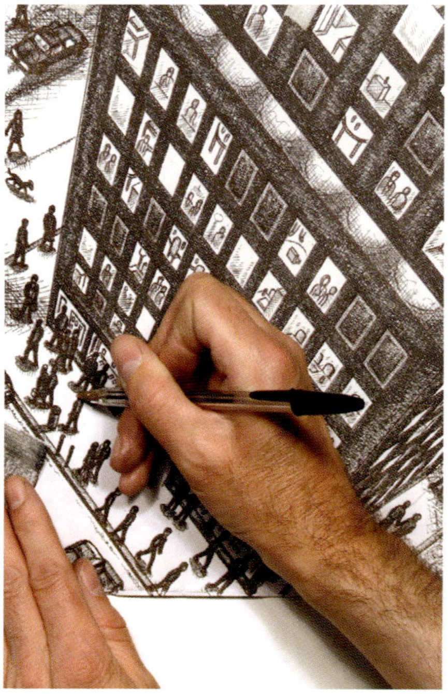

Big City, 2007. Etching, 38 x 25 cm (15 x 9⅞ in.). Transferring the image to a copper plate

Studying in the mid-1980s among artists that the media would later christen 'the Britart group', I worked hard and made good progress. My first experience of etching came in the second year; I enjoyed the drawing that it entailed, since it felt similar to my approach to pen and ink drawing.

I feel that I actually have very few secrets to divulge regarding the making of my prints. I seem to have followed a very pared-down approach to making etchings that involves making direct marks onto a wax-covered copper plate with a sharp needle, biting the revealed metal with acid and then printing the results in the blackest ink on the whitest paper available. In a way, perhaps, that simple and direct approach is the secret of my work.

I produce work that is inspired by and reflects the urban environment. I make many drawings and sketches when walking in towns and cities and these feed into my work. I often make prints based on my paintings, choosing compositions that will lend themselves to a black and white etched image. The key to choosing an image is the composition: if it has an energy and a dynamic then I can see that it will become an etching in its own right, a black and white original print distinct from the painting.

Once I have chosen a painted image from which to make an etching I am faced with how to transfer the composition from the painted surface to the copper plate. As I have worked very hard to achieve the compositional balance of the image in the painting, I seek to preserve this as accurately as possible. I have therefore developed a method of transferring the composition that is very close to the painting. I photograph the painting, which can then be reduced or enlarged on a photocopier or a computer to fit the size of plate I have chosen to work on. I then attach the print to the surface of a copper plate covered in a hard wax ground, and carefully draw firmly over the compositional outlines with a biro pen. This leaves a ghostly impression on the plate as a guide for my drawing with an etching needle. This is a relatively slow process but is worth it in the long run as it means I am working on a plate that has a very accurate composition on it. This is my update of the method of transferring a pencil line drawing onto a hard-ground plate by running the drawing through the press, in contact with the plate, leaving faint marks on the hard ground's surface as a drawing guide. These are no doubt tasks that could be carried out by studio assistants, but as a one-man band in my studio I do it all myself and, in a way, enjoy the slow pace of making the print; the process and methodical approach all help, allowing me to focus and hone my ideas for the final image.

I then work on the plate in the

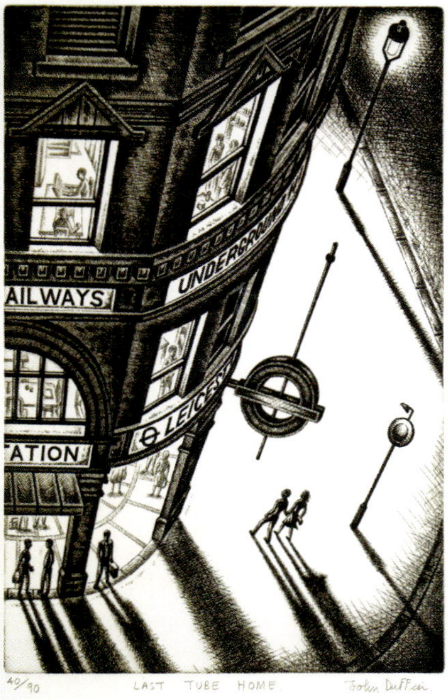

Last Tube Home, 2007. Etching, 38 x 25 cm (15 x 9⅞ in.)

traditional method, building up lines and cross-hatching to create space and depth. Each time the plate is bitten in the acid I make a proof, allowing me to ascertain which areas require more line work or need burnishing out. The plate is then continually worked on until I have the atmosphere, contrast and mood that I want. I often find that the etching can distil the essence of the image, sometimes becoming more successful than the original oil painting. The reverse can also happen: a print can be made that will then be transferred onto a canvas and become a painting. The real secrets of printmaking are in fact in the imagination of the artist, that strange world in which an idea scratched onto the back of an envelope in a bar can lie in a drawer in the studio for several years, only to be seen later and inspire a painting or a print. Ideas, of course, are only as good as their realisation, and it is in this that the

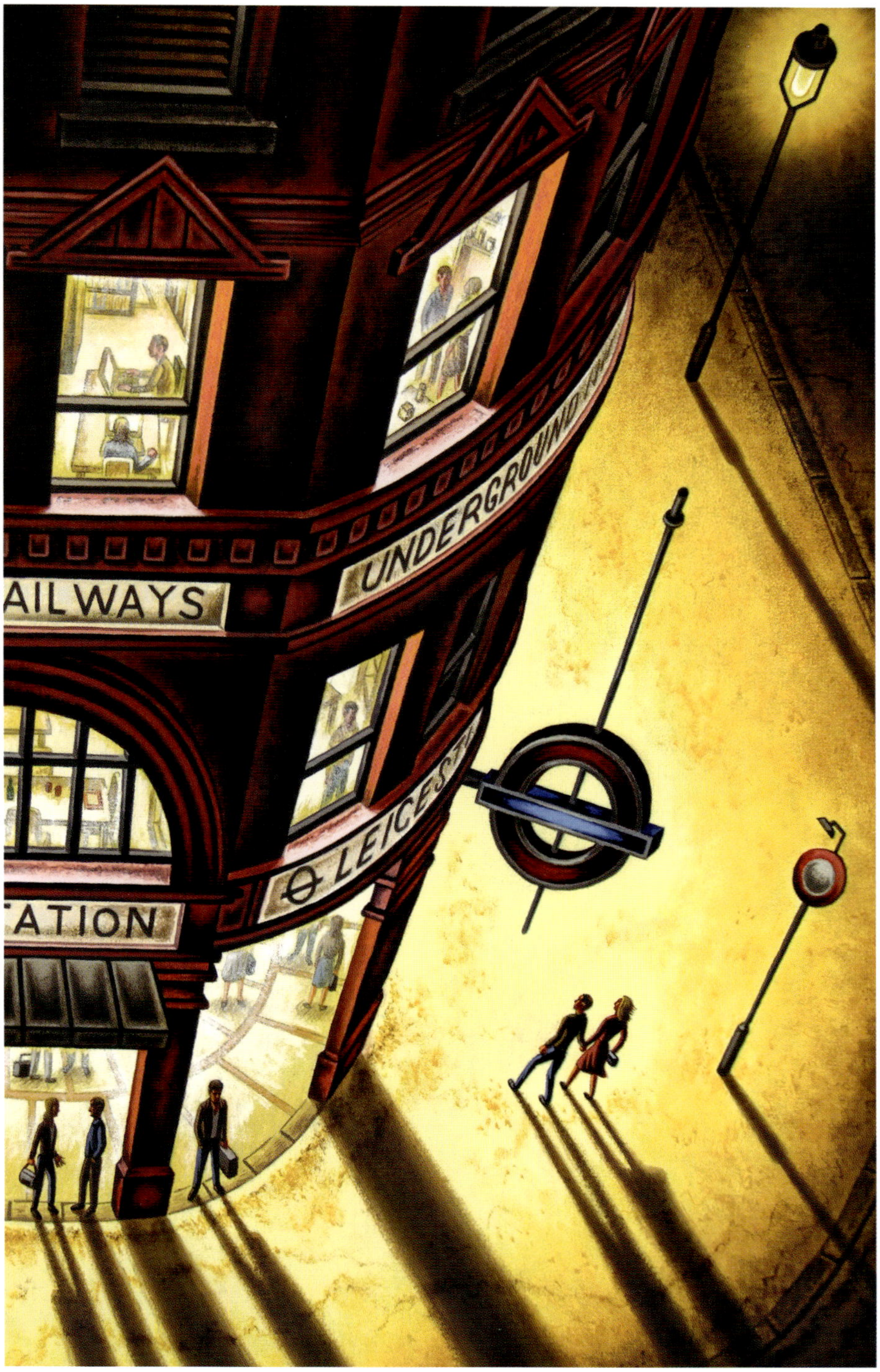

Last Tube Home, 2007. Oil, 56 x 38 cm (22 x 15 in.)

enjoyment of printmaking lies: the slowness of the process can allow the idea to breathe and grow. Your duty then is to follow where it leads, stay with the essence of the original idea and not lose faith in it.

Fernando Feijoo

Working for four years at London's Curwen Studio as a master printer, and collaborating with such artists as Quentin Blake, David Gentleman and Paula Rego Hon. RE, taught me much about the rich possibilities of lithographic printing with the use of photopolymer plates.

When creating my *Contemporary Street Alphabet* book, in which I illustrated characters one might see on the street, I wanted to push the boundaries of what could be achieved with lithography. Therefore I drew my images on the photoplates in a rough, loose style with a thick chisel-tip brush loaded with Indian ink, and scratched back into the lines with a scalpel to tighten up the graphic composition. This added a scraperboard effect and allowed more detail. I also placed different grades of sandpaper under the film and made rubbings to give different textural patterns. I used a candlestick, rubbed it over the film and washed different concentrations of ink over it to give a negative repellent wash effect. Photos taken from the streets were printed onto acetate, then collaged into the street billboards and frames on the walls of the bar scenes. Spray paint was also used to give an explosion effect in one of the images. I worked with a variety of old wooden type as well, being interested in type and image working together to make a striking graphic composition, combining old and new printmaking methods. The images were printed in grey and black, with one plate being more burnt out than the other, making it darker and giving the image less tone and more of a linear quality. A spot of red printing ink was also applied, making an overall powerful image and highlighting the important parts. The text on the left-hand side of the page gave an opportunity for wordplay, rhyme and slang to reveal what the character was up to.

My inspiration comes from seeing and experiencing scenes and situations in an urban environment – bars, clubs, street festivals, cultural events – and through observing different social classes interacting. What these characters might engage in is seen as a sequence of events in my restaged versions of Hogarth's Progresses: *Crack's Progress* (The Rake's Progress) and *Charlie's Progress* (The Harlot's Progress).

Influences on my drawing style come from such artists as Goya, Posada and Masereel as well as Hogarth. I often include small, unobtrusive details: for example, there might be a street scene with people digging tunnels to escape from some predicament; or illegal activities taking place behind closed doors. Pub signs, street signs and posters often appear, sometimes subverted to add different social and political comments to the overall composition.

My dual nationality is also often reflected in my work, the Spanish bull sometimes appearing on the horizon of my landscapes and British yobs boozing in typical English pubs abroad. I enjoy travelling and bringing all my experiences of different customs, cultures, colours and architectural styles into my prints. Recently I have been collaborating with other artists and producing joint prints. This process involves allowing others to start drawing with no restraints. Once they are happy, they hand the film over to me, allowing me to draw over and add my part to the picture in my own style. This way of working can spark off interesting and unexpected solutions, complementing the usual approach of a sole practitioner. I practise all printmaking methods and enjoy the excitement of going on a journey and not knowing exactly where it will end. I think this is what really attracts me to printmaking.

Pages from the book Contemporary Street Alphabet, 2007. Hand-drawn lithograph, 17 x 25 cm (6¾ x 9⅞ in.)

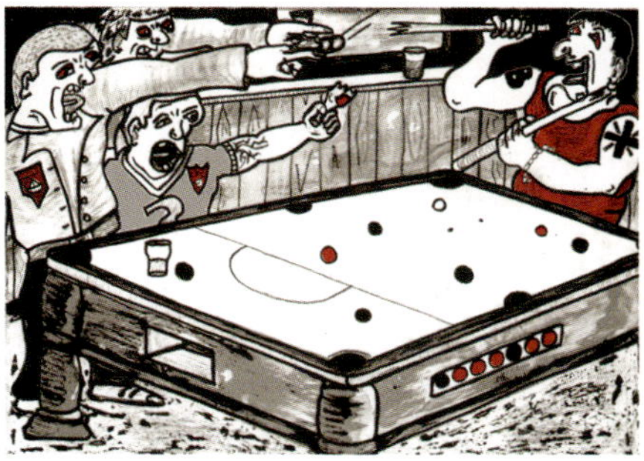

Bruiser Bruce never knows when to call a truce

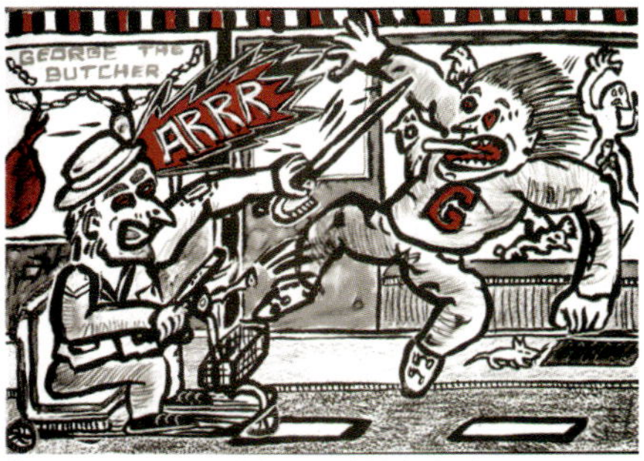

George was gerry a trick over which he had no mastery

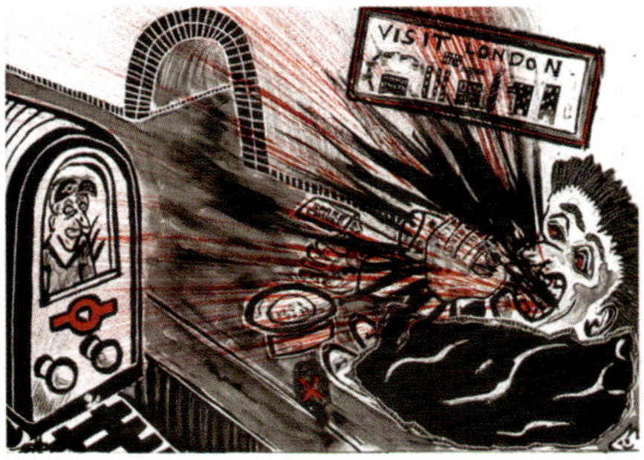

Mike drinks meths the cause of most explosive deaths

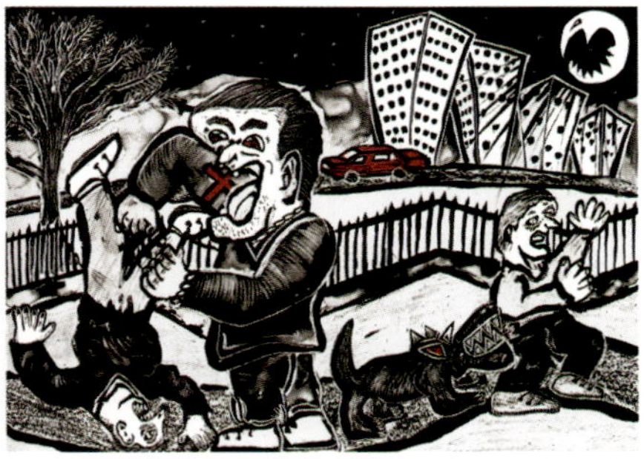

Quentin is a queer basher with his dog nicknamed gnasher

Early Hours of the Morning, 2007. Linocut hand-coloured with Indian ink, 60 x 80 cm (23⅝ x 31½ in.)

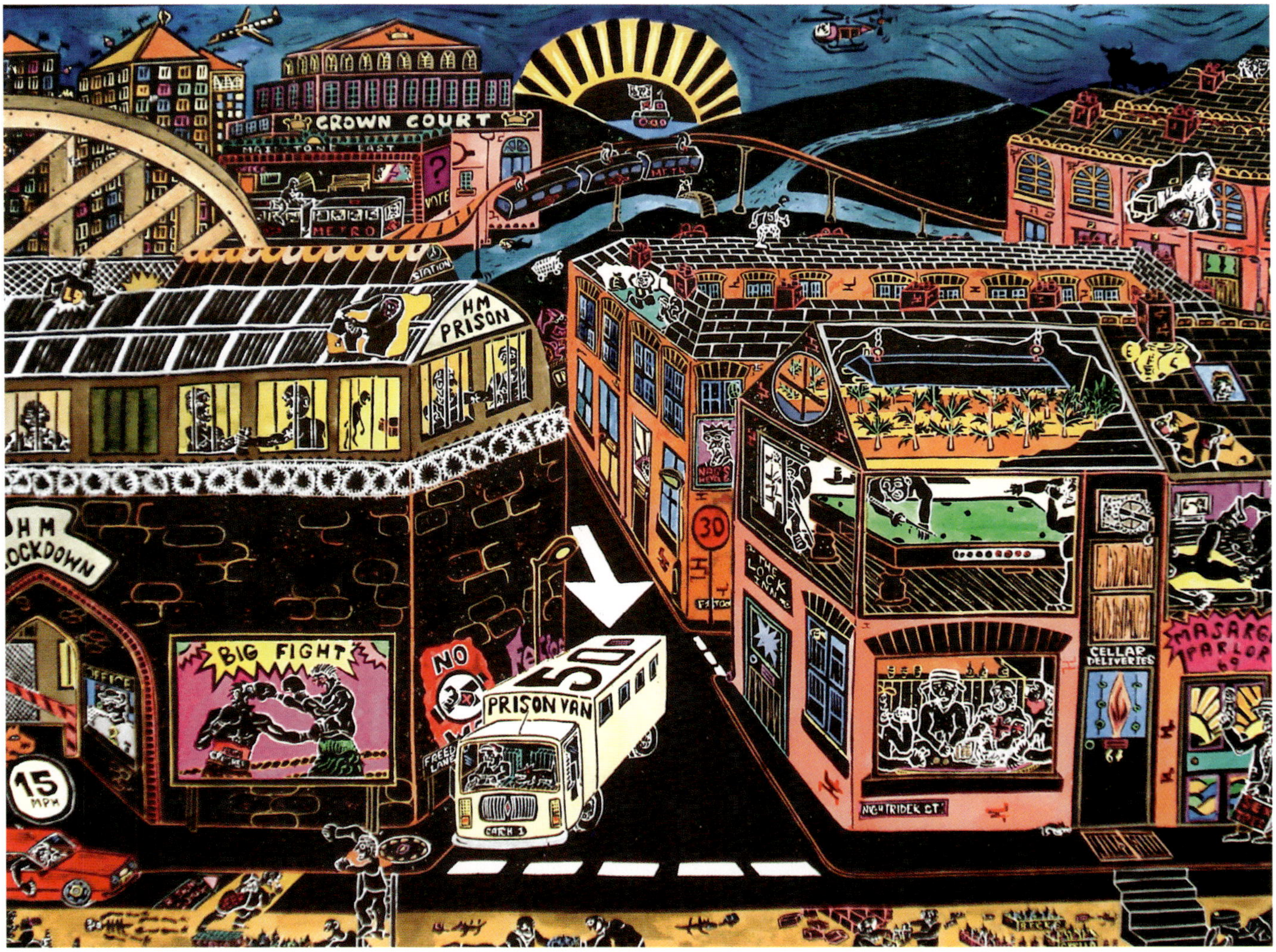

David Ferry

I begin with an idea about how I can alter, change or tamper with an existing published book. I choose a book that has plenty of photographic images in it and text that relates to these images. I like the total freedom of choice that this brings about; it is like an Aladdin's Cave of possibilities. Photomontage is a good starting point, and I very simply but deliberately set about the task of sticking additions to pre-existing published material. A new image has now been created and this new image has a different relationship with the pre-existing text. I am drawn to coffee-table books where text and image establish a simple and non-threatening view of the world.

A Picture History of England mainly in Black & White, 2001–3 (Double-page example). Original photomontage over existing published material, 30 x 21 cm (11 x 18 in.)

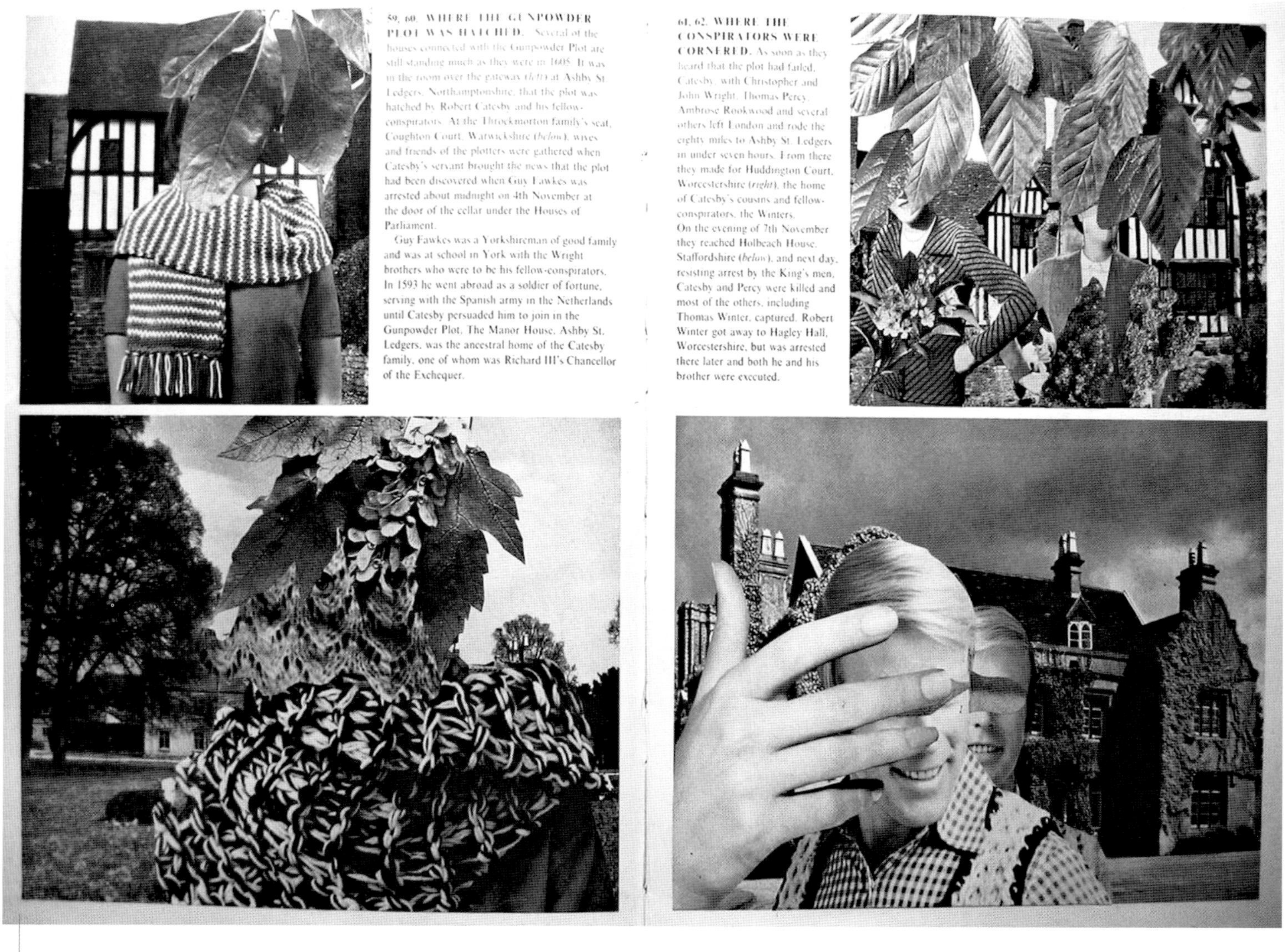

Once every page in the pre-existing publication has been rearranged, altered or defiled, I can then claim that it is, and that I have created, an Artist's Book. This part of the creative act can take months or even a couple of years to complete. I therefore work on a number of themes (books) at any one time.

However, that is not the final chapter in the creative process, and I now scan every page in my artist's book so that I can rearrange and add further complexity of tone, colour, etc. to the scan using Photoshop software. Once I have made inkjet printouts of these scanned images, I then tile them on the studio wall to see what else I can do with them creatively. I may add more montage material or new areas of colour or indeed recut the images to create a new photomontage altogether. This is a very 'analogue' way of working and very much an additive process, where new material is placed on top of pre-existing data. I can of course take things away at this stage, and this is also done straight on top of the inkjets. It also makes for a balance between the 'hands off' and the 'hands on', which is more tangible and interesting for me. It is a fine balance between traditional montage and collage practice (which of course includes traditional printmaking) and the digital formats that are readily available to the artist. I am now in a position to scan the reworked inkjets straight from the studio wall (that is, the second scan in the operation) and refine these, again using Photoshop software on the computer. In short, I have created from the same starting point both a unique artist's book and a set of prints that can be editioned on a large-format digital printer.

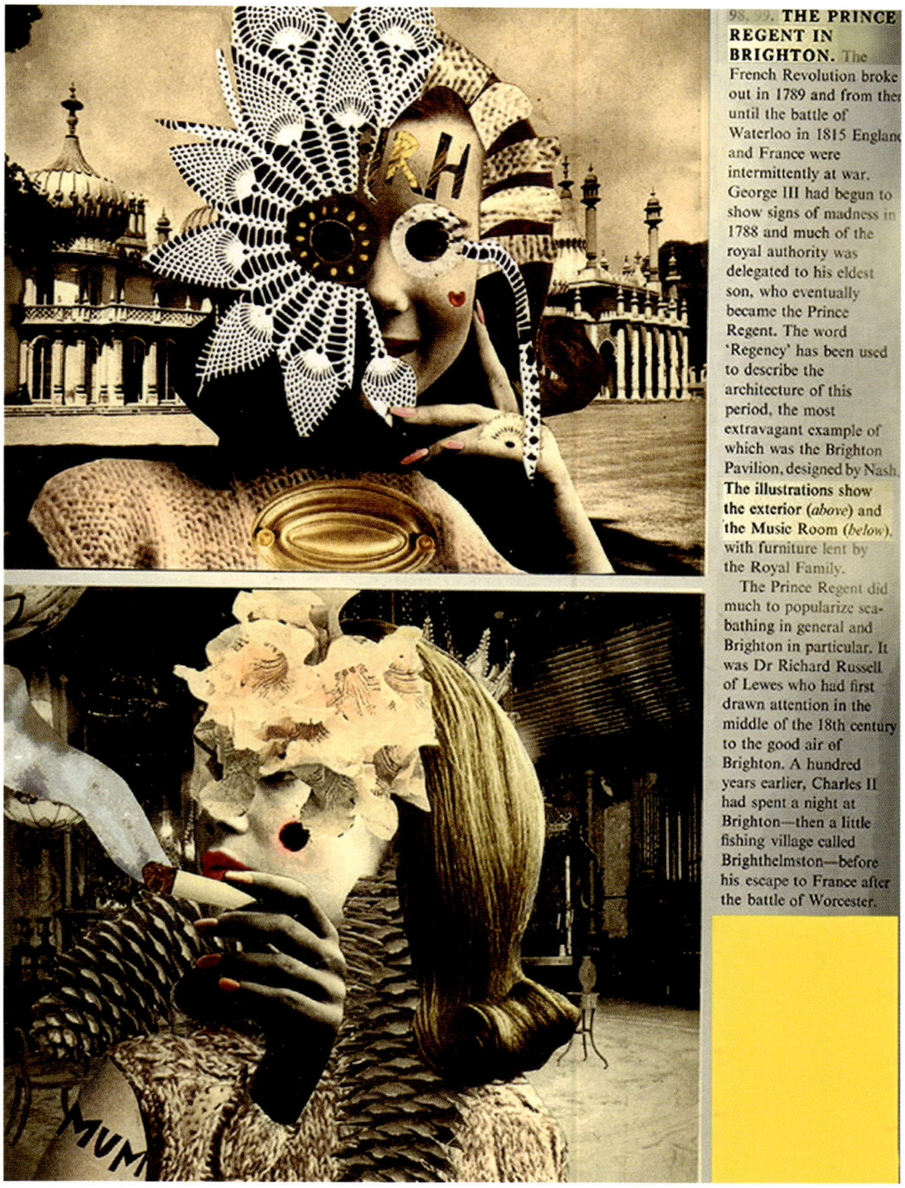

Prince Regent, A Picture History of England mainly in black and white, 2006, Original archive digital colour print. Size variable

I cannot, in this process, overlook my former years of making offset lithographs (initially during my postgraduate studies at the Slade School of Fine Art and later at the Curwen Studio), as the lessons of lithography (colour, overlay, tone, texture, transparency, etc.) are implicit in the qualities of the final digital print.

Trevor Frankland

My move from intaglio to relief printing was to exploit the linear and planar contrasts that lino-cutting could give and to develop ideas within these boundaries. My work relies on making an accurate drawing onto the lino block. To expedite this process I photograph my original design so that it can be reduced in size on my printer and at the same time copied onto a transparent film. I then project the image onto the lino block using an overhead projector; this guides the initial drawing in soft pencil, subsequently completed with a felt-tipped pen to provide clarity of detail.

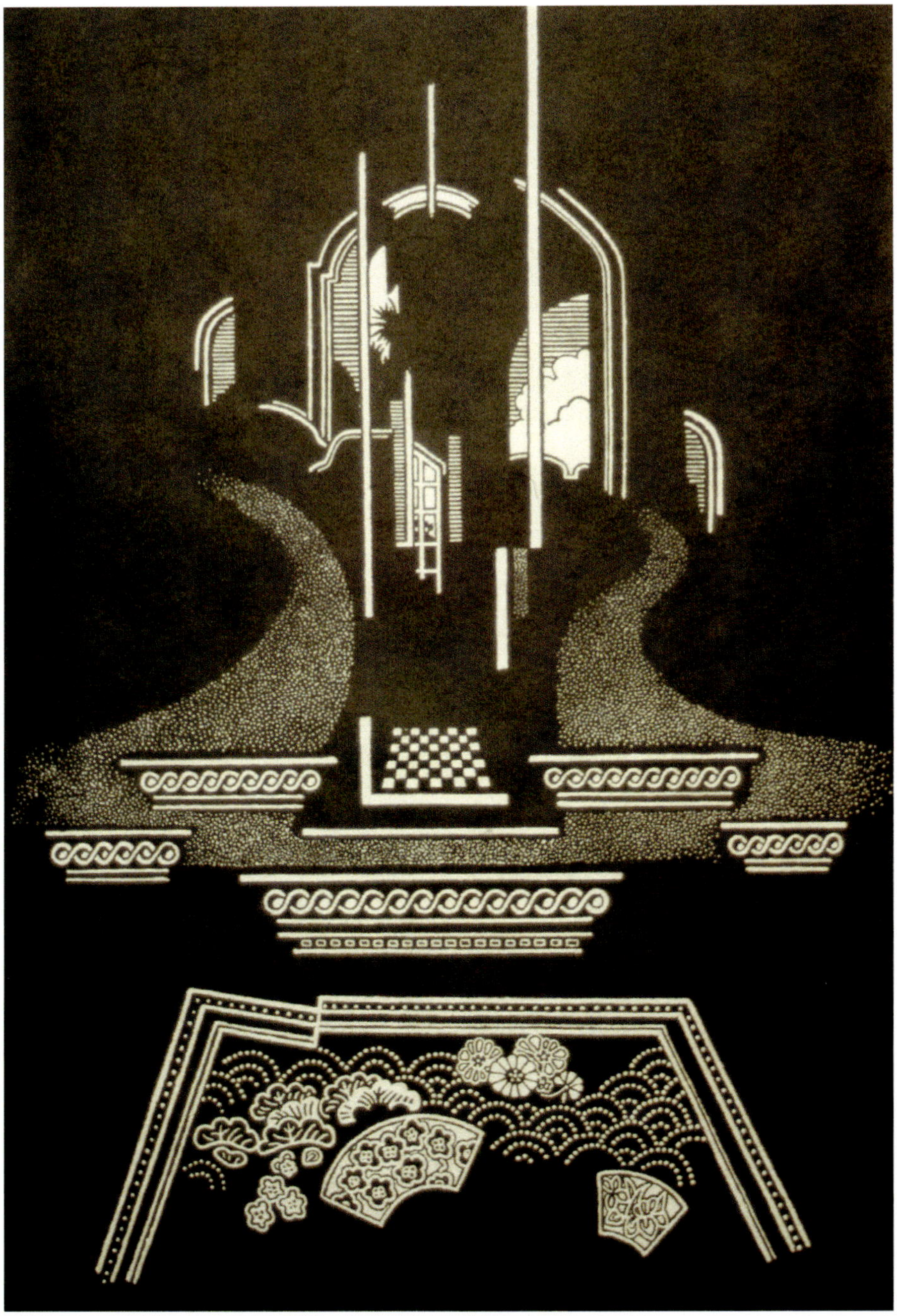

A Summer Afternoon, 2001. Linocut, 68 x 46 cm (26¾ x 18⅛ in.)

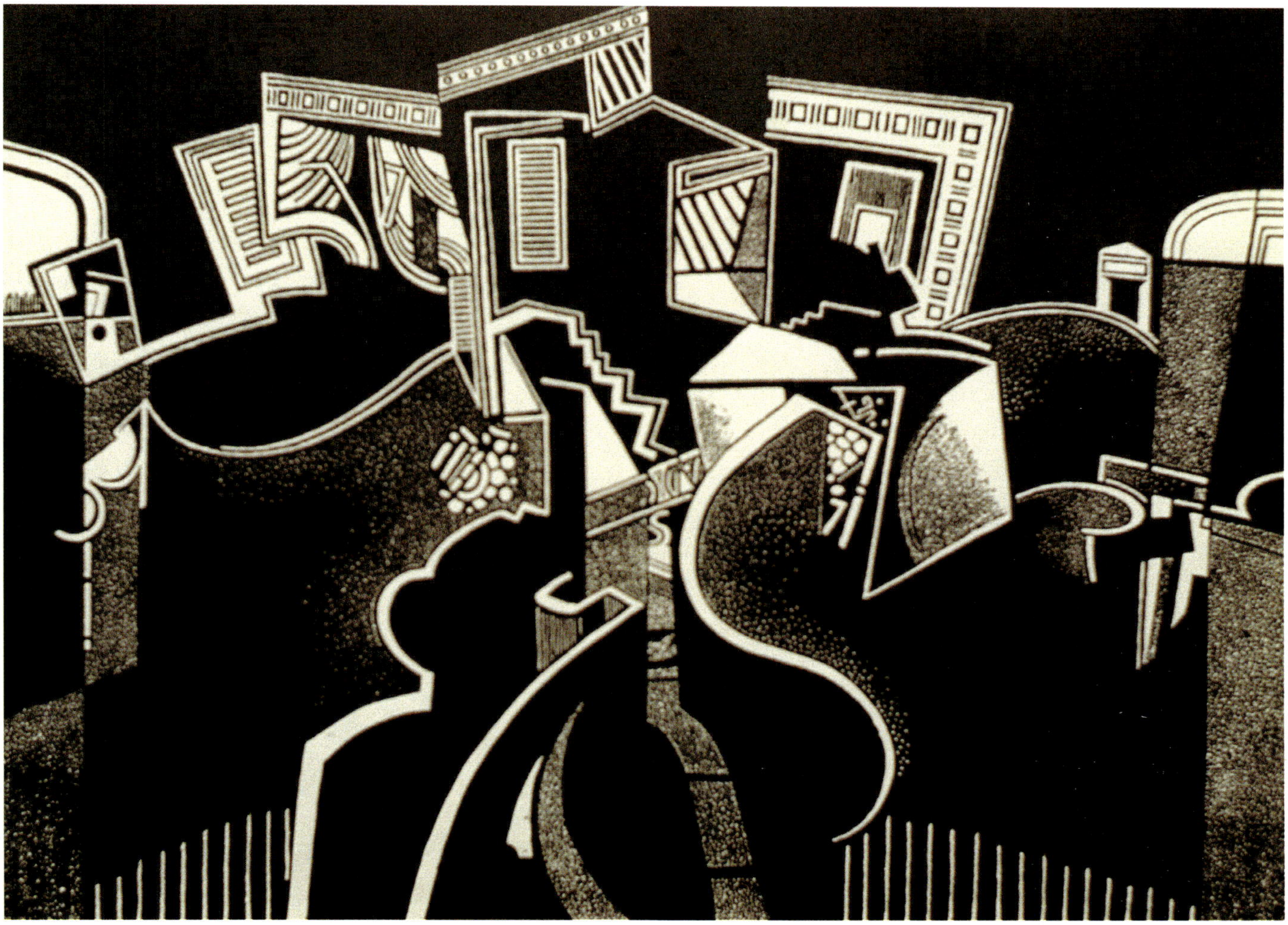

The House at L'Estaque, 2000. Linocut, 43 x 61 cm (17 x 24 in.)

Dense black areas together with fine detail require a different approach to the traditional cutting and printing of a lino block. Through initial experimentation I found that fine cutting could be done with an electric flexi-drive router, using a variety of bits, and that the larger areas could then easily be cut away with traditional tools. I knew that bonding the lino to a piece of thick, medium-density fibreboard was necessary for deep cutting, stability in printing and the possibility of epoxy-resin repairs. After preliminary cutting I take a print to gauge the overall effect and decide if alterations are necessary. It is at this stage that I use an epoxy resin filler to level unwanted cutting. Once the filler has set, sanding and polishing enables the recut block to print without a blemish.

When inking the block with a roller I have to take care, as a heavy viscous layer of ink tends to fill in fine detail, whilst a thin layer does not give the rich, intense blacks I am trying to achieve. Lifting the paper to re-ink or to remove surplus ink from the block could cause registration problems, so I have chosen a heavyweight, handmade Japanese paper called Aku-shi, which I hold in position with heavy iron weights when portions of the paper are lifted to re-ink the lino block. The Aku-shi printing paper is light straw in colour and provides an excellent base for dense blacks (which a white mount can emphasise to advantage), whilst its heavy weight prevents stretching or creep during re-inking and burnishing. My method involves printing by hand, using a large stainless-steel spoon as a burnisher so that I can, by varying the pressure, create dense blacks while at the same time leaving details sharp and unclogged.

Peter Freeth

It was in 1971 that I got the postcard which, as they say, changed my life. Sadly, I didn't keep the card; in it my uncle, Andrew Freeth, described a way of making an etching by offsetting imagery from the current day's newspaper directly onto a clean plate, reinforcing the image with a ghostly dusting of resin and biting the plate all in one go, with no stopping out at all.

I tried it out and was completely hooked. The fact that I hadn't done any work at all for two years due to moving to a new house certainly meant that I was willing to experiment with something so totally at variance with anything I had done before. I am still very fond of some of these prints from the 1970s. The complexity of the collage images and the subtlety of the biting I've never quite managed again. After five years or so, my convert's ardour was beginning to dim and I felt the need for something more personal than tearing up *The Sun* every day. But I certainly wanted to use the experience I had gained and to retain the main principle with its special characteristics. I began replacing the newsprint with monotypes, using ordinary etching ink: I have made virtually all my prints like this ever since. Etching ink, even the faintest smudge, is obviously a lot stickier than the grubbiest (pre-Wapping) newspaper ink, and tended to hold too much resin, so that the distinctions between all the greys and the blacks were lost. Bit by bit, I managed to adapt.

Here is some of the detail of my own way of working: a pale monotype is printed on a clean etching plate, using the press. (It could be transferred by hand or with a roller or by scribbling with a pencil.) Now shake resin over your plate, using as little or as much as you feel and more in some places if you want. Before melting the resin, bang the plate down on its edge, or bash it with a

Reflection on a Theme of Canaletto, 1996. Aquatint, 55 x 49 cm (21⅝ x 18⅞ in.)

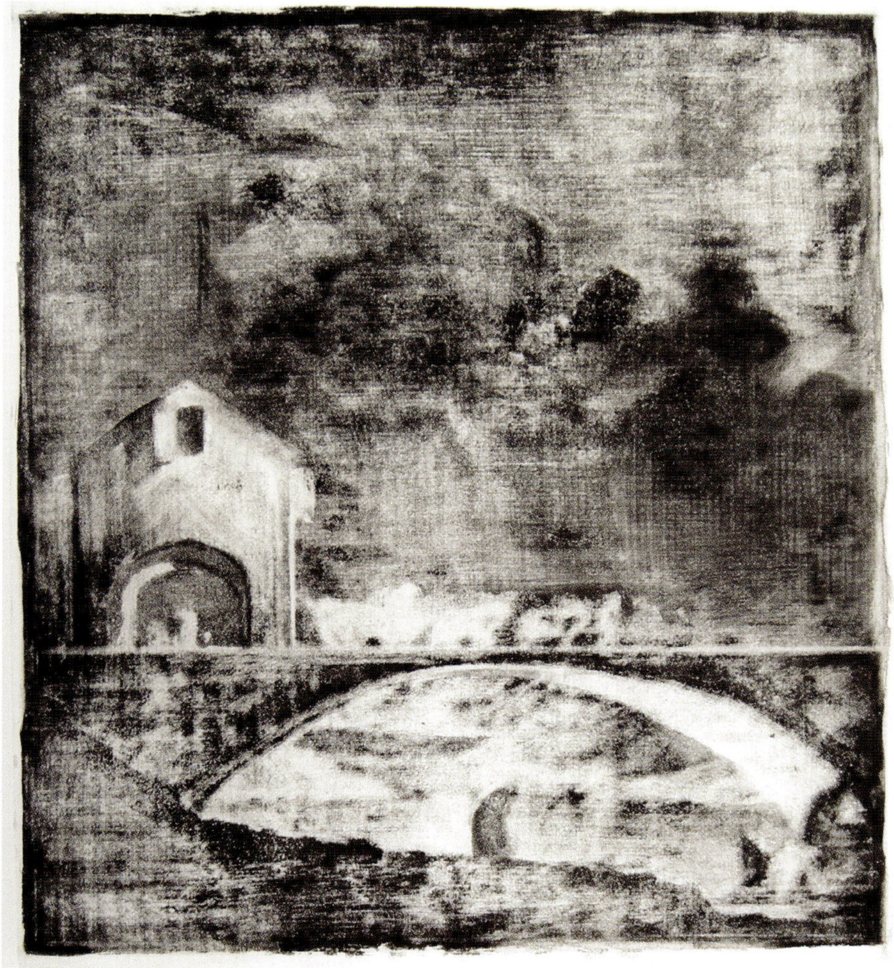

wooden club, to remove the loose or excess grains. Now the white areas of the monotype should be resin-free, the pale greys will have a little resin, the dark greys more ... and so on. This for me is the uniqueness of the process: the differing amounts of ink and resin produce a rich texture (a bit like a halftone plate) with the irregular pattern of the resin changing with the tonality, quite unlike the uniformity of conventional aquatint. Compared with the ruthless efficiency of stop-out varnish, etching ink is infinitely subtle and flexible: it can be rubbed, smudged, patted, dragged. The pressure of the press, the roughness of the blankets, the melting of the resin – all affect the outcome.

At this point you have two options: 1) go ahead and bite the plate – though just one bite! The white, unprotected areas will open-bite and the rest should be a rough, gutsy version of the original monotype; or 2) add a further layer of resin with the aquatint box (or two layers or hand-shakes) all over in the normal way and melt it. Now the whole plate has some resin. In the acid, the original whites (having only a thin covering) will bite fastest and the blacks (with most ink and most resin) will bite slowest. The result – you've got it! – is a negative, a tonal reversal of the original image. All you have to do now, to get back to the original tones, is to take a print of this negative plate, offset it onto a clean new plate and ... start all over again!! Why on earth jump through such a preposterous set of hoops if you don't have to? Two reasons: firstly, the negatives are often beautiful in their own right; and secondly, as in photography, a negative means you can create as many positives as you like (etching in different ways) or retransfer and re-bite the same plate as many times as you like. When melting several layers of resin together with ink also on the plate, it is clearly important not to overdo it. I still occasionally get plates with so much resin on them that I can safely put them in the acid and pop out to Sainsbury's!

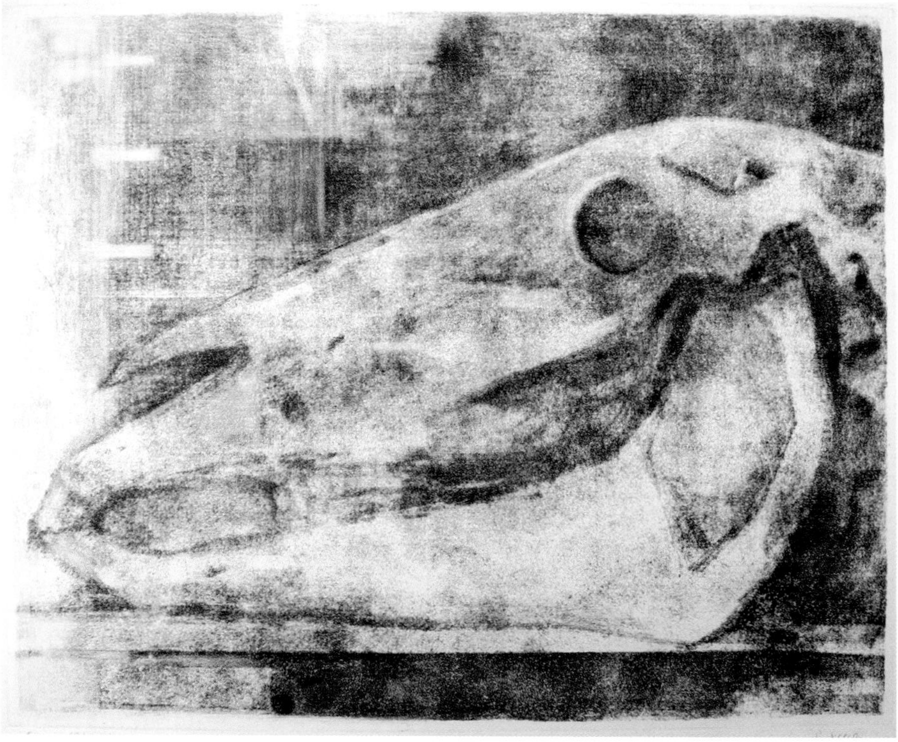

Equus, 1998. Aquatint, 49 x 60 cm (18⅞ x 23⅝ in.)

The preparatory stages are long but, in compensation, the drawing and biting are greatly simplified, the transitions are painterly and the texture rich and varied. One of the nicest compliments I ever received was at an opening at London's Bankside Gallery. A fellow-printmaker whom I did not know, but whose work I much admired, asked me if I had anything in the show. He looked at my prints for a few moments and said, 'What do you know that we don't know?' Thank goodness, we all do things differently.

Carmen Gracia

I started to make prints quite by accident in 1960. Having just arrived in Paris from Mendoza, my home town in Argentina, after finishing art school, I felt quite lost and miserable as I knew no one. Then just by chance someone told me about Atelier 17, founded by William Hayter Hon.RE. I had come to France to pursue a career in sculpture but I went to the Atelier and found the experimental atmosphere stimulating and the new technique of colour etching fascinating. Coming from a background in painting and sculpture, working with the plates was the perfect way to combine both elements of my work, to create a sculptural dimension within the flat plane of the paper.

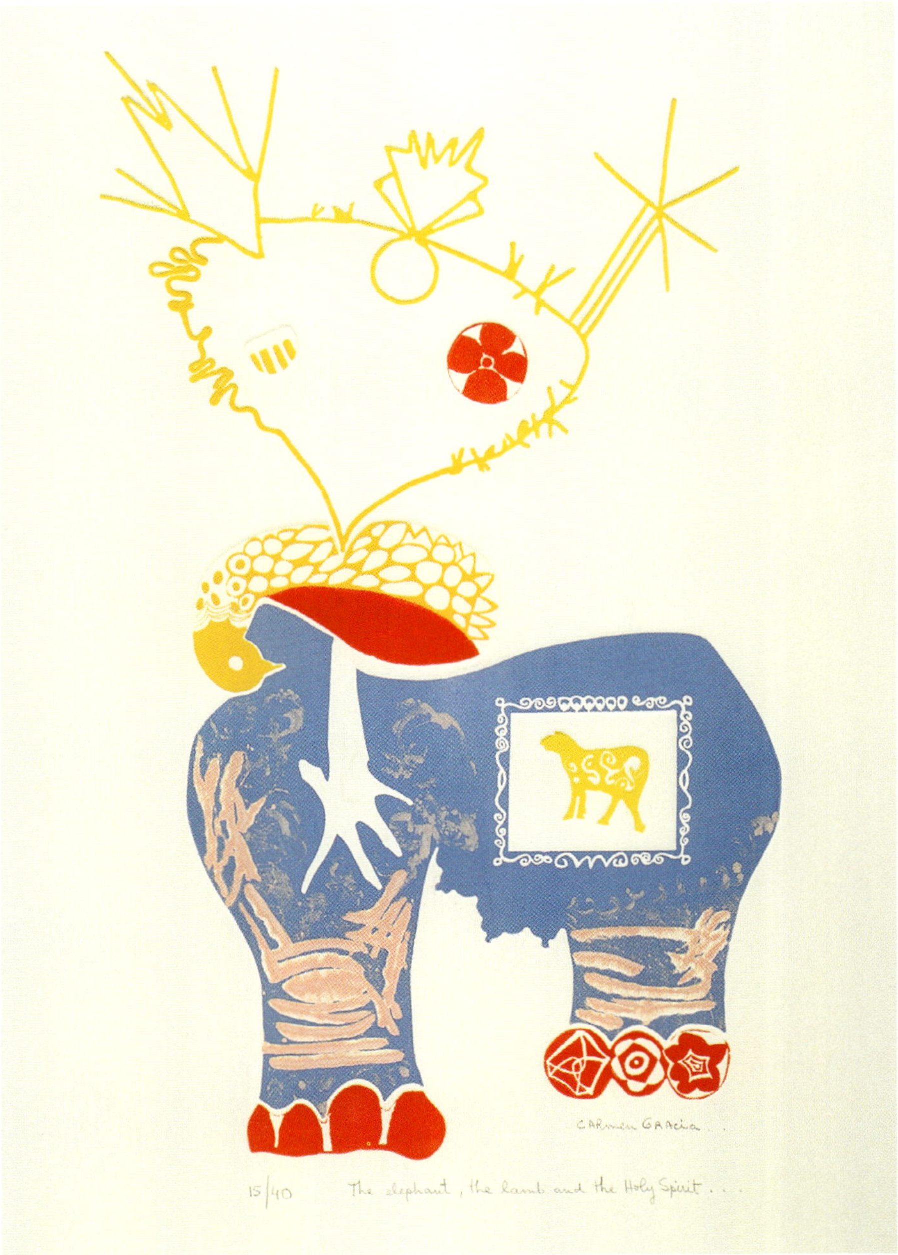

The Elephant, the Lamb and the Holy Spirit, 1977. Etching, 71 x 56 cm (28 x 22 in.)

Bill Hayter's enthusiastic help and innovative methods of printing opened my eyes and liberated my imagination; he was a great inspiration. I remember one day going to him as he arrived at the studio around midday, as was his custom. I showed him two pieces of work, both from the same plate but printed in different colours, to ask which was better. What he said I have always remembered: 'If you are not convinced yourself, how are you going to convince others?' I never asked again!

Bill was one of the first to develop the viscosity method of printing, which I learned and practised at the Atelier. However, I have not continued to use it. I started to move away from the traditional rectangle filled with image and colour and to experiment with cutting my plates to

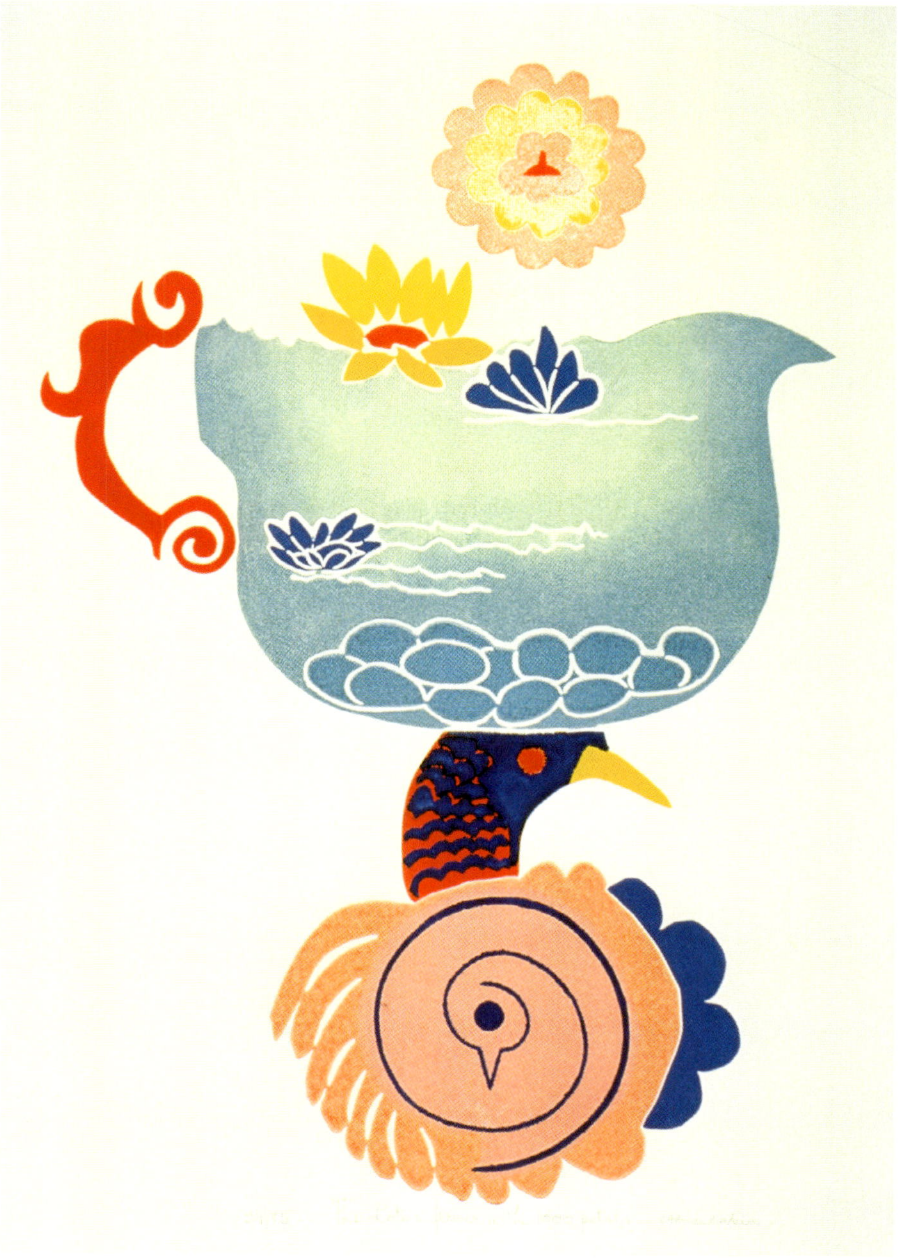

The Lotus Flower with 1,000 petals, 1987. Etching, 72 x 56 cm (28⅜ x 22 in.)

create many separate shapes which can then be assembled. Sometimes I superimpose them, but generally I place them, as in a jigsaw puzzle, in the bed of the press and print in one go. I feel this method offers me more possibilities, more ways to express what I want to create.

Once, quite by chance, I left a plate in the acid for too long and a hole appeared. I suddenly saw, as if for the first time, the dimension offered by the apparently blank space and the possibilities it opened up. I see this, the white of the paper within and around the image, as playing an intrinsic role in the whole work and now use it as one of the primary elements of my work.

Later, when working in a collective studio in Norway, I observed the girlfriend of a colleague working with silver wire to make the jewellery she designed. I was inspired and started using soldered copper wire in my work. This may be seen in *The Elephant, the Lamb and the Holy Spirit.* All the lines forming the Holy Spirit – the upper image – are created using the copper wire. Also, the image of the lamb appears within a hole in the plate.

From Paris I came to London's Slade School of Art, where I studied under the tutelage of Anthony Gross RA, Hon.RE, a friend of Hayter. I feel particularly indebted to these two early mentors. Gross told me one day, 'The only thing I can teach you is the discipline of work.' The rest was up to me. But I feel he did impart the importance of this discipline, as Hayter also communicated the importance of extreme care when working with potentially dangerous chemicals. Such good advice is as valuable as the techniques, which, after all, are relatively simple to learn.

Peter Green

My involvement with printmaking, and particularly the magic of repeating an image, has its origins for me in trade-printing. The realisation that printmaking enables images and ideas to be accessible and affordable for a mass audience coincided with my early development as an educationalist; I have therefore always seen myself primarily as teacher-printmaker rather than 'artist' (a title with which I feel uncomfortable) – 'printmaker' sounds like a valid job!

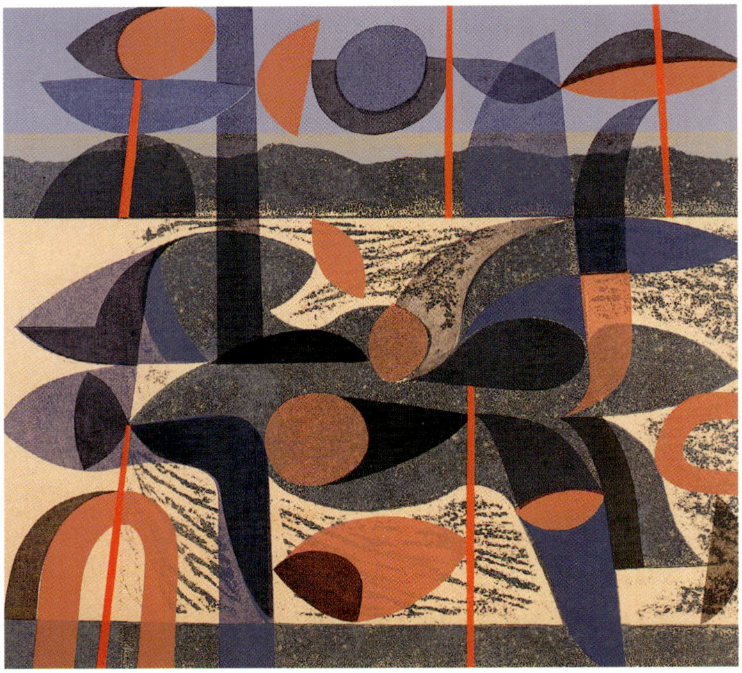

Desert Phantom, 2007. Woodcut and stencil, 33 x 35 cm (13 x 13¾ in.)

As a teacher-printmaker I am also uneasy with the idea of 'secrets'; knowledge is about common ownership – we learn from each other and the processes I use have developed through shared experiences with students and colleagues. I have been anxious to demystify the printing process, making it simple and accessible rather than in any way promoting the idea of special techniques and craft mythology.

As a relief printmaker, I do not use a press. This approach was a practical response to limitations of space and money. But then I realised the advantages – you are not limited by paper size and you can flexibly explore the full depth of the block. Presses are not readily available in schools and, with any large college group, waiting to get onto the press can be a real deterrent, so we developed easy ways of printing. With relief printing, the ink is on the top surface and needs little pressure to transfer it onto paper. Having placed the paper onto the inked block, I normally roll it with a large dry roller; then I use a pad of clean rag if I want to press the paper further down into the block to reveal the texture of the lower areas and the trace marks of the cutting tool.

Another method I use is offsetting with a hand-roller. The block is inked up in the normal way and then a clean hand-roller is rolled over the inked surface and the image transferred onto it. Once transferred, it can be printed or 'offset' onto any two- or three-dimensional surface by simply rolling the 'image roller' onto the surface. As I frequently print from found objects or irregular surfaces, offsetting these images onto paper is a very direct process.

Among the simple methods we have developed (my wife Linda works with me both on teaching courses and in the studio) is the use of paper stencils. The idea grew in response to the problem of how to print large areas of colour quickly without a press – the principle is very direct and requires no complex craft skill. Basically, my prints develop by first printing a key block (or blocks) and then developing a series of

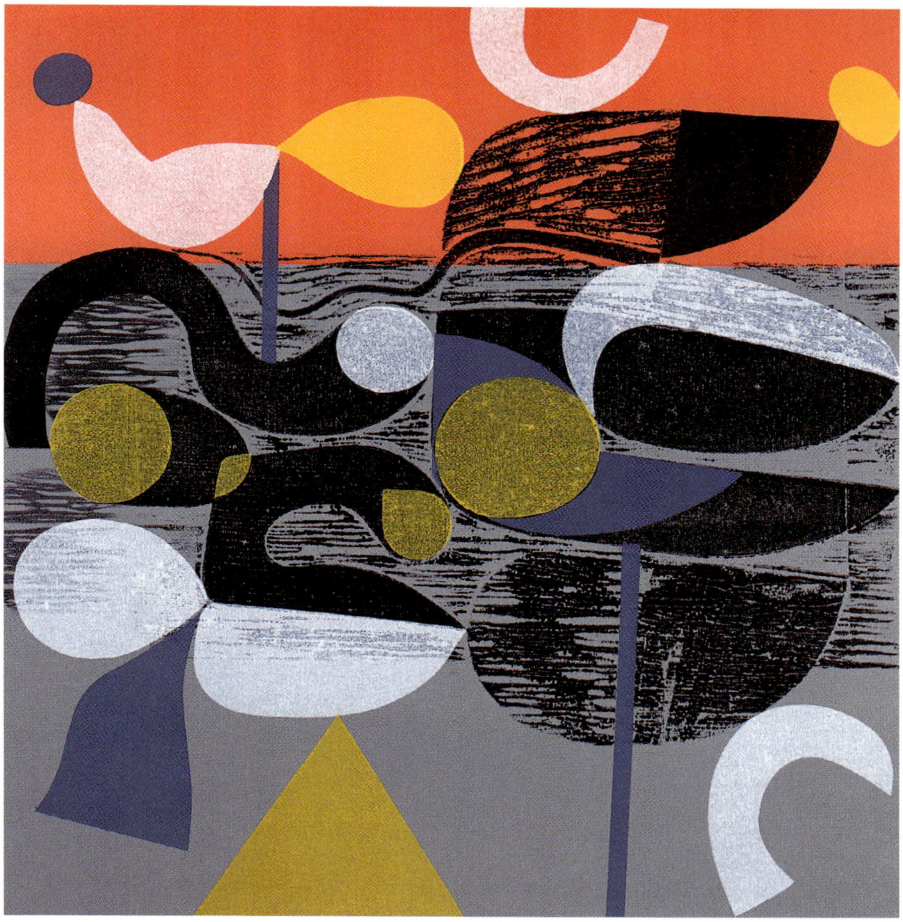

Red Night Fantasy, 2007. Woodcut and stencil, 38 x 38 cm (15 x 15 in.)

overprinted colours using paper stencils. We use ordinary 'typing' paper or any thin paper, cut out the required shape and then place the stencil over the print and roll the colour, through the stencil, directly onto the printing paper. This provides a perfectly flat colour area; and registration is simple, since you can see exactly where you are putting the stencil over the print. Once the ink has dried on the stencil paper, the stencil itself becomes very strong; we have printed large editions in this way. This paper-stencil method naturally and easily produces flat opaque areas but by using reducing medium (an agent that reduces the density of a colour) we can get subtle transparencies, especially as we often lift excess colour from the print by blotting with clean newsprint.

These methods of printing have grown initially from practical necessity but have subsequently been reinforced by encountering historical and industrial precedents such as Japanese paper-pattern stencils, Nigerian metal stencils for Adire textile printing and examples of early offset trade printing for metal cans and bottles.

My images have a variety of origins but usually emerge as part of the printing process rather than from extensive preliminary drawings. It has always seemed to me rather perverse to use the autographic printing process to reproduce an existing drawing – there are plenty of mechanical processes that do this better. I see image-making and printing as an integrated activity – the drawing and printing are not separated, as one grows out of the other. I usually start with a basic image, either discovered or drawn from imagination or some stimulus such as the human form or a found natural or mechanical object. The image is printed directly from a found object or cut onto wood or lino. It is then proofed and that is when the creative decision-making process starts. I work from what the initial proofed image may suggest (frequently a fantasy, dreamlike, landscape form) and it grows progressively with each proof; but the nature of the final print is not known when I start.

A further factor in the way I work has been to consider the concept of collaboration. Printmaking is traditionally a collaborative activity; artist, block-maker, engraver, pressman, compositor – all contribute. So artists often cut blocks or draw on plates which are then passed over to technicians or master printers – yet it is only the artist who signs the prints. Many of my prints owe so much to people working with me – my co-printer and wife, or students and other artists. In recent years we have tried to acknowledge this sense of collaboration (breaking down the notion of the artist as a special kind of person) with some prints being signed jointly to reflect the collaborative nature of our printmaking.

Brian Hanscomb

I live in Cornwall and my studio is a small converted stable and pig-house in our steeply sloping garden on the edge of Bodmin Moor. It's a marvellous place in which to live and work – the moor, although small compared with others, gives the illusion of great space and has an ancient, timeless beauty. The studio overlooks the Camel Valley, which has been for me a source of great inspiration for creating densely worked, moonlit, miniature engravings. I much admire the small engravings and etchings of Edward Calvert (1799–1883) and Samuel Palmer (1805–1881), and indeed we have named one of our favourite walks down to the Camel Valley 'The Samuel Palmer Walk'.

Airfight, 1982. Line engraving, 26.5 x 37 cm (10½ x 14½ in.)

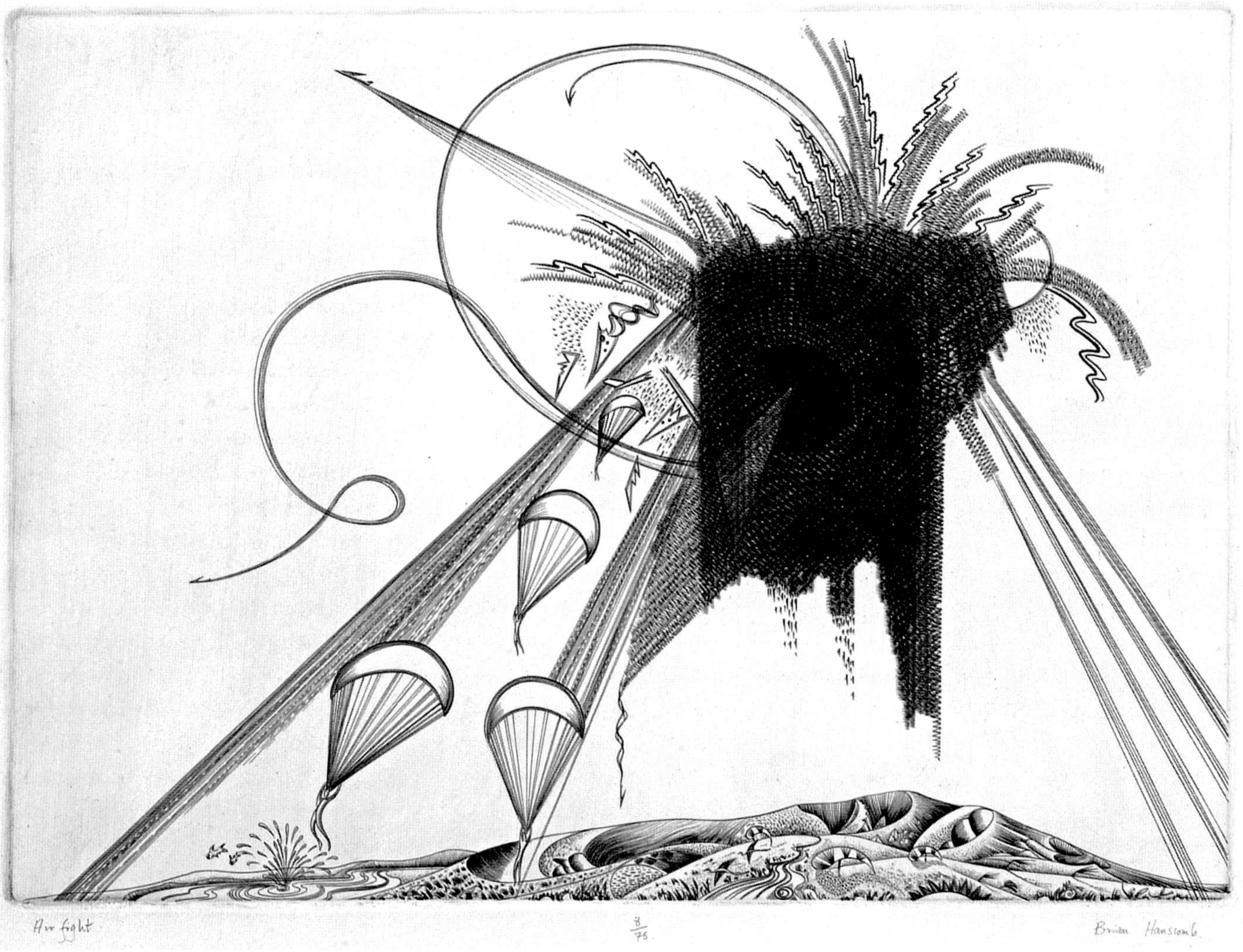

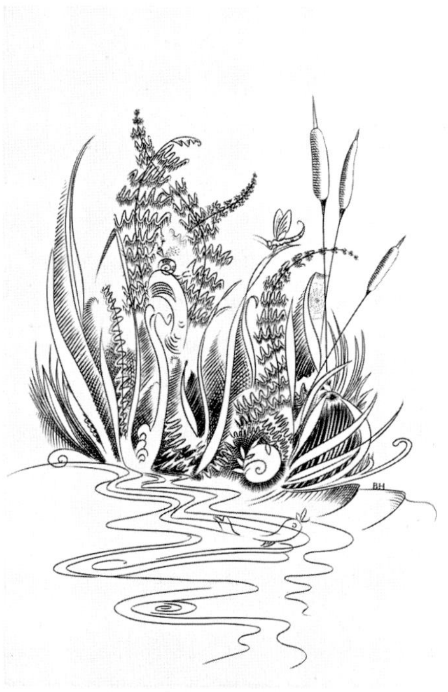

Water's Edge, 1989. Line engraving, 21 x 13.5 cm (8¼ x 5¼ in.)

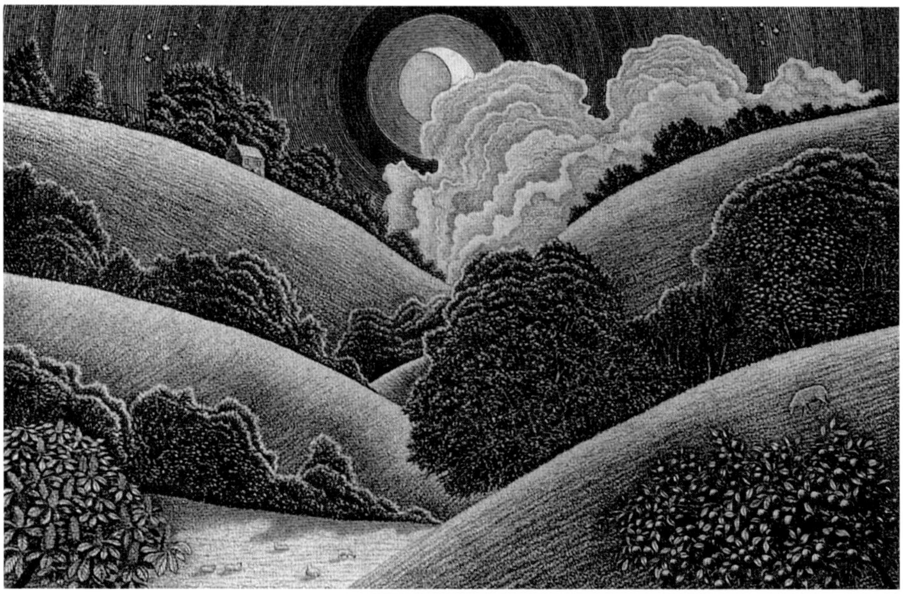

Camel Valley, Cornwall, 2007. Line engraving, 8 x 12 cm (3⅛ x 4¾ in.)

After a serious studio fire in 2002 I was very fortunate to salvage my beloved French, Victorian and Edwardian engraving tools from amongst the débris – I had been given them by my journeyman during my industrial-engraving apprenticeship, and he in turn had received them from his father. They were re-tempered and re-handled and I am now using them again, and feel I am reliving the past times of unhurried skill and craftsmanship when I am handling them. I love the feeling of peeling a cut swathe of copper from the plate, and the clean quality of the cut line. I once read this described as giving 'tonic value' – a good therapeutic description!

Having the full range of tools from my early industrial-engraving days, I have since experimented and taught myself the use of various techniques suited to certain subject matters. I remember avidly studying the line of Dürer's masterwork *Melancholia* under a 10x magnifier, trying to reproduce his quality in my own symbolic and mystical work. Dürer's style of fine line work inspired my *Christ Appears in the Factory* (1978–81), especially in the portrait studies required for it.

I have engraved many landscapes from my love of the West Country, evolving a personal style of lyrical curves inspired by the varied music to which I listen while working. I have tried to enrich my engravings through the beauty and power of sound: music enables me to 'loosen' my line work, allowing relaxed lines to flow and swell. This can be further enriched by adding texture, creating the illusion of colour, for I feel that the use of coloured inks is unnecessary, even a distraction. A full range of tool marks can be seen in my engraving *Airfight*, one of a suite devoted to the 1982 Falklands War. The dynamic use of scorper and multi-line tools in this work creates dense 'explosive' blacks and vigorous movement contrasted with single tool lines creating, to my mind, an empathy with some of Shostakovich's symphonies.

I find the most important aspect in creative engraving is to empathise with and, through the power of imagination, even to become one with the subject matter; my Zen meditation practice helps me towards attaining this state. This, allied to a control of craftsmanship, is paramount. Line engraving is a beautiful and neglected medium but its possibilities are endless, and, for over 45 years, I have tried to bring it more to the public's notice. To quote the French engraver Roger Vieillard, writing in 1989: "Joseph Hecht, an excellent engraver of the first half of this century, called the burin "the violin of gravure". The moment the burin enters the copper-plate is the most passionate and creative moment of the artist's life."

Marcelle Hanselaar

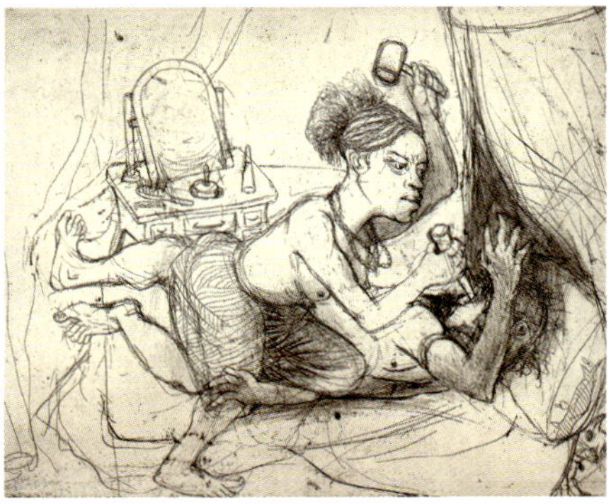

Some time ago I saw Rembrandt's wonderful pen and ink drawing of Jael lustily hammering a tent peg through Sisera's left temple. Typically for Rembrandt, the focus was on Jael's very feminine way of concentrating not on the murder at hand but on hitting that nail on the head. I particularly liked the way the angularity of the pen and ink line emphasised the brutal subject matter. Etching is made for drama and darkness and very suitable, I felt, for trying out this combination of medium and mood.

Right: **Jael and Sisera 2,** 2007. Etching, 21 x 28 cm (8¼ x 11 in.)

Below: **Jael and Sisera 1,** 2007. Etching and aquatint, 20 x 25 cm (7⅞ x 9⅞ in.)

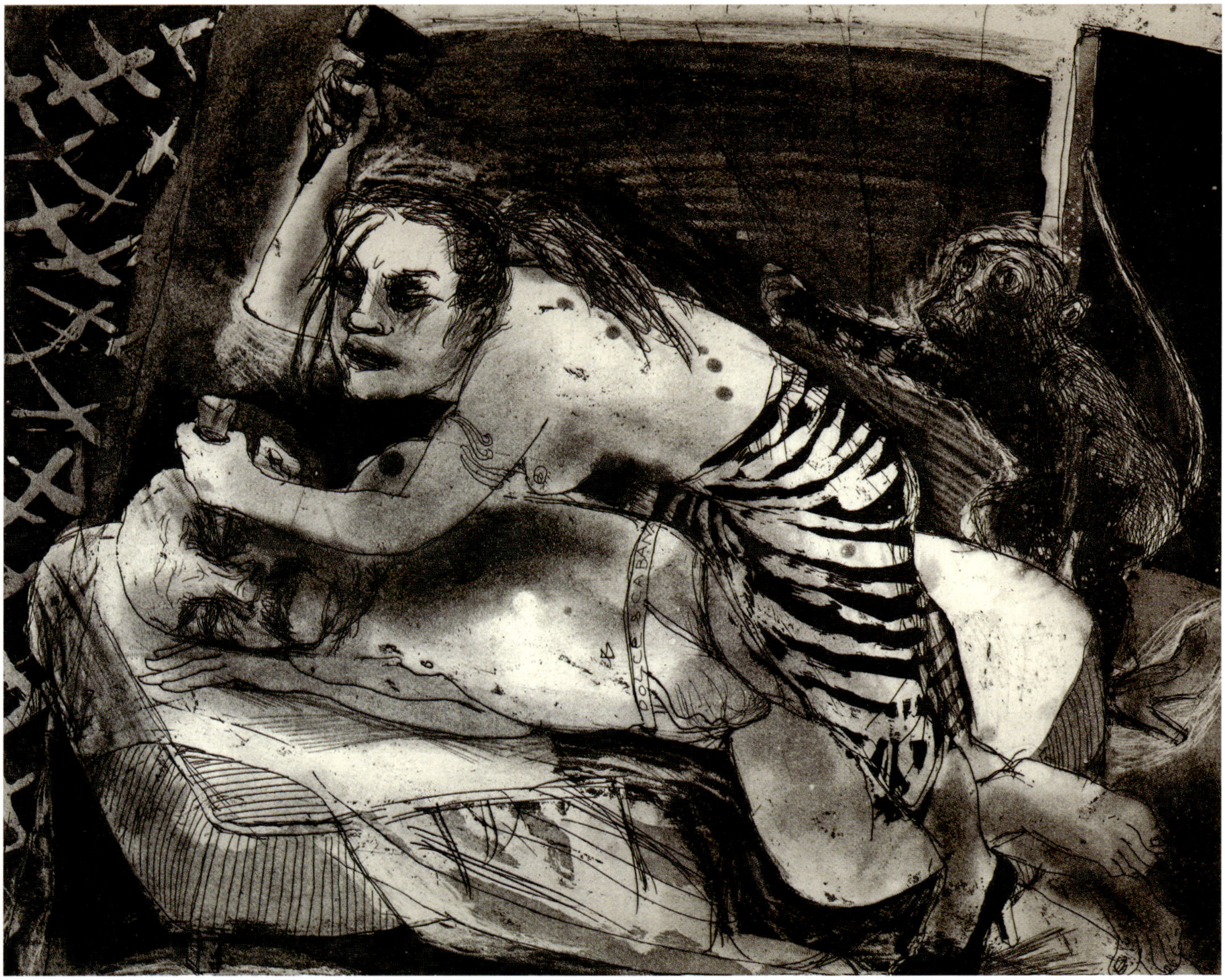

Above: **Lot and his daughters 1,** 2007. Etching and aquatint, 20 x 25 cm (7⅞ x 9⅞ in.)

Below: **Lot and his daughters 2,** 2007. Etching and aquatint, 20 x 25 cm (7⅞ x 9⅞ in.)

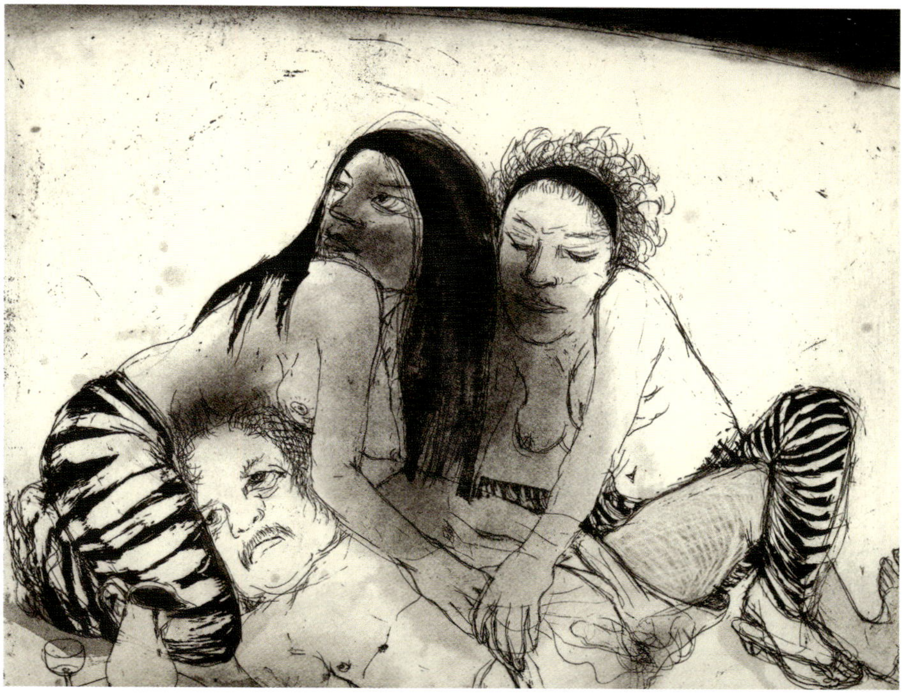

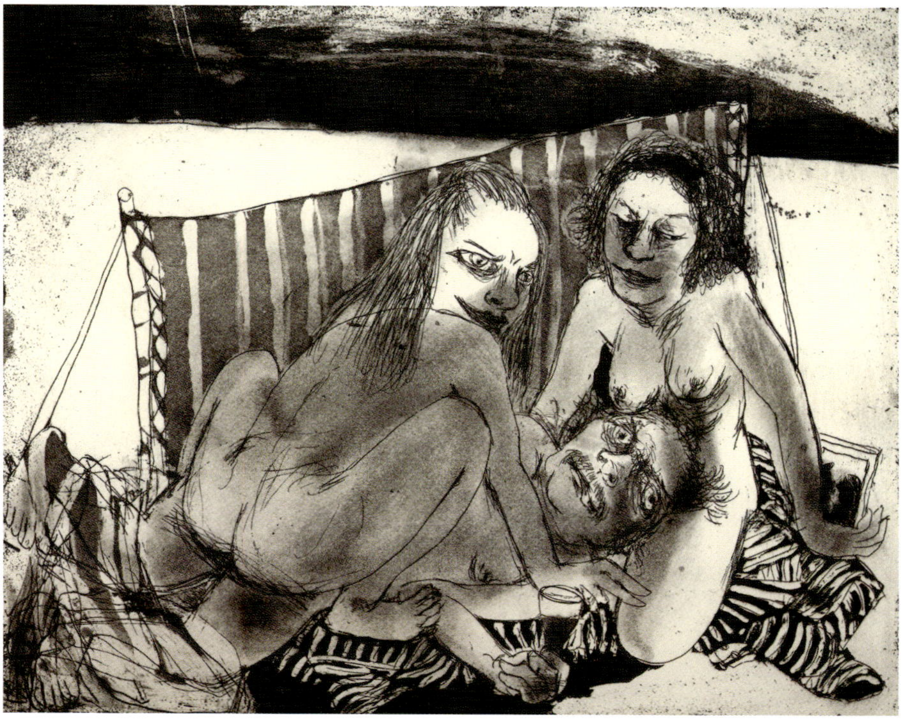

The legendary tales of the Old Testament are full of retribution and tribulation, murder and sexual mayhem enacted under the shadow of the Law. The liberating quality of these stories manifests itself the moment we realise how they in actual fact mirror our subconscious world. Take the tale of Lot and his family, for example. After Lot's wife turned into a pillar of salt for looking back at what was being lost, his two daughters found themselves with their father out in the middle of nowhere. There, forced by the circumstance of being the sole survivors of their tribe, they seduced their father so that he would impregnate them. I like portraying these heroines as ordinary women whose conspiratorial 'a girl has to do what a girl has to do' expression places the scene resolutely in the present. Props like stripy beach screens and Calvin Klein briefs mixed with objects as found in genre painting give the image an eclectic source reference.

My definition of etching lies somewhere between cooking and concocting a witches' brew. I always work on several plates at the same time to keep my momentum going; equally, it gives me the chance to play around with certain effects from one plate to another, choosing copper or zinc as the mood takes me. As a painter, I like to counterbalance the harsh bitten lines with the poetry of aquatint and I especially love using spit bite, the danger and unpredictability of that method being part of its appeal.

In addition to their great drawing skills, the sensual and playful approach to printmaking techniques of artists like Beckmann, Dix, Goya and Picasso is a constant source of inspiration and delight to me.

Roger Harris

I can see that drawing has literally shaped my life. I drew from an early age; I drew on the wallpaper, on the windows with my mother's lipstick and in the margins of books, which was my introduction to the idea of a printed picture on a page. I was born in 1942, in days when drawing paper was scarce; the best available to me was lined writing paper, and virtually the only plain sheet I could find would have been the flyleaf of a book. Though I have drawn for as long as I can recall, it has taken me a very long time to learn to see. Drawing is about seeing, about acquiring a language of marks that makes the world visible.

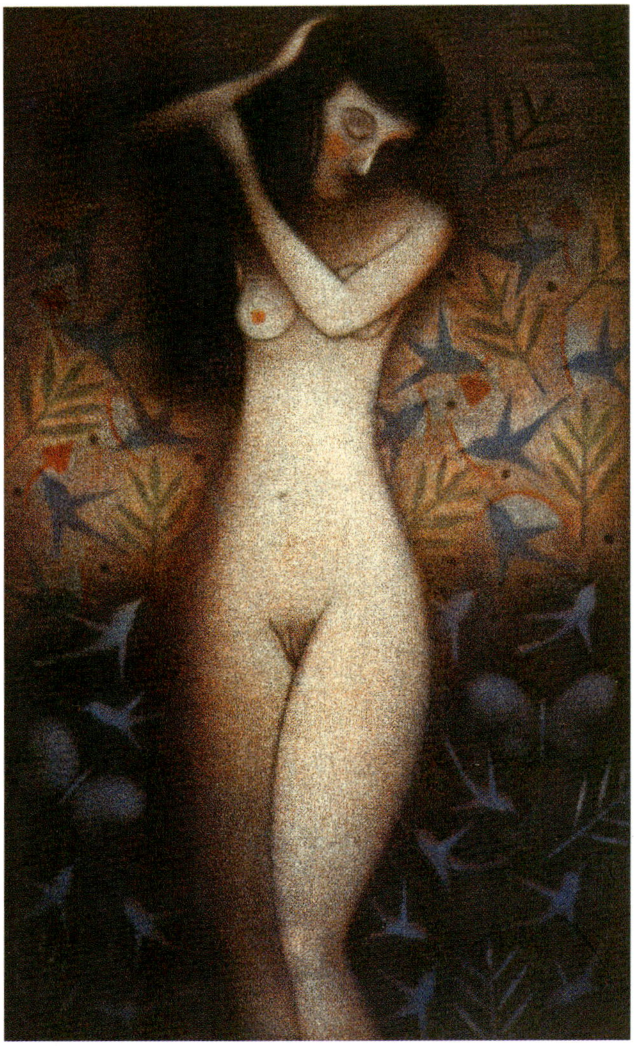

Etude No. V, 2000, Mezzotint, 13.7 x 8.2 cm (5³⁄₈ x 3¹⁄₄ in.)

In the 1960s and 1970s the *Radio Times* was a rich pool of drawings with small, magnificent, black and white images – all gems – by artists including Eric Fraser, Paul Hogarth, Robin Jacques and Leonard Rosoman. This was also the age of the Penguin paperback, with more priceless images for a visually hungry person. Like a magpie I collected all these things; they fired my imagination. In the 1970s, on seeing the superb etchings by David Hockney for his *Grimm's Fairy Tales* series, I realised that I wanted to turn my own drawings into etchings.

I know now that drawing embraces many approaches, but my inclination is towards the figurative. My heroes are Michelangelo, Brueghel, Rembrandt, Degas, Seurat (beautiful Conté drawings!), Picasso, Leonard Baskin, Kitaj and many more. I have also found the work of naïve artists such as Edward Hicks, Alfred Wallis and Bryan Pearce stimulating: though not conventionally tutored, there is an inherent rightness in the way they place images on a piece of card or wood. In my work I am always conscious of the shape of the plate and the potential life within it, seeking to hold the viewer's attention within this space.

Around 1978, Holly Downing RE (see p. 50) gave an illustrated talk on mezzotints to our etching class and showed examples of her work and those of Japanese printmaker Yozo Hamaguchi – deep, rich and mysterious coloured images. I immediately knew I had to find out how they were created. Information at that time was very thin, with only very few artists making mezzotints in this country and books on printmaking referring only fleetingly to the subject, so I visited the V&A

Mother & Child, 2000. Mezzotint,
4.7 x 4.7 cm (1⅞ x 1⅞ in.)

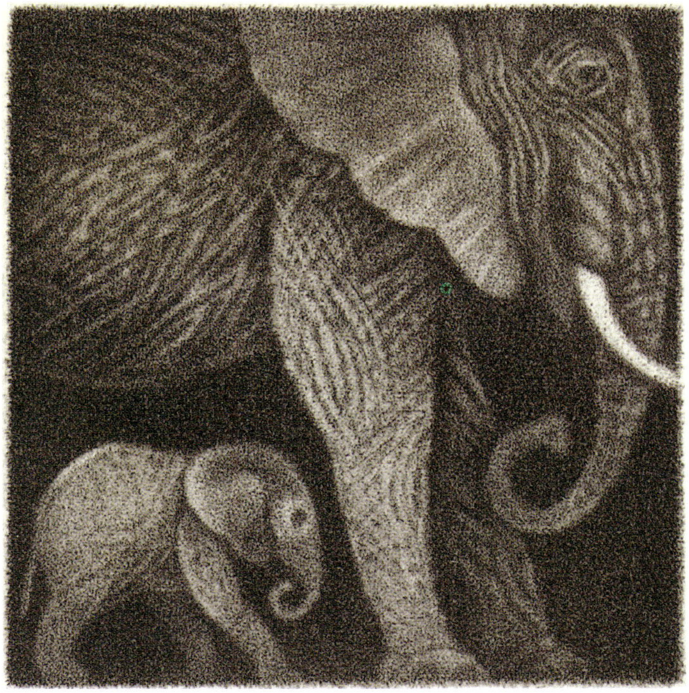

and the British Museum to study prints. Tools were few: I had a mezzotint rocker and a small knife. I started to make small prints, loved the effects and the plates grew in size. My first attempt at a coloured print involved a plate inked in green and printed under a black-inked plate, which proved difficult as the green overpowered the black; from this I realised that a black-inked plate is very delicate and that any colour printed under it has to be quite subtle. I am now working with up to four plates, one for each colour, with their subtle interplay finely balanced. A plate can take a month or more to rock before drawing and scraping can commence. I create my image with a small knife and a burnisher.

For me, mezzotint is the most beautiful form of printmaking. It is like drawing with light; the image seems to be in the paper, rather than lying on the surface.

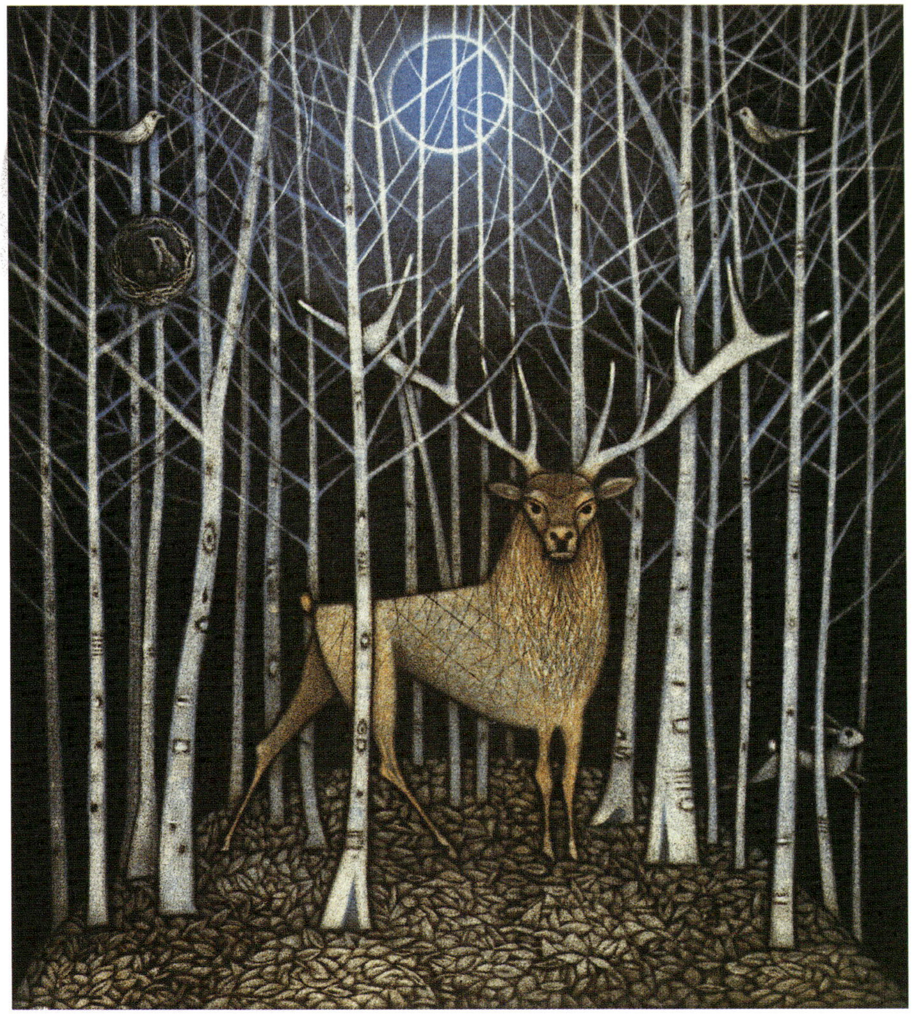

Spirit of the Wood, 2007, Mezzotint,
21.5 x 19.5 cm (8½ x 7¾ in.)

Brenda Hartill

1. Collagraph plate construction

Collagraphs are printed from built-up, collaged plates. Materials chosen for this should be thin enough not to tear the paper or the etching press's blankets, yet should be thick enough to create a satisfying embossing. A 600 gm^2 paper is ideal for editioning and protects the blankets best, but for proofing 300 gm^2 paper backed with blotting paper is adequate. It is important to keep an eye open for textured materials: leaf and plant skeletons, plastics, cork tiles, grasses, various boards, card and chipboard, for example. Natural materials should be stuck to the plate with a contact adhesive spread onto both surfaces, and the plate should then be covered with a chalk-powdered paper to protect the blankets before putting it through the press under moderate pressure. Afterwards, any concave areas can be filled in with plaster filler and the whole sealed really well with PVA then water-based matt varnish. I experiment with different fillers (always adding some extra PVA), glues, metal paints, varnishes, carborundum (I always use fine), sand, grit, etc. Plaster fillers can be scratched into or carved with woodcut tools. Above all, you should try to be brave and be prepared to fail! However, plates tend to settle down after a few pulls and any necessary repairs can be made with superglue.

2. Collagraph printing

Many people take far too long to ink and wipe an intaglio or collagraph plate. Ink can be applied with stubby brushes – either stencil-type or small, trimmed house-painting brushes. They don't need to be completely cleaned, just stored in jars of vegetable oil classified red, yellow and blue, and simply dried off well onto a rag before being used again with a similar colour. A large piece of medium scrim should be used for wiping the inked plate – it's a false economy to use little bits; a metre square is best – softened by pulling across the weave in both directions. First, densely inked areas should be wiped firmly with well-used scrim, and surplus ink cleaned off the scrim from time to time on newspaper which is frequently changed. The scrim should be constantly shaken out and a clean part found for the wiping, and a neat pad should always be formed by tucking in the trailing tails. Wiping moves into gentler mode when the plate has a very thin covering of ink. I always keep clean scrim for the final wiping and finish with a piece of tissue paper flat on the plate, spitting on my hand to stop it from slipping, wiping in a circular motion and constantly changing the hand's position so that clean parts of the tissue are in contact with the plate.

3. Chine collé and metal leaf

When adding chine collé or metal leaf to a print, the plate is inked and wiped first. Shards and sheets of metal leaf are laid directly onto the inked plate, either roughly torn or precisely cut as the image requires. Then the back of the leaf is pasted with cornflower paste or neutral pH PVA, which will stick it to the dampened paper as it is run through the press. The joy is that the inked image will overprint onto the leaf. When applying chine collé you should brush paste thinly onto a piece of glass, then press the tissue evenly onto it, lift it gently off and lay it paste side up onto the inked plate, to which, as in the case of metal leaf, it adheres during printing. Never use spraymount adhesive as it is not acid-free and will discolour quickly.

4. Marking up and printing tips

Before printing, it's a good idea to mark up a layout on the underside of a thin sheet of Perspex or heavy plastic, indicating the position of plate and paper. With several basic layouts to tape onto the bed of the press there need never be an off-centre print. After each impression the Perspex can be cleaned by wiping with a soft rag and baby powder – not solvent. The simple way to keep paper off an inked plate preparatory to printing is to trap its leading edge in the roller, then clip the opposite edge

Blue Grass I, 2007. Collagraph with plant material, 40 x 50 cm (15¾ x 19¾ in.)

Blue Inferno I, 2003. Collagraph with silver leaf, 49 x 46 cm (19¼ x 18⅛ in.)

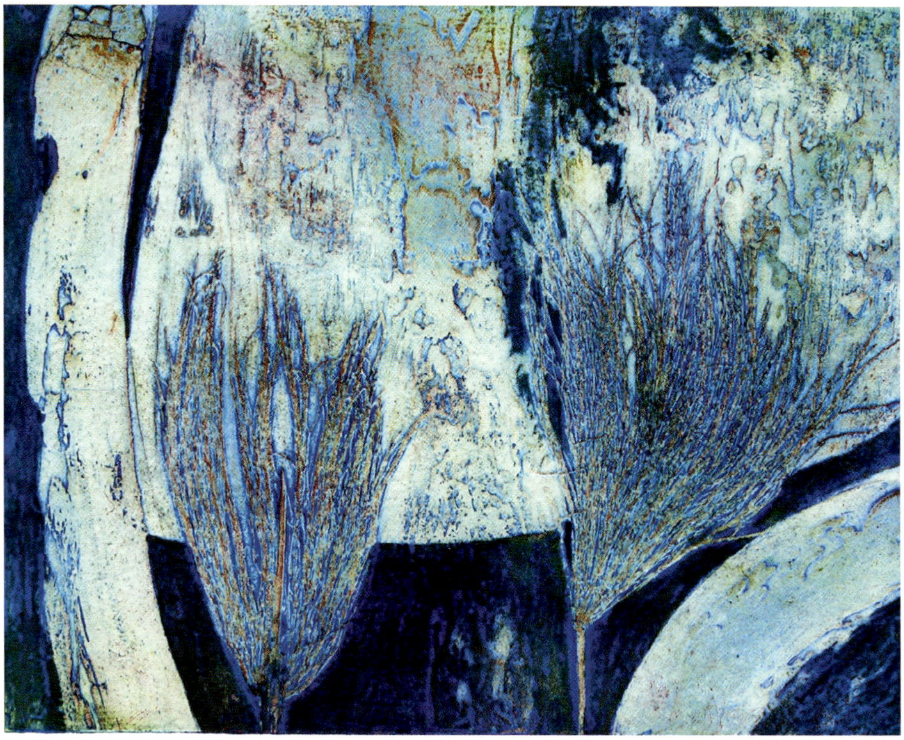

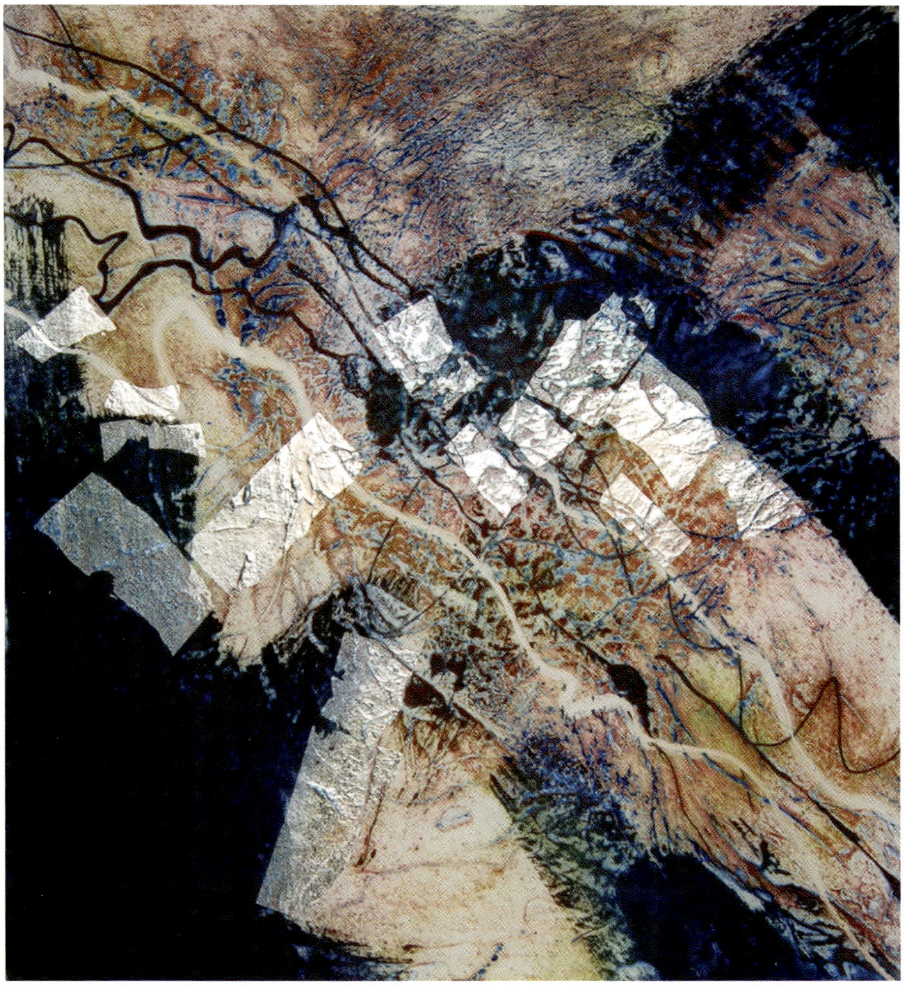

with a padded bulldog clip attached to a weight at the end of a 30 cm (12 in.) piece of string, and drape it back over the roller. This is better than laying paper flat on the inked surface, since it avoids undue paper stretch and creasing; but don't forget to release the clip before it gets trapped as the bed travels between the rollers!

5. Cleaning and touching up prints
Most ink and dirt smudges can be removed from prints with masking tape pressed firmly over the mark and lifted vertically, holding both ends rather than peeling. In the case of dried ink an alternative is to scrape gently with a sharp Stanley knife blade and smooth down the disturbed paper fibres with the back of your fingernail. Once prints are dry, good-quality watercolour is best for disguising blemishes in the printed area. Passages that have printed weakly owing to worn aquatint can be strengthened with coloured pencils. Plates and inking surfaces can be cleaned with a cheap, soft nailbrush and vegetable oil (safer than white spirit), of which only a tiny amount is needed to remove the last traces of scum. Hands can be cleaned with the vegetable oil, with sugar added as an abrasive, and finally washed with liquid soap. Surgical gloves should be worn whenever possible.

Paul Hawdon

I get great pleasure from making etchings. I find all aspects of the activity have for me a natural and spiritual quality: the use of a simple sharp needle to find possibilities of expression, along with the immersion in acid, take the work out of my hands and into a realm of aggression. Then, in the inking of the plate, one can caress the drawing into a sense of abstract atmosphere culminating in the final reversed image that on the paper never fails to surprise.

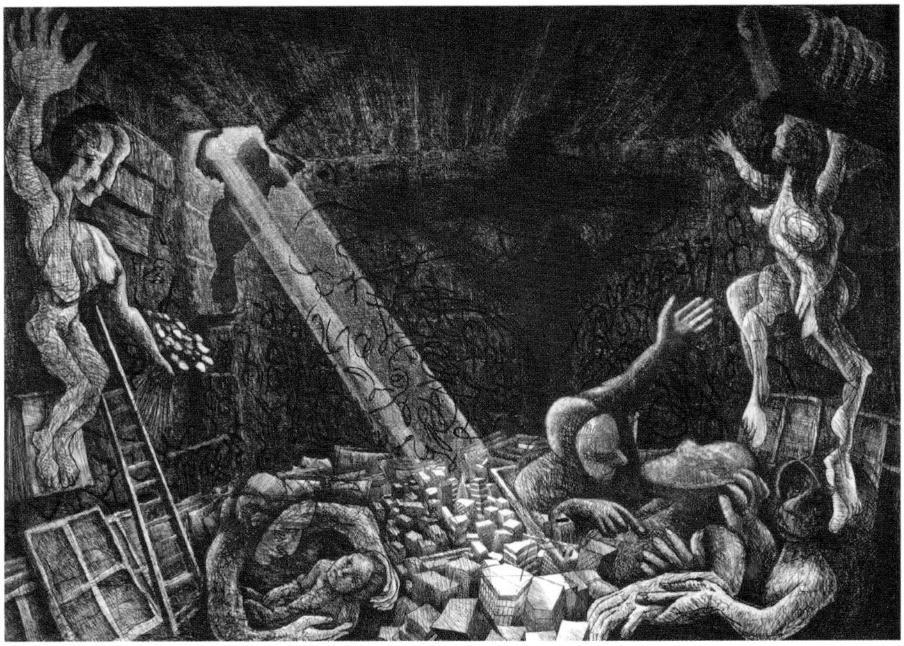

Depart and Forget. Etching, 60 x 83 cm (23⅝ x 32⅝ in.)

Steer for the Deep Water Only. Etching, 50 x 100 cm (19¾ x 39½ in.)

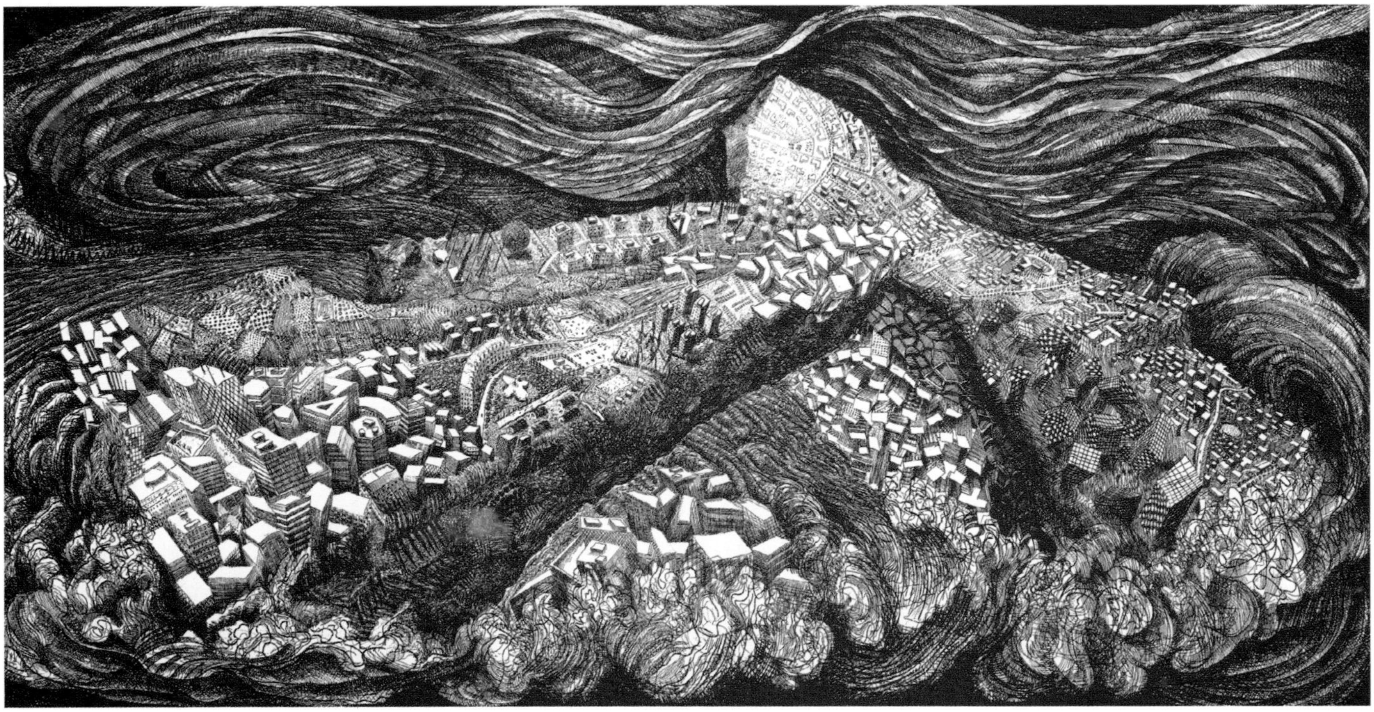

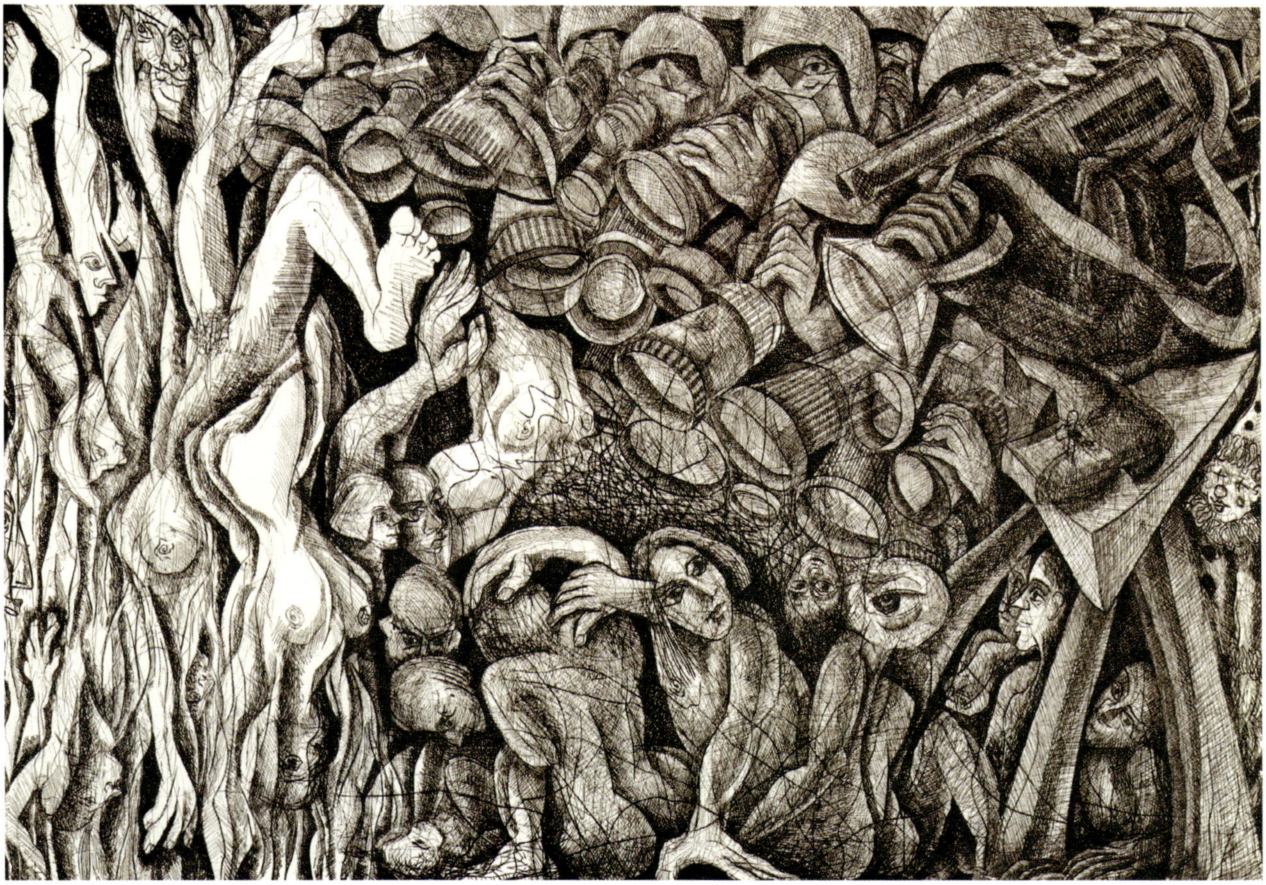

Ambiguous Situation. Etching, 60 x 83 cm (23⅝ x 32⅝ in.)

This essentially contemplative process and its associated search relate to my particular personality. I am a rather quiet person who finds it hard to interact with others, so for me the etching becomes about investigating this inner world in relationship to the outer world. It feels paradoxical to turn materials that in the world would be more useful as wire or cardboard boxes into something that has an emotional presence. Through etching, and this sense of contradiction, I am able to work through conflicts that I have within myself and conflicts that I have in the wider world, so that the work becomes my collaborator and conscience. Sometimes it is an external world and I look outwards to draw from things seen in an attempt to engage, but often I become confused and dulled. At other times, I look into myself and it becomes a private world, an uncrowded space that initiates within me a sense of reflection, meditation and introspection so that I feel mentally alive. In the world, in the crowd, I have a sense of being disembodied and lost, but once I begin the creative endeavour I begin to feel alive. The etching can be fought with by being attacked and devalued, or made love to and idealised. It can be sacred or secular, moving between the lowest of material worlds and the highest of spiritual worlds. It becomes an experiment and a source of life that allows one to feel both anger and love as innocently and intensely as a child. In this oscillation between childhood naïvety and adult sanity, I aim to surprise myself, to shock myself out of the sense of oppression that I feel when I try to engage with others; to attempt, for a brief moment, to escape from the adult world. In this futile effort to escape, I enter a no-man's-land where I strive to reflect and to antagonise modernity yet try not to produce a 'brand' style in which the work becomes neutralised into thoughtless banality. I constantly rebel against myself in an act of self-destruction to seek a form of authenticity. Paradoxically, in doing so, I arrive at a sense of inner peace and integrity that I think is rare in life.

Carole Hensher

Rummaging through old boxes in the attic and looking through their contents for 'precious objects' stored long ago by myself or my mother; emptying the contents of drawers, which in my house can have a kind of sedimentary-layered effect – these are activities that fascinate me and also provide a rich source of inspirational material for my printmaking activities. There seems to be a direct link in my imagination between these objects, stored for random reasons often many years ago, and my need to communicate, in a visual, non-verbal way, ideas and obsessions that have intrigued me since early childhood. Not only do objects such as these have a very personal resonance for me, I find that this is also recognised by people viewing my work, almost as if there is a link with their own personal experiences. All of this, of course, happens retrospectively. In the early stages of finding and sorting I feel as if I am just playing around with my found objects, almost returning to those early childhood days of the sorting and collecting and putting together that make up imaginative play.

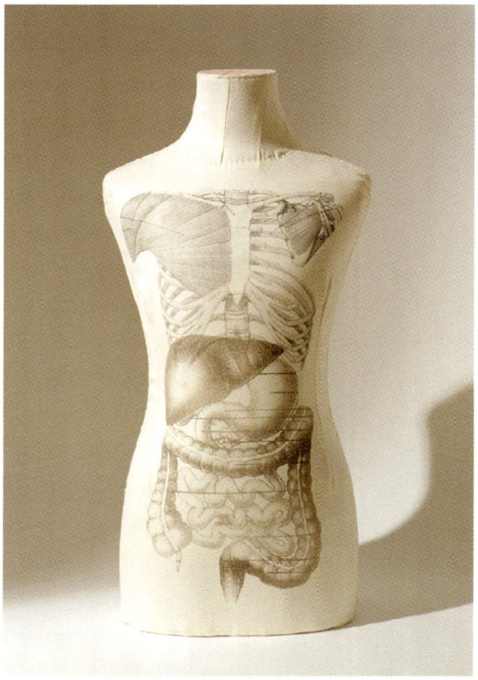

Anatomy Lesson, 2004. Lithograph on fabric, 59 x 20 cm (23¼ x 7⅞ in.)

I think it was Paula Rego Hon. RE who claimed that her studio was her play or nursery area, a private space where she could interact with her work and the objects and stories that provided her inspiration. Another artist whom I greatly admire and who has proved inspirational to my own methods of working is Louise Bourgeois. She freely admits that her childhood memories and experiences are the springboard for her work. She actually includes old dresses and other clothing that belonged to her in some of her installation pieces.

An inveterate 'maker' of things from fabric for as long as I can remember, I had always kept this very separate from my fine-art activities in painting and drawing. It was only when I started studying the work of early surrealist artists such as Meret Oppenheim, Hans Belmer, André Breton and Man Ray, while on an MA Printmaking course at London's Camberwell College of Art, that I began to realise the undervalued power and impact that everyday objects such as gloves, shoes and so on can have in the visual arts. It was during this time of investigation and reflection that I began to see the possibilities of printing images onto fabric pieces and then making these up into garments or three-dimensional objects. After experimenting with screenprinting I came to the conclusion that offset lithography provided the perfect solution to this type of tricky printing. This method allows great flexibility of registration and avoids flooding the fabric's surface with too much ink, a danger when printing on less absorbent fabric such as silk.

I print on a variety of textiles and papers and, using the offset method, I rarely have any problems of bleeding: that is, the migration of ink into areas where it is not wanted. I generally use photolitho plates since these enable me to use photographic material in my prints; they also allow me sometimes to expose actual pieces of

Stomacher II, 2004. Lithograph on fabric, 75 x 55 cm (29½ x 20⅞ in.)

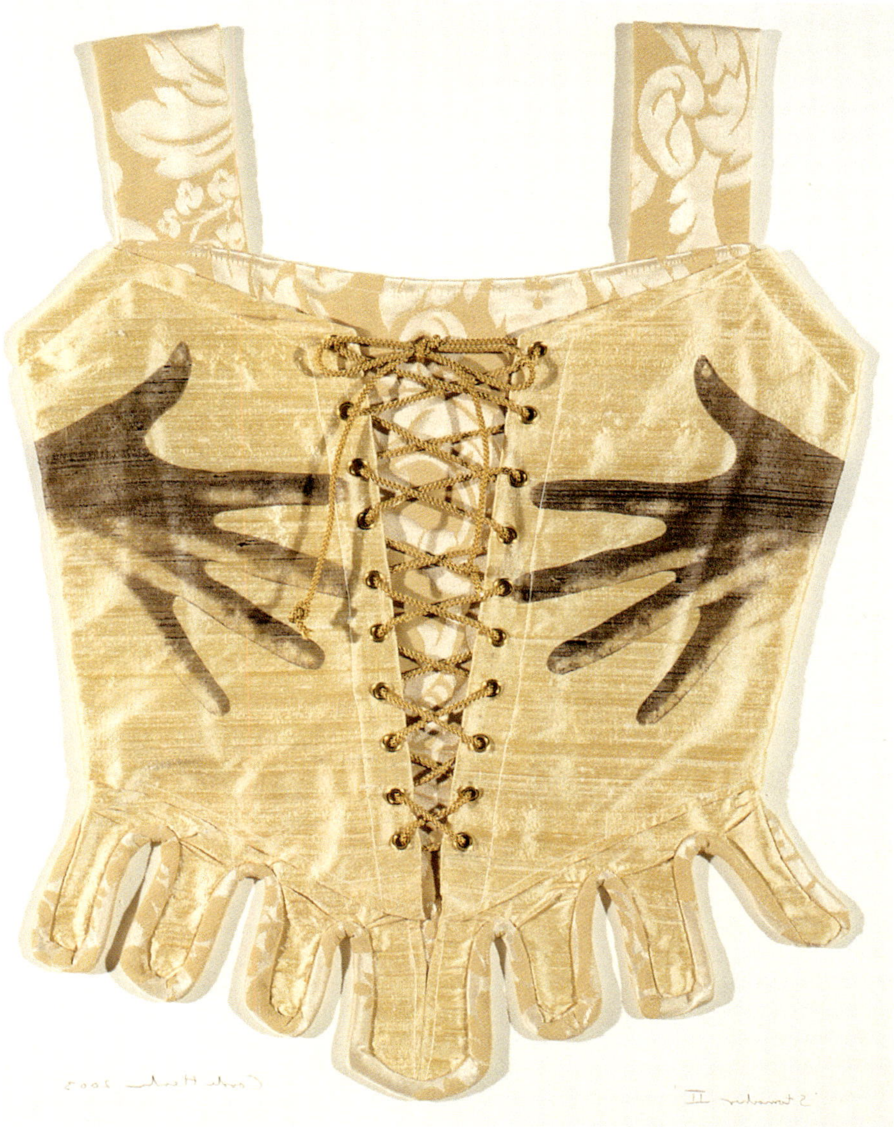

lace or small garments directly onto the plate, a process that I always find really exciting as one never quite knows what the final image will look like. I suppose that this element of my work is what I could call my 'printmaker's secret' because it is something that never fails to inspire and amuse me. I now own a small offset-litho press and can experiment to my heart's content on any materials I choose – a real back-to-the-playroom experience!

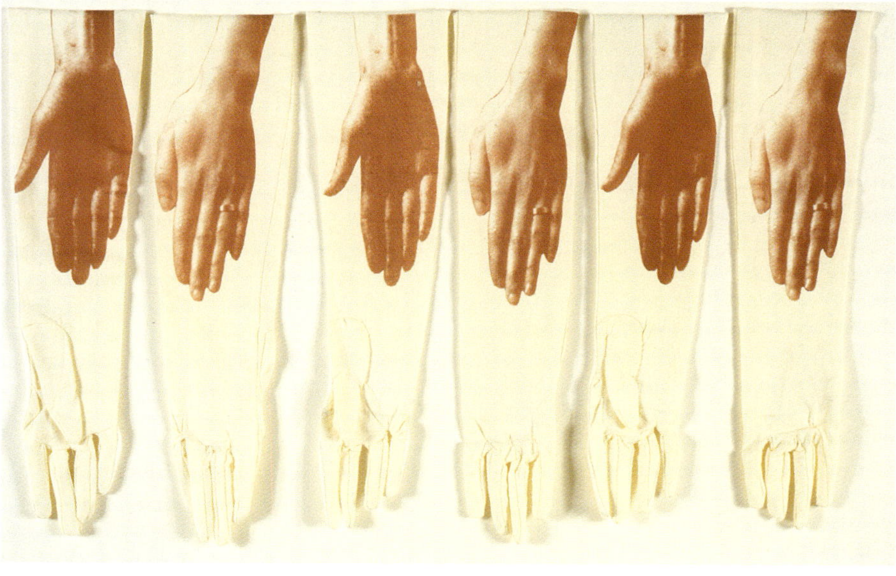

Gloved Hands, 2003. Lithograph on fabric, 57 x 75 cm (22½ x 29½ in.)

H.J. Jackson

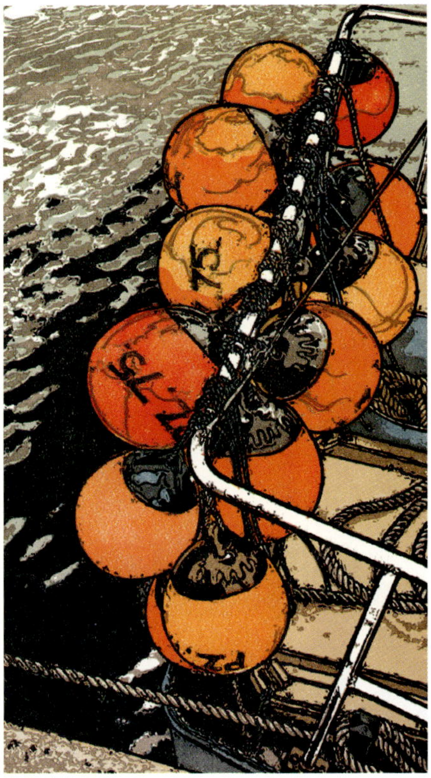

Floats, 2004. Linocut, 51 x 28 cm (20 x 11 in.)

Due to the size of my linocuts and the number of colours and blocks I use, people assume that I have a printing press. However, when I left art school in the late 1950s, having spent the previous four years creating lino prints on a large press, I suddenly found myself without access to such equipment. I had to improvise and the answer lay in the flat base of my tobacco tin, which I discovered I could use to hand-burnish my prints, as it glided over the back of the paper, bridging the cuts in the lino. I further discovered that the waxy inner bag of a cornflake packet, opened out and laid on top of the printing paper before burnishing takes place, provided the perfect material to help my tin slide across the paper. I roll oil-based ink onto the cut lino and use a paper mask to cover up any non-printing areas of the block. I lay printing paper in position and the tin is used to burnish this firmly onto the inked surface.

I generally work from photographic reference. I can take many shots of a subject covering different angles, which enables me then to produce a finished full-size drawing. In my head and using thumbnail sketches, I divide this image into the different blocks, some of which will carry just one colour, while others can be used to print different colours in different areas.

The drawing is photocopied onto tracing paper, which is then reversed and transferred with carbon paper onto the various blocks, the lino having been covered with a thin wash of white emulsion paint that helps the visibility of the carbon line. Using coloured drawing ink, I identify which areas are to be left and which need to be cut away. I only use two cutting tools: the first is a V-tool used for the detail; the second is a small gouge used to cut larger areas. This means that the tool I require is either the one in my hand or the 'other one'! This greatly simplifies my working practice.

I have developed my own registration process; it involves using two pairs of drawing pins. With one pair, holes are located on the drawing, the tracing and each block and mask. With the second pair, two more holes are located on the edge of the printing paper, away from the image itself. These also appear on the tracing, which is used to register each successive block into position. During printing, the pins are fixed into small separate squares of lino carefully positioned adjacent to the longer sides of the printing block. In this way, I can accurately match as many different lino blocks as required and can register the paper perfectly. Furthermore, whilst I am burnishing I can lift at least half of the print at any given time, check progress and add more pressure if needed. I have used this method for the past fifty years.

A typical print might consist of six blocks, eight printings (two blocks being printed twice but with different areas masked) and sixteen different colours. I only ever mix white into the first printing. All subsequent printings contain reducing medium in varying amounts, thereby building up layers of transparent colour, one upon another. Since I live near the coast, the declining fishing industry features strongly in my work, and I like my boats to look as if they have been to sea. The multiple layers of colour result in a 'treacly' appearance which helps to give the boats the look of working vessels.

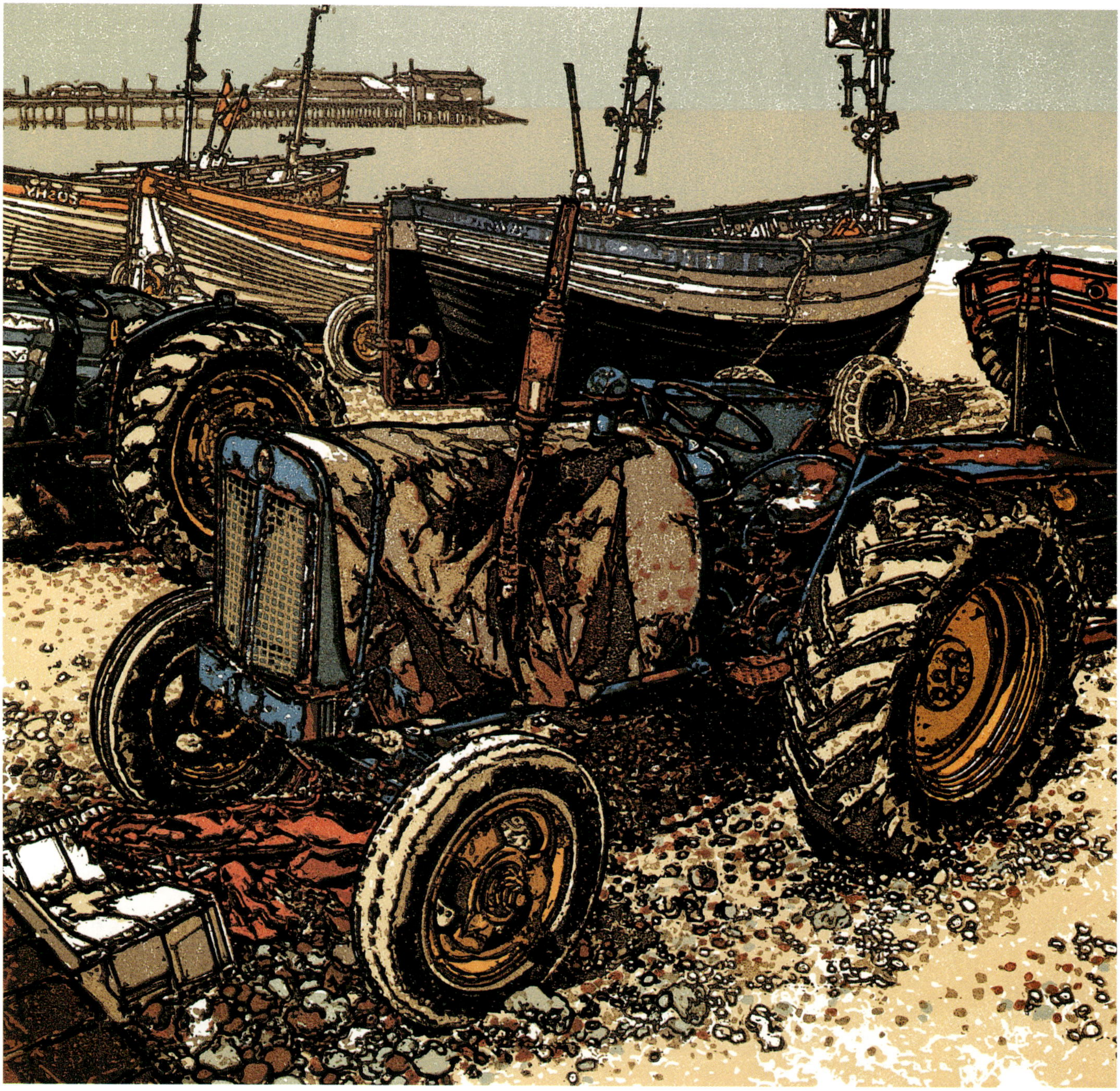

Boats and Tractors, 2002. Linocut, 42 x 44.5 cm (16 ½ x 17 ½ in.)

Each new printing alters the previous colours where they overprint. As a result, I have a seemingly endless palette of colours with which to work, yet they actually stem from a very limited range: black, white, light chrome, yellow ochre, cobalt blue and scarlet. Other colours are occasionally bought in for a specific use – for instance, a rose pink which cannot be mixed using the above selection. Cobalt driers are added to the ink to speed up the drying process, enabling me to overprint on successive days. However long I have spent drawing, tracing and cutting the blocks, it feels like magic when I ink up and take off that first print. As I build up the colours with subsequent printings, the magic increases. The feeling when that final key block overlays the previous colours and binds them all together is nothing short of amazing.

Howard Jeffs

The monotype printmaking method is one of the least complicated means of creating prints. Its direct method encourages spontaneity and the acceptance of chance – so important for the creative process. A monotype can be defined as a unique print made by drawing or painting with printing ink, watercolour, oil paint or another suitable pigment directly onto an unworked printing surface such as glass, metal or acrylic sheet, and then transferring the image to paper by hand-burnishing or with a press. Usually, a single print is produced.

Frequently, my prints are produced very quickly and many are discarded. I usually work with a series of images on one theme. It is not strictly correct that a monotype allows only one print to be made. Subsequent prints are possible, sometimes referred to as ghost, or trace, prints. After a first print has been taken from the monotype plate, traces of the image remain on the surface. If one were then to take another print

Four Black Sunflowers, 2003. Monotype, 38 x 56 cm (15 x 22 in.)

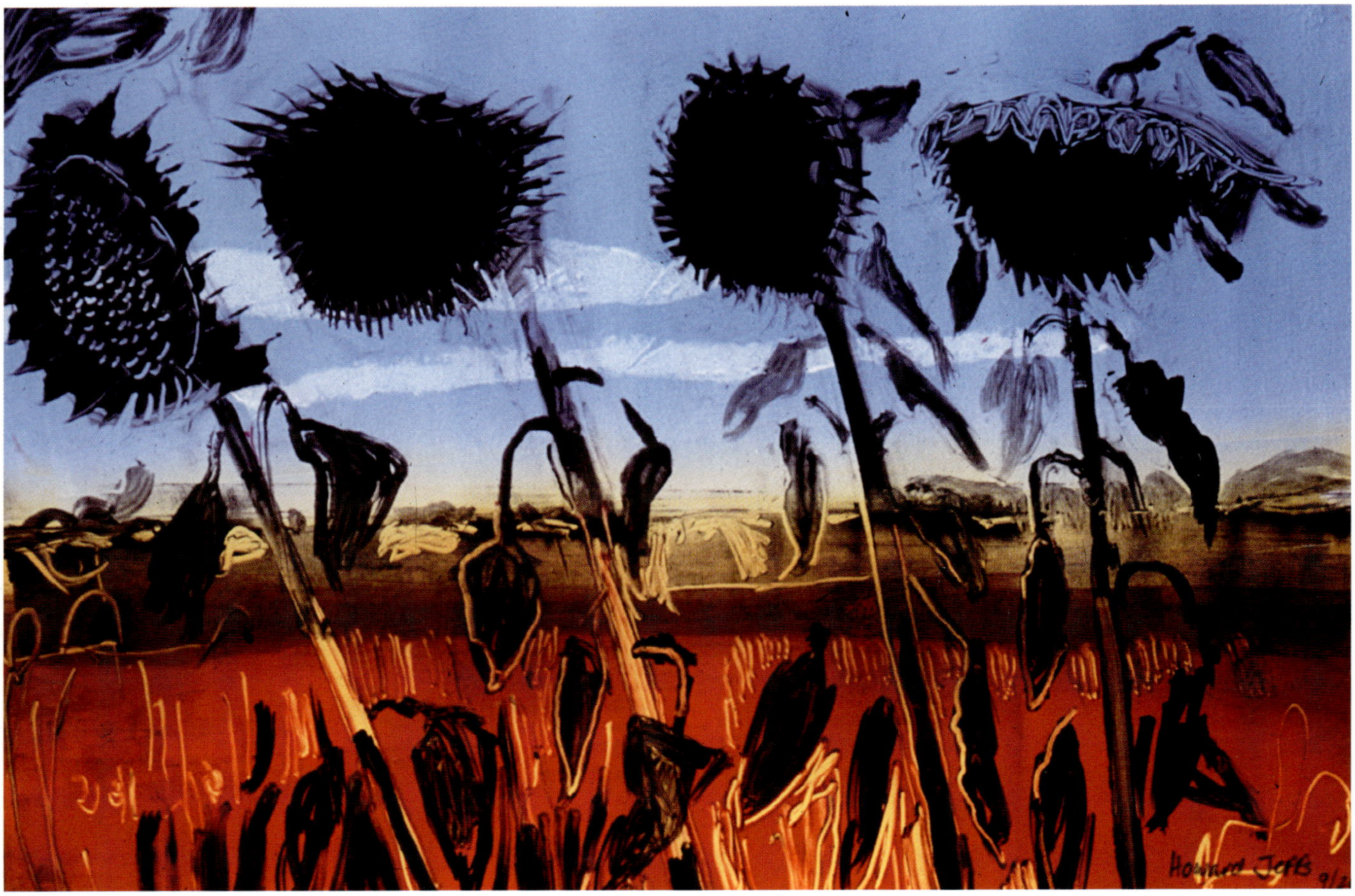

without adding anything more at this stage, it would be much paler than the first pull. Sometimes it is even possible to take a third print, but this would be very pale as hardly any ink would be left on the plate at this stage. I often start adding stronger, darker colours to the plate after the first monotype print has been taken, since what is left on the plate is the ghost or skeleton of the first image and offers unique possibilities for subsequent development of the print. It is a very similar approach to that of a painter using oil paint thinned with turpentine as a basis for the subsequent layers of thicker paint.

The monotype *Stars in the Night Sky* was made by devising my own individual methods and techniques. First, I sprinkled small particles of magnesium powder on the deep-blue ink of the sky to form small stars, while for the larger stars I used a pipette to drop spots of white spirit, which dissolved the deep-blue sky ink. The black shapes of buildings and trees against the sky were drawn by means of removing black ink with the tip of the handle of a painter's brush. The brown shape of the road was the colour that was laid on the first plate with the blue sky; and I also dissolved part of the night sky's blue ink with white spirit to give the impression of clouds.

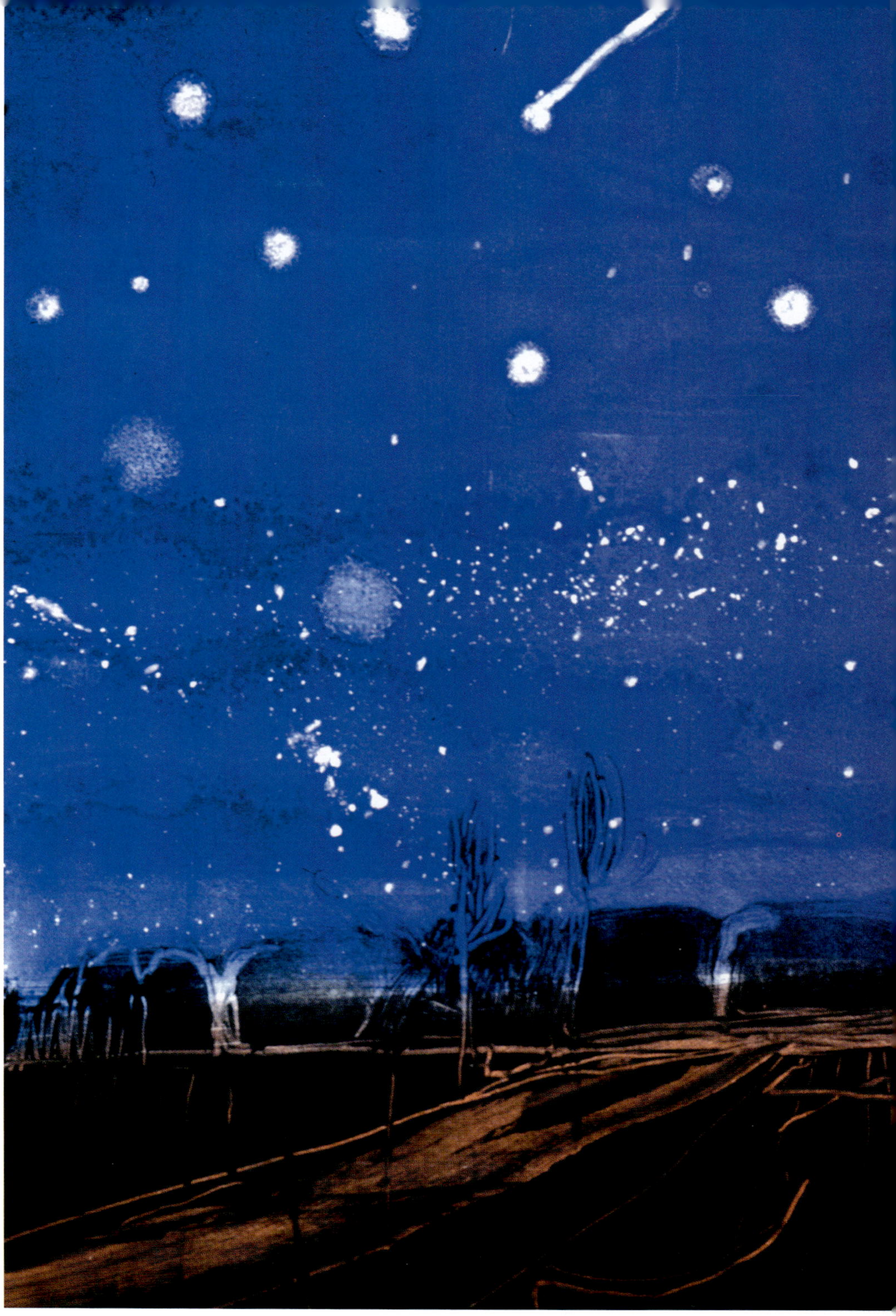

Stars in the Night Sky, 2004. Monotype, 38 x 28 cm (15 x 11 in.)

I can understand why painters from Degas onwards have been attracted to making monotypes. The method offers a direct approach, similar to making marks on a canvas or sheet of paper, and allows a high degree of spontaneity. Often, monotypes are not seen as being part of the main tradition of printmaking – that is, techniques such as lithography, intaglio and relief printing. Making monotypes produces no editions, leaving print galleries with little to sell. However, there are still certain artists working today, such as Mimmo Paladino, Hughie O'Donoghue and Barbara Rae, who seek to exploit the special, free characteristics of the monotype. I share their enthusiasm for this approach to making prints.

Frank Kiely

I like to work with big screens and on large screen-printing beds. I enjoy the whole screenprinting process, but my favourite part of the process is the mixing of colour – this, for me, is all-important. I enjoy the smell and consistency of the ink, whether water-based, acrylic or oil-based. I have great fun inventing colour names with whimsical reference to tastes. This, for me, is more precise than a reliance on the usual colour names: a synaesthesia that may well have its origins in my childhood. When I was a boy I would sometimes have lunch at my father's works canteen. I have vivid memories of sliding my wooden tray past all the goodies on offer. Among all the desserts, jellies and ice creams, yogurt was my favourite. I remember the chemical smell and bright colours that would burst out when I removed the foil lid and I loved stirring the deep containers with my plastic spoon. I still think of these experiences when I mix my inks, as if I am conjuring up a new flavour.

Dream a Little Dream, a title taken from the Mamas and Papas' song of the same name, illustrates well the use of colour in my prints. Whilst this print refers to *Absinthe*, Degas's painting of a woman in a Paris café, it does not share its sombre, depressing aspect. Degas's woman seems melancholy and only the bright green of the liquid in her glass enlivens the scene. In my image, the sitter is dreaming of being in a café in London. We do not see from where she dreams this – probably sitting at her kitchen table. Hers is a simple dream, a dream of happiness found in the independence of living in the metropolis, where she is anonymous and left in peace. I have only coloured part of the image. The parts left uncoloured are the magical regions intervening between the different dimensions of reality.

Transparent screenprinting inks can be overlapped so that a few colours can create the effect of more. I have chosen not to do this. In my print there are eleven colours, all separately mixed and juxtaposed. *Dream a Little Dream* reflects my admiration for Eduardo Paolozzi, whose screenprints are especially enjoyable for their colour. In my print there are many variations of yellow. I wanted the image to be illuminated by them, as if the woman's reverie became more real the more she dreamed; as if it was being coloured in her imagination whilst she envisaged a new life. Again, my palette evokes such tastes as sugar-coated banana, marshmallow sweets and hot mustard.

Another print from the same series is *December-Coloured Weather*, part of a body of work based on my experiences of London as a person originally from abroad, in my case from Ireland. The print contains images of people in my life, set in a London context. One of the inspirations for the print is a poem by the celebrated Irish poet Patrick Kavanagh, entitled *Memory of my Father*. In it, Kavanagh writes of grieving for his deceased father and how he mistakes strangers for him on the streets of Dublin and London. In one line, he writes of 'October-coloured weather' – words and mood adapted by me for my own title. I wanted to evoke in the print the feeling of a wet, wintry day in the city. To achieve this I have used a range of greys and blues. Kavanagh's idea of mistaking strangers for people known intimately also became linked in this work with missing those close to me. In fact, the man in the foreground represents my father, who, unlike Kavanagh's, is alive and well. Shown simply in line, with no colour added, he appears ghost-like and leaves the viewer wondering whether or not he is actually there.

Right: **Dream a Little Dream,** 2004. Screenprint, 54 x 76.5 cm (21¼ x 30⅛ in.)

Below: **December-Coloured Weather,** 2004. Screenprint, 52.5 x 75 cm (20⅝ x 11½ in.)

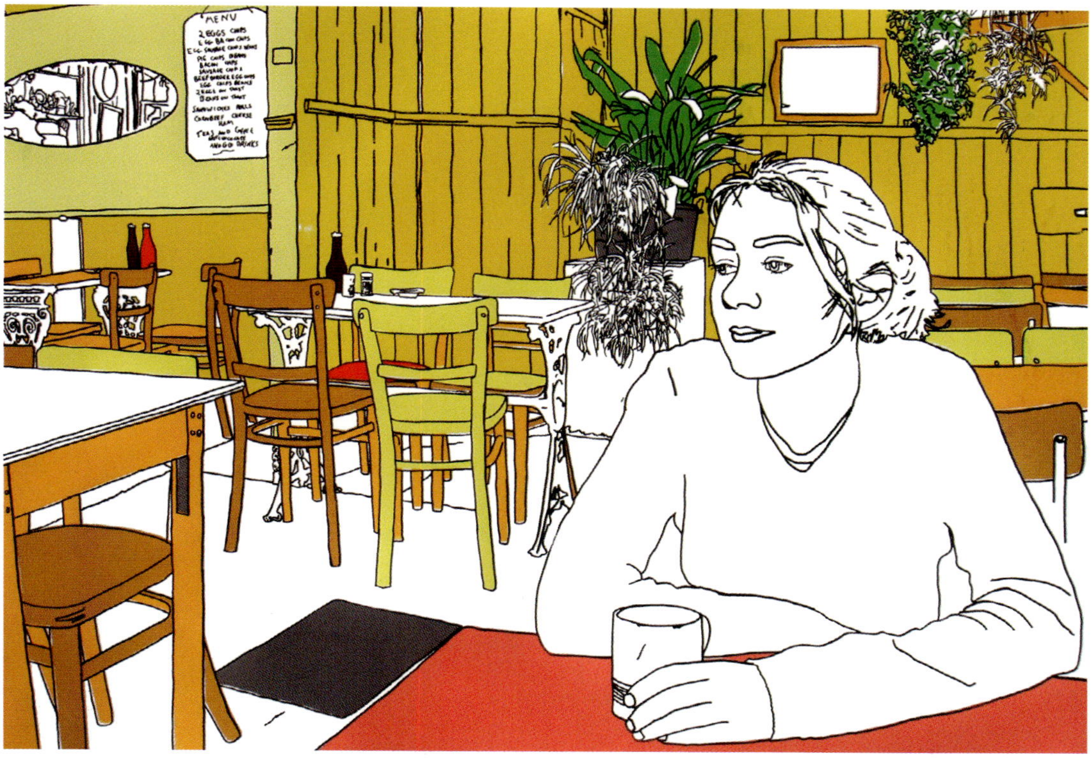

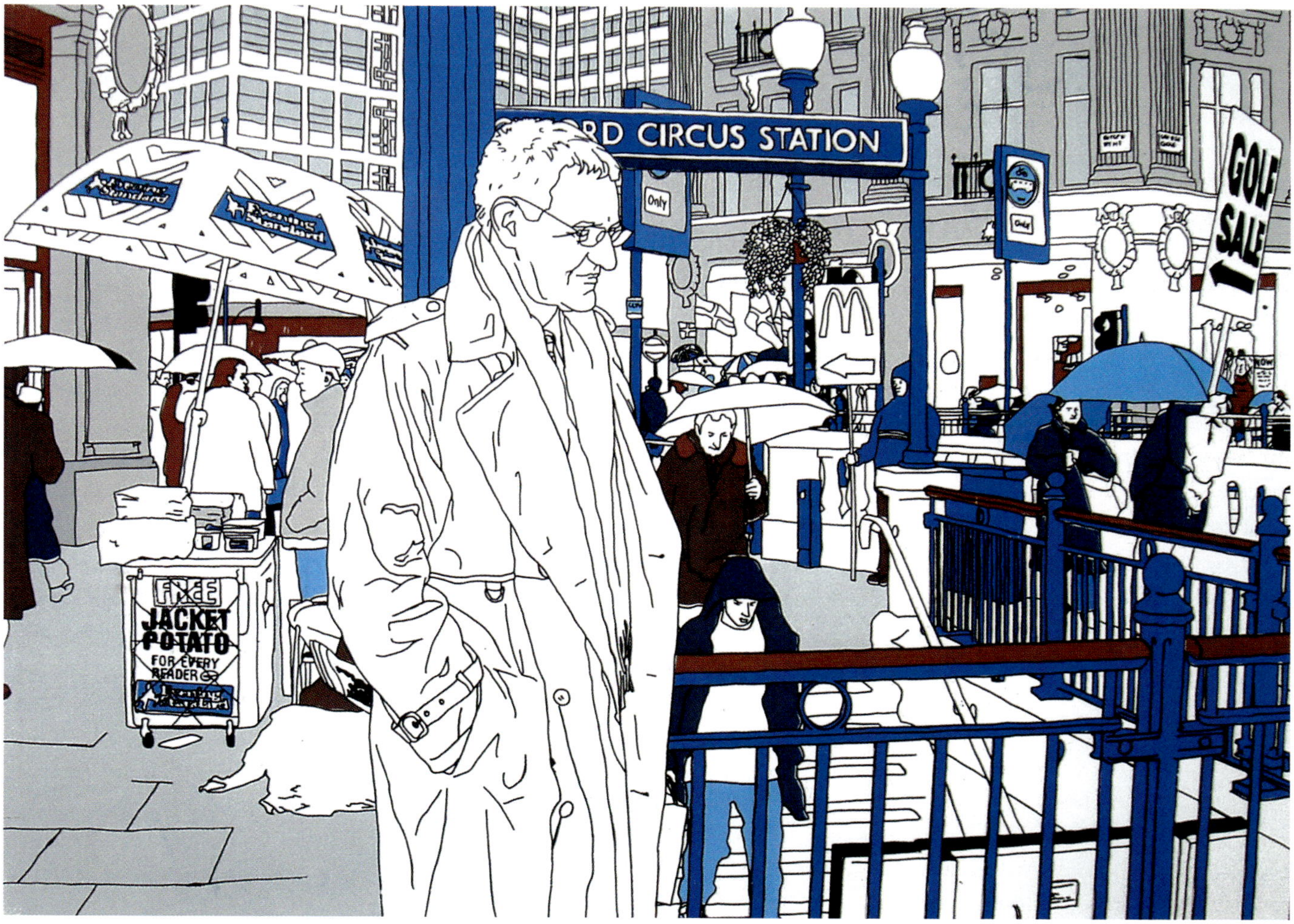

Anita Klein

Printmaking for me is an extension of drawing and I like to keep techniques as simple as possible so as not to distance myself from the finished picture. My favourite techniques are drypoint and woodcut, and, as I like my images to be clear and simple, I inevitably find myself wanting to cut away completely large areas of a woodblock. This used to be a laborious and time-consuming process until I discovered the wonders of power tools.

First I draw my image on a block of plywood. I like ply with a little grain showing, but it needs to be of good quality to stop layers underneath splintering; I use marine ply. I paint my image in diluted Indian ink as, working on a small area at a time, I need to be able to see clearly where to cut. A router is very noisy and makes lots of dust, so I do the cutting in my garden, protected by ear defenders and a face mask. I used to clamp the block down, but recently I have discovered rubbery cutting mats that effectively grip the block without the need for clamps. As I cut, I am looking at my drawing inside the small cutting circle of the router and following my painted lines carefully. I use two routers, one with a large cutter for big areas and one with a fine point for details. Of course it is possible to change blades on a single router, but having two saves time.

When the block is fully cut I go over the surface lightly with sandpaper to remove any hairiness in the wood, then take a proof. At this stage I need to decide whether the image is successful in black and white or if it needs a second colour. With this particular print I felt that the top edge, where the tops of the heads were cut off, needed defining a bit more, so I experimented by hand-painting in green. In the end I decided that a single overall background colour would be better than a second cut block. I used the back of the original block for this, and printed in a 'wrapping paper' mid-brown – a colour I am fond of as it is an exact mid-tone between black and white. When this first colour was dry, I printed the original block on top of it in black, registering by laying the block onto the printed paper, then flipping over for printing.

Stages in printing a woodcut. Photographs: Nigel Swift.

The image drawn on the block

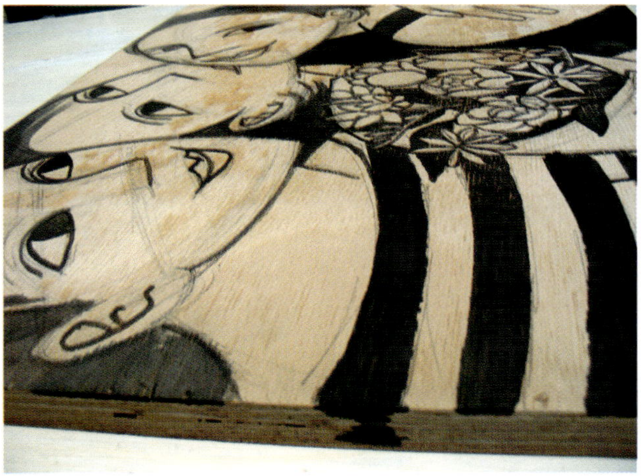

Cutting the block with a router

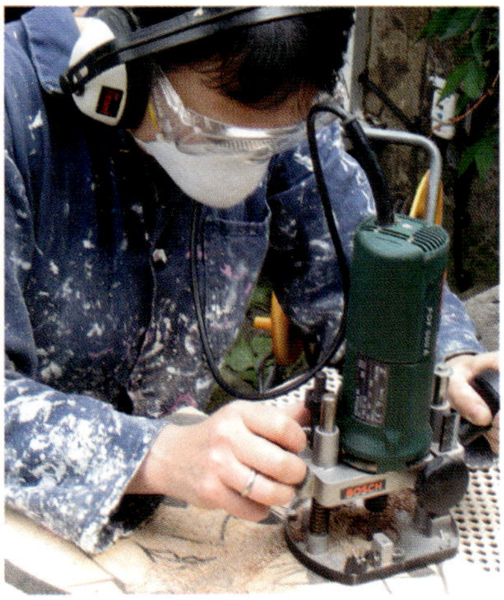

Fine cutting

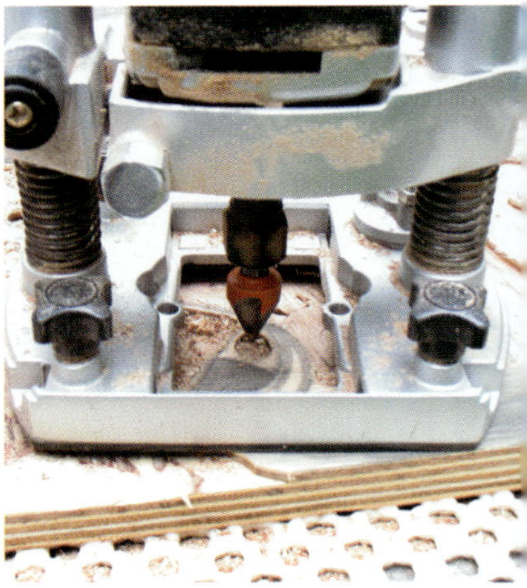

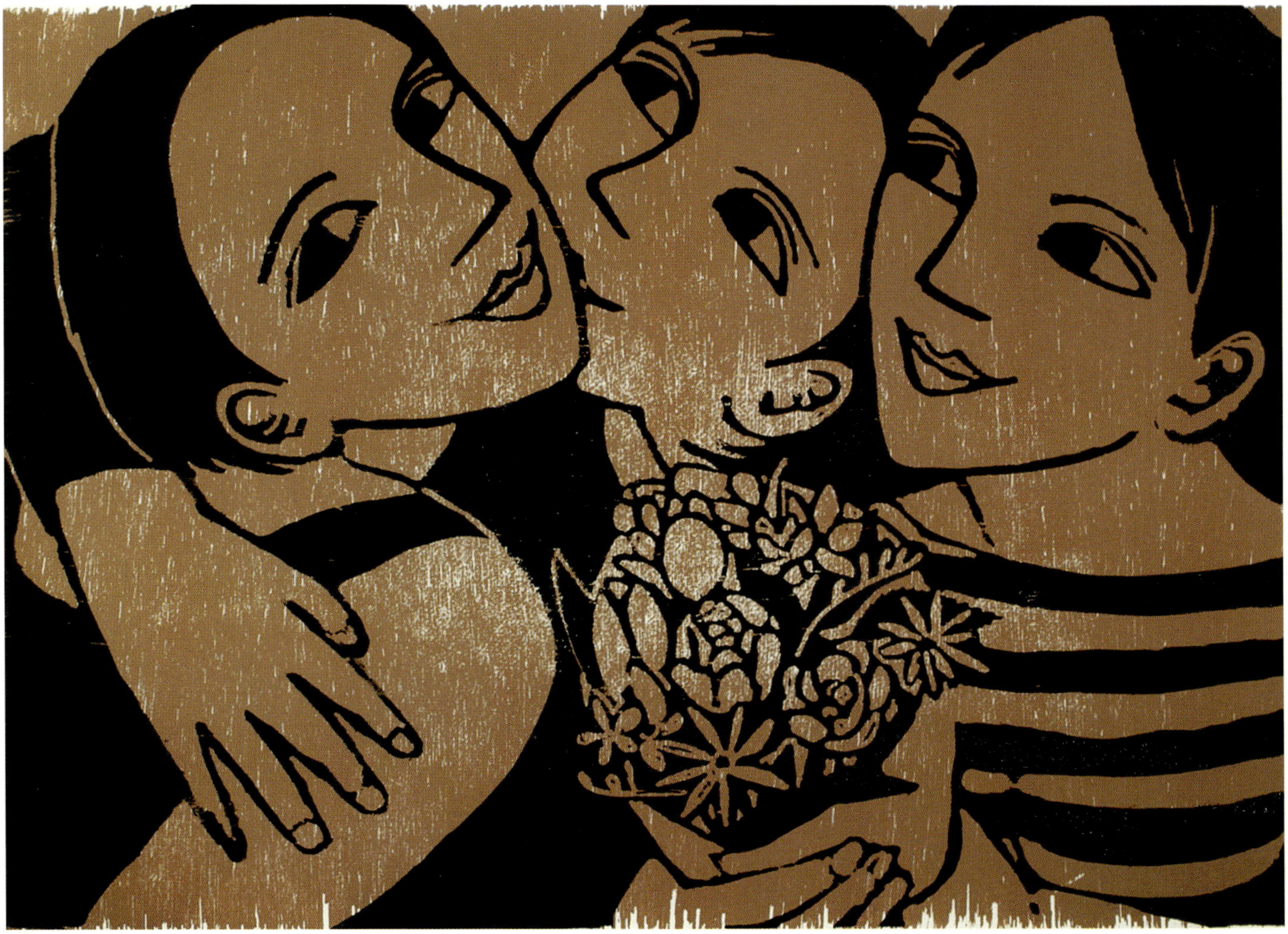

The Bunch of Flowers, 2007. Woodcut, 43 x 60 cm (17 x 23⅝ in.)

The block partly cut

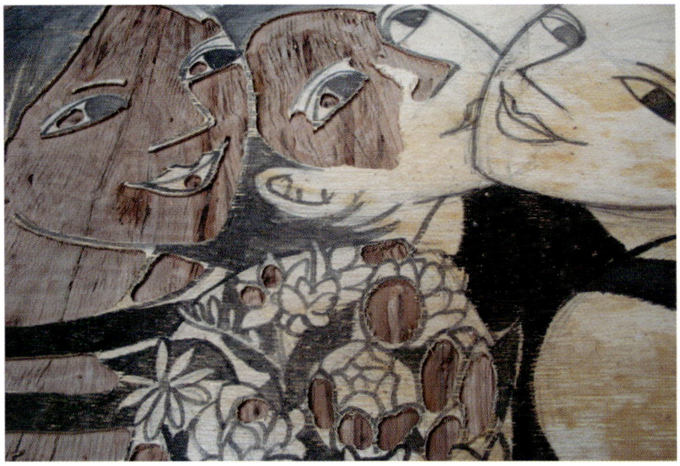

Lifting a print

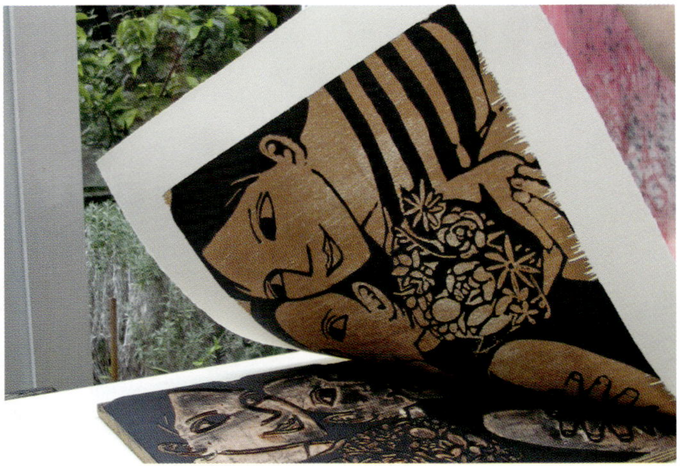

Peter Lawrence

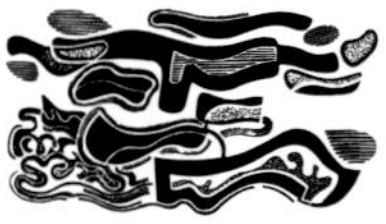

Ah ... the familiar scrunching sound of the spitsticker cutting its little channel through a block of perfect type-high boxwood. Not for me. My wood engravings are done on Resingrave, an artificial substitute for traditional box. Of course, it's the spirit and the tools that make it a wood engraving, but the switch to Resingrave is not completely insignificant. It was bound up in my move to larger prints allowing greater freedom of expression. It seems to suit my modernist predilection. The cutting of curves can be more a continuous movement, less a series of joining lines (scary if I want to do these freehand, but fun). I use the tint tool as my basic drawing tool, rather than the spitsticker; it gives a clean, even line. The whiteness of the cut lines is a bonus. Photocopying the block (darkened with brown ink so that I can see my black drawing and the white cuts) at various stages gives a 'proof' to work on without the need for inking and printing.

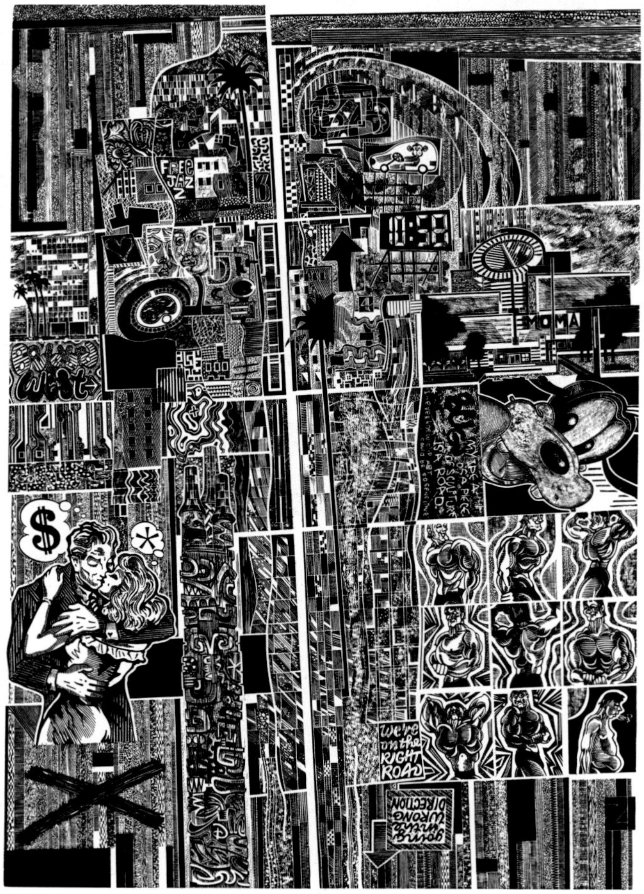

Way Out West, 2004. Wood engraving, 41 x 26 cm (16⅛ x 10¼ in.)

Breaking out of the one rectangular block is important, if only as a possibility. Multiple blocks, blocks off square, allow for the shape of the print to become a key element in itself. For me, the design of the whole as an abstract shape comes first. The individual shapes then create opportunities for infill with pattern or images. With a print such as *Transform* the design is transferred from my imagination directly onto the paper at its final size. The detailed pictures within the overall image come from a huge resource of past sketches, ephemera and ideas that have been awaiting their moment of fame. I'll do a separate drawing for each of the small elements. They don't all make it through the 'auditions' to appear on stage! There's some logic, for me at least, in the combination of elements, but I enjoy mixing styles and making unusual juxtapositions.

Planning is all-important in engraving. It's an unforgiving medium that prints every mark as an equal, both those carefully crafted and those done in error. But my methodical approach must be countered by risk-taking: I like to wander off the map, as long as I get there in the end.

The patterns and textures are coded on the tracing of the final design, though not always followed in execution. For me it's like chess, thinking a few moves ahead as I

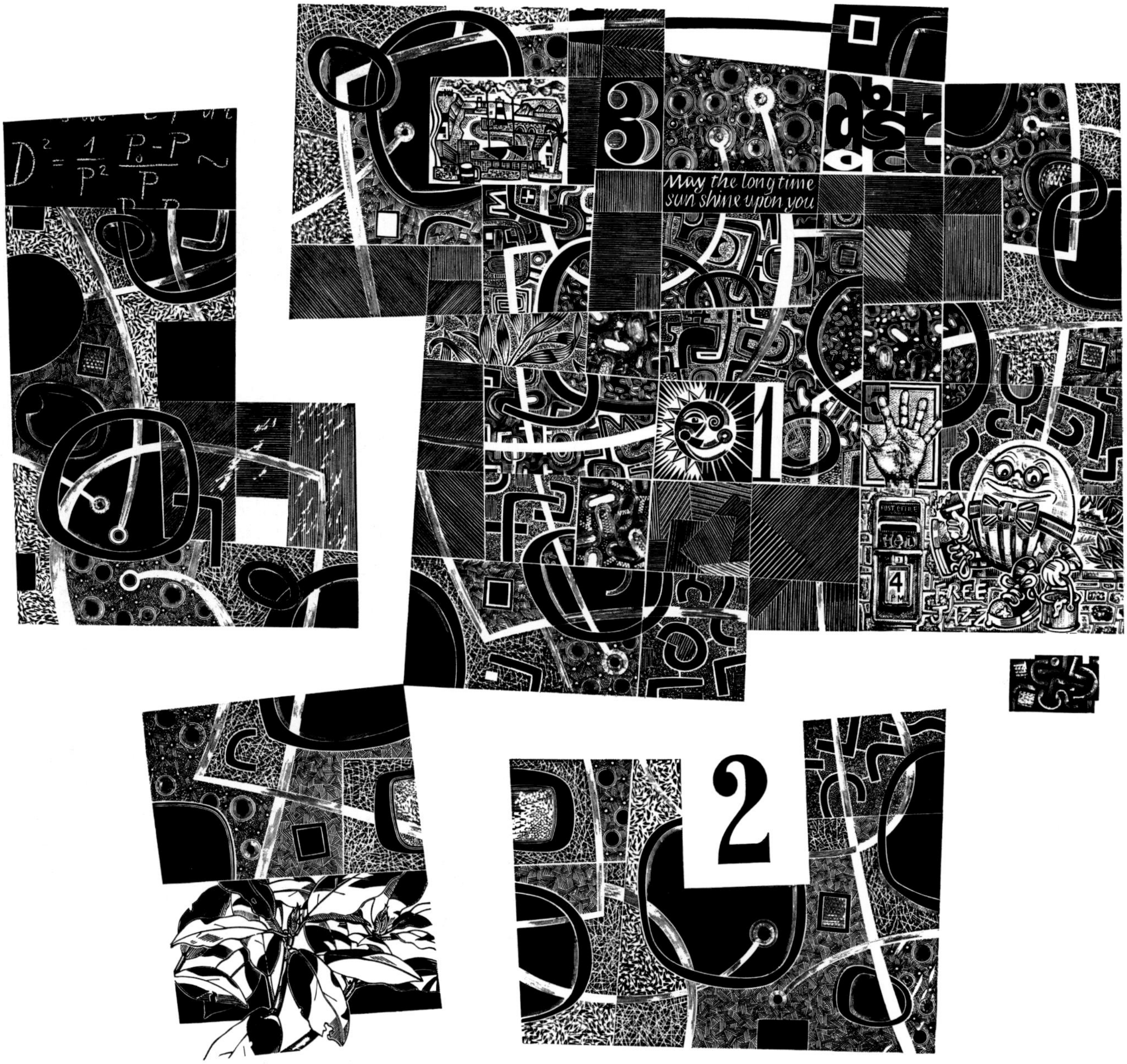

Transform, 2006. Wood engraving, 31 x 33 cm (12 x 13 in.)

work, revising my strategy as I go. Freedom of choice whilst cutting is increasingly allowed, balanced by the essential safety net of the reference drawing. I want the image to appear lively even when, in execution, it has been painstaking. Like modern jazz, I want structure and improvisation. There's a lot of time whilst engraving to think about what you're going to do next … and then change your mind and do something else.

I also work on paintings or on collages and then consider these as starting points for engraving. It can be liberating to engrave equivalents of painted marks or to work in a variety of styles. You can't really do an abstract-expressionist engraving, but you can scratch and scribble with the point of a nail and then, as necessary, engrave carefully along those spontaneous marks. I enjoy working out of control within strict guidelines. It satisfies the extremes of my personality.

Ursula Leach

I walk and draw almost daily in the chalk landscape of Cranborne Chase. Drawing seems the first step to really seeing and understanding the territory. I walk over the same area of land continually and am always finding new aspects of interest and inspiration. Subtle and not so subtle changes are always occurring in this mostly arable landscape. I notice the changes that take place in contemporary farming techniques as one farm manager succeeds another and global warming takes effect. I try to incorporate these facts into my prints. Colour is an important indicator of the nature and condition of crops and also of climate change. Huge fields with thin topsoil and little hedgerow or tree protection alter dramatically in colour in drought and deluge.

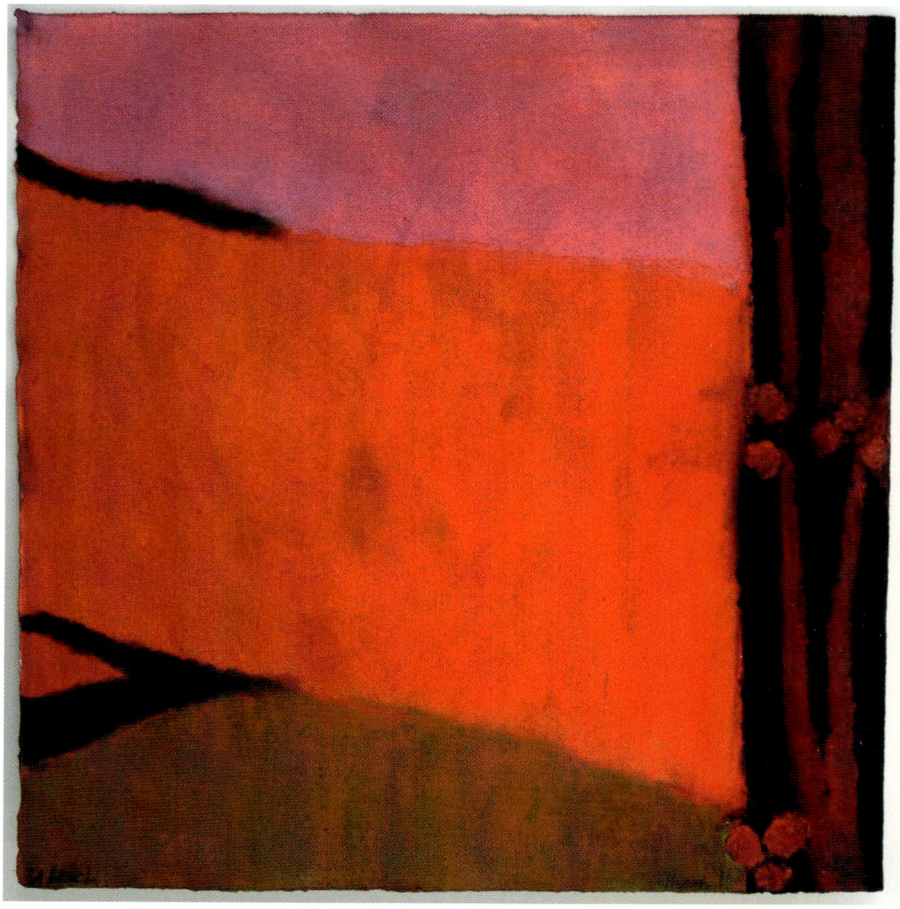

Thorn II, 2006. Carborundum and hand-colouring, 36 x 36 cm (14⅛ x 14⅛ in.)

When I first started making prints I made monochrome etchings; these were quite romantic images concerned with texture and scale. As I looked more, I became aware of the destruction that was occurring on the land through agribusiness and the requirement for bigger fields. Also, being conscious of the huge amount of artificial fertilisers and pesticides put on the land, I decided I did not want to use nitric acid for my etchings as disposing of it was a problem; so I looked to find a more eco-friendly way to make prints. This coincided with a growing dissatisfaction about printing colour from an etching plate; I wanted to use colour more directly and strongly. Also, last but not least, I had had enough of wiping large etching plates – this was beginning to feel like scrubbing floors! I decided to proceed using cardboard for the plate and carborundum mixed with PVA to hold the ink. I began rather timidly using colours in a way that was quite close to those of the landscape itself – yellows and greens along with hand-coloured tissue paper for the more defined areas. I found this fiddly and time-consuming so, after ten years of doing only printmaking, I returned to painting so that I could really put one colour against another. Colour is for me the most important aspect of my prints, and I value what I discover of this through painting. Whether this has to do with global warming or new and different-coloured crops, or

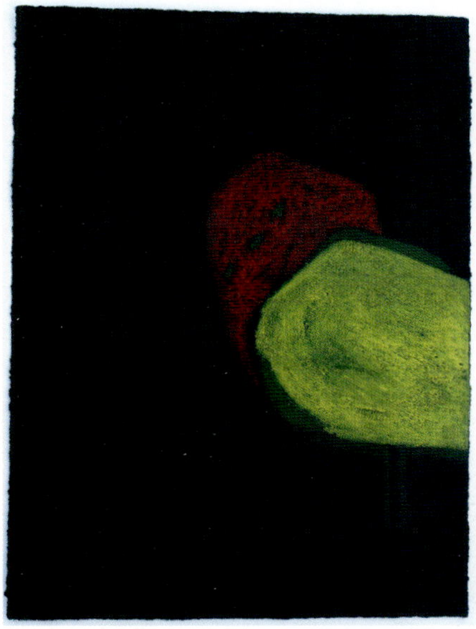

Three Trees, 2008. Carborundum and hand-colouring, 41 x 31 cm (16 x 12¼ in.)

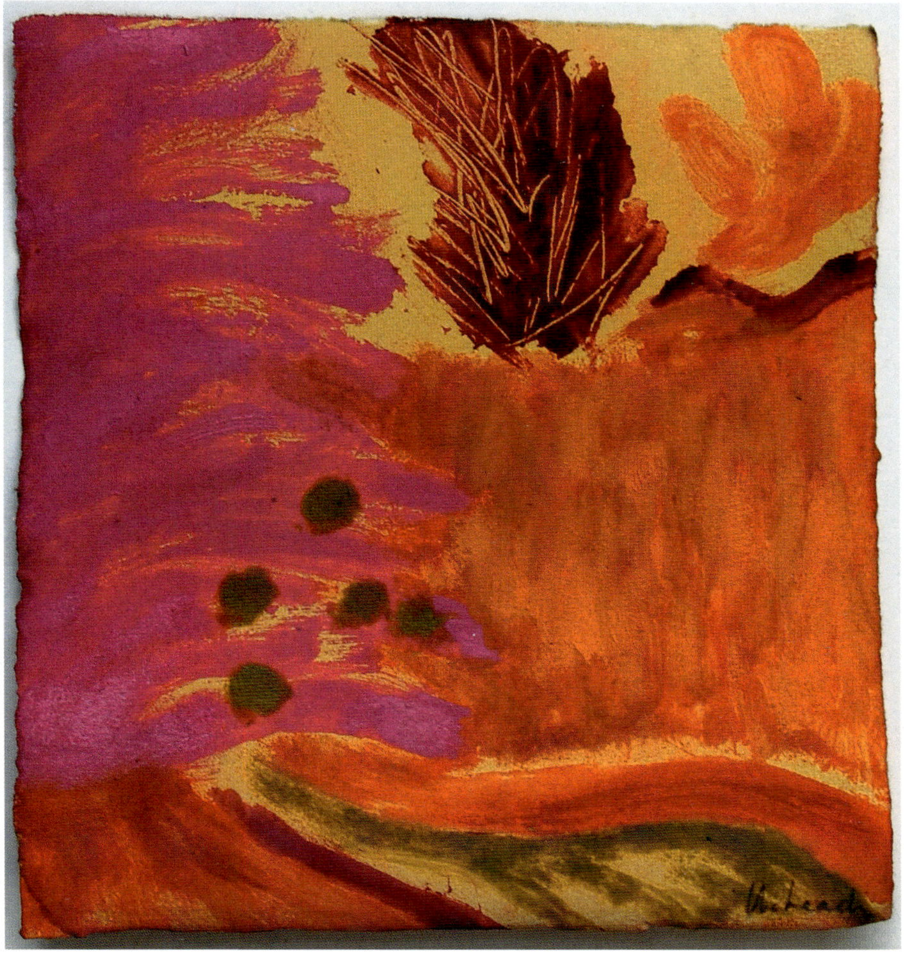

Colour Fields, 2007. monoprint, 18 x 18 cm (7 x 7 in.)

whether it is an expansion of my practice, I do not know. I do know that I am influenced by painter and printmaker William Crozier, who is a wonderful colourist and seems to find continual inspiration in the landscape, as I do in this landscape I love.

To overcome the problems of colour and immediacy I hand-colour in one colour the 'field' of the image – that is, the printing paper. This has some reciprocity with monoculture in the fields. I then make an image on the cardboard plate using carborundum and gouging out areas; this is very physical, in some way corresponding with manmade marks and plantings on the land, and sits on top of the 'field' when printed. The paintings generate the prints because a painting can be radically altered and the sort of prints I do cannot. This, hopefully, results in a bolder and more vigorous image.

Ann Le Bas

For me, it is a sad fact that so few printmakers are using line-engraving now. Exmoor Beeches *is a line engraving pure and simple, with no other methods added; there is no messing about with acid – just a graver, or burin, to cut every line into bare copper.*

Exmoor Beeches. Line engraving, 27.7 x 34.7 cm ($10\frac{7}{8}$ x $13\frac{5}{8}$ in.)

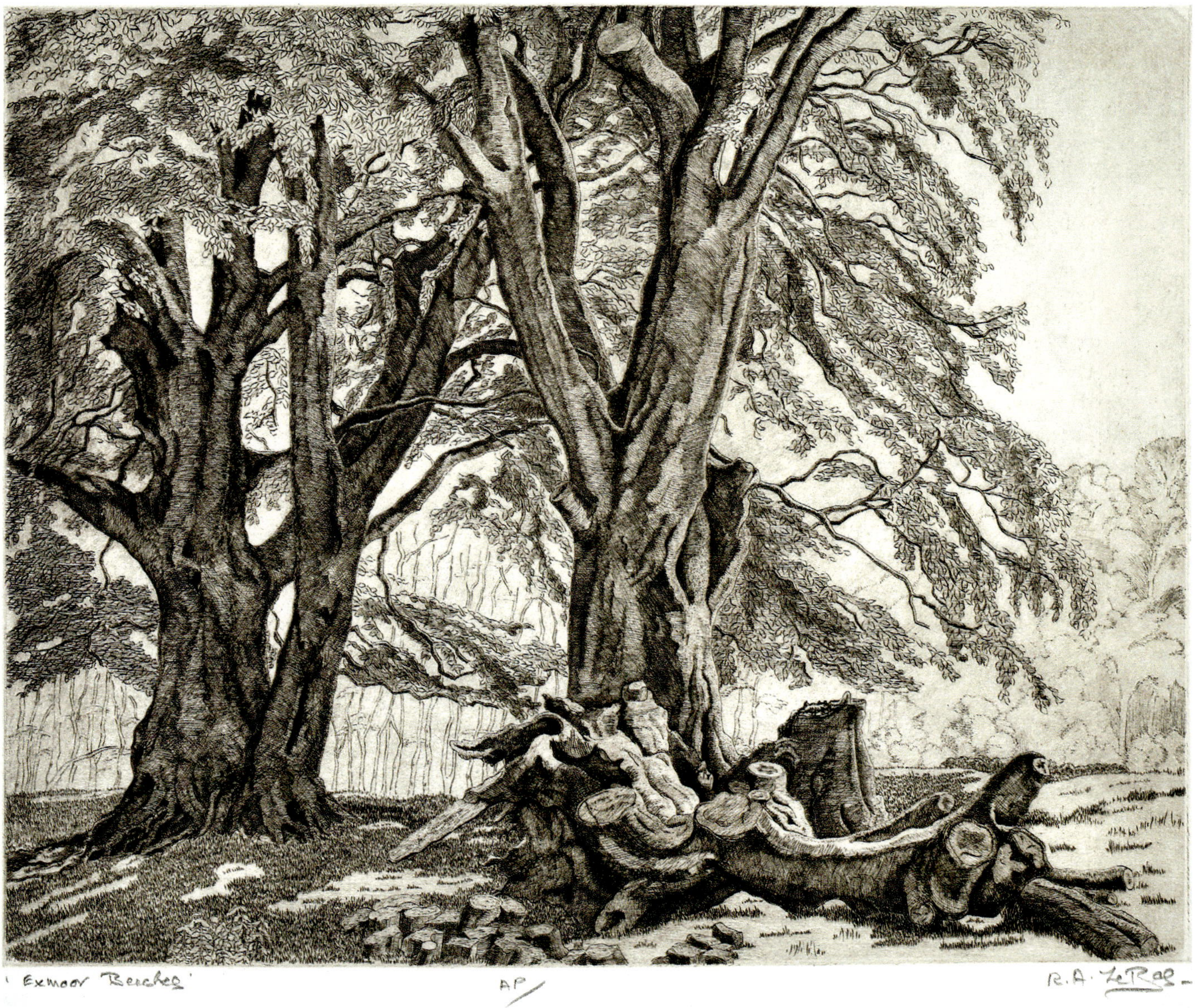

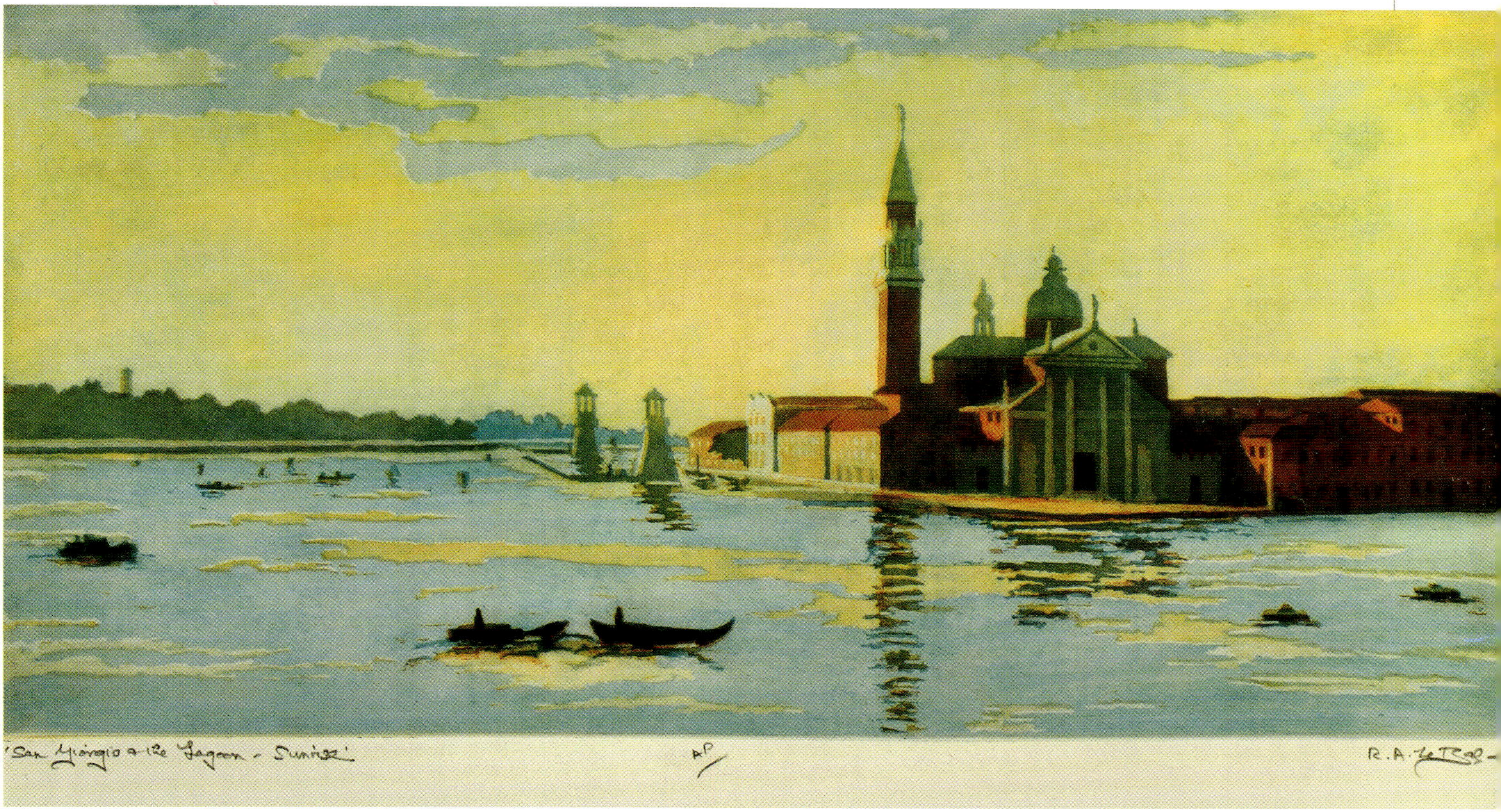

Venice and the Lagoon – Sunrise. Aquatint, 23.5 x 49 cm (9¼ x 19¼ in.)

Engraving is one of the oldest methods used in the production of prints and is, I find, one of the most satisfying. My introduction to it came in the late 1940s at the City and Guilds of London Art School, under the guidance of Henry Wilkinson RE. The fine quality and delicacy of line which can be produced with the graver far exceeds anything that I, at any rate, can achieve with the etching needle and acid. I never really trust the acid; however carefully a wax ground is laid, there is always the chance that foul biting can intrude in all the wrong places and ruin the plate, or, at least, make for hours of corrective scraping and burnishing.

Line engraving requires only a sandbag and possibly a free-standing magnifying glass in addition to the tool itself, so it is possible to cut a few lines at any time without elaborate preparations. Sharpening the tool is perhaps the main difficulty, and good-quality sharpening stones, as well as practice and experience, are needed for this task.

I think, though, that *Venice and the Lagoon – Sunrise*, an aquatint, is the most difficult print I have ever attempted. To try to do justice to the subject and to preserve the atmospheric feel, I wanted to avoid any etched line and just use pure aquatint. I needed to try to produce accurate and detailed drawing and to use pure, unmixed colour with which, if the selective biting and therefore the tone values of the aquatint were correct, the colour would be right. For those of us who edition our own prints and so probably don't produce the whole edition at the same time, it is very difficult to achieve uniformity if anything other than pure colour needs to be mixed before application.

To keep the colour of this print pure and clean I needed to use three plates, one for each colour – pale yellow, blue and red – so registration had to be exact. There are various ways to achieve this: for example, some studios use a pair of square-section steel bars to be placed against the edges of the first plate after it has been printed, so that the precise location of the next is established. I prefer a simple method: I have a sheet of white Formica fixed to the bed of the press, and on this I draw a pencil line right round the first plate and lay successive plates within it to ensure correct registration. I have often used aquatint in conjunction with engraving but it is my hope that the latter, in its pure form, will not be allowed to die.

Jean Lodge

Faces, portraits, most often unidentified, have fascinated me since early childhood. For about half a century I have been searching faces. There have been many imagined images alluding to women of history and of legend: Pasiphae, Dido, Veronica, Eleanor of Aquitaine, Ophelia and Joan of Arc. I have used them freely as characters who, though known and recognised through their traditional stories, are in my work not fixed in their conventional roles; I use their names but give them free choice to act in new ways, allowing them to disclose my own dreams and desires.

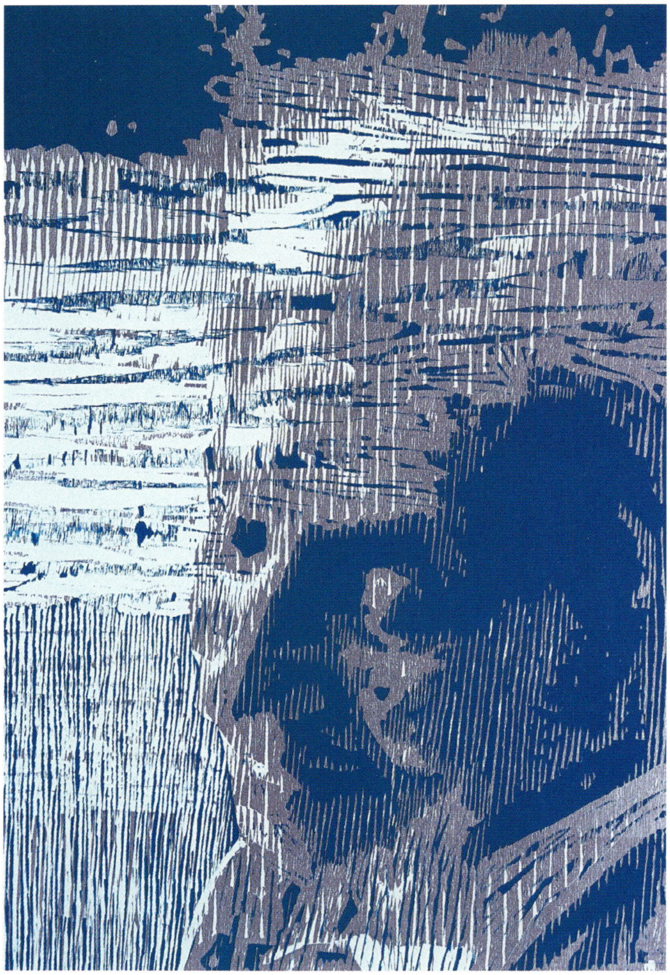

Portrait III, 2007. Woodcut, 54 x 39 cm (21¼ x 15⅜ in.)

Alongside these references to old histories and myths there are elements of self-portrait and invented images of my immigrant ancestors, those who left England and Germany to make new lives for themselves in America. I have played with the fact that I myself have reversed the direction by setting my life back here in the Old World. In my prints all these feelings and sources have become freely mixed, combined and overlaid, sometimes torn apart and recreated as a patchwork of new faces, new realities.

These portraits could not have been created in any other way than by cutting into successive woodblocks and gradually discovering the image as I overprint the various blocks. When I begin, I do not know how many blocks will be needed or quite what the conclusion will be. I go on cutting and layering the colours, allowing the wood itself an important role, until the image develops into something I can consider a final state. The final result is something I could not have imagined without going through this lengthy and indirect process.

At present I am working on a series for which Angélica, my long-time friend and colleague, is often the model, but her likeness may be overprinted with that of my mother as she might be were she alive today. Rather than representing an individual, the work goes on to say something to all of us about life and memories, dreams and desires. My mother died when I was an infant; at present I wonder if, on some level, all these faces I make and have searched out and created through printmaking over the years are not attempts to identify that Mother I hardly knew.

Portrait IV, 2007. Woodcut, 54 x 39 cm (21¼ x 15⅜ in.)

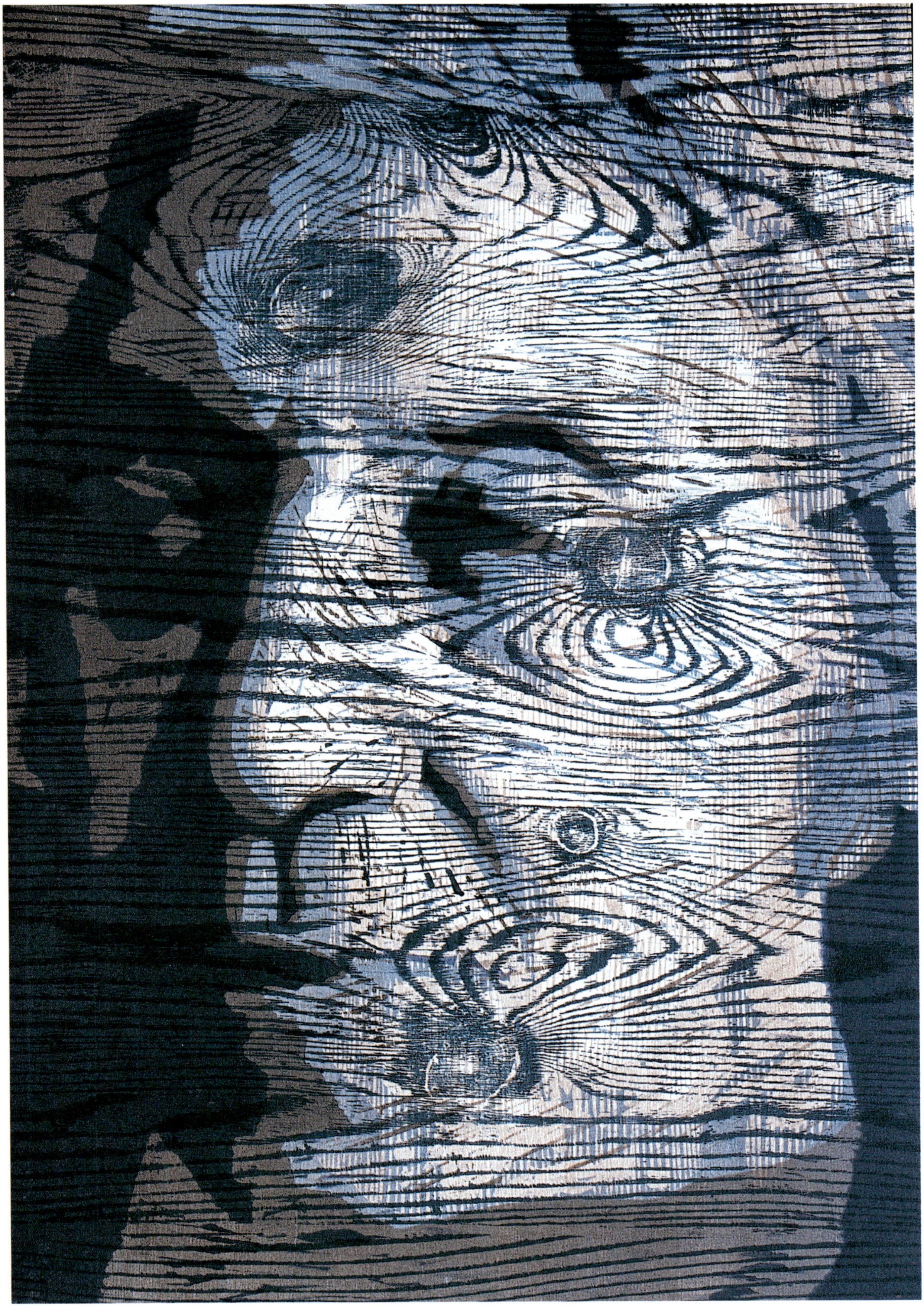

Irvine Loudon

I began drawing seriously at about the age of fifteen. I soon found that I had subconsciously developed the habit of looking at all kinds of things as possible subjects for a drawing. However, owing to a previous career as a doctor in a very busy general practice, I knew absolutely nothing about printmaking until, in my sixties, I found by pure chance that there was a local printmakers' workshop where courses were available. By this time I had been granted a research fellowship in the history of medicine; this gave me more freedom, so I enrolled on the etching course and from the first day I became, and remain, addicted to prints and printmaking. I have produced more than 250 prints, of which I consider at least a quarter have been failures. I resented the waste of copper until I found that commercial metal polishers can remove all traces of etched lines and so enable a new start.

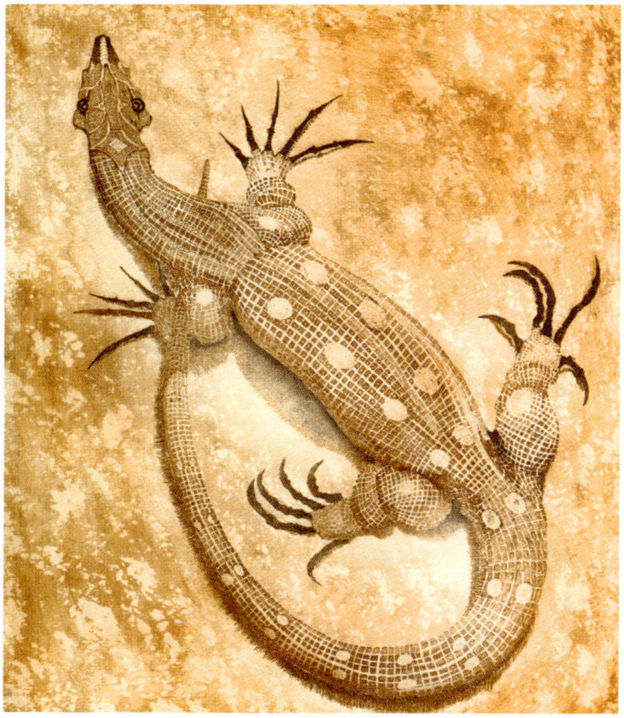

Sand Lizard, 1990. Etching, 31 x 27.5 cm (12¼ x 10⅞ in.)

Many of my printmaking colleagues work from photographs. I have tried to do so, but photographs never work for me. The reason is, I think, that my drawings are not an end in themselves, but the first stage in the exploration of an image which will become an etching usually far removed from any photographic record. I begin an etching by transferring the outline of the resolved preparatory drawing to the grounded plate. I establish the image in detail with the etching needle and bite it into the surface of the copper with ferric chloride. I tend to overbite, so I next lower the overbitten areas with an electric sander and wire wool, which is quicker than using the traditional scraper and burnisher, although some polishing is usually needed. I may then re-ground the plate and superimpose another layer of detail. The final stage is the addition of aquatint, for which I use salt. I cover the plate with a thin layer of hard ground and, whilst it is still hot, I sprinkle household salt evenly all over the surface. I lift the plate, shaking off the excess salt that has not adhered to the warm wax, and reheat it over a gas ring to a temperature much higher than is needed for a resin aquatint. As a result, the wax ground liquefies and the grains of salt sink through it into direct contact with the copper. When the plate cools it is held under a gently-running tap of lukewarm water which washes away the salt, leaving a porous ground containing many thousands of tiny specks of bare copper that will be bitten by the acid to create a speckled texture. I use diluted nitric acid for this task, with which it is easier to judge the progress of the biting than with the brown-coloured ferric chloride. Though not as straightforward as resin aquatint, a salt ground has its advantages; for example, it is more resistant to wear during printing.

After each stage I take a proof – essential guidance, since the printed image is often very different from what the bitten plate promises.

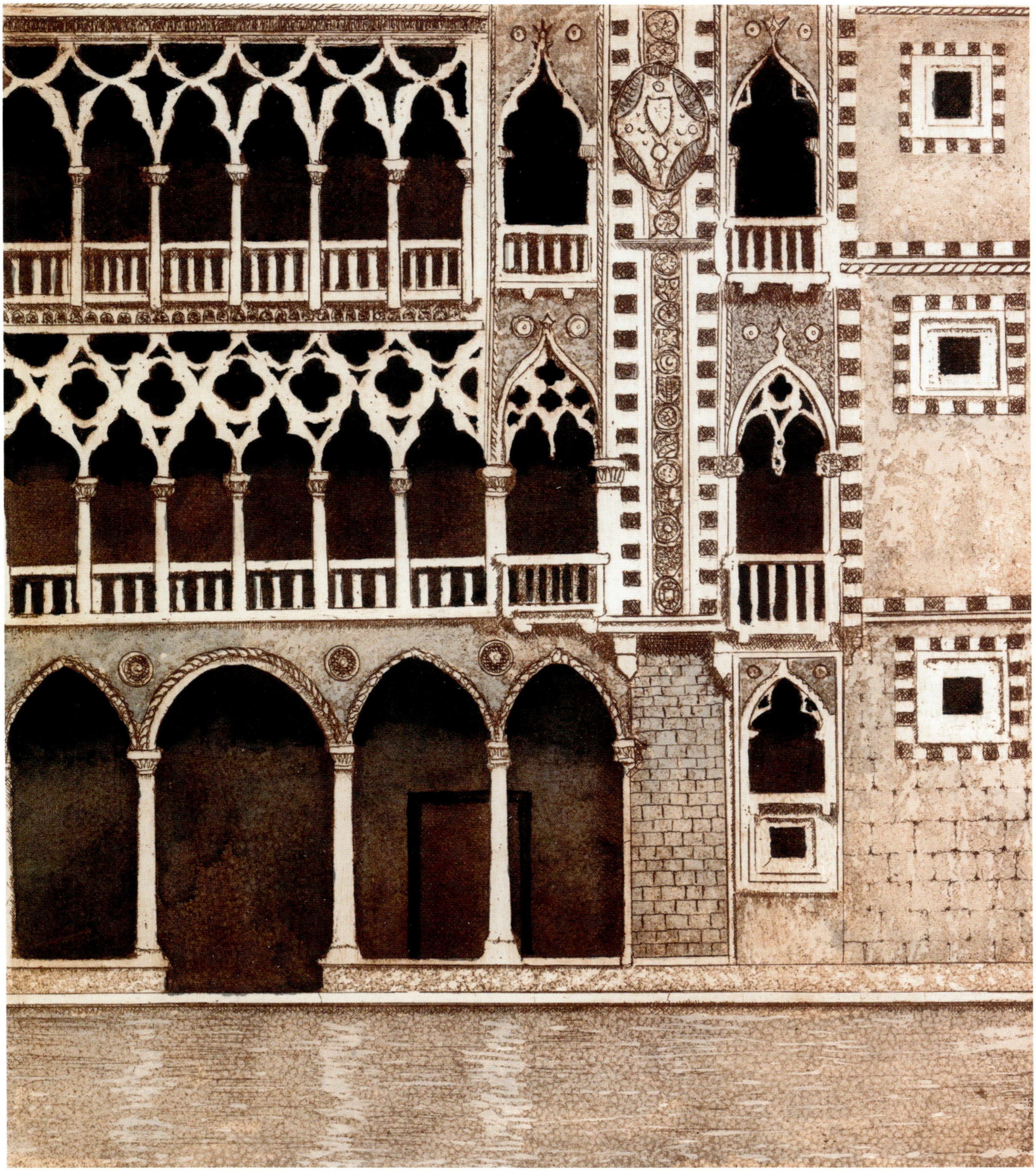

Ca'd'Oro, Venice, 2002. Etching, 26 x 24 cm (10¼ x 9½ in.)

Sasa Marinkov

I discovered relief printmaking in my thirties. I immediately responded to the physical nature of the cutting and to working with resistant materials to produce hard-edged lines and shapes. I relished the challenge of varying the cutting to express solids and space, pattern and tone. Coinciding with having a baby, my work tended to become less abstract as I found myself looking more to the outside world of appearances. When I felt the need to make bigger work I went to woodyards to buy Malaysian and birch ply; the appeal of fractured lines gouged out of the solid mass of the wood confirmed my choice of medium.

Fallen Leaves, 2007. Woodcut, 38 x 56 cm (15 x 22 in.)

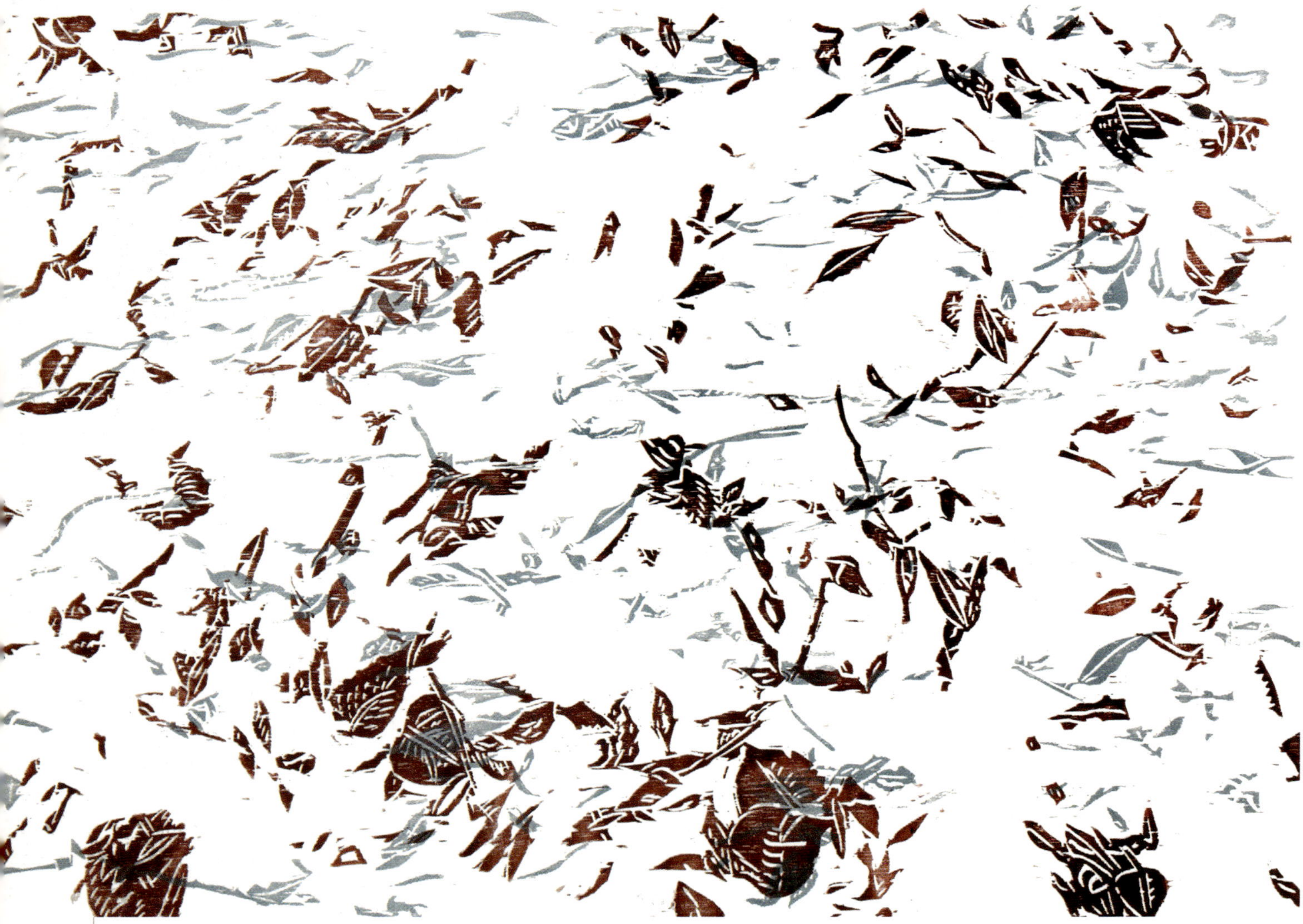

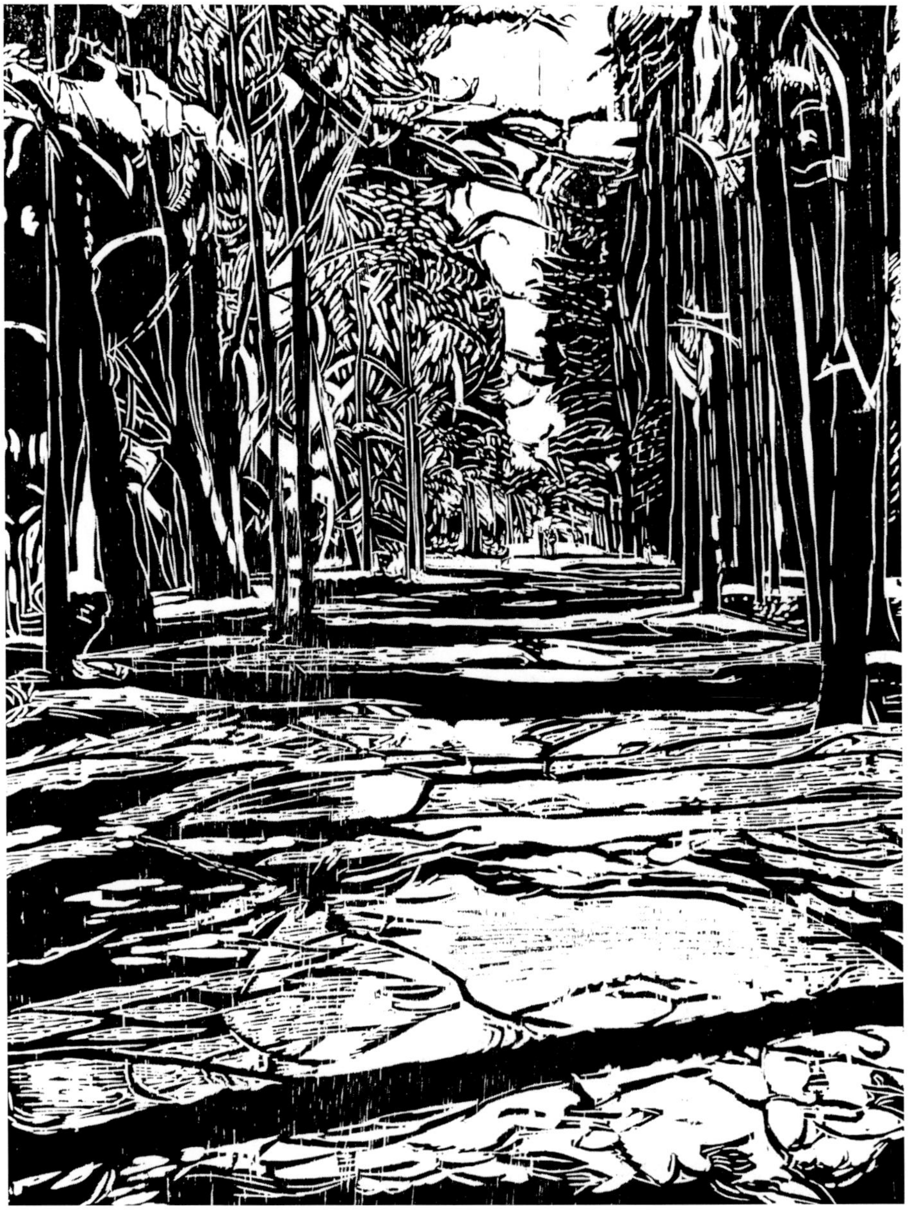

Inside the Forest, 2005. Woodcut, 88 x 58 cm (34⅝ x 22⅞ in.)

Ever since, my work has been a dialogue between positive and negative, representation and abstraction. The excitement is in the constant alternating between incised line and solid mass, and in not knowing how the image will look after its reversal in print. If I want instant gratification, I will make rubbings of the cut surface with tissue paper and graphite, or just apply graphite directly on the block to give shapes greater prominence. Immersion in my work transports me into another world – a world of low technology. My happiest times have been spent in the British Museum among the artefacts of older civilisations, enjoying scripts I cannot read, noting the patterned surfaces of early sculptures and metal objects, admiring brush marks on early pottery and paper. This, together with my interest in contemporary architecture and design, has been my apprenticeship.

I track down my subjects with a camera. The viewfinder isolates particular locations and details, and the photographic image, even when contemplated years later, renews the experience of the original enthusiasm. Although these images are usually recorded in colour, I translate them into black and white, which I believe gives the image an iconic quality, freezing it in time and giving it meaning and mystery. The labour of the physical cutting is a journey, an essential means of defining the image as an idea. Sometimes I make a tracing by projecting a slide, rather like using a camera obscura. This provides shapes to play with that are quite different from those obtained by drawing from life. Throughout the whole process I hope for happy accidents to complement the deliberation, not only in the cutting but also in the printing. By visually (and according to the sound it makes) controlling the layer of sticky oil-based ink as I roll it onto the block, then floating Japanese paper onto the inked surface, and finally by uniformly rubbing the back of the paper with the bowl of a wooden spoon to make the print, I am repeating a process which is the oldest form of printmaking. I am in control of the whole process; in a sense, acceptance of the occasional happy accident is part of that control.

Toni Martina

My images are largely inspired by cities and their inhabitants; this interest began whilst travelling as a child. The impact of journeying back and forth, between Italy and the UK, to my father's home town during the 1950s and 1960s forged vital images. The noise, heat, chaos and smells were exciting and unnerving. I was pushed through train windows into a marketplace of livestock and humanity and occasionally abandoned until my father appeared through the mayhem to rescue me. This period of waiting and watching on railway-station platforms, surrounded by suitcases and boxes, while the lives of street vendors, hawkers, beggars – and some whose occupations I struggled to find a name for – were played out around me, set the scene for my future work.

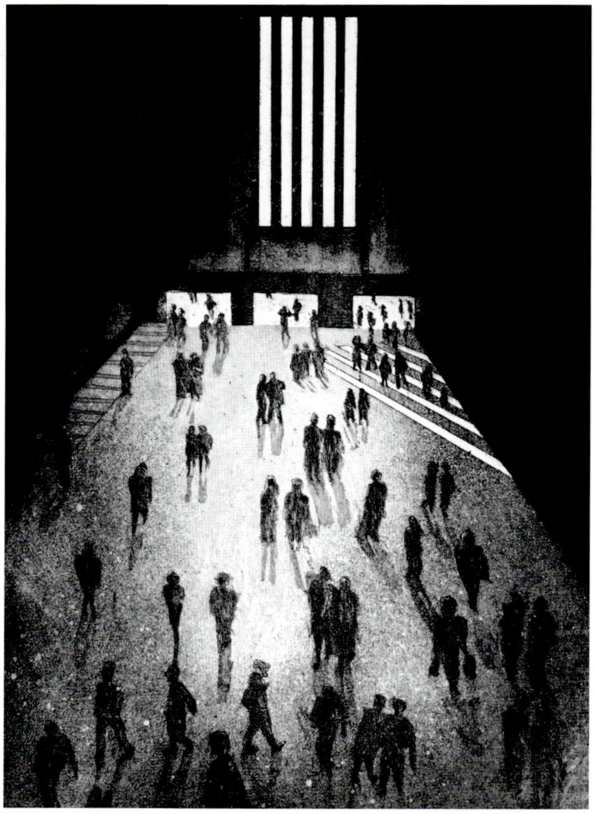

Turbine Hall, Tate Modern, 2001. Etching and aquatint, 35 x 26 cm (13¾ x 10¼ in.)

The process of galvanising these ideas into prints and paintings is both mysterious and straightforward. Working from life, photographs and sketches, I draw directly onto the grounded etching plate. This becomes the reference from which to infuse memories and ideas, to see what might happen through line drawings of groups of figures or heads. The method or technique depends largely on the starting point and can range from the physical use of power tools to light aquatint and sugar lifts. The choice is made intuitively.

The contrast between places feeds my imagination. For example, during an afternoon siesta, as adults slept off rustic lunches washed down with wine the colour of ink, I would go walking in the towns, looking at the deserted streets, bleached white and with a spattering of humanity glimpsed from afar; people snoozing while leaning against buildings in the distance, their faces covered by broad-brimmed hats; farmers on horseback and wild dogs; the hard-edged shadows casting geometric shapes onto the stone walls and pavements, heightening my sense of awareness.

What I observe as a participant in the movement of people is how they interact in physical space. It reconnects me to early memories of the weird and wonderful locations in London: Petticoat Lane, Brick Lane and Club Row; moments held in eternity by a photograph with parrots perched on my shoulder or suited monkeys on my arm. These magically atmospheric recollections also relate to the central market in Turin, where I would help my uncle to sell fruit and vegetables after a precarious ride on a three-wheeler vehicle.

The sense of displacement through the diaspora of migrants has always informed my work. As I walk through public spaces now, I am aware of this connection. The tall buildings in London's Canary Wharf reflect their neighbours and the steady stream of people moving across squares. The shadows touch through streams of light, while the abstract forms and shapes link the organic movement of people. An early spring walk along the Thames between the London Eye and Hungerford Bridge creates a perfect

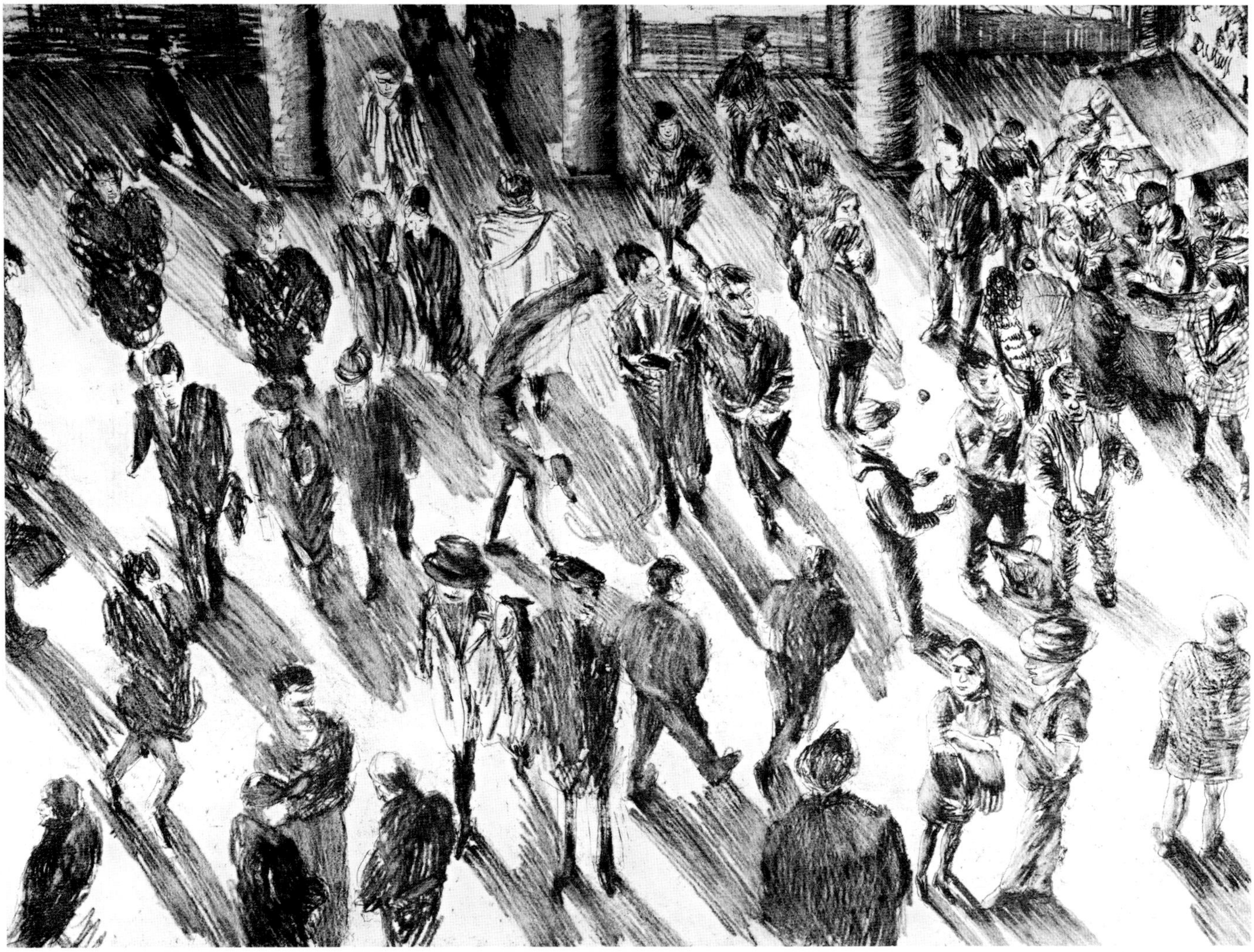

Above: **Covent Garden Piazza**, 1992. Etching, 46 x 61 cm (18⅛ x 24 in.)

Right: **Ridley Road Market**, 1992. Etching, 46 x 61 cm (18⅛ x 24 in.)

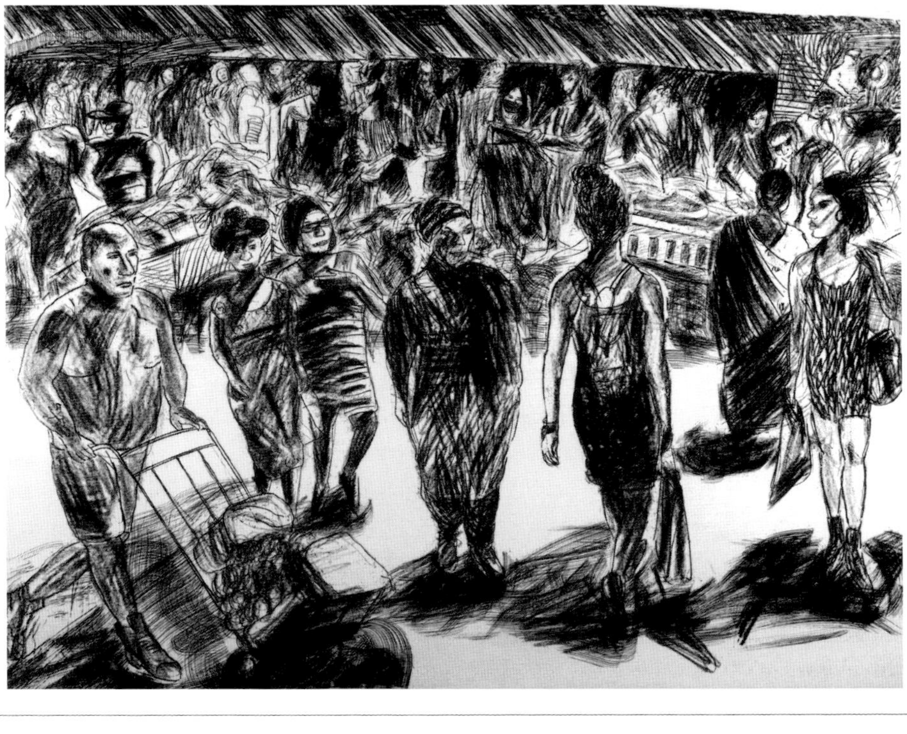

play of silhouettes, from the leafless tree to the dark shadows of people dancing in a rhythm.

The moment of completion of a new print creates a special excitement, partly because the work is finished but also because the search for the next image can begin. Ideas emerge from the filing cabinet of stored memories, where places suddenly become alive through the play of light.

Sally McLaren

In 1961, while still a student, I was elected to membership of the Royal Society of Painter-Etchers, as it was then called. At the time I considered that very little innovative work was being produced by the members. I had a very thorough grounding in etching techniques at the then Central School of Art & Crafts in London under the inspirational tuition of Merlyn Evans and Tony Harrison. We explored everything from line etching and sugar-lift aquatint to deep etch, using colour on separate plates and working ink into the crevices as well as applying it to the surface. We used stencils to protect parts of the plate's surface from a rolled colour and took advantage of the variety of depths in a bitten plate and the effect that this has on the tonal quality of an inked-up area.

Scratchells Bay, 1995. Etching, 57 x 74 cm (22½ x 29⅛ in.)

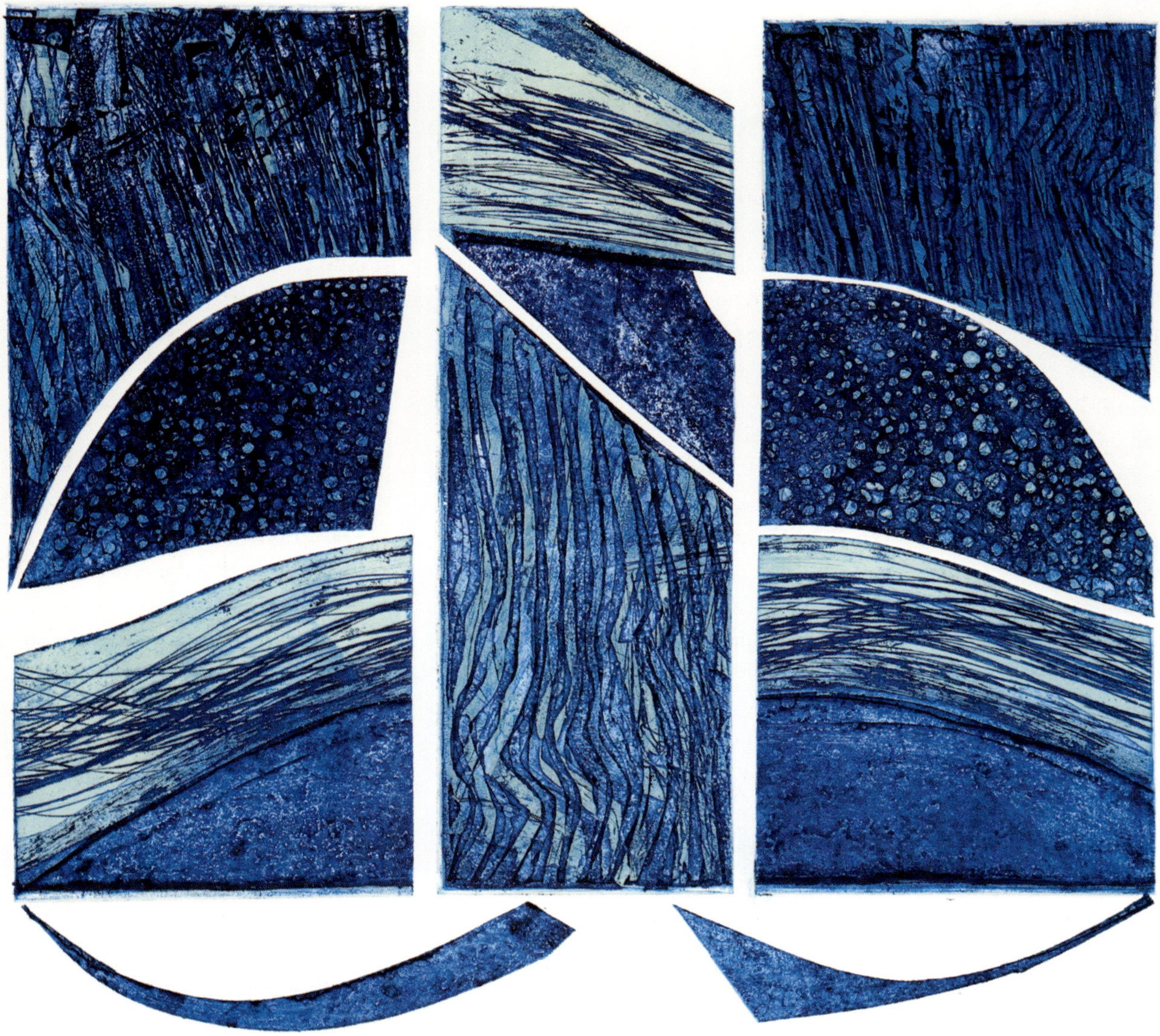

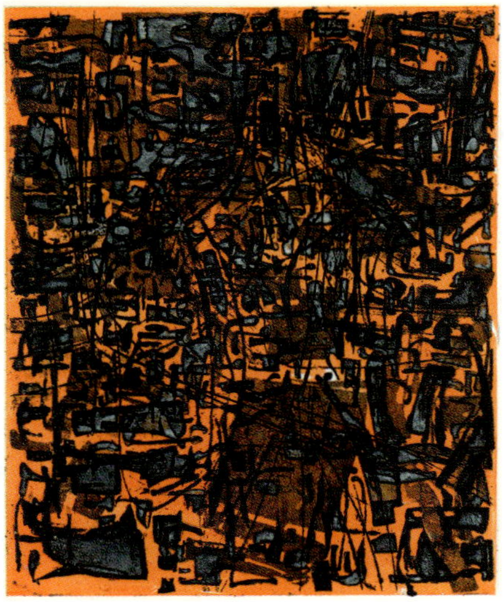

Thème Japonais, 1962. Etching, 44 x 37 cm (17⅜ x 14½ in.)

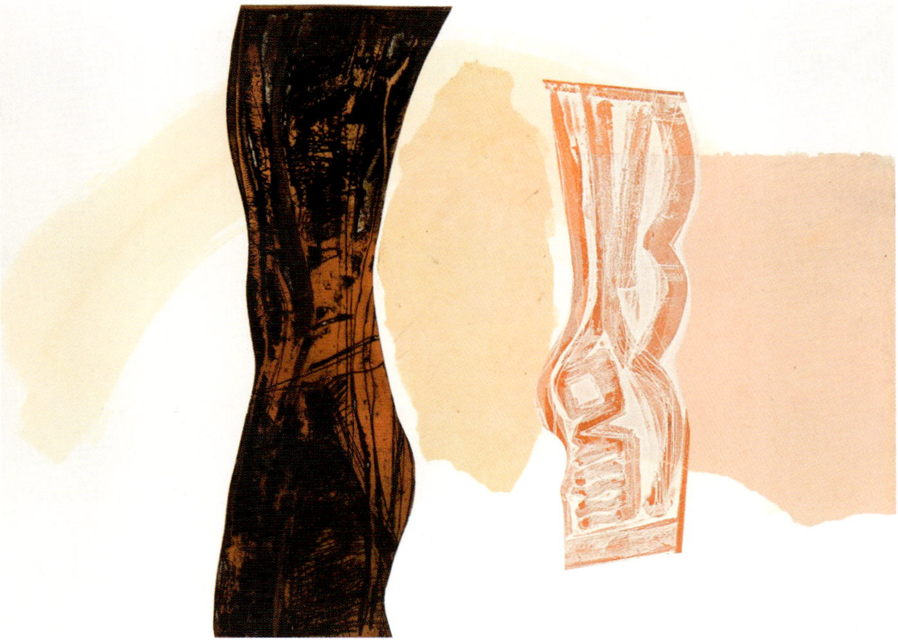

Land series, Fragment I, 2001. Etching and chine collé, 75 x 104 cm (29½ x 41 in.)

However, I went on to work in Paris with S.W. Hayter, who didn't recognise any techniques acquired prior to one's arrival at his celebrated Atelier 17. I learned his method of applying different viscosities and colours of ink, with rollers of different degrees of softness, to a single plate bitten to various depths. This meant that the plate could be passed through the press just once to produce a print with several colours. I found, though, that if there were larger areas of open bite this method could result in a rather messy combination of inked intaglio overlaid by a touch-down of a different colour or colours from a subsequent roller or rollers, thus creating a patch with an indiscriminate edge. On returning from Paris I felt that somehow I had to separate myself from what I viewed as a formula and adapt just those parts of Hayter's method that suited my way of working. So, in order to force myself to change, I started cutting up my plates, first of all to escape the rectangle.

Inspired always by rock faces and the geological patterns formed where the ground has moved through volcanic activity or cliff slip, I decided to go further and to cut the plate into sections using ragged edges and negative spaces to emphasise the shapes, to float the image, unrelated to the confines of a rectangle, and to abstract it from any surrounding interference.

Recently I have been introducing *chine collé* to provide an extra colour, with a softer texture to suggest the atmosphere of a particular day and overprinted by the ruggedness of a heavily bitten plate. I love strongly textured plates, much worked on, deeply bitten layer upon layer, put in and out of the acid, line-etched, aquatinted, scraped back; and then perhaps overbitten, leaving wide areas that need more 'tooth', which I sometimes supply with carborundum paste. I have been experimenting with the paste, applying it to roughened Perspex and drawing into it to create a printing surface. I prefer ferric chloride as a mordant. It bites cleanly and, unlike nitric acid, it gives off no noxious fumes. There are also happy accidents when, if I leave the plate in the ferric for some time without agitating the mordant, it acquires a very organic texture. I also prefer to apply one rolled surface colour at a time to my plates rather than employ Hayter's technique, which he nevertheless practised to great effect.

I hugely enjoyed my time at Atelier 17 and valued Hayter's enormous enthusiasm and encouragement. I recognise to this day the influence he and other masters of the original print – notably Julian Trevelyan, Anthony Gross and Michael Rothenstein – undoubtedly had on my work. All of them championed the print as an art form in its own right and were an early inspiration to me.

Mike Middleton

My ideas originate in often unexpected ways. In the case of Holiday Camp circa 1990 *it was the glimpse of a landscape seen from overhead, from afar. It looked for all the world like a Mediterranean vision, perhaps the Elysian Fields, whereas in reality it was the corner of a postcard depicting Colchester Institute of Further and Higher Education in about 1990. I think it was the effect of the light as it shone through the trees, on what was obviously a warm sunny summer day in July or August, that made me look at the tiny fragment with a view to using it as the basis for a print or a painting.*

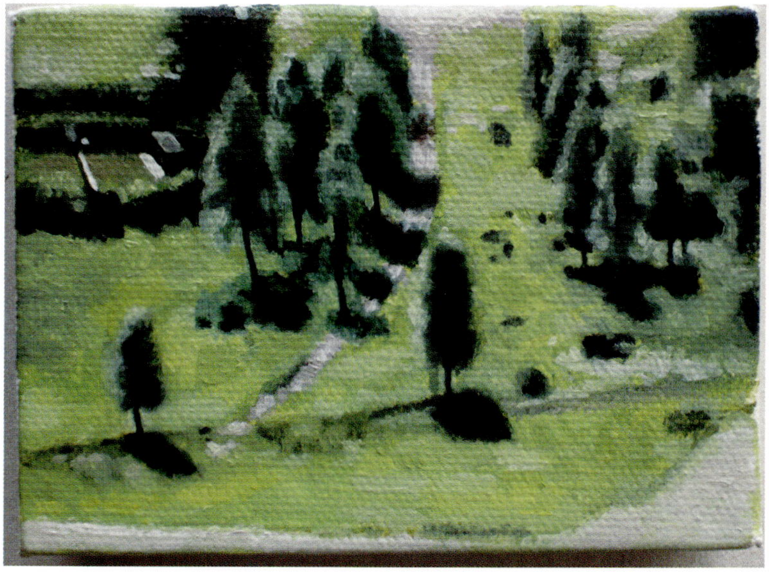

A Distant Prospect, 2006. Oil on canvas, 7.4 x 10 cm (2⅞ x 4 in.)

On further reflection, it probably reminded me of a drawing, the *View of Aventine* by Nicolas Poussin, which is in the prints and drawings collection of the Uffizi Gallery, Florence. This drawing shows similar intense sunlight filtering through trees and conveys an almost tangible effect of summer heat. Cézanne said famously that he 'wanted to do Poussin again, from Nature'; in my fanciful way I would redo Poussin from a postcard fragment. It appealed to my sense of irony.

Drawing the scene several times in my sketchbook, I was sufficiently enamoured of its qualities to try it out as a small painting, working in oil on a tiny canvas three inches by four. I then turned to an etching plate, recklessly biting the scene on a small piece of zinc. I attempted by deep biting to give the shadows an intense quality, the look of dark shadows in sunlight, and relied on the white of the paper to express the bright sunlight bouncing off the grass and the surrounding buildings. The first plate didn't seem quite right. The drawing didn't satisfy, and the low huts in the corner, rising in a diagonal across the plate, didn't give me the effect I was after. I etched a second plate, slightly more sure of what I wanted. This time it worked. However, I wanted to do more, and the screenprint grew from a desire to explore further, to see the image in a different medium by returning it to its origin in a photographic matrix. I scanned the corner of the postcard into a computer and changed the scale, making the image much larger. The tear in the corner, the image skewed at an angle – these were deliberate decisions. I then produced both positive and negative transparencies to give myself the freedom to print and overprint. To me, the beauty of the screenprinting process is its facility for putting down layers of flat, transparent colour. By using both positive and negative images on the screen I attempted to reintroduce an element of unpredictability – even though I was using a photomechanical dot – to penetrate below the surface and re-present the image with intensity and vision. Eventually, I settled on printing in black and white and greys so that the image took on a silvery hue, travelling away from the predictability of the cyan, magenta, yellow and black of commercial printing. Bleached out and bright, the

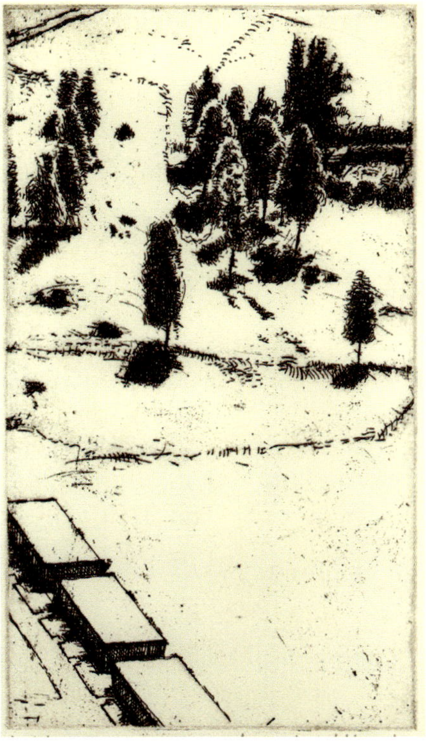

A Distant Prospect 2, 2006. Etching, 14.8 x 8.5 cm (5⅞ x 3⅜ in.)

grass looked as if it was covered in snow or as if the sunlight was so bright that it was draining all the colour out of the scene. Finally, I varnished the print with a solvent-based varnish, using the process both to seal all the layers of the water-based inks and to intensify the hues.

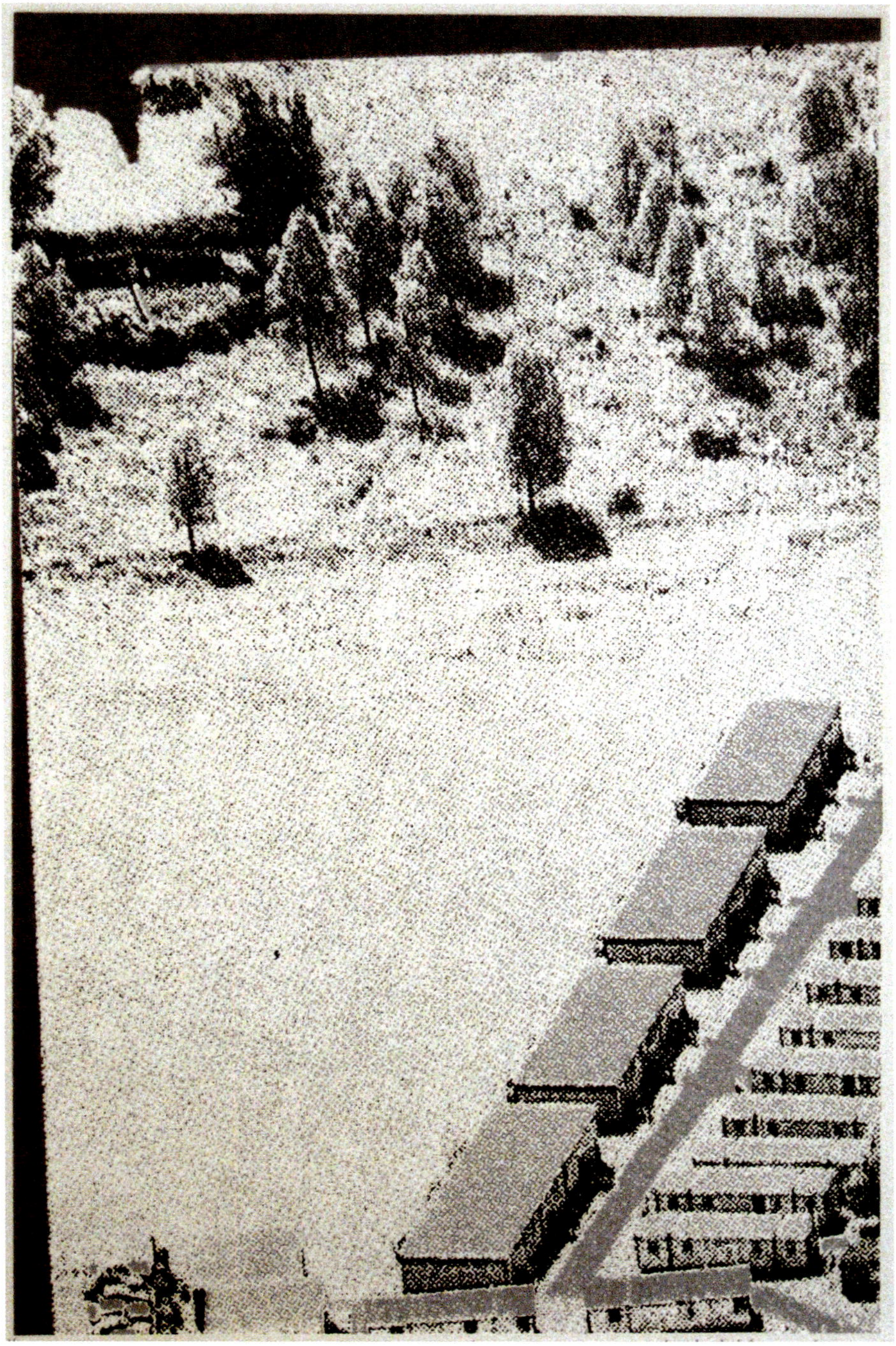

Holiday Camp circa 1990, 2007. Screen print, 30 x 20 cm (11¾ x 7⅞ in.)

Julia Midgley

I draw all the time, mainly recording from direct observation. Sketchbooks provide aides-memoires for future works. From the sketchbooks an idea is formed for a new image. Drawings and design sheets are then developed until the finished piece is resolved. When preparing a new print, sketchbooks pile up on my desk and I riffle through them for any relevant little drawings. These could be of artefacts, travel sketches, horses or simply characters that have intrigued me. I will test my compositions on different coloured papers, then in black and white, to consider the effects aquatint may have, since this can have a major impact on my composition.

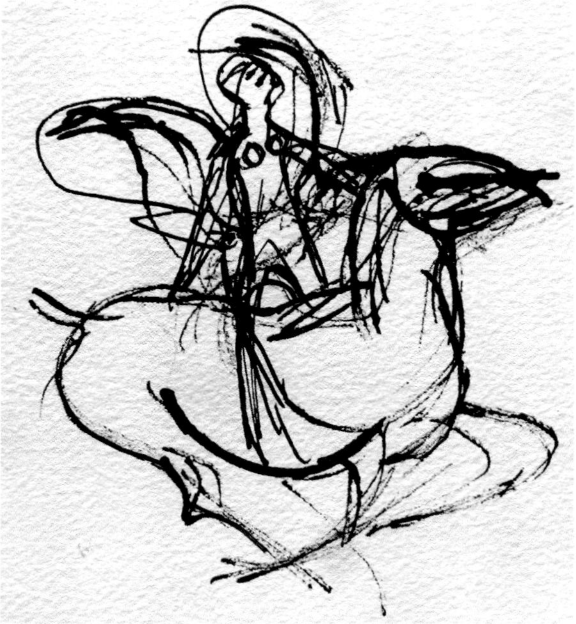

Ink study 2, 2006, pen and ink, 11 x 11 cm (4³⁄₈ x 4³⁄₈ in.)

Unlike many people – and contrary to orthodox advice – I draw my design directly onto the grounded zinc plate. I do not transfer to the plate a mirror image of the drawn design and I happily accept a reversal in the eventual print. If I had to think about reversing an image whilst drawing, I might lose that spontaneous quality of line which is of paramount importance to me and which I cherish. For me, reversal is only really essential where lettering or numerals are involved. Another thing I sometimes do, also contrary to advice, is to repeat the application of an aquatint ground if the first has been underbitten through premature removal from the acid bath. This can happen all too easily, since accurate timing is vital when etching aquatint. The problem about laying and biting a second ground is that the characteristic sparkle of the aquatint can be muddied – and yet, interesting effects can result.

In 2006, Chester City Council hosted a festival to celebrate the work of Charles Baudelaire, and artists were invited to respond to his suite of poems, *Les Fleurs du Mal.* I was asked to create a new etching but I found the poems bleak, dark, embittered pieces and was unable to sympathise with them. On the point of declining the commission I came across *Les Vins des Amants* ('The Wine of Lovers'). As I read the following lines I realised that here I had a vehicle for venting my feelings about the poet:

'Let us ride away on wine
To a divine, fairy-like heaven!
Like two angels who are tortured
By a relentless delirium ...'

My etching, *Avenging Angels,* depicts angel sisters riding the wind whilst their winged horses (a favourite metaphorical device of mine) trample the poets below, releasing them from the misery of the 'relentless delirium' of which Baudelaire writes. The struggle to find inspiration from a suite that I had initially found unappealing had become stimulating and my initial distaste had invested the etching with energy and drama. I find that the sense of movement has been heightened through the use of sugar lift to complement the line work and the aquatint.

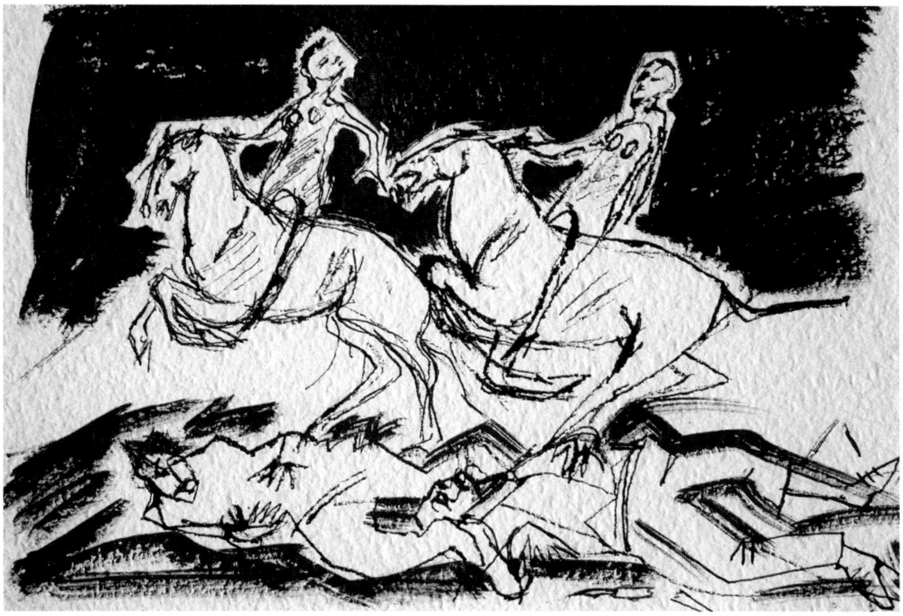

Ink study 3, 2006, pen and ink, 26 x 35 cm (10¼ x 13¾ in.)

Avenging Angels, 2006, Etching and aquatint, 26 x 35 cm (10¼ x 13¾ in.)

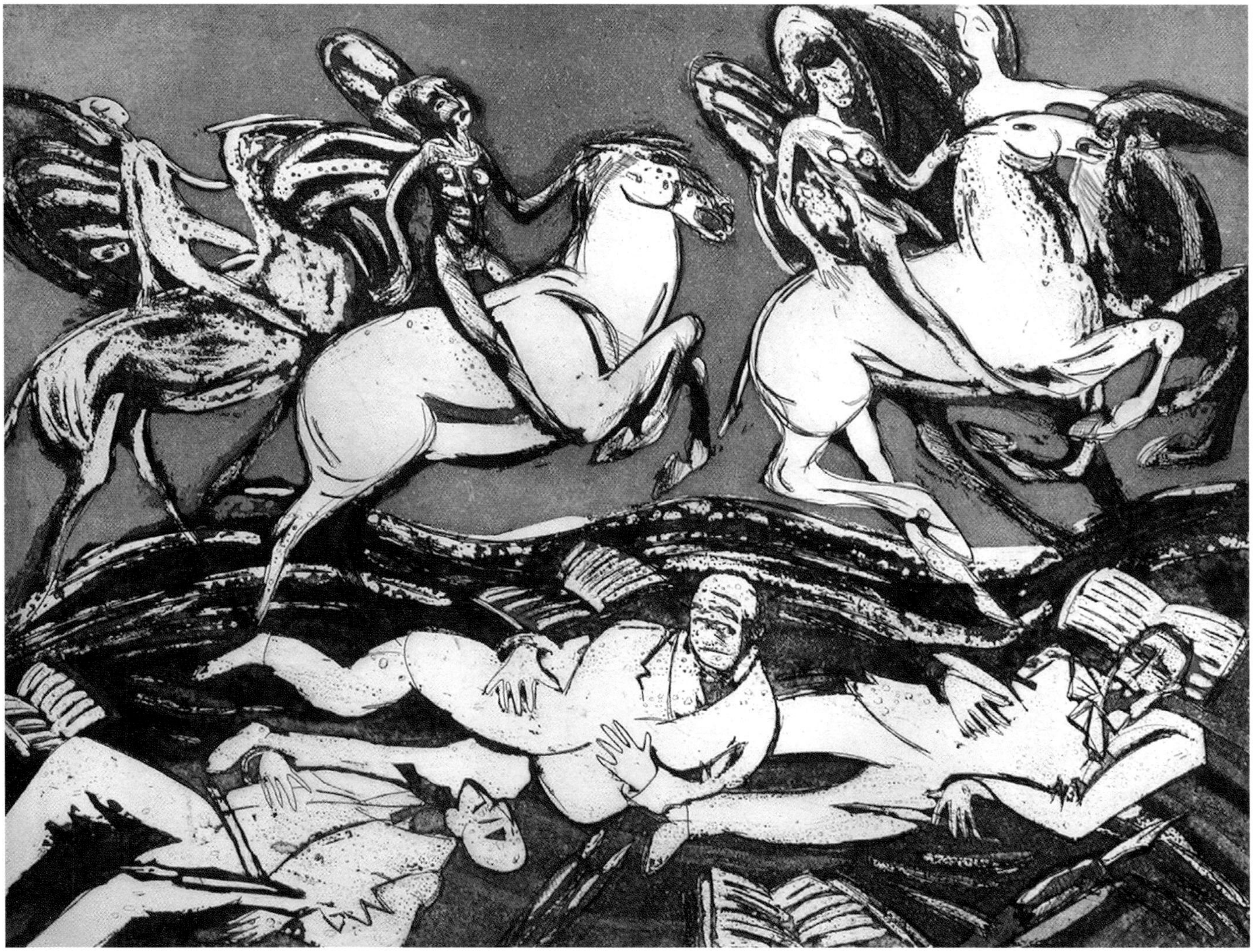

Stephen Mumberson

Printing on unconventional materials and in difficult circumstances came from my experiences of working abroad in remote print workshops in Germany, France, Finland, Zimbabwe and Zambia. Often the workshop would have little beyond very basic means: a space, tables, a set of inks and well-used rollers. I found that I had to be very inventive and resourceful in finding materials and simple methods to produce prints.

Hand-burnishing and printing from relief blocks offers the most flexible and direct approach, one which could be used on a variety of potential surfaces. It did not take me long to realise that clothes could offer a fruitful area in which to work, as I later found that both second-hand clothes and old furniture carry their history on their surfaces. This led me to make a series of print, installation and sculpture works, each piece creating new problems and demanding fresh approaches to placing a printed impression on

Stephen Mumberson in his studio

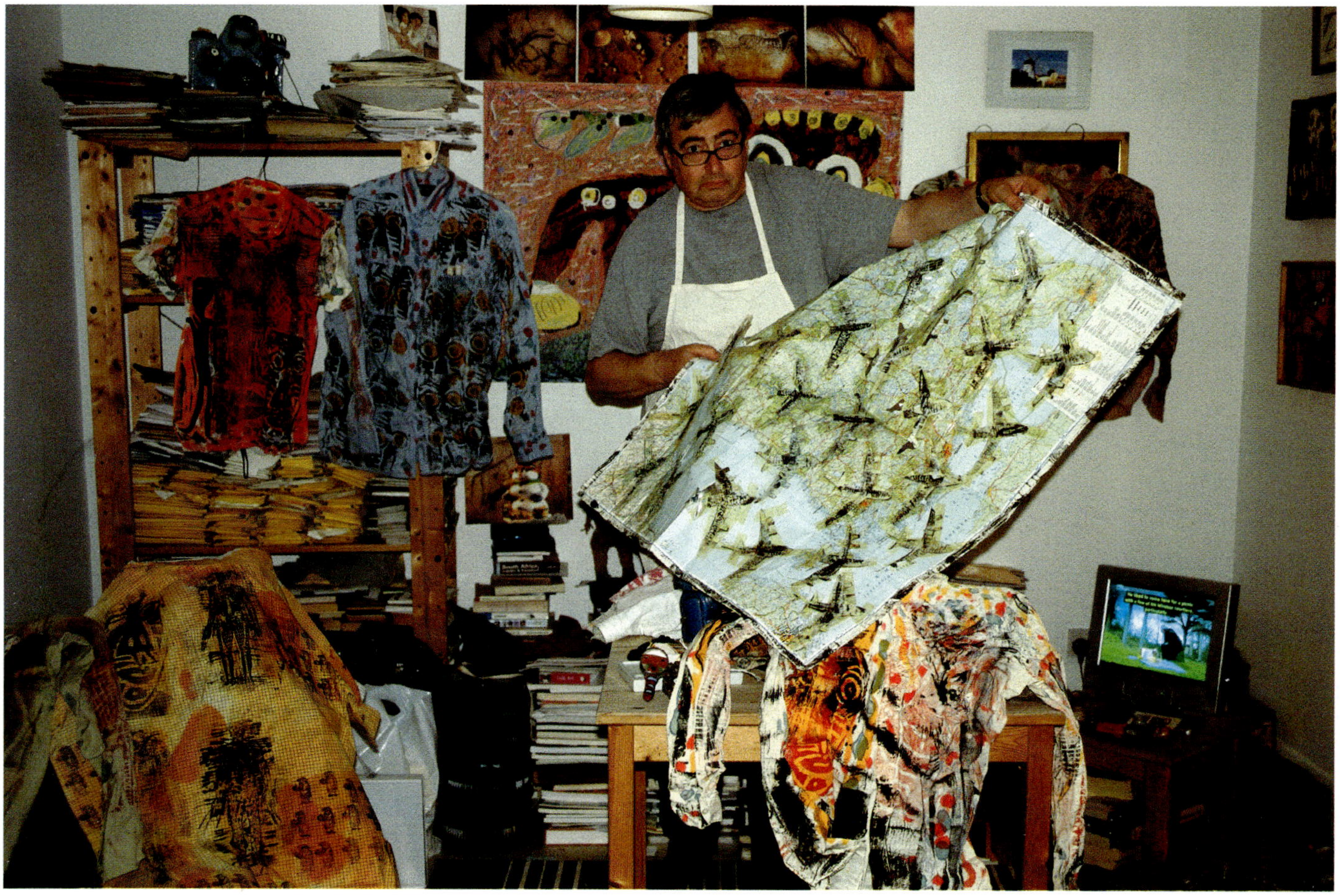

Untitled, Printed garments: hand-printed relief print and mixed media

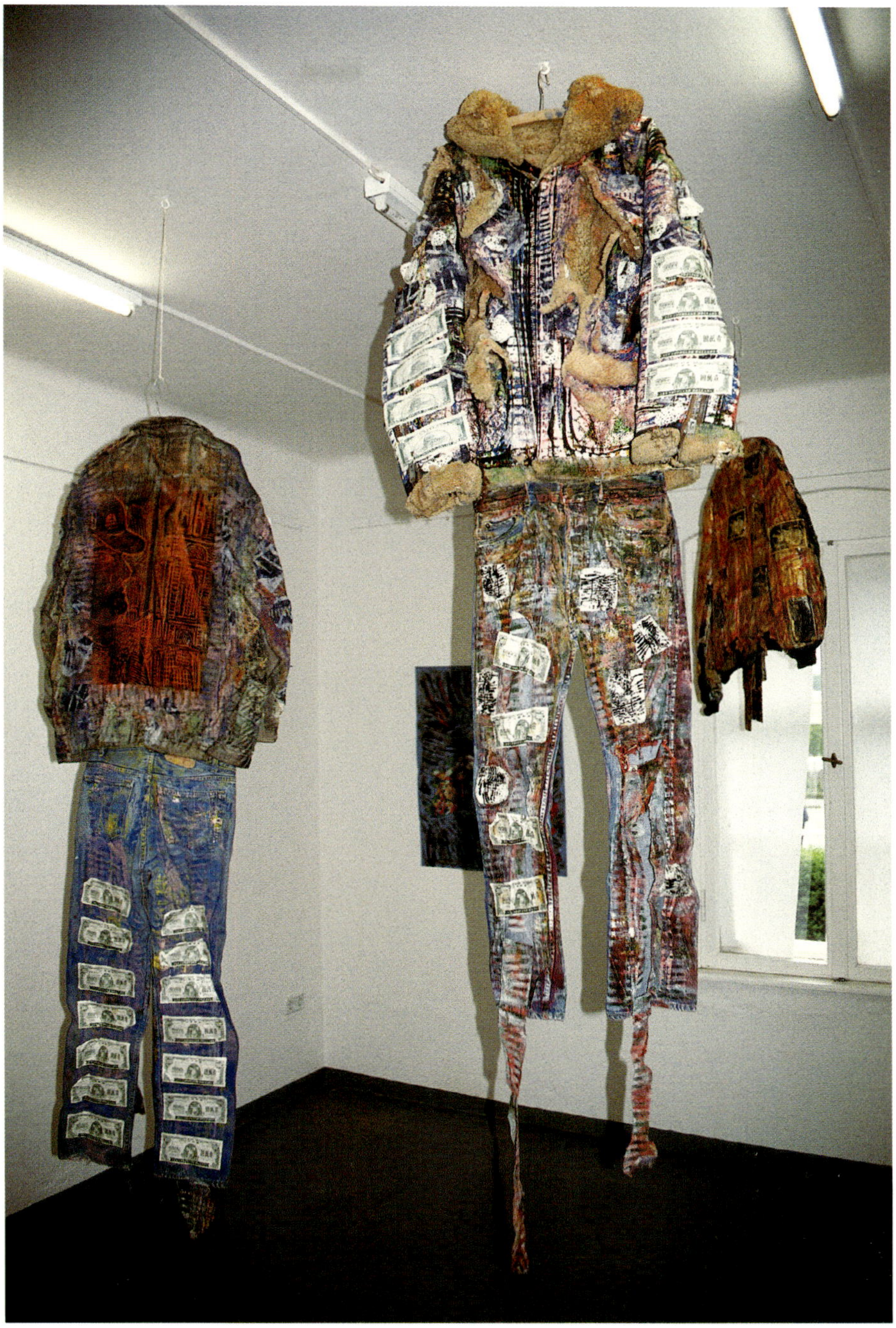

textile or other unconventional surfaces. The clothes and textile works were particularly interesting to develop, since even quiet imagery gained a different character and meaning once printed on a jacket or shirt. There was also the implicit reference to fashion, or rather anti-fashion, since strong imagery would be too difficult to wear even when compared to extreme fashion, in which much is underplayed. For me, these pieces work best in their suggestion of the presence of a human body, of the individual who could be imagined wearing them. Printing these works became a constant game of invention and careful work, calculating the way in which each block was inked or printed on the fabric's surface. I found that I could modulate the surface in much the same way as a painter does with oil and canvas.

Despite having worked for many years as a printmaker, these are deeply entrenched methods that I learned right at the start of my career. In that period, I vacillated between sculpture and painting, never sure which was my chief interest. It was through the medium of printmaking that I found a sense of order that could progress my ideas and love of imagery, though my experience of painting has always influenced that approach. So, finding myself in a studio with only basic facilities, it seemed constructive to employ looser and less formal approaches to the use of traditional methods in order to facilitate a free play of those qualities that are particular to printmaking, though applied in my case to unorthodox surfaces. This experience has become a great aid in the making of my prints in that I now use studio time very well, knowing that I can adopt a freer approach at any time, without requiring a complexity of different resources.

Pilar Muñoz

The most important subject in my work is the concept of time and how it affects the individuality of each human being. My inspiration comes from my daily routine: my obsessions, worries and thoughts appear constantly in my imagery. Artists who influence my work are Louise Bourgeois and Juan Muñoz, in particular.

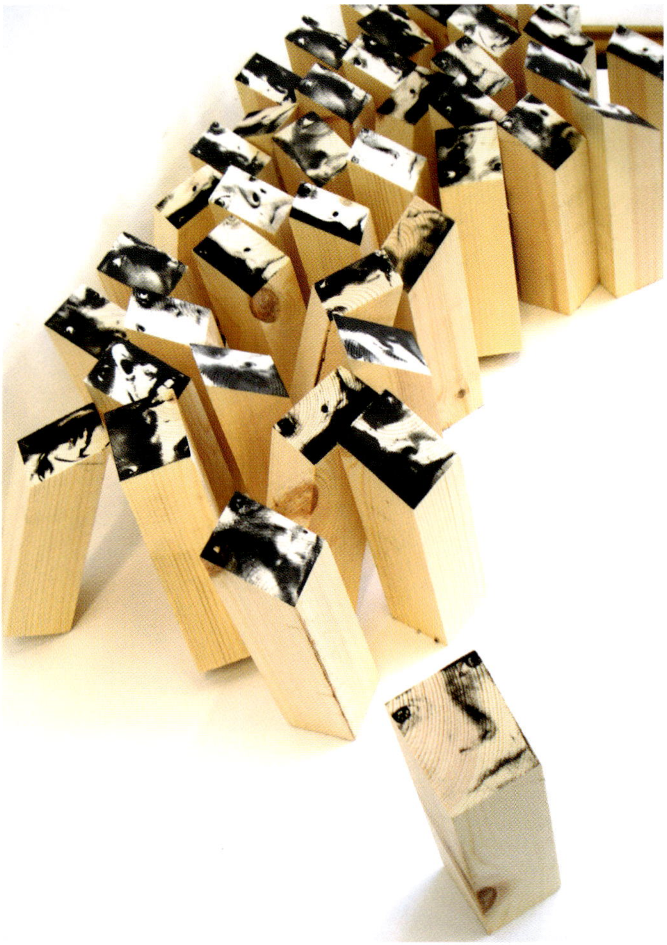

Normality, 2007. Screenprint on wood, installation of 50 figures, each 20 x 5 x 5 cm (8 x 2 x 2 in.)

I employ a mixture of different techniques including painting, photography, sculpture, collage and printmaking. Focusing on the printmaking: I normally use everything connected with this technique, from the tissue I use to clean the plates, to the registration acetate used in the screenprint table. My work is built up by collaging different materials found during my daily routine, for example: tissue paper, envelopes, wrapping paper and so on. Again, this relates to time, the moment when something was collected and the reminiscence of the place.

With puppets, I have found a format for experimenting with and communicating how time makes us act in different ways. The human being has become an object and time the subject. As a result the human being is managed by time. So the puppet is managed by the puppeteer and represents both the manipulator and the manipulated; it takes on an identity of its own. Also the puppet is made and frozen in one expression; that is its physical form, but in its movements – through space and time – it is seen to change. The puppets are made in different materials depending on what I want to say at any one moment.

I also enjoy experimenting with print onto different materials, as in my works *World* (screenprint on canvas) and *Normality* (screenprint on wood). I had a very clear idea about what I wanted to create. With *World* I was aiming to make a ball of connected faces; so the procedure was to screenprint onto canvas a series of small faces, which were later cut out and finally stitched to each other with red thread, following the shape of a plastic ball which forms the inside structure. In the work *Normality,* my intention was to make a group of small figures in a very simple way, with realistic faces. So I prepared 50 wooden cuboids, each of which had the top cut at a 30° angle. I then screenprinted faces onto them,

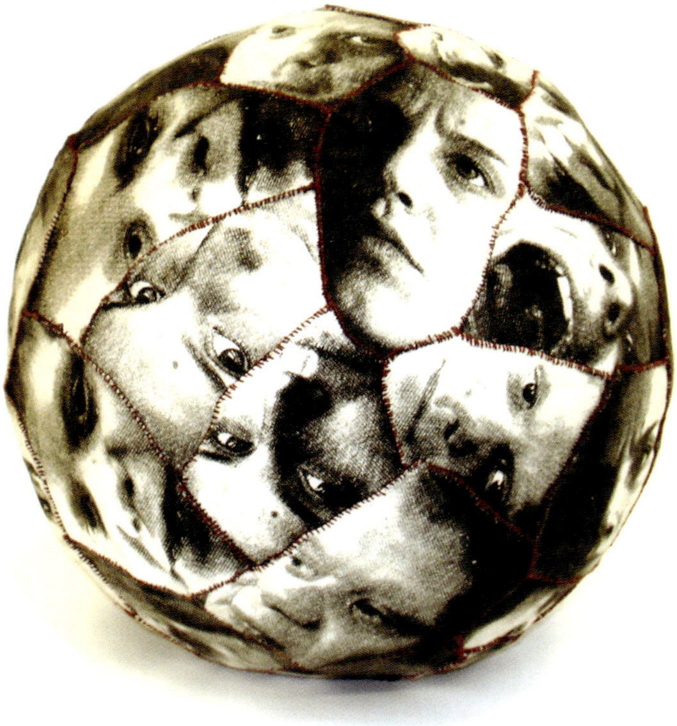

World, 2007. Screenprint on canvas, 30 x 30 x 30 cm (12 x 12 x 12 in.)

manipulating the screen by hand in a very simple way, using a small card as a squeegee and my free hand to locate the wood without any registration, just calculating where the face would be and printing onto the angled top of each cube.

Printmaking, seen in isolation as a technique, can be very frustrating when one seeks to achieve a perfect final result. That is why I am more interested in concentrating on the journey of the image, using bits of mistakes to create a new piece of work and mixing print with sculpture, painting or whatever I am enjoying at the time, and expressing what I need to at a particular moment. I am more interested in using the inspiration of what occurs at any one instant in time rather than planning something too precisely. For me, the accidental represents the essence of time.

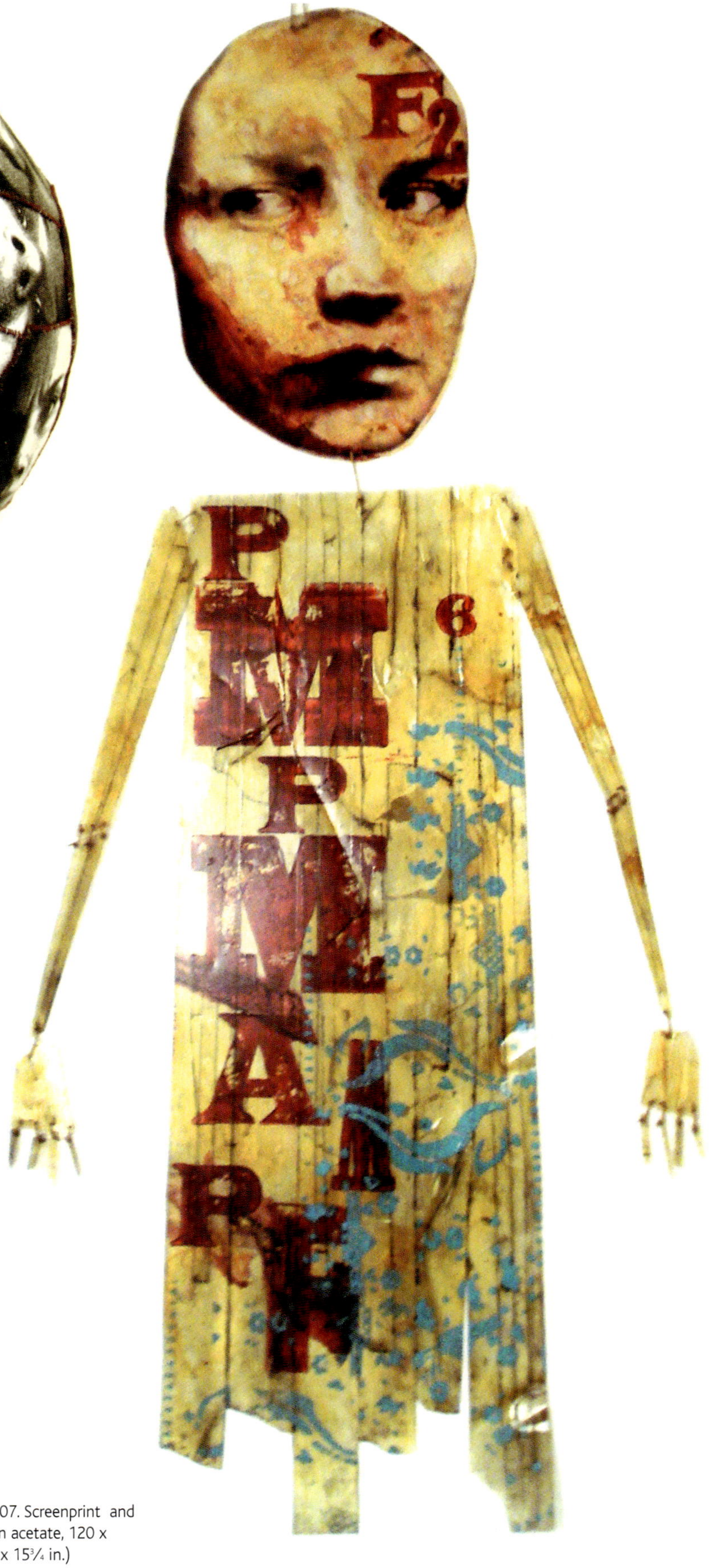

Puppet II, 2007. Screenprint and woodblock on acetate, 120 x 40 cm (47¼ x 15¾ in.)

Chris Orr

I often startle students by telling them my golden rule: 'You should never remember anything you learn in a print workshop.' My theory is that you should leave at the end of the day and forget everything you have painstakingly acquired. When you return, reinvent, rethink and relearn. Printing and printmaking hold inherent contradictions, being at the same time both instigators of creativity and a conservative force. They can codify and restrict as well as liberate. The appearance in print of Gutenberg's Bible was not all good news. The conundrum is: how do artists use what are essentially rigid industrial processes to make art? How do we make poetry through mechanics?

Mind Boggling, Petty Fogging Detail, 1998. Counterproof etching, 58 x 77 cm (22⅞ x 30¼ in.)

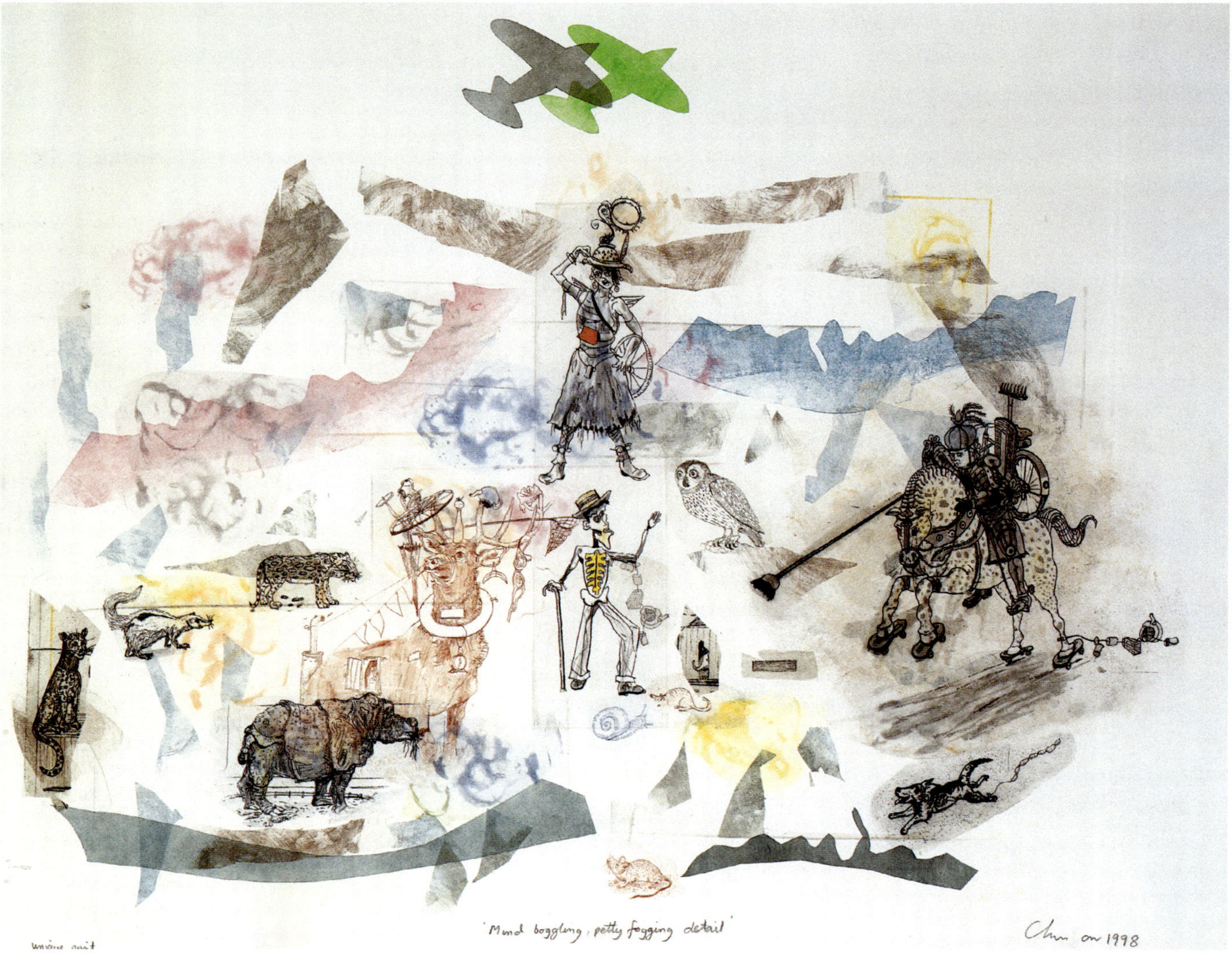

The Small Titanic, 1993. Counterproof etching, 67 x 103 cm (26⅜ x 40½ in.)

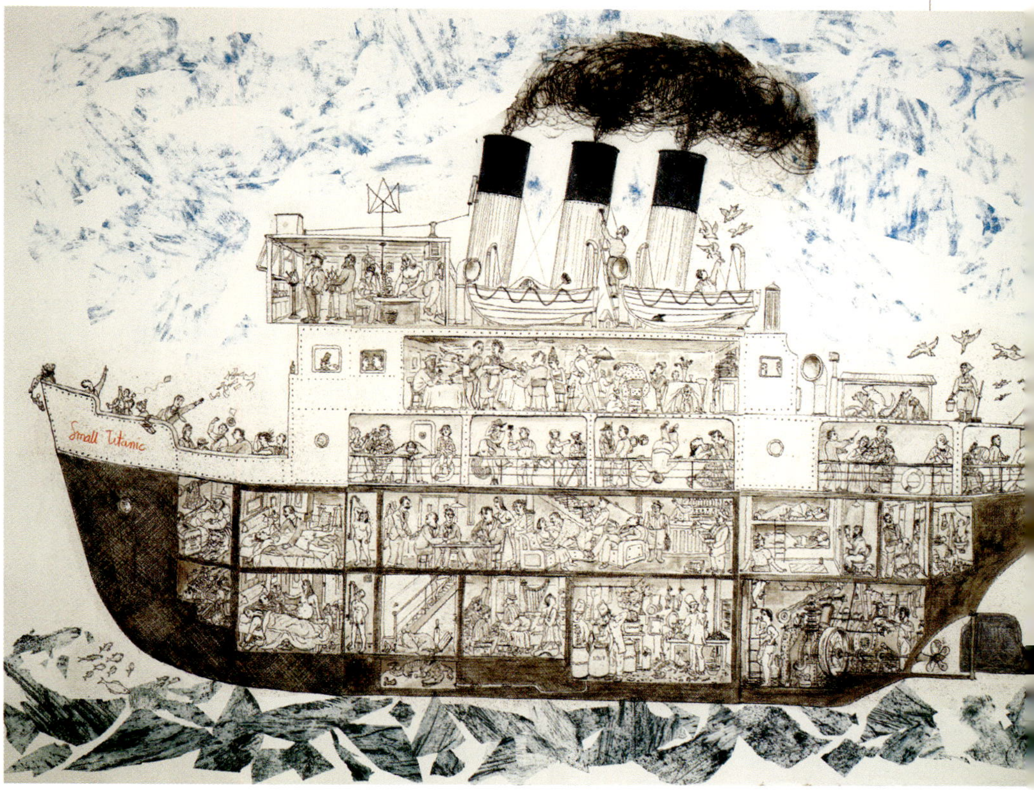

The wonderful craft of printmaking and the history of technological development are to be enjoyed and respected, but they must be the servant of the ideas. The term 'printmaker' should be used sparingly. I am a printmaker when I am in a workshop making prints, but it is artists who make original prints. We have a powerful history at the Royal College of Art of artists coming to us with no previous experience in the technology and yet making collaboratively wonderful works. In the process of learning skills and mastering techniques, the reason for making images remains profoundly important but can be easily lost. The difficulty with technology is that so many effects and so much manipulation can be achieved so rapidly that much of what is produced is adrift from the artist's original intentions.

I was lucky that, at an important period of my career, I had a very well-equipped print studio and the freedom and resources to play with the possibilities it offered. I had burning ideas and feelings waiting to find expression. My multi-layered surreal ideas like *The Small Titanic* demanded new approaches, leading me to the rediscovery of counter-proofing, an offset etching technique that allowed me the opportunity to use the full size of the press bed and took me away from the tyranny of the rectangle imposed by the standard shape of an etching plate. I also developed relief printing from inked-up waste film and paper, as well as a variety of monoprint techniques.
The print workshop became my alchemist's den, any material or method my base metal, and the realisation of my ideas the golden goal.

The flatness of counterproofing allowed an easy marriage with my other print love – lithography. In *Bones*, (see p.151) a print about evolution, based on the University Museum in Oxford, I used drawings done on the spot to make a lithograph and etching plates that fuse description with puns and fanciful narratives. In this visual essay there is a concern to return to the role of the artist as witness. It was Wenceslaus Hollar's *Long View of London from Bankside*, produced in the mid-17th century, which set me on another course with my prints and paintings. I have always drawn *en plein air*, both for pleasure and as an essential discipline. As a result of trips to China and Japan and a life-long obsession with my home city, London, I began to treat the print as a topographical medium allied to books and maps. The complexity of cities requires detailed description, and the precise graphic disciplines of both etching and lithography lend themselves to this delineation.

My inclinations since I was a student back in the 1960s have always been populist. Printmaking seems to offer a strong means of expression and identification with a bigger world. Pop art and the re-evaluation of all forms of printed material was a formative influence. I have continued to see print and printmaking in all its forms as a fluid route to new things. The print workshop is for invention. Invention must come from a mind open both to the completely new and to the wealth of the past. My golden rule seeks to strengthen the creative dynamic of printmaking.

Hilary Paynter

I have never had enough time for engraving. Commitments to the RE, to the Society of Wood Engravers and, via my former career as an educational psychologist, to children with special needs, have always been heavy but usually irresistible. Leaving aside the case for priorities, the advantage is that I was forced to develop rapid engraving techniques. My preference is to work directly into the wood with only rudimentary sketches. This can be risky, but the results are often more dynamic. When I have to reverse the design and trace it onto the block, I keep only the essential outlines and details.

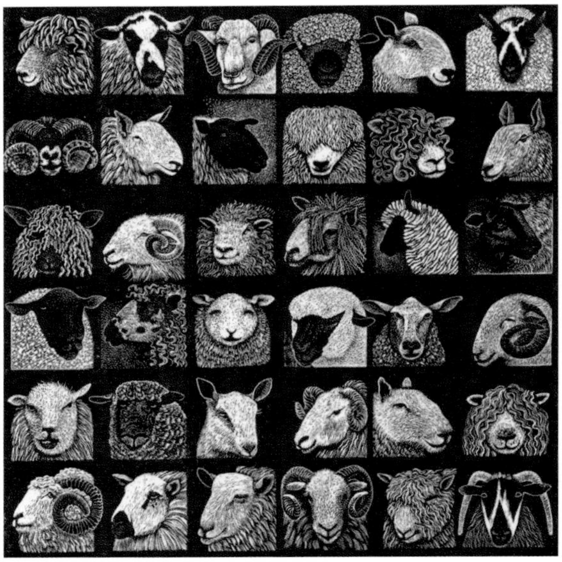

The Sheep Show, 2006, Wood engraving, 17.5 x 17.5 cm (6¾ x 6¾ in.)

Fallen Angel was started at a demonstration, with only the vague outline of the figure, and I began gently but rapidly stabbing in the texture of rough ground around the edge of it. I didn't want anything such as vegetation to detract from the impact, so I covered most of the block with barren, stony ground. The tiny spectators were added to establish the scale.

I always have about six to ten blocks on the go. They may all be part of a series, such as my Newcastle Metro project (unveiled in 2004) or illustrations for a book, but are often totally unrelated. There is no time to sit around wondering where to go next so, when I get stuck, I simply move to another block and work at that one until I need to pause again. Loads of time can also be saved by proofing several blocks in the same printing session. When I am close to finishing a block, I usually pin the latest proof on a wall somewhere and forget about it for a while. I will come across it later, unexpectedly, and immediately understand what needs to be done next.

My woodblocks are prepared by painting the surface with the thinnest coating of dark-grey gouache. On this I can draw with black biro or white pencil. As the engraving develops it is easy to see the design emerging. My main subject at art college was sculpture, and stone-carving has been enormously influential in the way I draw and engrave. This is most obvious in my landscapes and figures, where I rough out the general forms on the block and refine them until they seem right. The marks I make define the structure. It is crucial for me to know what is happening below the surface, physically as well as metaphorically. Once the wood has gone, it cannot be replaced.

The most frequently asked question is, 'What happens when you make a mistake?' I learnt to keep my tools sharp and my left hand below the parapet. A worse problem is finding a crumbly area or disguising a block that is starting to part at the seams: all large wood-engraving blocks have been assembled from smaller pieces. I have sometimes incorporated these straight white lines into the design or broken down the surface so that they do not show. With a design that is not too rigidly set, I can relish the challenge of accommodating the vagaries of working with organic materials. Sometimes when a proof is examined, I wish that I had left an area blacker, but this can be rectified by making adjacent areas lighter so that the contrast makes it appear darker.

Sometimes the block warps or the centre sinks, which complicates the printing process. I don't have time for 'make ready' when I am changing the blocks so frequently, so I keep a simple device to remedy this problem: a series of torn concentric circles of paper lightly glued together and placed over the problem area on top of the packing. Happily, new blocks made by Chris Daunt in Gateshead do not seem to have these problems.

Rejected prints are kept in a

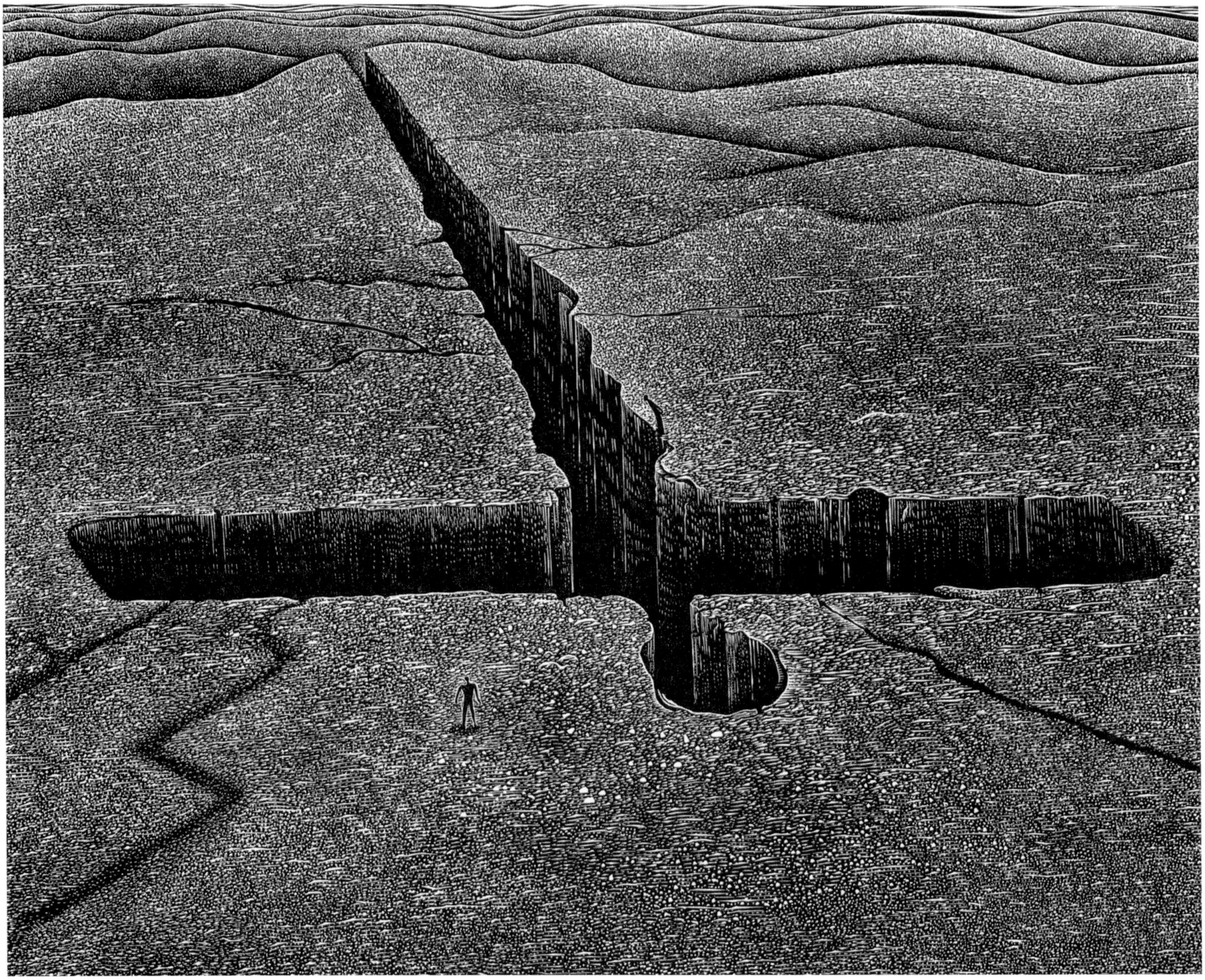

Fallen Angel, 2006, Wood engraving, 20 x 25 cm (7⅞ x 9⅞ in.)

folder in case they could be useful. During proofing, I might wonder whether to lighten an area and can cut out pieces of rejected prints and stick them on the working proof to try out the tone, texture and scale of the marks. Often there is only a small part that has not successfully printed, and I can use the good parts of the print to collage birthday or Christmas cards.

In the early years, my landscapes were almost the only prints that were accepted in exhibitions, and there was scant interest in wood engraving then. I made other prints for myself that were political or social comments on what was going on around me and enjoyed producing a Christmas card each year for friends, unfettered by what was acceptable. Enoch Powell featured in *Pandora's Christmas Box* (1969) with a tiny Biafran figure of Hope in the box; Thatcher and Reagan were depicted as children fighting over their missiles in *Christmas Presents* (1982). *The Sheep Show* was born of happy hours at the North Devon Show with all the wonderful and rare breeds. They also have alpacas, llamas, goats, cattle and poultry ...

Wood engraving is an intense and often lonely occupation and can ruin your posture. I listen to stories on tape when I am working and this helps to shut out the world and stops me composing letters and reports in my head. Engraving animals with all the different textures of their coats is wonderfully therapeutic and amusing and makes a great balance with the more serious subject matter.

Melvyn Petterson

Drypoint has always been a special medium for me, with its own set of rules, which are different in many ways to those of etching. My own drypoint tools are a mixture; some I have purchased from printmaking suppliers, some come from DIY stores and some are household implements. Over the years I have built up quite a collection and I'm still adding to it. Having a good range of mark-making tools allows me to create more variety in drypoint marks. Because drypoint wears fairly quickly, it is better to work the drypoint to a nearly finished state before proofing, as the first pull will normally be your richest print, with the burr sitting at its most ink-retaining height. The last thing you need is to pull four to six proofs before you're ready for the edition, especially when working on aluminium or zinc.

Snow on the Wold, 1997. Drypoint, 90 x 61 cm (35½ x 24 in.)

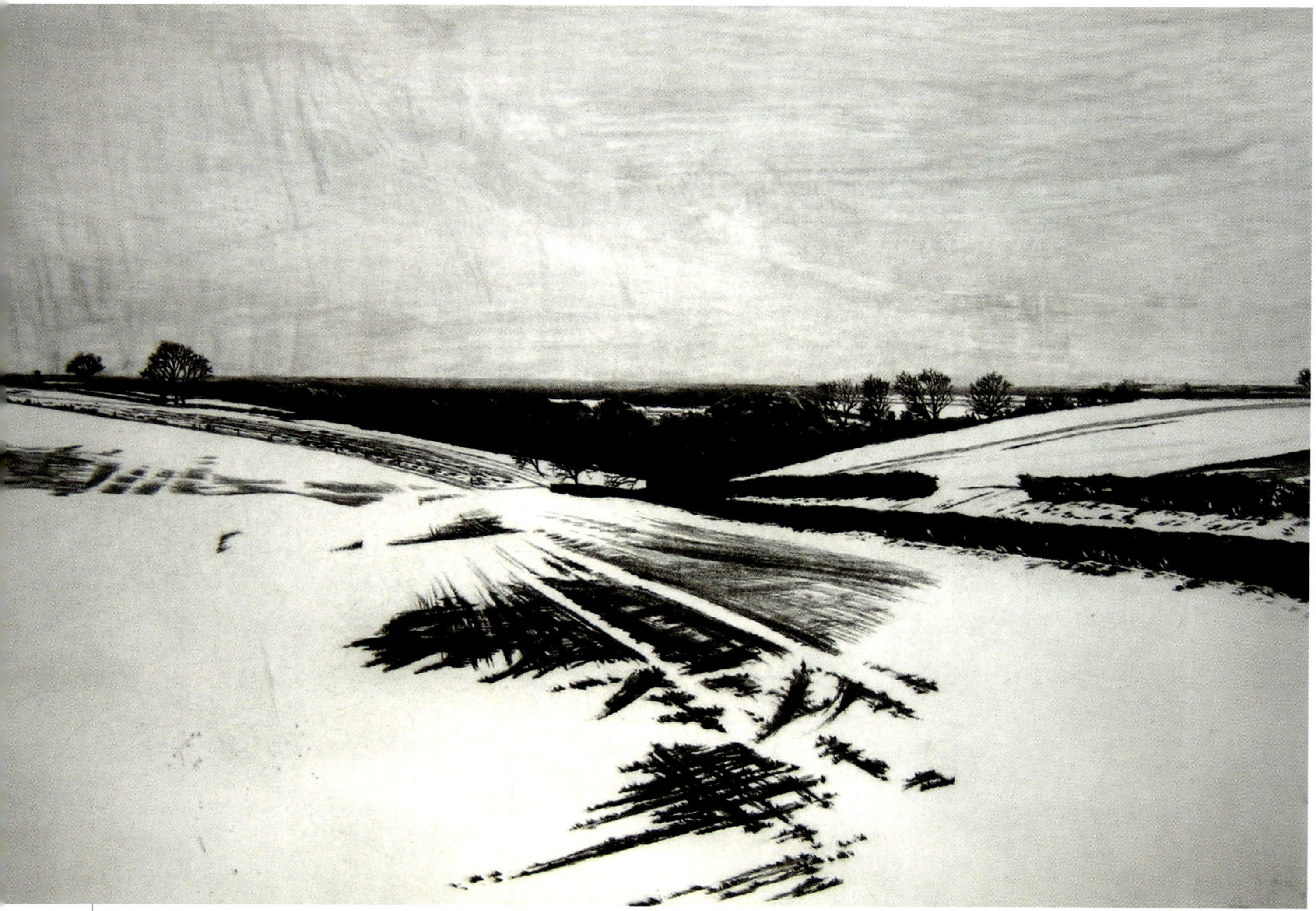

Greenwich Evening, 1988.
Drypoint, 14 x 21 cm
(5½ x 8¼ in.)

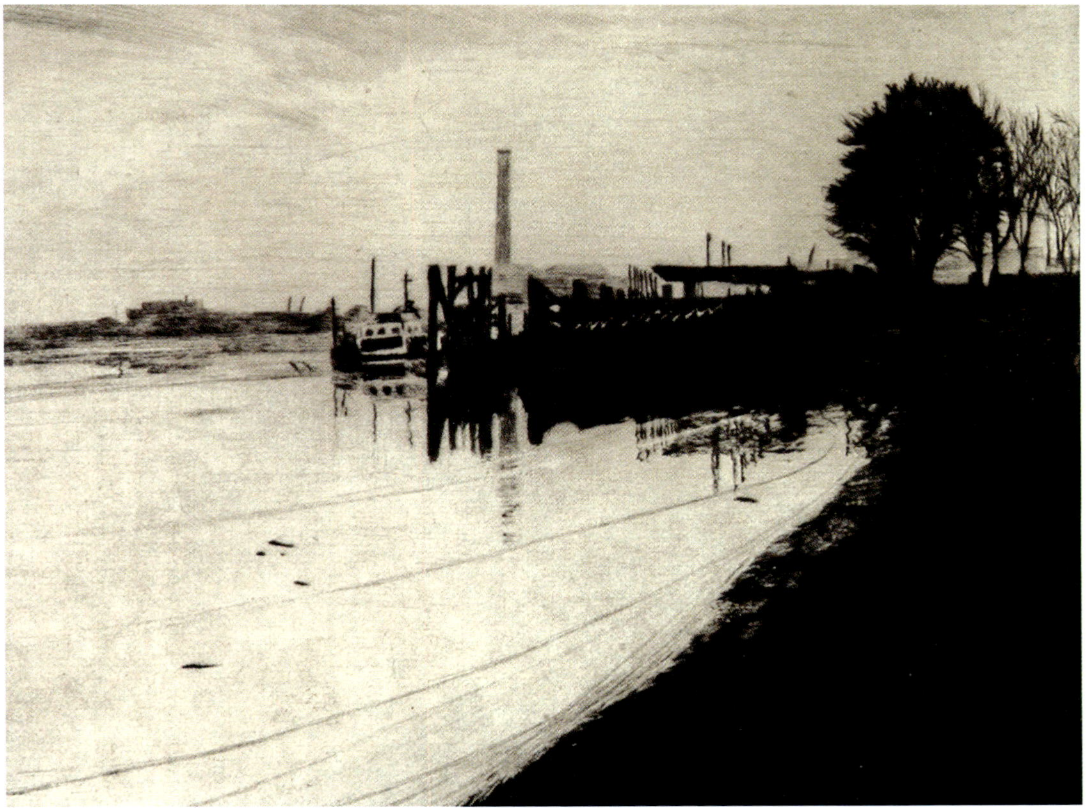

The wiping of drypoint is very important, so my technique is to wipe across the drypoint marks whenever possible, as this traps more ink in the burr, giving me more rich prints in each edition; this is preferable to wiping along the lines, which tends to push ink out of the grooves and burrs, thus reducing the print's richness. I remember printing a hundred drypoints some years ago from a smallish copperplate after having had it steel-faced, a good way to make sure you achieve rich prints and avoid the plate wearing prematurely.

Snow On The Wold was made in drypoint on copper, using a tungsten-carbide drypoint needle; most of the time I kept my incisions in one direction, quite close to each other and very deep in order to ensure very heavily inked lines. Roulettes were used in the foreground to suggest soil showing through the snow, and then a very large, fine roulette was used to represent a cold wintry sky typical of the Lincolnshire Wolds. Often if I work on an accidentally scratched plate I can quite easily incorporate the incidental blemishes into my landscape.

With *Greenwich Evening*, again on copper, I have whilst wiping left quite a bit of plate tone to help give the scene an early-evening atmosphere. Areas that need to show a little detail have to be wiped more, though without losing too much ink. When wiping drypoints I normally try to create a soft scrim pad, about the size of my hand, which is firm to hold but has no loose ends that might catch the burrs when wiping and break them off. Certainly, having a good, sound, sympathetic wiping technique and the right amount of pressure on the press can make the difference between achieving your edition and falling short. The sky in this print was done with an old biro pen that was empty but can dig out a subtle burr to create a moody evening sky.

The shafts of the most well-used drypoint needles in my collection are wrapped in masking tape to reduce the pressure on my finger ends when digging into copper. There is certainly more to drypoint than many artists would believe; it's all about preserving the burr and trying different tools and ways of making expressive marks. It's a whole skill in itself and if you are patient it can, like all other printmaking media, be very rewarding and satisfying. But don't take my word for it – give it a go and with a little time and effort you might well surprise yourself.

Tom Phillips

Two recent prints that I have made contain much implicit knowledge since every artist's work refers, in some way, to the cloaked hinterland of an emotional, intellectual and private world.

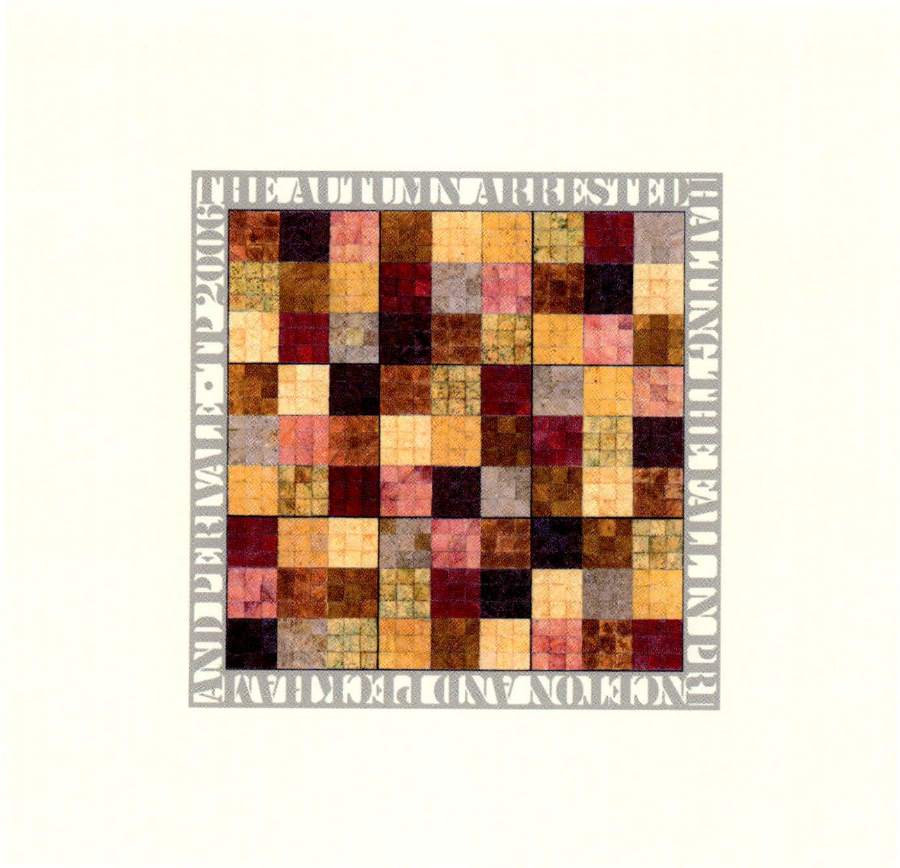

The Autumn Arrested, 2007. Inkjet and screenprint, 81 x 81 cm ($31\frac{7}{8}$ x $31\frac{7}{8}$ in.)

Of these two prints, only one could be said to feature a 'printmaker's secret' as such. *South London Dreaming: Life Seen from Above* announces the existence of autobiographical enigmas without any specifics. Dots on a paste-up of old A to Z map pages designate places of pith and moment in my life and are colour-coded, though without a key. Otherwise, it is a good old-fashioned screenprint robustly done, using hand-drawn stencils and produced with the help of Ray Dennis at Brighton University.

The Autumn Arrested uses inkjet (giclée) printing on an Epson machine, a method currently as frowned upon as was silkscreen using photostencils when I started making screenprints in 1964. Although thought to be a short cut to producing graphics, the computer image can be as laboured over as anything else, and this print, done with Brad Faine at Coriander studios in Greenford, Middlesex, took much more time to produce than did *South London Dreaming*. It is not only work with the hand that counts. The basis of the inkjet work was a collage, a fugitive artefact of actual leaf fragments gathered at the Institute for Advanced Study in Princeton. The only mystery in the making was the falsification of the paper colour, whose whiteness underlies the image to make the ink glow, but outside the image area it is darkened to the paper's edge, a secret that the print keeps convincingly and one which allows the leaves to sing.

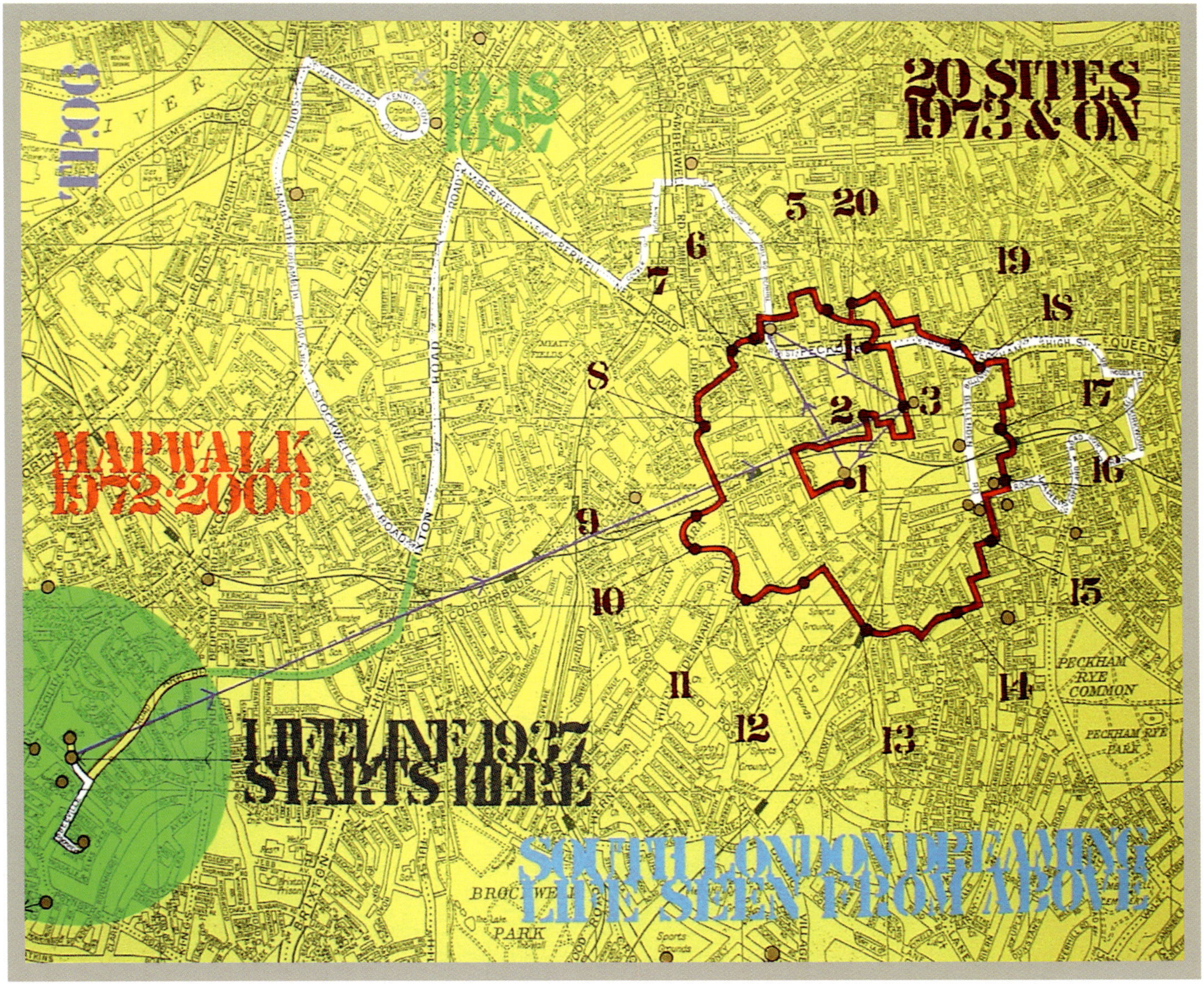

South London Dreaming: Life Seen From Above, 2006. Screenprint, 65 x 74.5 cm (25½ x 29¼ in.)

Neil Pittaway

In intaglio works I often use European themes from past empires to the present day. I create microcosms of these worlds, reinvented to offer a highly personalised view. I use ideas from different periods and bind them together using contemporary themes that offer the spectator a fresh look at how we view our heritage.

The Glory of Victory, for example, explores Britain's imperial past and its relationship to modern London and Europe through symbolic images. The work, although based on London's Trafalgar Square, uses ideas from my imagination and evocative images from the 19th and early 20th centuries. The central theme of this etching focuses on the events and significant places of the Napoleonic period. Humour and satire are used symbolically. The title is there to prompt the spectator into questioning the meaning of victory and our interpretation of the notion today. I have deliberately made this ambiguous in the work. Victory can result in a triumphant celebration or it can raise questions about what real victory means years after the event. This work is also about how the spectator uses the narrative as a vehicle to question not just the wider role of empire but his or her own relationship, perception and placement of it in relation to the present.

The London Connection portrays the development of the modern metropolis. Split into three sections, the left-hand panel represents the early 20th century, travel and links to North America. The middle section concentrates on the lifeblood, the heartbeat of the metropolis based on Britain's imperial past. Everything in this section is for display – a false paradise where the past is brought to life as a theme park. The right-hand panel represents the modern vision of the metropolis and Britain's wider role in the contemporary world, now symbolised by its links to Europe.

My prints are based on careful research, using primary and secondary source material. My idea may be very broad at first but through further studies becomes gradually more focused. I work intuitively to enliven the work and bring the concept to fruition.

The use and quality of line in the etching process is very important for me, and the rich qualities of the intaglio process reflect the emotional and other characteristics found in the subjects I explore. Seeing a print for the first time fresh from the press, seeing my concept come to life on the paper, is magic. Drawing in line on an

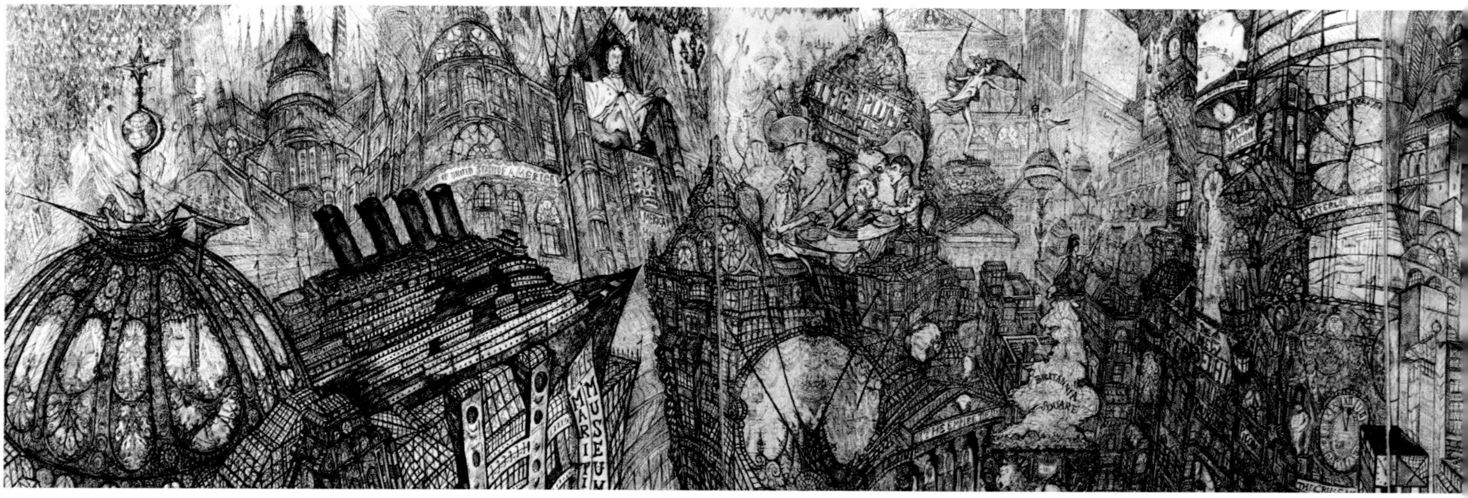

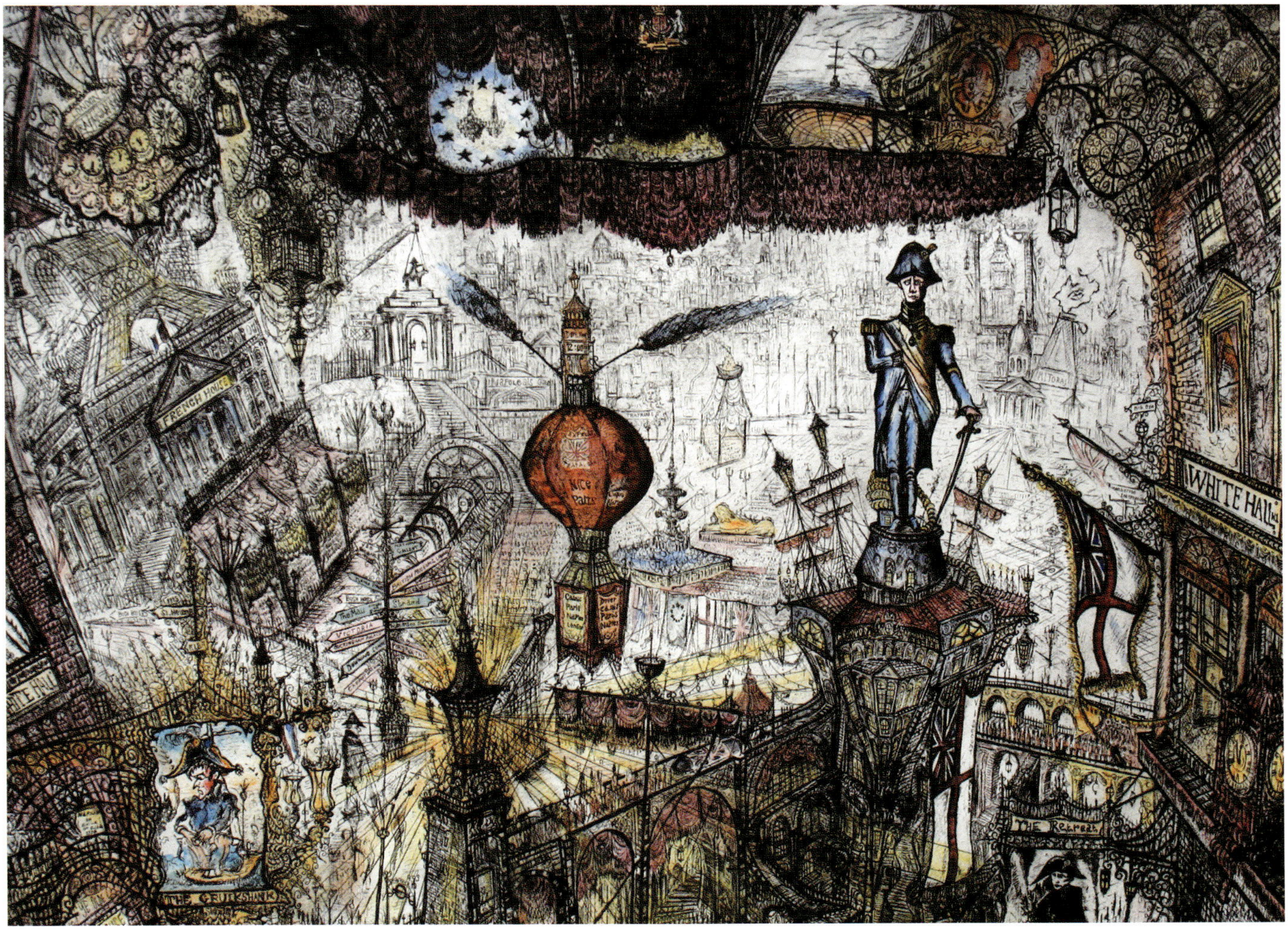

The Glory of Victory, 1997. Hand-coloured etching, 68 x 85 cm ($26\frac{3}{4}$ x $33\frac{1}{2}$ in.)

The London Connection, 1998. Etching, 77 x 256 cm ($30\frac{1}{4}$ x $100\frac{3}{4}$ in.)

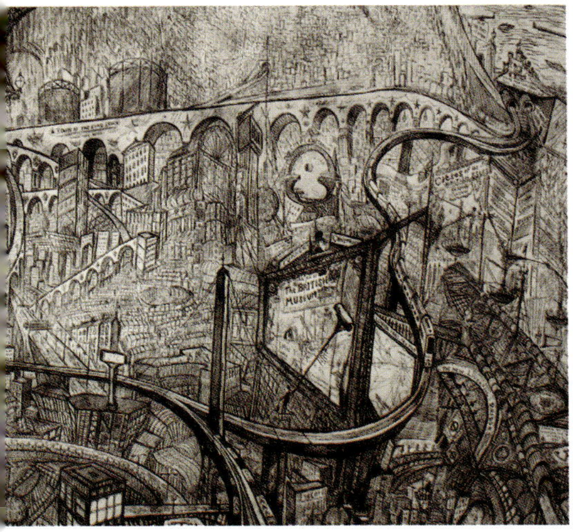

etching plate's ground is like drawing on silk: I do not need to apply much pressure, just let the drawing hand glide across the surface, creating varying emphases and linear movement. To get the maximum quality from my idea I draw as much detail as possible on the plate, varying the quality of the drawn lines. I often use a magnifying glass to help me achieve even finer detail and create a tapestry of intricate lines, like lacework.

After the plate has been bitten in acid and a proof print made, more work is usually undertaken. This can include adding a further hard ground, drawing more detail and then biting the plate again. Alternatively, I add drypoint line. I use various sharp tools to scrape and draw directly into the surface of the plate. Drypoint produces different qualities: a softer, more fuzzy line which contrasts well with the hard, sharply bitten, etched line. With drypoint I can also create areas of subtle tone, much like shading with a pencil. When using the drypoint method it is important to test the weight of line first, because the line can end up being too dominant compared to the original etched lines. I find that building up the etched image, working into it with further detail, works well in capturing the overall effects needed to convey my concepts.

Bryan Poole

My love of making etchings of botanical subjects stems from my close association with Kew Gardens, where I worked as an illustrator in the early 1980s. There I had access to the Herbarium Library, where the rich history of printmaking in the service of botany may be traced. Most of the Herbarium's prints record plants collected from many parts of the world and brought back from voyages of discovery over the centuries. In 2006, true to this tradition, I collected from Tahiti a frangipani plant (Plumieria rubra), symbol of the tropical paradise of the South Pacific. Whilst in the island I made the sketches and watercolours on which is based the master drawing for my aquatint of the plant.

The important principle when preparing a master drawing is to envisage from the outset all the technical problems entailed in the making of the plate and its eventual inking and printing. Once the drawing is resolved I transfer it, back to front, onto a copper plate prepared with a smoked hard ground. Using a fine etching needle I then build up the image as a line drawing, which will provide the basic structure of the plant in an almost subliminal way underneath the aquatint. In the case of the frangipani, the wooden stem is left as a line etching, but the leaves are rendered as a flat aquatint in which the veining and glossy highlights are achieved by burnishing. These burnished areas hold less ink and consequently print as a lighter colour.

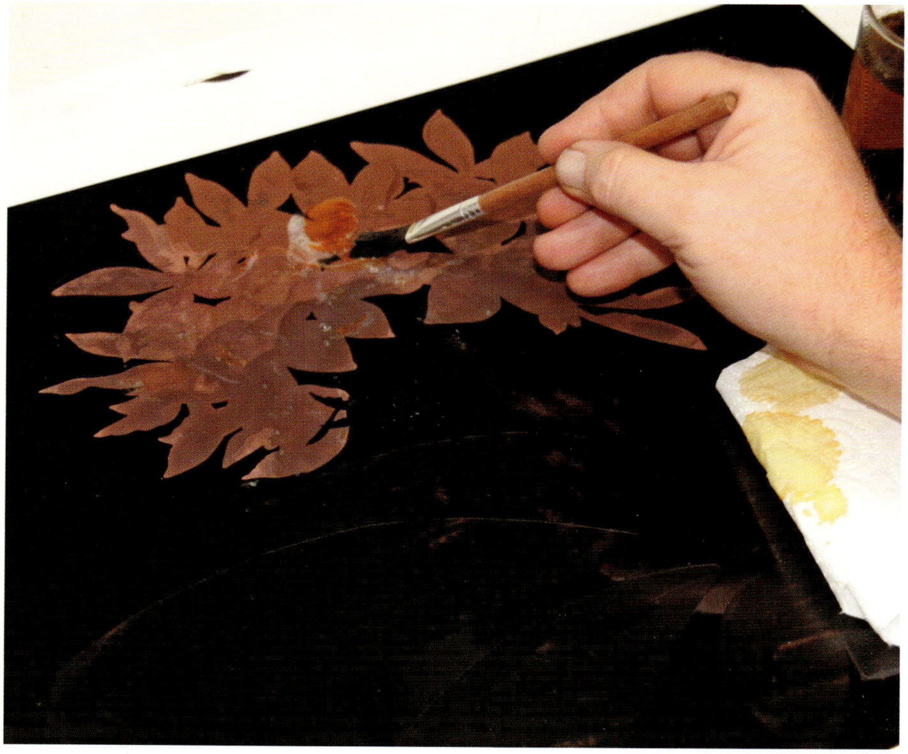

Applying spit bite to the **Frangipani** plate. Photo by Helena Poole

The lush flowers, however, are done with spit bite. The rest of the composition is stopped out with protective varnish, carefully leaving the flowers exposed. A conventional aquatint ground is applied to the plate, and a mixture of ferric chloride and saliva is brushed onto the flowers, petal by petal. The viscosity of the saliva causes the biting to be more random but also enables precise areas to be bitten, since the extent of the mordant can be controlled. The whole process is time-consuming and nerve-racking, as I dab off the mixture in a painterly way, attempting as I go to capture the three-dimensionality of the flowers. From time to time, I check the biting with a linen prover, to make sure that the aquatint texture remains strong enough to print as a saturated colour. Once I'm happy that the aquatint has bitten sufficiently, I

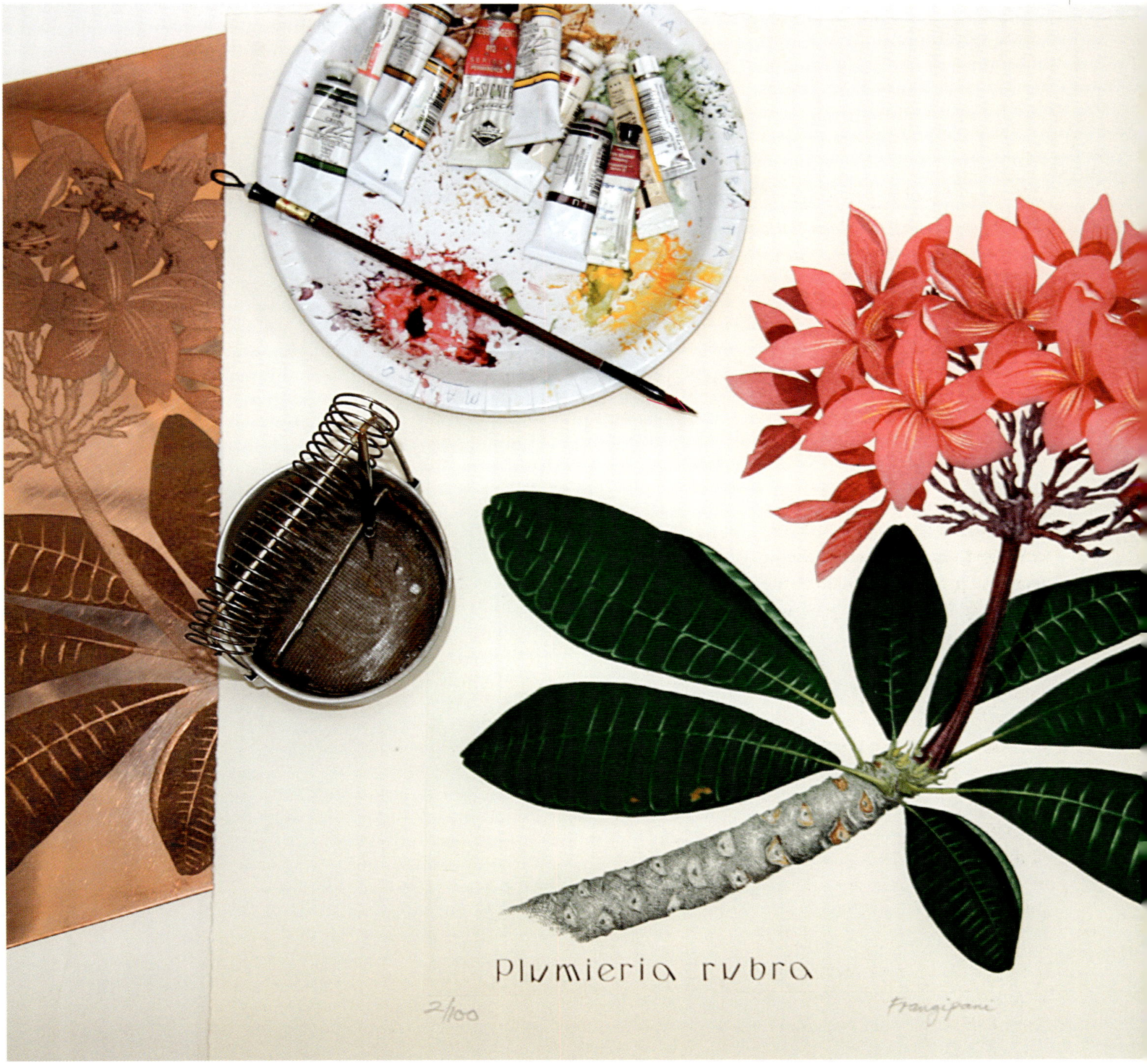

The **Frangipani** etching in progress, 2007. Photo by Helena Poole

clean off the stop-out varnish and pull a black and white proof; if this is not satisfactory the whole process has to be repeated. Once I get a successful result I use a soft charcoal block for some subtle burnishing of the petals, to reinforce their form, and finally I have the plate steel-faced to protect the delicate aquatint.

I make a *bon à tirer* proof in full colour, using my preferred method of inking *à la poupée*, in which the multiple colours are applied to the plate, giving a full-colour print for each pull. In the tradition of botanical printmaking, I hand-finish in watercolour, applying the small botanical details essential to the taxonomic integrity of the subject.

Martin Ridgwell

For me, the starting point for a new piece of work can come from anywhere: a moment from an old movie, a sentence from a book, the fashion spread from a magazine – anything can provide the germ of an idea. From this beginning I start to amass a hoard of images torn out of newspapers and magazines, images that in themselves may not finally be used, but that in some way illustrate what it is I am trying to express.

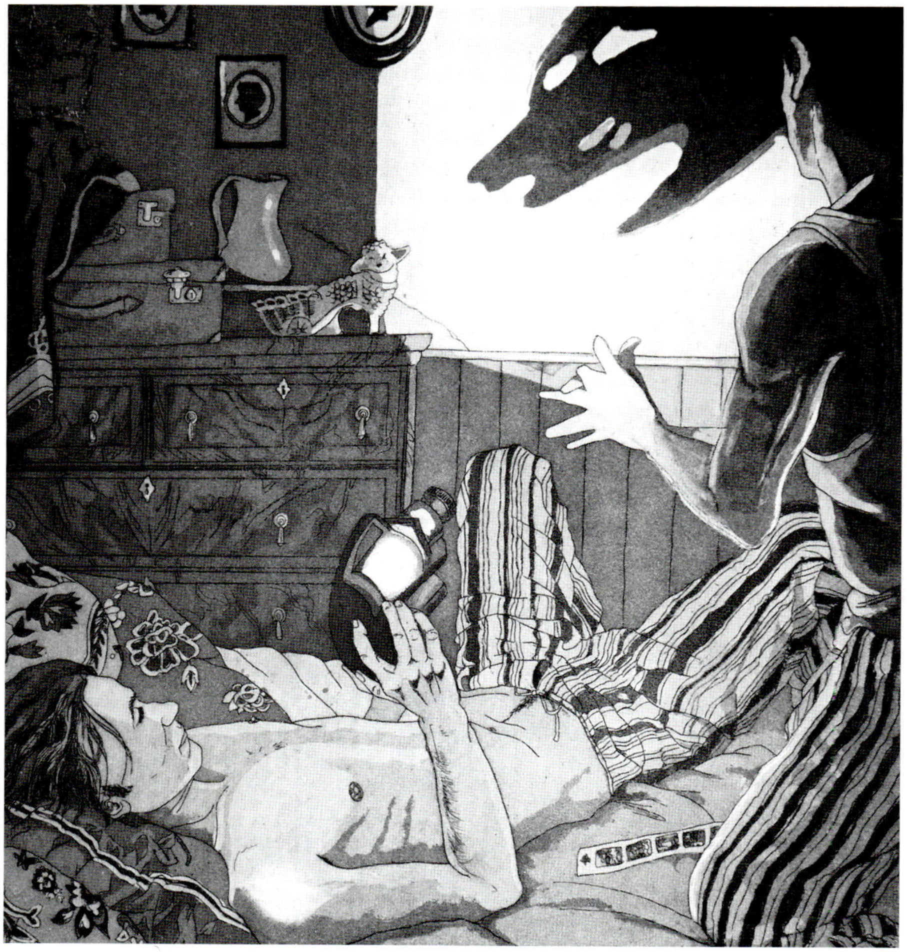

Shadow Play, 2007. Etching, 32 x 31 cm (12⅝ x 12¼ in.)

Recently, my work has been concerned with the way men interact with each other; how men's social role-playing can be at odds with their own personal desires. For my *Shadow Play* series of etchings I wanted to explore the moment that we, as men, are expected to invest in the 'psychological armour' that society demands of us and leave behind our more natural and impulsive childish selves – to examine that point at which, as adults, men learn to mask their personal desires and wishes with the habitual role-playing that goes hand in hand with modern urban life.

Whilst working on the *Shadow Play* series, I found that there was one particular movie that I constantly returned to: Jean-Pierre Melville's 1950 film based on Jean Cocteau's *Les Enfants Terribles*. Briefly, the film concerns a brother and sister in a quasi-incestuous relationship, who live in one room which becomes a shrine to their childhood and which, as adults, they later recreate in an empty chateau, where their endless games and strange rituals prevent reality and adulthood from encroaching into their lives.

From this strange, darkly funny film I began to fashion the scenario of two childhood friends who years later find themselves alone in a once grand but now decaying old house.

Cut off from the outside world, the two young men resume their old childhood rivalry through ceremonial games and baroque rituals. What were once childish games that helped them, as children, to examine the psychological tensions that they were too young to articulate, have now taken on a darker, more menacing aspect.

In *Shadow Play*, the youth on the bed aims an old toy slide projector at a bare wall, whilst the other young man uses his hands to cast animal shadows. An age-old game, quite innocuous amongst children, suddenly takes on a more threatening character. The vast shadow of the wolf looms down at the youth on the bed, whose state of undress exposes his vulnerability, which is wryly echoed by the model of the cute lamb who is seconds away from the jaws of the hungry wolf! Just as children use the props of an adult world to explore their own awareness, these men use the paraphernalia of childhood to examine their latent emotions – emotions that in the outside world they would leave unformed, unlabelled and barely acknowledged.

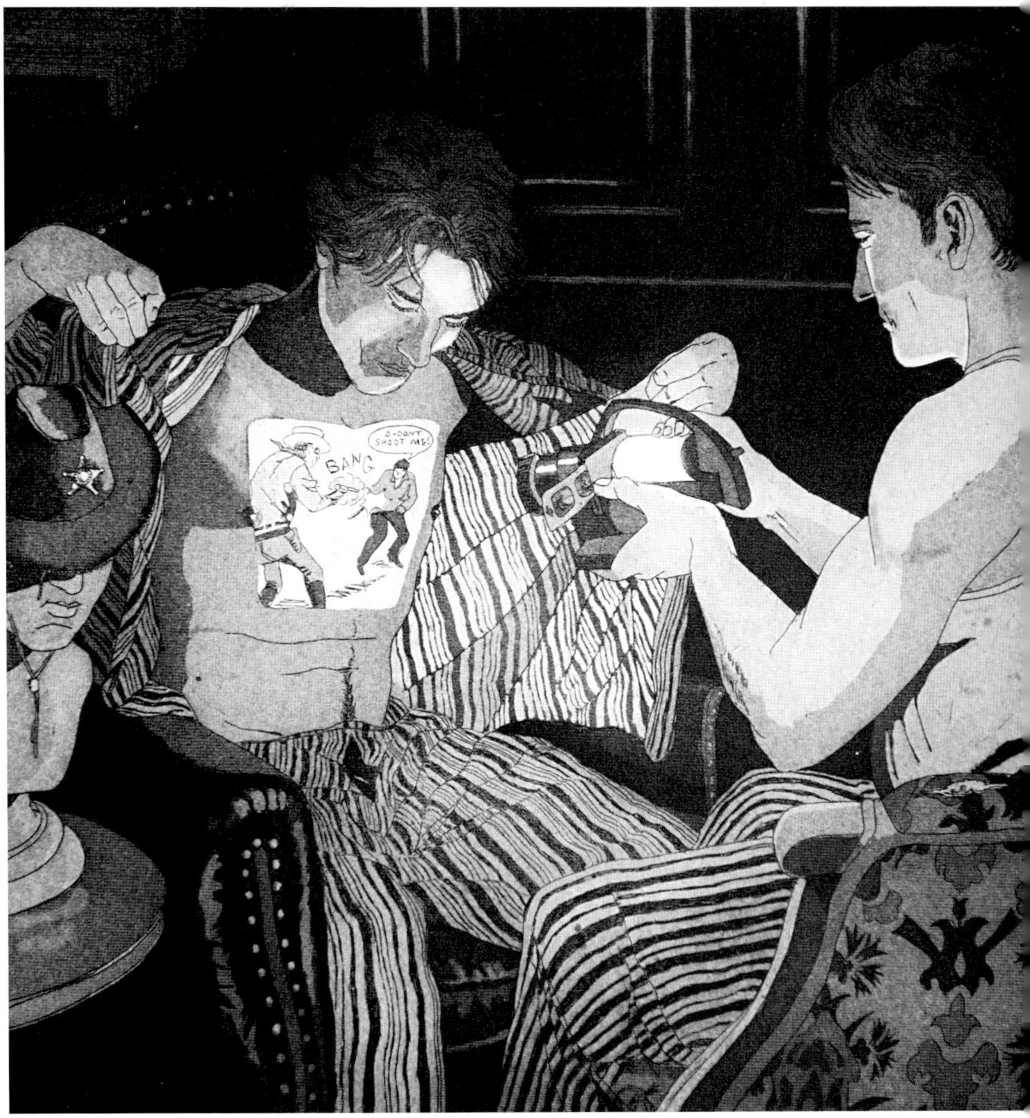

D-Don't Shoot Me!, 2007. Etching, 32.5 x 32.5 cm (12¾ x 12¾ in.)

For all my talk of dark, menacing tones, what I really want to transmit through these etchings is a sense of fun and humour. One of the initial starting points for this series was coming across a batch of old *Jack and Jill* comics and rediscovering a character that I had almost forgotten: Walter Hottle Bottle. Each week young Charlie would, within the first two frames of the cartoon strip, encounter some new problem. At night his parents put him to bed along with his hot-water bottle. In the middle of the night the hot-water bottle would come alive, and Walter Hottle Bottle would take Charlie (always in his striped pyjamas) to a magic land to be taught how to solve the difficulty in his life. If you care to look, you will find Walter Hottle Bottle hiding under the bed in one of my prints, *Hand Puppet*: a kindly reminder that the past is ever-present and the present is rooted in our past.

Nana Shiomi

The woodcut is the oldest method of printing; it has a two thousand-year history in the East. A major difference between the woodcut prints of East and West is the ink. In the East, we traditionally use water-based rather than oil-based colours. Water-based inks are easily absorbed by the Japanese paper and so are not only on the surface but also thoroughly integrated, making the colours more vivid and clear. Other differences in our printing are that we use brushes rather than rollers to apply the ink and traditional circular barens for hand-burnishing.

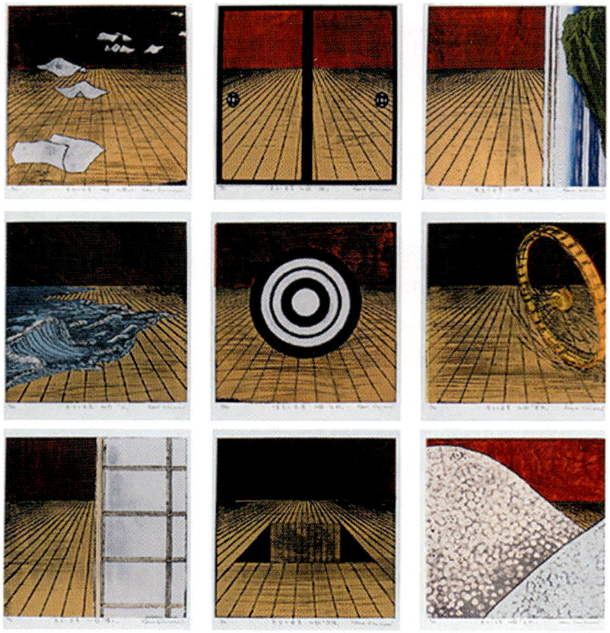

Nine works from **One Hundred Views of Mitate** series, 1998–2002. Woodcut, each 34 x 34 cm ($13\frac{3}{8}$ x $13\frac{3}{8}$ in.)

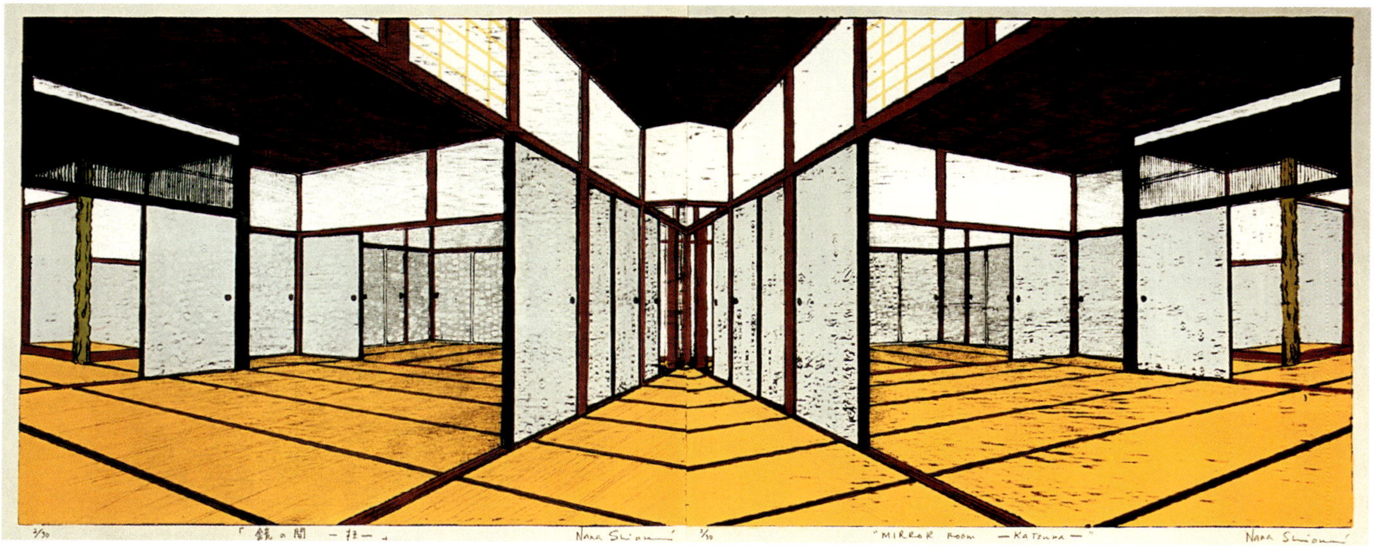

Mirror Room, Katsura, 2006. Woodcut, 45 x 120 cm ($17\frac{3}{4}$ x $47\frac{1}{4}$ in.)

When planning a colour print I mark out the composition on tracing paper in pencil, simply marking the outlines of each colour area and the position of the black lines which will form the framework of the image. I cut a number of birch-faced plywood blocks, identical in size and shape, one for each colour (except that more than one colour may be printed from a single block if they are apart on the surface and therefore can easily be inked separately). Next, I transfer the outlines from the tracing paper to the appropriate blocks using carbon paper and a ballpoint pen. An important departure from traditional methods is that whilst all my colour blocks are printed in relief, my key block prints the black lines in intaglio – that is, the lines are incised rather than cut in relief; this is because it would be more difficult in big sheets of plywood to cut fine lines in relief, and in any case my aim is expressive rather than simply to follow tradition. I use a modern knife and gouges for cutting the relief blocks; these should be kept very sharp with frequent use of a whetstone. I also use an electric

7th May 1956, 8th May 1956, 2005. Woodcut, 93 x 62 cm (36⅝ x 24⅜ in.)

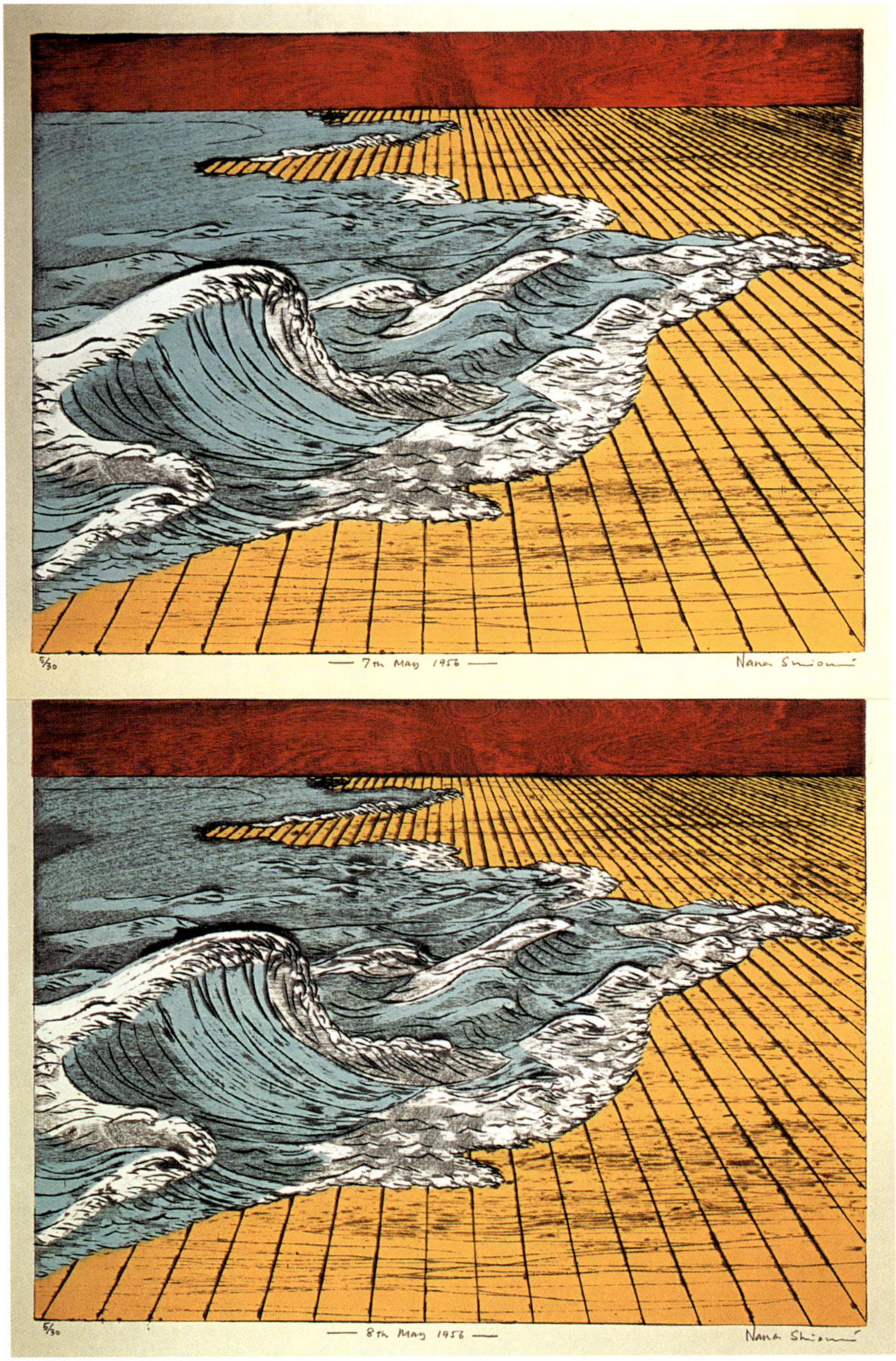

router, which makes removing extraneous wood much easier. When the cutting is complete I smooth all the printing surfaces, using fine glasspaper for a perfect finish. Japanese paper is extremely strong and durable, with long, intertwined fibres. I prepare twelve to fourteen sheets at a time, cutting them to size so that the prints will have a margin exactly as marked on an L-shaped registration board. I dampen the sheets, interleave them with blotting paper, wrap them in vinyl sheet, apply a weight and leave them overnight. I also soak my printing brushes to make them expand and to avoid losing hairs during printing.

For printing the relief blocks I use watercolour, gouache or Japanese poster colour. Water is a very important element in Japanese art, so I soak the block first and wipe it well with a wet towel. This helps the brushes to apply ink smoothly and also to remove excess ink if necessary. The damped paper is laid on the inked block and is burnished firmly to receive the colour. Burnishing is done either with a traditional baren – a coil of twisted fibre – or a modern version with small ball-bearings on its surface.

After each colour block has been printed in turn, the intaglio block is inked. This block will have been given several coats of satin varnish before being engraved. Like the relief blocks, this one will also be soaked and wiped well. Acrylic paint with a retarder medium is worked with a brush into the engraved furrows, and the surface ink is removed with a window-cleaning squeegee which glides easily over the varnished block. Again, the traditional baren is used to press down the paper and receive the ink, transferring the framework of black lines to the coloured sheet. This is basically the method used for printing etchings and, indeed, an etching press could be used for this part of the process, though a wooden bed and thick blankets are kinder to the block. The baren gives a soft, delicate result; the press a stronger print. After printing, the sheets are placed on a flat surface to dry and are then stacked and flattened under weights.

Sheila Sloss

I think I am slightly unusual for rarely sketching things first; I prefer the spontaneity of working directly onto plates or adding to prints. I like the excitement of not knowing exactly what will happen in a process of layering and collaging images. Image and concept are definitely to the fore in the final print, but I revel in having a wide technical vocabulary. Personal photographs are often incorporated into my prints and manipulated in some way, although I also value the handmade mark linking them. There is always a story unfolding behind my images if one keeps looking. Sometimes right at the start I have a moment's insight as to what the final image might look like and I quickly do a thumbnail sketch of it. When it's going off the mark, a glance at that thumbnail usually tells me why!

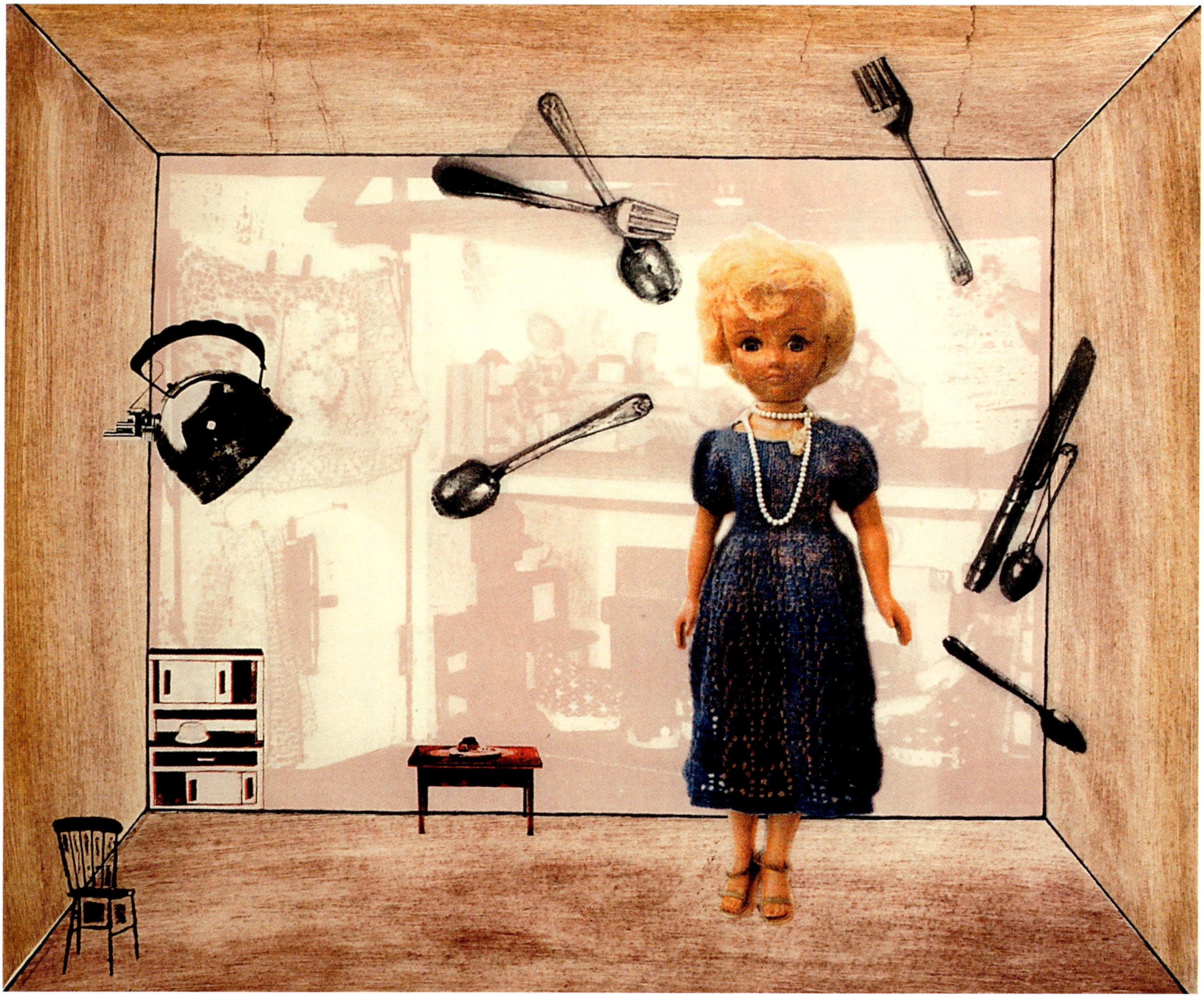

Watching – Dancing Dresses II, 2004.
Photolithography, collagraph, screenprint, 45 x 55 cm (17¾ x 21⅝ in.)

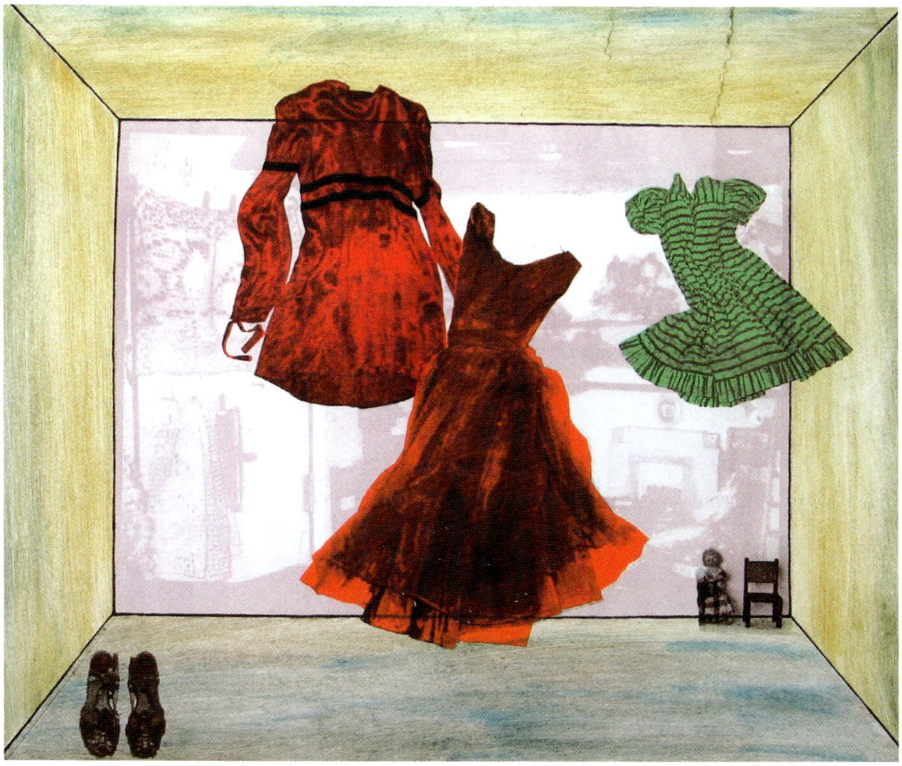

As a child I used my dolls' house and dolls to enact what I thought would happen in my adult life. When I looked at it again, 25 years later, I took the opportunity to reflect on what I had imagined.

The two illustrations shown here come from a series of five basic images. All the backgrounds are the same; they represent different scenes in the same room at different times of the day. The title of 'watching' in this series of prints refers to being an observer of life. It is signified by the empty chairs and the dynamic between them and the objects in view. The background 'wallpaper' is the interior of the dolls' house. It almost has the luminosity of a back projection, enhancing the viewer/watching theme. Each image is displayed with an equal white border, acting like a window frame. Although I had thumbnail sketches of the ideas, from the start I didn't want to define them exactly, preferring to let the image develop as I got immersed in it. I worked on four or five prints of each image, adding new layers or repositioning pieces of print as you might work into a painting until it achieves what you want. In that sense, each one is a monoprint. Each object in these prints has a significance to me. When I started using such personal references I feared it would be seen as narcissistic; but of course no one is unique and the viewer may see echoes of her or his own life in the prints.

Watching – Dancing Dresses II depicts three party frocks that were mine at different ages. They are fantasy wear for special occasions: a dress bought for a portrait photograph at age one; an expensive netting frock given to me when I was twelve and had nowhere to wear it; and a red-satin mini dress I purchased at twenty-one, to look cool. The dresses are empty because the owner has grown up; they are party memories and dreams recording time.

Watching – Domestic Chaos I features a 'grown-up' doll. Curiously, when I had finally packed her away as a child, she was wearing a knitted dress and a plastic set of pearls. I don't think this is what she was bought in. Her dilemma is that she is dressed to go out, but the domestic life threatens to keep her prisoner. The odd sizes of the objects in the image link importance to scale: the cutlery is enlarged from dolls' house size; the cupboard and table are almost true (doll) size; my current Alessi kettle flies in for good measure and, as ever, Grandad's empty kitchen chair looks on.

Technically, these are extremely complicated to print. What made it feasible is that they are images I had already worked on previously. The photolitho plate was made five years ago for an earlier work on the dolls' house theme, but then not used. The walls are simple, dry-printed collagraph. Some objects had already gone through other transformative processes before I added them in screen. Screenprint dances on the surface of the other processes, giving spatial layers.

I have made a lot of work on these themes since my father died ten years ago and I cleared out the real house. I think these will be the last; I too will move on to different themes.

Watching – Domestic Chaos I, 2004.
Photolithography, collagraph screenprint, 45 x 55 cm (17¾ x 21⅝ in.)

Sandy Sykes

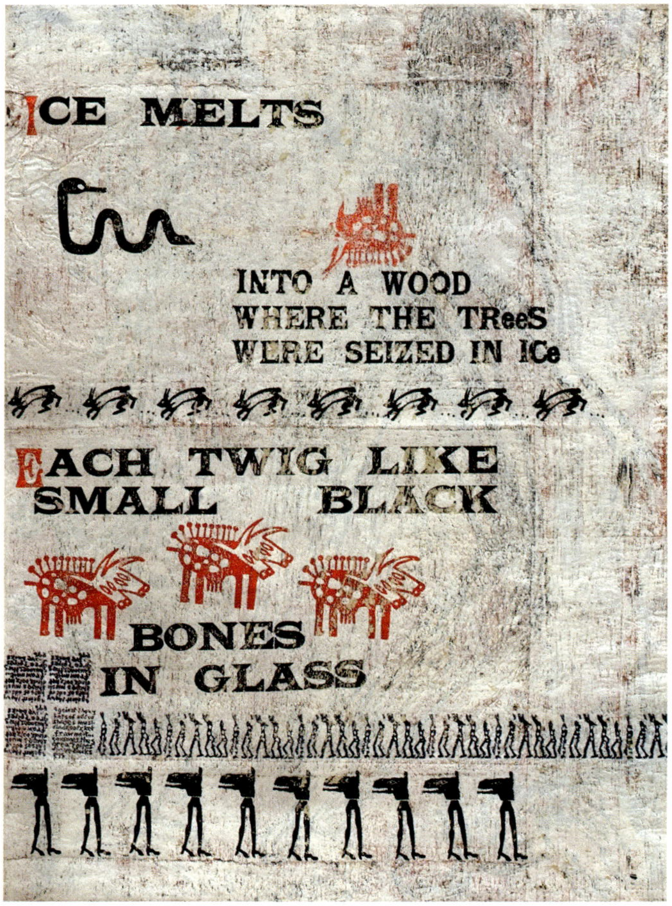

Manuscript 1: Ice, 2007. Hand-rubbed woodcut, *chine collé* and collage on Khadi ecological papers, approx. 150 x 100 cm (59 x 39 in.)

I live in the bleak wilds of the Essex marshes, beside the sea, though I was born and raised in Yorkshire. The loneliness of the views ache in the mind. My studio is an old wooden barn surrounded by fields, the estuary and the sky. Landscape is an essential part of my being and integral to my production. I do not paint landscapes but absorb them along with their inhabitants. I watch the behaviour of animals, birds, and insects; I take photos of clouds, the sea and the fields. These creatures and the natural movements of the elements leave significant marks and patterns in their wake. I record these shifting and ephemeral traces in sketchbooks, which are essential to the development of my ideas. The comedy and tragedy of animal posturing does not escape me; indeed it appears in my images, alluding to the social and political conduct of humans and its inevitable consequences.

I love the areas of margin – where the sea meets the land, and where earth and the sea meet the sky – just as we humans push or are pushed to the margins of passion, anger, despair and longing, where the edges bleed or blend as does colour in water on paper. Books, too, have long inspired me, from the Brontës to *Brer Rabbit* and from Dante Alighieri to Michael Ondaatje.

My latest prints are a series of 1 x 1.5 m (39 x 59 in.) hand-rubbed woodcuts on constructed Indian ecological paper; embodying many combinations of media and method, they are multilayered, collaged and complex of surface. Taking short texts from Cormac McCarthy's poetic novels, set in the pioneering days of the North American West, the prints refer obliquely to threatened changes in our landscape and the awesome repercussions for inhabitants of the earth. Entitled *Manuscript*, the series (containing 21 images) indicates my lifelong interest in ancient manuscripts and palimpsests, their accumulated dilapidation and their captured history held within the boundaries of the bindings. Fire damage, wormholes and mice nibbles taped and restored, text over text, cut and defaced, sewn and conserved; each century adding and taking away.

As history overlays itself within the confines of books, so structures are devised to keep nature useful for indigenous populations. I walk the tarred boulders of my local sea wall, cross the Roman earthwork with its ancient stone chapel and gaze over the worn wooden groynes stretching out into the mud at low tide, a forlorn attempt to tame the sea. I am aware of and in awe of earlier generations, each of which have devised solutions which are assimilated endlessly into the grand pattern of the next.

In this way I work at my prints, laying down surfaces and rejecting the smoothness of a single large sheet, preferring to join paper together to create seams, joins, inconsistencies and problems. The paper is thin,

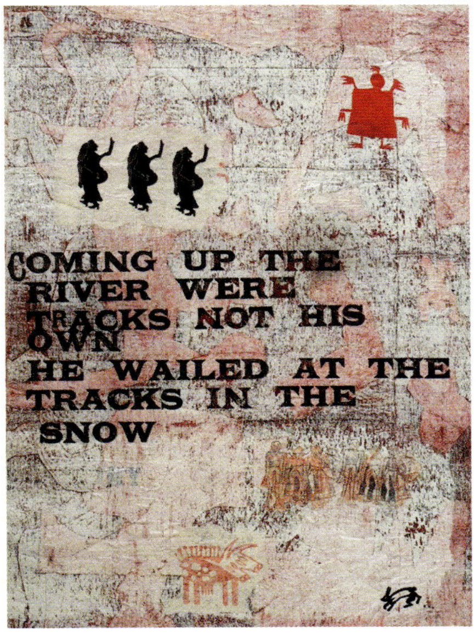

Manuscript 2: Tracks, 2007. Hand-rubbed woodcut, *chine collé* and collage on Khadi ecological papers, approx.150 x 100 cm (59 x 39 in.)

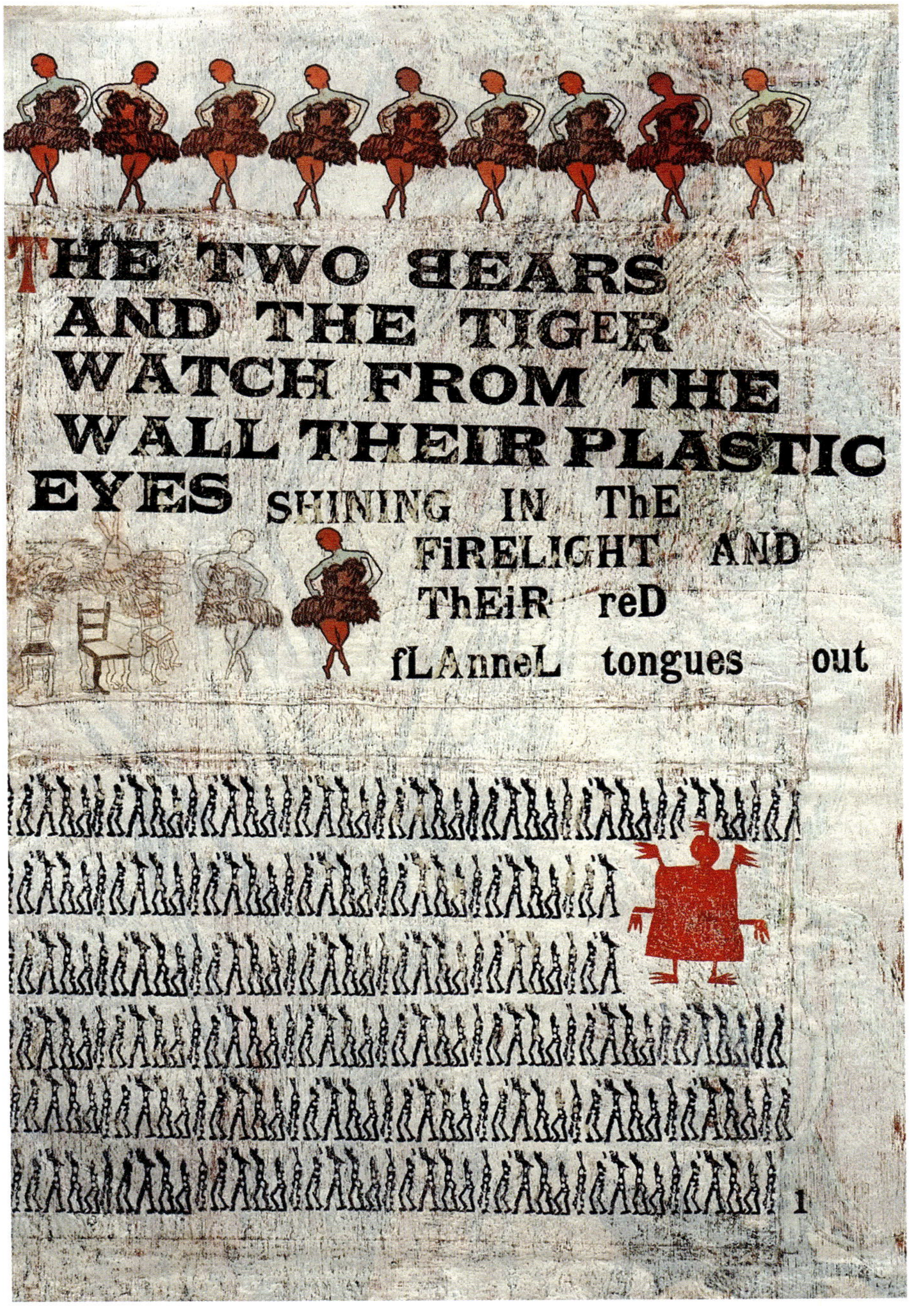

Manuscript 3: Bears, 2007. Hand-rubbed woodcut, *chine collé* and collage on Khadi ecological papers, approx. 150 x 100 cm (59 x 39 in.)

often fragile and misshapen, allowing ink to seep through and stain the other side. I ink up large weathered boards which have had other purposes before I found them. They hold evidence of former human intervention and the marks of rain, sun and wind, nails and mechanical tools. I am building on history.

I mix inks – sometimes thick, sometimes thin – with slow- or fast-drying medium. I consult the sky. Is it winter or summer? How long have I got? How long an intervention between inking and drying do I need? Do I want to add imagery through collage or *chine collé*? Or not? Get on with the rubbing, wooden spoon, glass mortar, baren or cloth. Pencils to scratch imagery, tissue to remove ink, tears to mend with patches selected from my box of accumulated print remnants on papers and tissues, gleaned carefully through the harvest of former printings. Text, image – plain or fancy – all are grist to the mill. Do I need more carving? What wood, what tools? What if I make a mess? All mistakes can be rectified, nothing is too risky. Sew it, stick it, replace or cut out, stencil, blot, scream! Leave it for another day – I have plenty of others to work on. When will I know it's finished? When I cannot add or take away any more. When it invites the quiet contemplation of landscape.

Tobias Till

I have always been drawn to architecture and was impressed by the underlying physics governing the curves of this rollercoaster, Colossus. *Not only did I find the structure beautiful but it also reminded me of Paul Klee's description of drawing as 'taking a line for a walk'. I made many drawings, some from ground level and others from an aerial perspective.*

The drawings became progressively more complex as I attempted to describe almost the entire rollercoaster and found that the aerial viewpoint gave a greater feeling of involvement with the ride. In order to enhance the visual elegance of the track's curves I had to reposition and omit many of the supporting posts.

All my lino prints up to this point had been printed in two or three colours. With *Colossus* I wanted to describe the turquoise of the track contrasted against the orange/ochre sandstone and ultramarine sky. This complicated the process in that each object needed a corresponding shadow colour, and these also had to be blended and modified to create a feeling of distance and space. As I was using the reduction method, I was aware that there was no going back and that with each additional layer I was increasing the potential for mistakes. In order to get the most accurate registration, I printed on a board that had two protruding nails on two corners. The paper was then perforated by the nails so I could be confident that I could repeatedly align the paper with the plate. I have found that variations in humidity affect the size of the paper and this has to be compensated for in the registration. It may also be that the slight indentation of the paper into the block during previous printings has an effect on a large-scale print.

Since I was unsure if I could get so many overprintings aligned correctly, I printed two versions of the image. A dozen were printed with only two colours in the foreground faces, and a further twelve were printed with three. I also experimented by printing some colours light over dark and others dark on light. The water area was deliberately under-inked by lifting some of the ink from the plate. I did this by placing tracing paper on the inked plate and rubbing with my fingers the areas that were to print lighter.

Westway was printed from one lino block, again using the reduction method. The block was printed three times before I did any significant cutting. I cut small markers into the lino to indicate an intended colour change, since all my drawing would be obscured after the block had been inked up. These cuts would mark the transition from the orange glow of the sky to the dark brown that is the base colour for the majority of the buildings. The areas of light were printed, allowing the ink to fade out as it got further from the source of light. The tower blocks were difficult to roll, given their shape and size, so I used a scraper to apply ink directly to the block. I didn't mind an uneven inking since it would be closer to the natural variation in colour that one might expect to see through windows at night. The beams from the floodlights were under-inked and then blotted before printing so as to leave a haze of colour. The same colour was then re-used, but thicker this time to print the lighter tone of the figures. Before the final printing I realised that some areas needed to be accented, so I applied some off-white ink with a finger; this was then blotted to remove any fingerprints and surplus ink.

All of my prints are pressed with a hand roller and a few specific areas are burnished occasionally with a spoon where necessary. I kneel on the back of the print, which helps to keep the paper still while I roll the reverse of the paper. This also allows me to put my full bodyweight onto the roller. The inks I use are oil-based.

Colossus, 2005. Linocut, 90 x 135 cm ($35\frac{3}{8}$ x $53\frac{1}{8}$ in.)

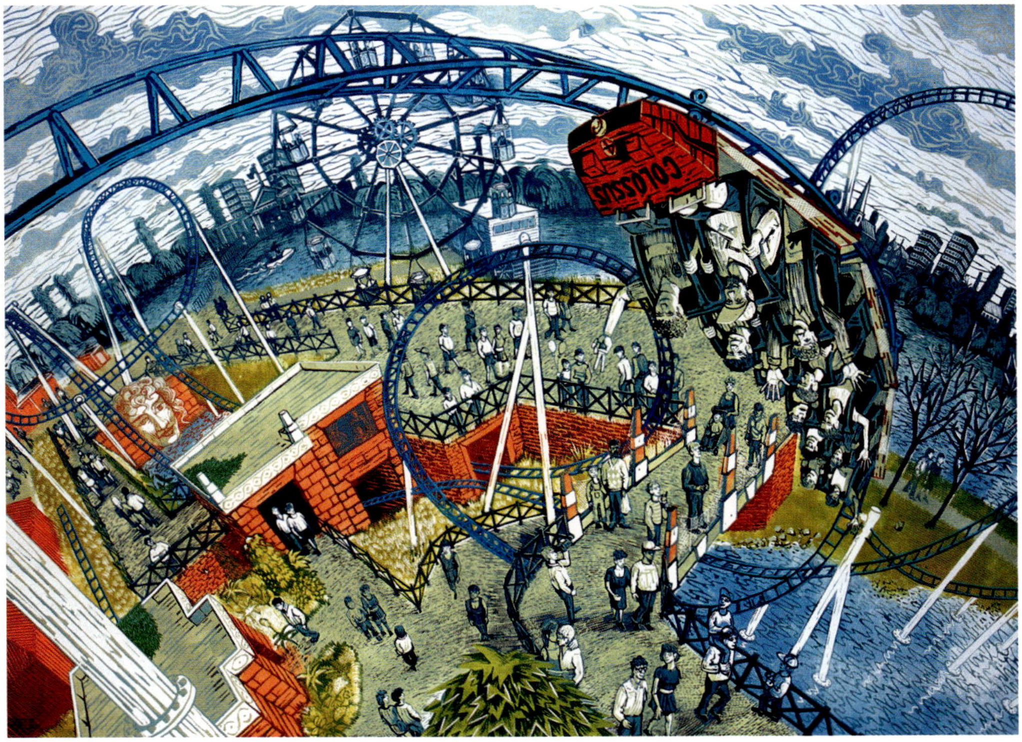

Westway, 2007. Linocut, 85.5 x 121.5 cm ($33\frac{5}{8}$ x $47\frac{3}{4}$ in.)

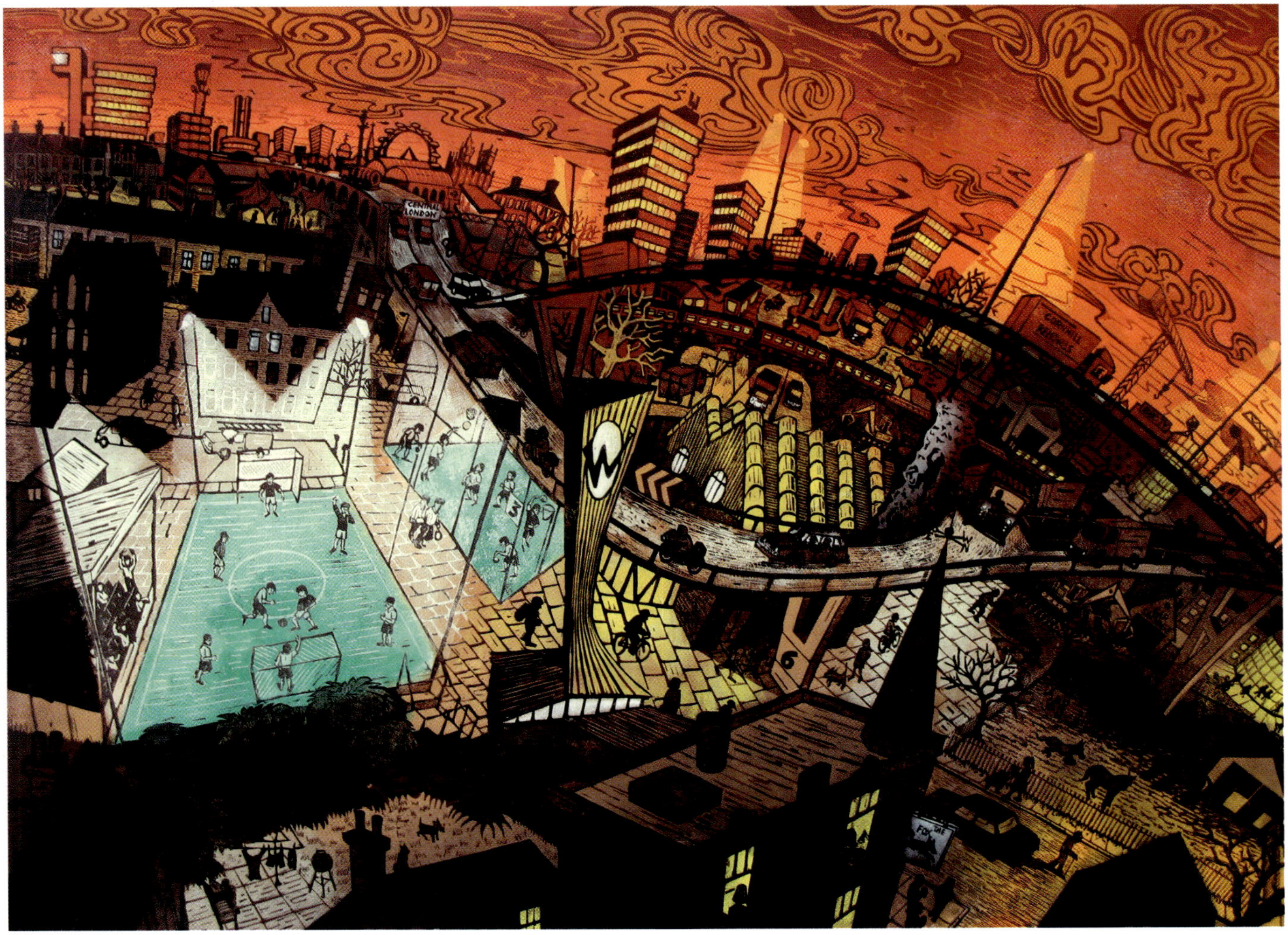

James Todd

I decided early in my career to try for, and was lucky enough to get, an academic position to teach art. I wanted a regular income so that I could keep my subjects and techniques free from the necessity of becoming a commercial artist or so that I didn't have to depend on a livelihood governed by the market pressures of the gallery world; both of these means of earning a living can, in their own ways, restrict artists in their range of styles, methods and ideas.

In graduate school I specialised in printmaking, and when I finished I could not afford the press that is necessary for intaglio and lithographic printing. However, relief printing allowed me to cut and print my wood engravings and woodcuts by hand and, since I travelled a lot, the few materials I needed for relief prints made it possible for me to carry my 'workshop' in a handbag. As the years progressed, I planned eventually to buy a press, but with time I came to prefer hand-printing because I felt that the burnishing I do to produce the final print is an extension of the original drawing and cutting stages. With time, I developed a spontaneous and layered method for cutting my engravings that is like my approach to painting and which accommodates my hand-printing: I engrave small cuts spontaneously, cut upon cut, with assorted tools, until I achieve the desired effect. My facility at hand-printing with a steel burnisher allows me to exert sufficient surface pressure to print my woodcuts on very heavy coloured papers. Moreover, a few years ago I began hand-colouring these prints with acrylic paint, used opaquely or transparently. Rather than going through pre-planned colour stages that require a block or stencil for each colour, I can approach the colouring of a woodcut with the same freedom as in my painting; and if I wish to make an edition, I can duplicate the colours of the print from a photo or a copy of the original.

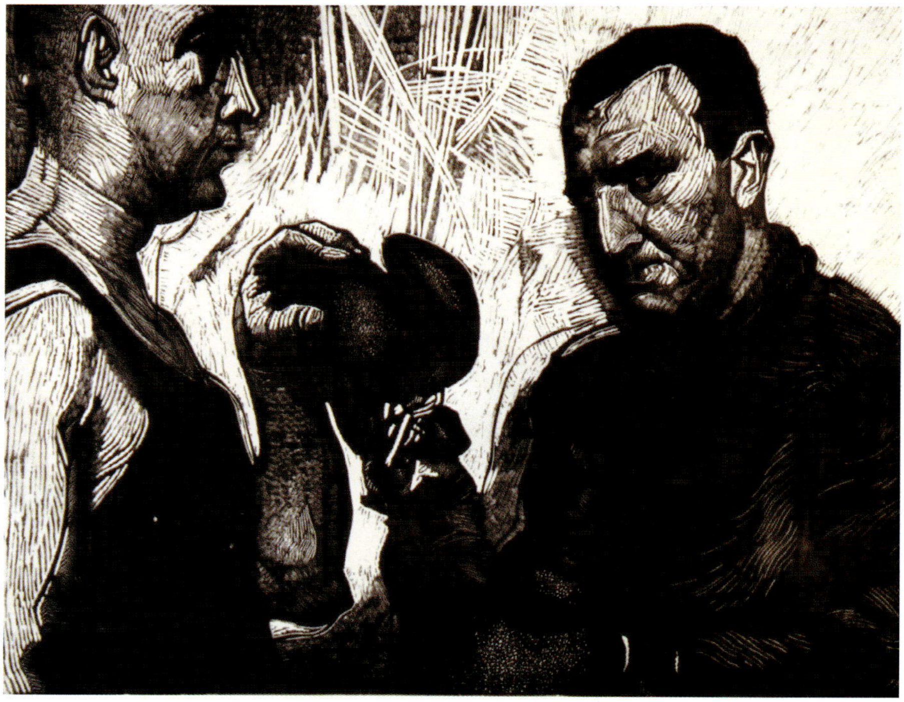

Georg Grosz with Boxer, 1984. Wood engraving, 30 x 40 cm (11¾ x 15¾ in.)

While these approaches are hardly practical for the efficiency and speed needed for commercial or commissioned printmaking, they give me the time and creative freedom to treat each print as if it is an original one-time affair, unique up to a point, but a monoprint rather than a monotype. And whenever it is necessary, I can and do use a press

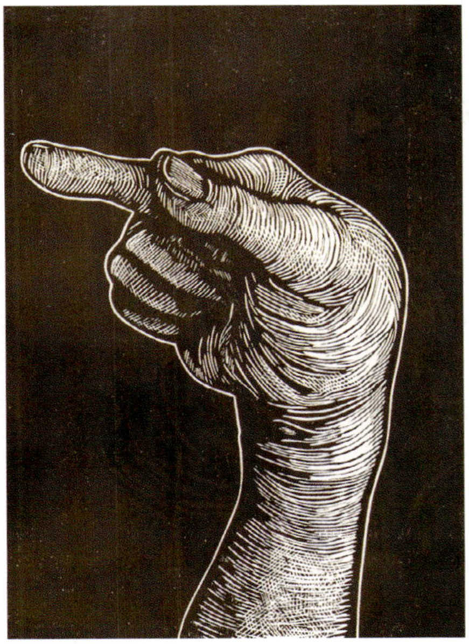

God, 2007. Woodcut, 40 x 30 cm (15¾ x 11¾ in.)

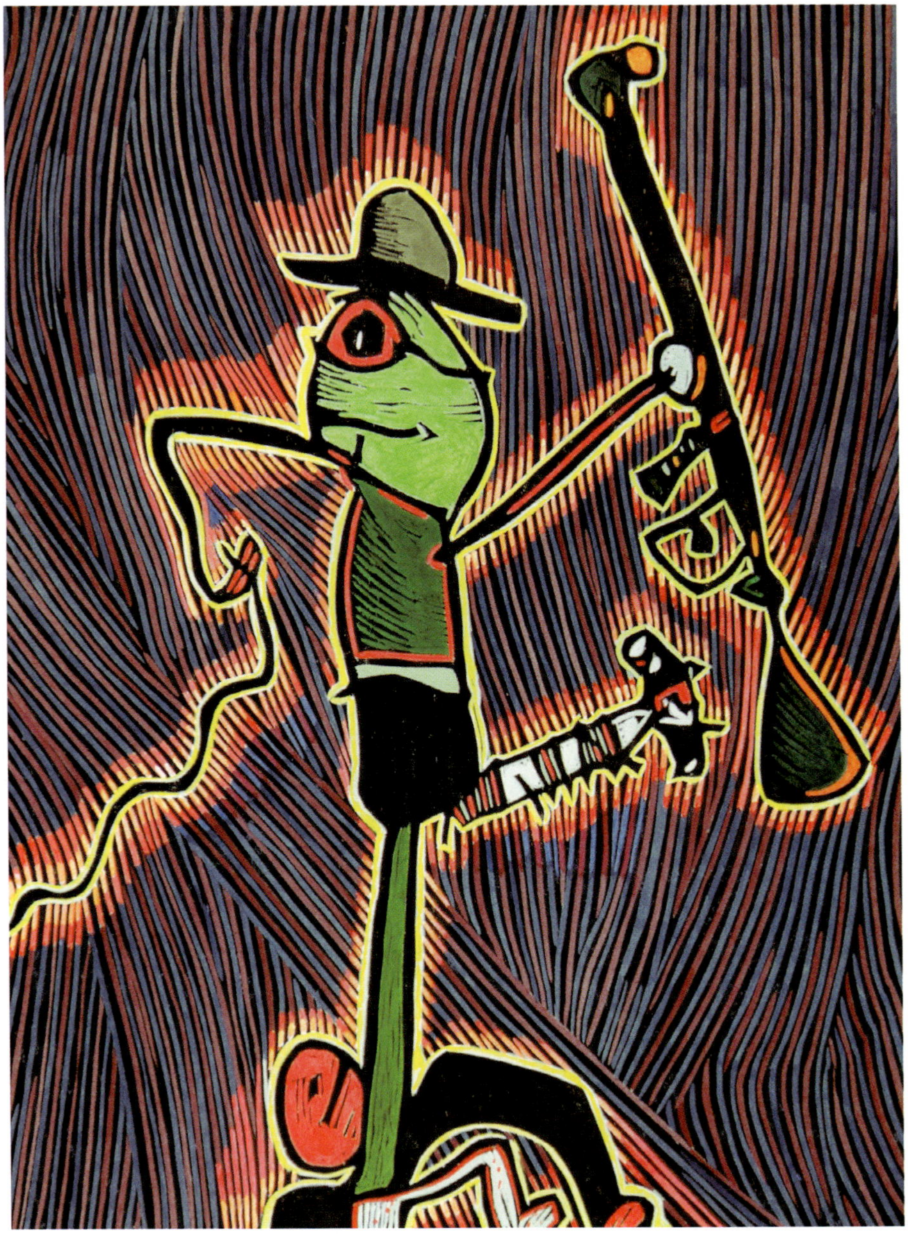

The Victor, 2006. Hand-coloured woodcut, 40 x 30 cm (15¾ x 11¾ in.)

despite my favouring burnishing.

In general, I believe it is helpful for artists to have a wide range of creative techniques to help them meet the different formal and expressive demands of their ideas and not consciously to confine themselves to a single 'signature' style; such flexibility I believe develops naturally and unconsciously on its own anyway, much as do our individual styles of handwriting. If nothing else, variation allows us to escape the monotony of always doing something the same way.

The content of my work tends to be social and includes portraiture. I have been influenced by early European Modernists and 20th-century Mexican and German political artists – Diego Rivera, Georg Grosz and Käthe Kollwitz, for example. I am interested in the new digital and computer methods of printmaking and, if I were a young artist, I might work more extensively with them, but at 70 I prefer to use my remaining years to try and complete my many unfinished projects with the means I know best.

Ann Tout

My first fruit engraving was inspired by the construction of the Newbury bypass, which prompted some of the largest protests seen in Europe. I gathered my ideas about this conflict in an engraving called Gravity*: a play on words, depicting a grave situation in an engraving about Newton's apple. In this print, I have distorted the perspective so that the tiny figure of Newton is surprised and threatened by the massive apple hurtling towards him. The print led to a growing fascination with various fruit and the symbolism embodied in them. I have since engraved a series of prints encompassing ideas surrounding particular fruit with a mixture of serious and light-hearted symbolism.*

There are times when ideas flow readily and I draw and engrave fluently. However, when I am blocked I go into the garden, where I get absorbed by tending the plants, pruning and weeding. Eventually, the tension eases and I am inspired to return to my block of wood.

Hospitality Unmasked was an extremely demanding subject because of the constructional twists in the pineapple. I started by drawing the fruit, to study and understand its idiosyncrasies, and the masked faces began to emerge. The title of the engraving is derived partly from the use of the pineapple in the 18th century as a symbol of hospitality, still to be seen on many of the grand buildings of that time; it is also partly a reference to the rather sinister traditional Venetian masks and beaked faces.

When I think I am ready to transfer the design to the block, I study it in a mirror so that I can see how reversal will affect the image when printed. This often surprises me and allows for a more critical appraisal of the design and perhaps further adjustments.

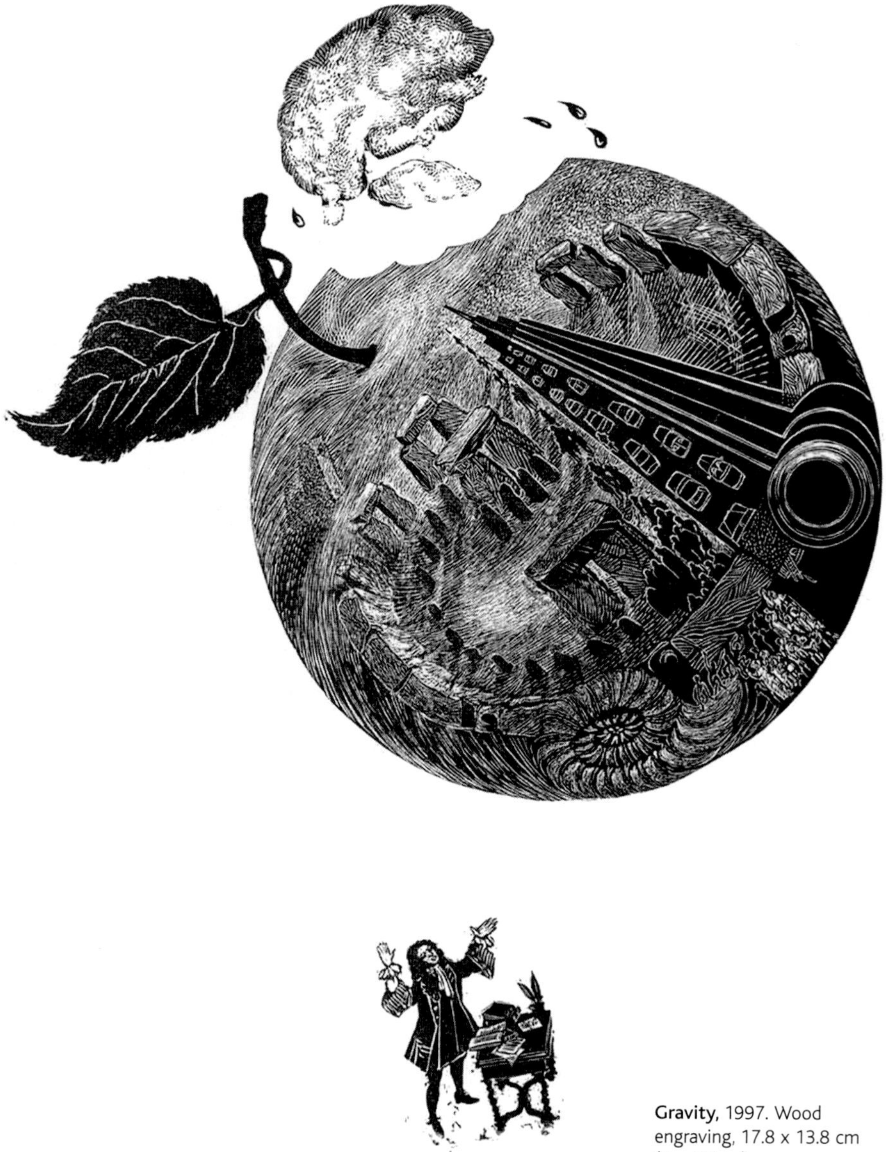

Gravity, 1997. Wood engraving, 17.8 x 13.8 cm (7 x 5½ in.)

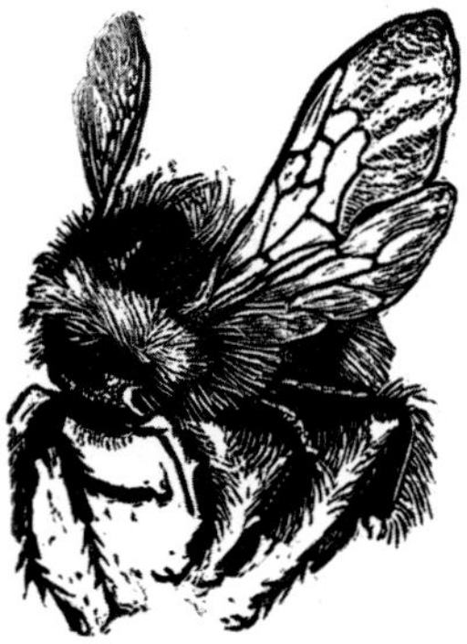

Bumble Bee, 1995. Wood engraving, 3.55 x 2.6 cm (1⅜ x 1 in.)

Occasionally, I work on very small blocks. Because these are often offcuts and therefore not as precious as the larger pieces of boxwood that I use for more serious prints, I am more relaxed and can freely enjoy myself, depicting scenes from life without any of the tension that normally builds up. These smaller prints are derived from studies in my sketchbook.

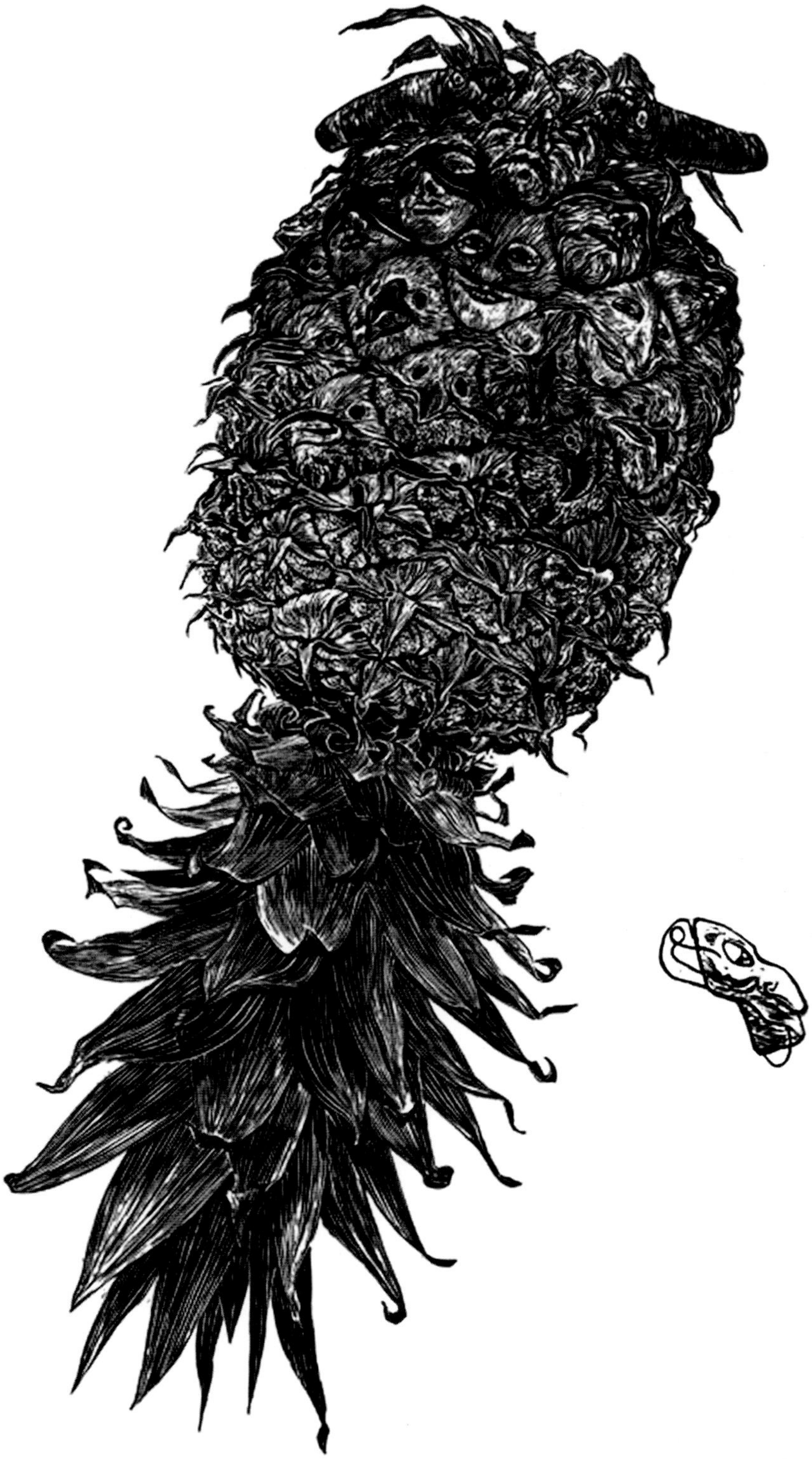

Hospitality Unmasked, 2001. Wood engraving, 21 x 12 cm (7⅞ x 4¾ in.)

Bren Unwin

In the far west of Cornwall, just off the north coast and on the south-facing side of a valley, in a landscape characterised by its wild and treeless terrain, is a small parcel of land that I know as 'the quillet' – an ancient term for a modest strip of ground. I took possession of the quillet several years ago and, over time, it has gradually become central to the ideas that inform my printmaking. This area of Cornish landscape is a place far from the multifarious challenges and pace of existence that distinguish life at the beginning of the 21st century; it has become a location for inspiration and reflection, and a practical resource for the many tools and techniques that lead to the marks created on the copper plates used within my printmaking.

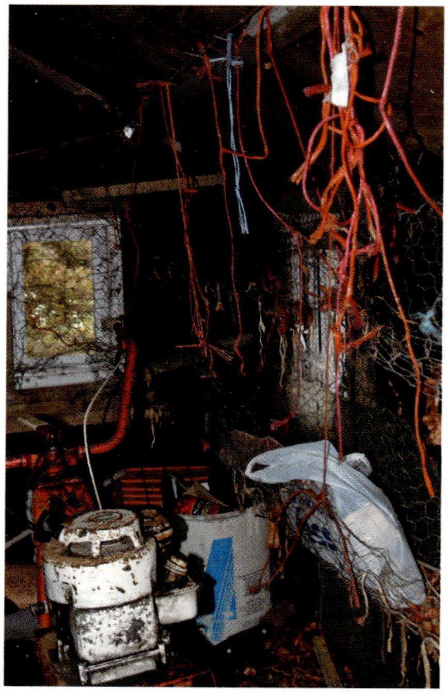

Onion Shed, the quillet. Photograph: Bren Unwin

The character and qualities of the quillet in the present era are significantly determined by its history. The land not only bears scars from its role in the tin-mining industry but also has strong traces of more recent activity. In particular, a range of tools and detritus that has accumulated over many years is contained in and around the various sheds that were intended both for shelter and for storing the implements used for working the land. Many of the tools and remaining artefacts have been incorporated into my printmaking processes. Also, for a while, I used an old mangle, purchased from a junk shop in the nearby town of St Just, and with it made rough-and-ready prints from all sorts of objects and imagery inspired by my experiences on the quillet.

As my repertoire of printmaking processes has developed, I have employed more complex techniques that use artefacts and ideas from the

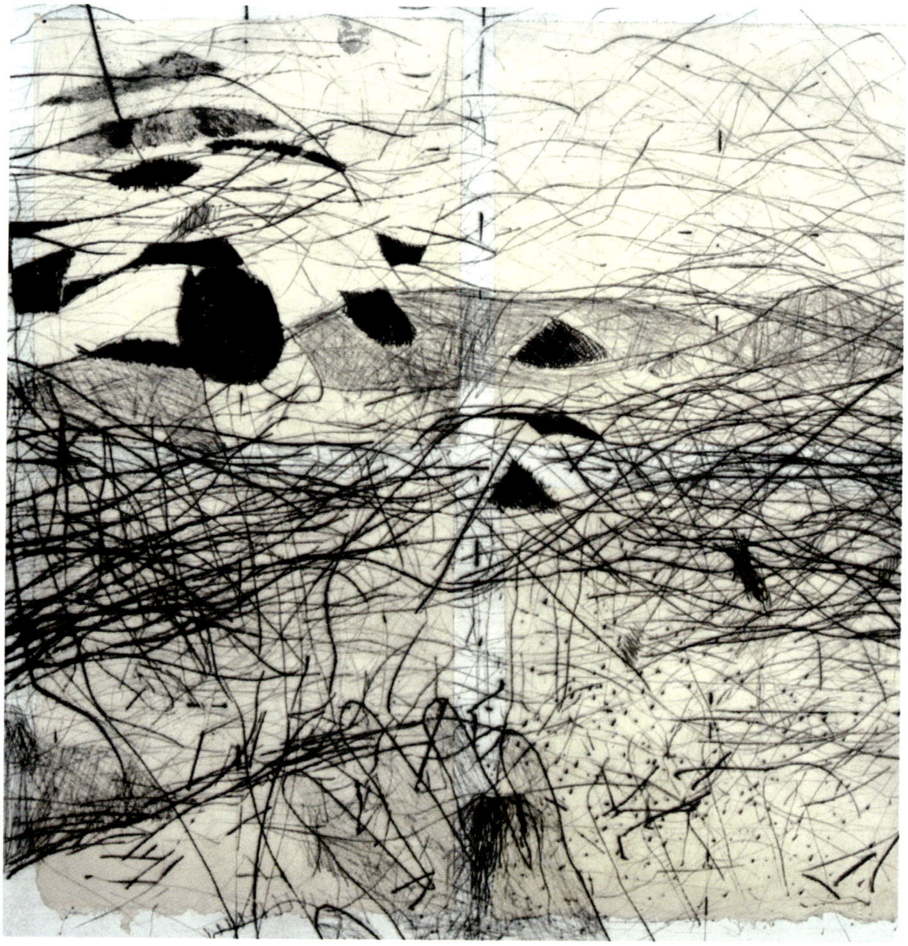

Above: **Chiasmus: Quillet series,** 11th state, 2008. Drypoint and etching, reverse relief, 40 x 40 cm (15¾ x 15¾ in.)
Opposite: **Chiasmus: Quillet series,** 7th state, 2008. Drypoint with *chine collé*, 40 x 40 cm (15¾ x 15¾ in.)

quillet. Various intaglio and relief processes are used in conjunction with collage, *chine collé*, drypoint, carborundum and many monotype techniques. Layers are built up within the work that might be considered analogous to the palimpsest of the landscape – a term used in this context to denote a change in land use whereby its current usage changes but doesn't completely eradicate its former use. As the prints develop, both through reflection and activity, within the landscape and also in my studio, the final artwork reveals evidence of my experience unfolding over time. Such evidence confirms both the experience of the processes involved in making the print and my ongoing association with the quillet.

Carol Walklin

My interest in art was evident when, as a child, I would sit at a table with my older sister's Phaidon book on Botticelli open in front of me and copy, in pencil, the detail of some of the faces. I was fascinated then, as I am still, with the infinite variety of the human face. I like to study the faces of the congregation on television's Songs of Praise, *and can be happily absorbed in observing people on a railway station concourse. As an art student I admired Rembrandt's drawings, the colour in Matthew Smith's paintings and, later, the deceptively simple illustrations of Edward Ardizzone. The printmakers who impressed me then (and now) are: Picasso, for his versatility and bravado; Gertrude Hermes and Edward Bawden, for their great technical skills; and Anthony Gross, for the delicacy of his etched line. When I worked in the publicity business as a graphic designer I sometimes used linocuts as the major part of a design; and my enthusiasm for printmaking was enhanced when, in the 1970s, I joined a print workshop and began to relearn and improve my skills in relief printmaking, lithography and etching, working just for myself.*

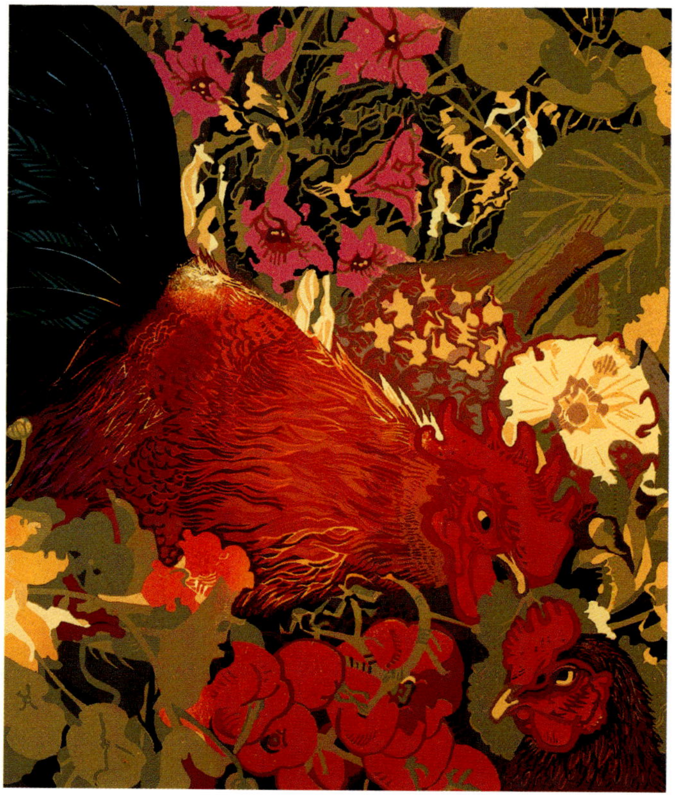

Compost Heap at Waterperry (detail). Linocut, 47 x 38 cm (18½ x 15 in.)

My subject matter is wide in scope. Some may be unusual in itself, while at other times ordinary things are juxtaposed and transformed into the extraordinary. The *Compost Heap at Waterperry*, with its assortment of natural forms, is comprised mainly of detritus, the discarded, but is reinvented to become beautiful.

I work in a range of media, each with its own discipline. When making a linocut (especially in the elimination method, as in the *Compost Heap*) I work progressively to develop and complete the single image; but when etching, I may return many times over quite a long period to adjust work on my plate. My resolution for the future is to experience more of the technical and expressive variations one can achieve with etching while continuing to work in relief printing in colour.

To return to subject matter, perhaps portrait prints give me most satisfaction. My own example here is the portrait of Maggie Smith, *The Lady in the Van or Mr Bennett's Dilemma.* This is different from my other portraits in that it was uncommissioned, evolving from a scribble done in the darkness of the theatre. Initially, I made a key drawing. Then to make the unique print, I assembled layers of printed paper, florists' wrapping paper and small jigsaws of lino, cut and overprinted to define the figure. The double portrait of Alan Bennett, puppets in Miss Shepherd's pocket, completes the image. It met with Mr Bennett's approval – an accolade of no small importance!

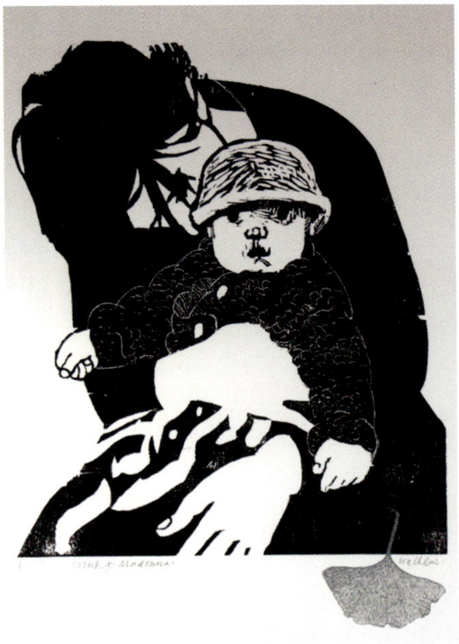

Ginkgo Madonna. Woodcut, 43.5 x 32 cm (17⅛ x 12⅝ in.)

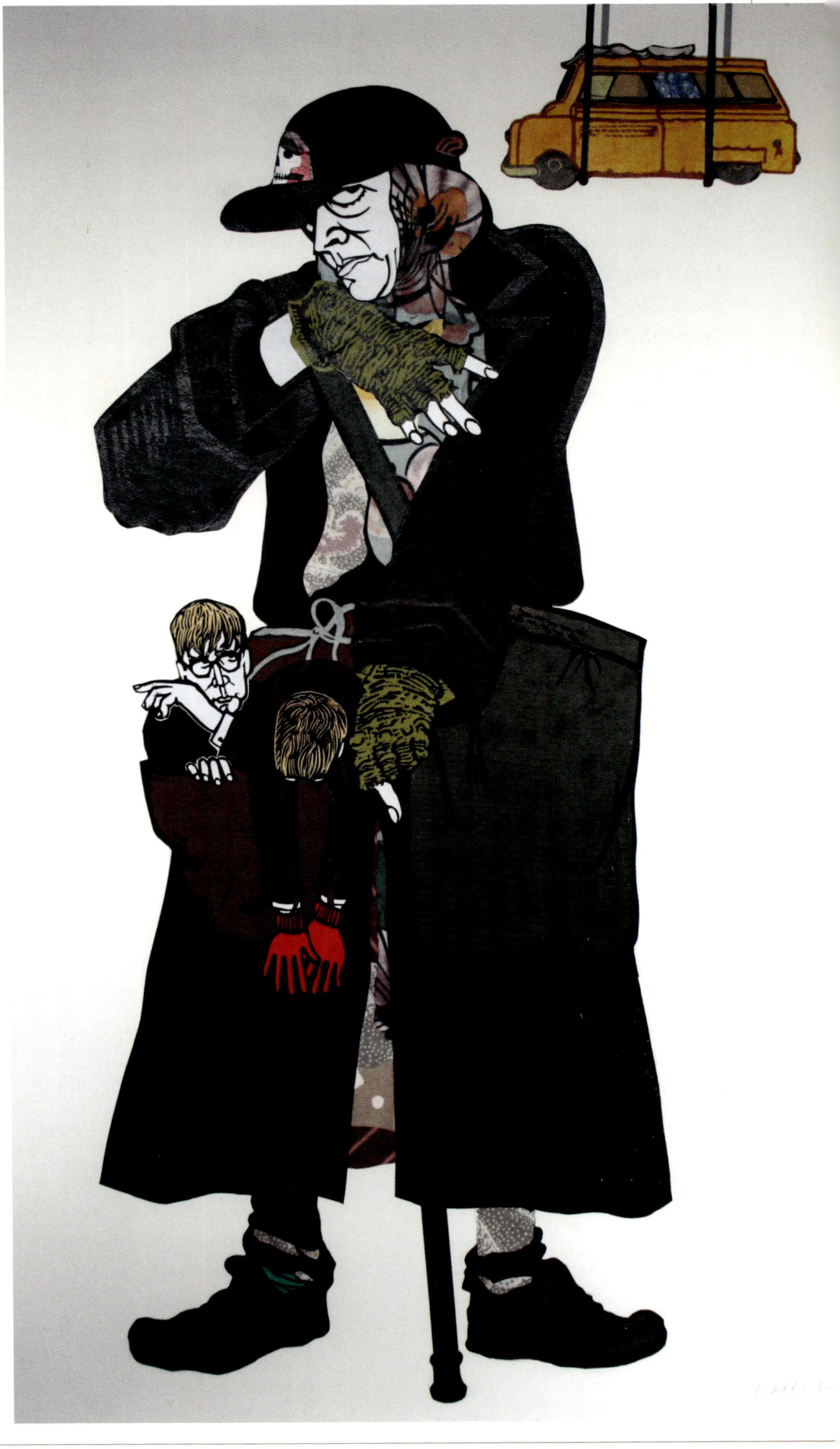

The Lady in the Van or Mr Bennett's Dilemma. Unique print with collage, 78 x 52 cm (30¾ x 20½ in.)

Jim Westergard

More than fifty years ago our high-school teacher of creative writing advised the class to search for topics within ourselves and to write from our own experience. That advice stayed with me because it seemed so absurd at the time. I figured that a lazy seventeen-year-old with life experience limited to choosing acne medicines, struggling to get an English essay written in twenty minutes and working out how to unhook a girl's bra from the front didn't have much worth writing about; but when my goal shifted from becoming a writer to becoming an artist I could still hear Mr Thornley's advice.

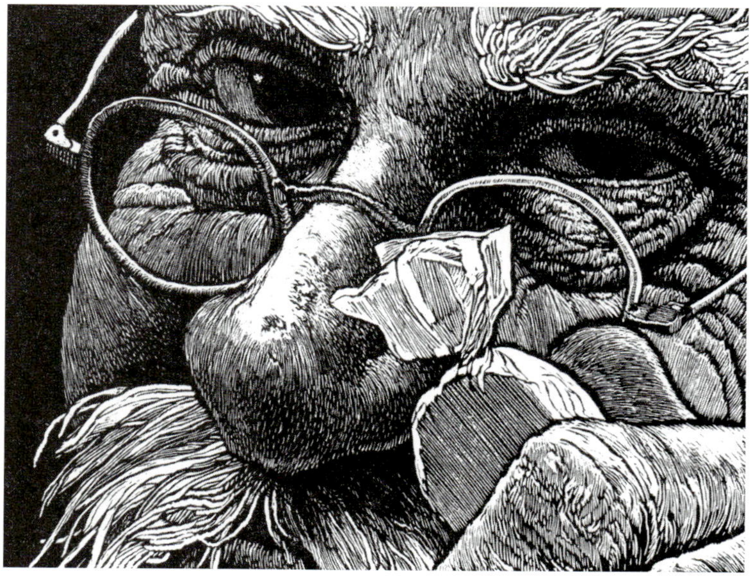

Georgy Porgy (ret), 2000. Wood engraving, 7.5 x 10 cm (3 x 4 in.)

Now, whenever I need to search for a topic or theme, I graze in my pasture of images. For years I have collected, from magazines and newspapers, photographs and articles that have caught my attention and have filed them in an old cabinet in my studio. Also in the collection are photographs I've taken myself, sketchbooks, written records of ideas and quotations. This collection is the measure of what intrigues me; in order to understand myself, I simply have to consider the kind of source material I collect. A patron who was studying my work once asked me, insightfully, 'Has anyone ever told you you're weird?' I smiled and nodded, knowingly.

Two themes have played a major role in the images I create. The first is the symbol of the mask, as described by Octavio Paz in his book *Labyrinth of Solitude*, which I read prior to a university term in Mexico; this had a profound impact on me. The second is the metamorphosis which occurs as we age. One day, I looked in the mirror and noticed on my face the same wrinkles and sagging skin which had fascinated me in my grandparents and, later, my parents. My prints and drawings have been strongly influenced by these themes since that day when I became aware of my own erosion.

Another moment from my past has had an influence on the direction of my work; it occurred during a seminar in graduate school while we were debating issues of content and processes in art. The professor asked the question, 'What good is having something to say if you don't have the technical skills to express it?' There was only a very brief moment of silence before a wise and quick-witted student retorted with, 'What good is having technical skills if you have nothing to say?' I would say that both questions are important, though I tend to value the second one rather more.

Now I Lay Me Down to Sleep, 2000.
Wood engraving, 10 x 12.7 cm (4 x 5 in.)

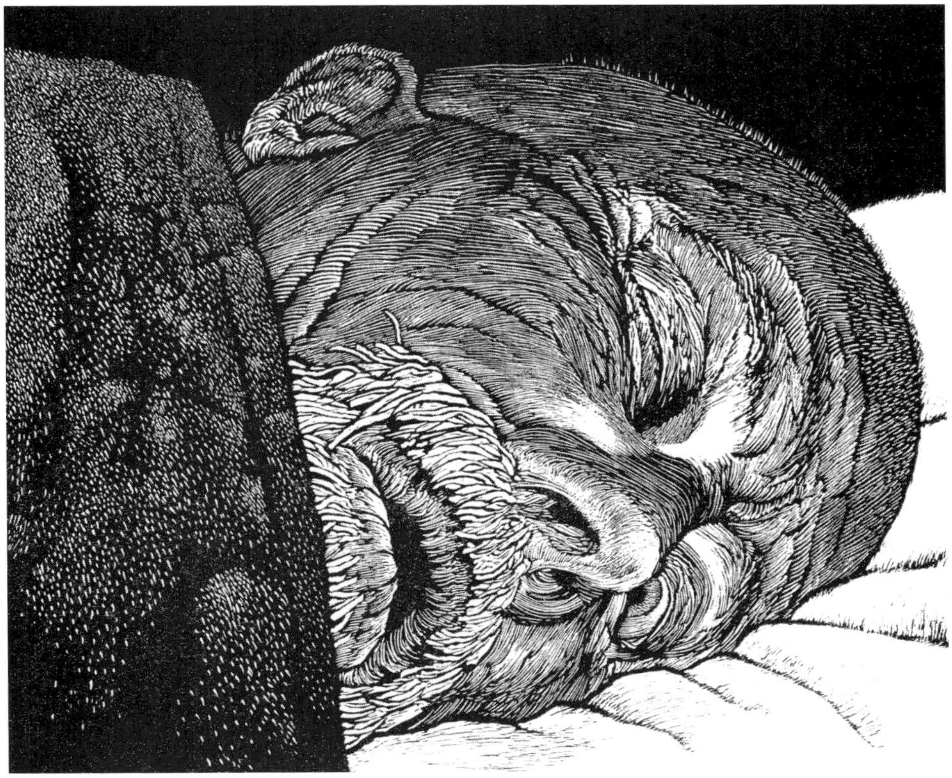

Loose Mask, 1994. Wood engraving, 12 x 20 cm (4 x 8 in.)

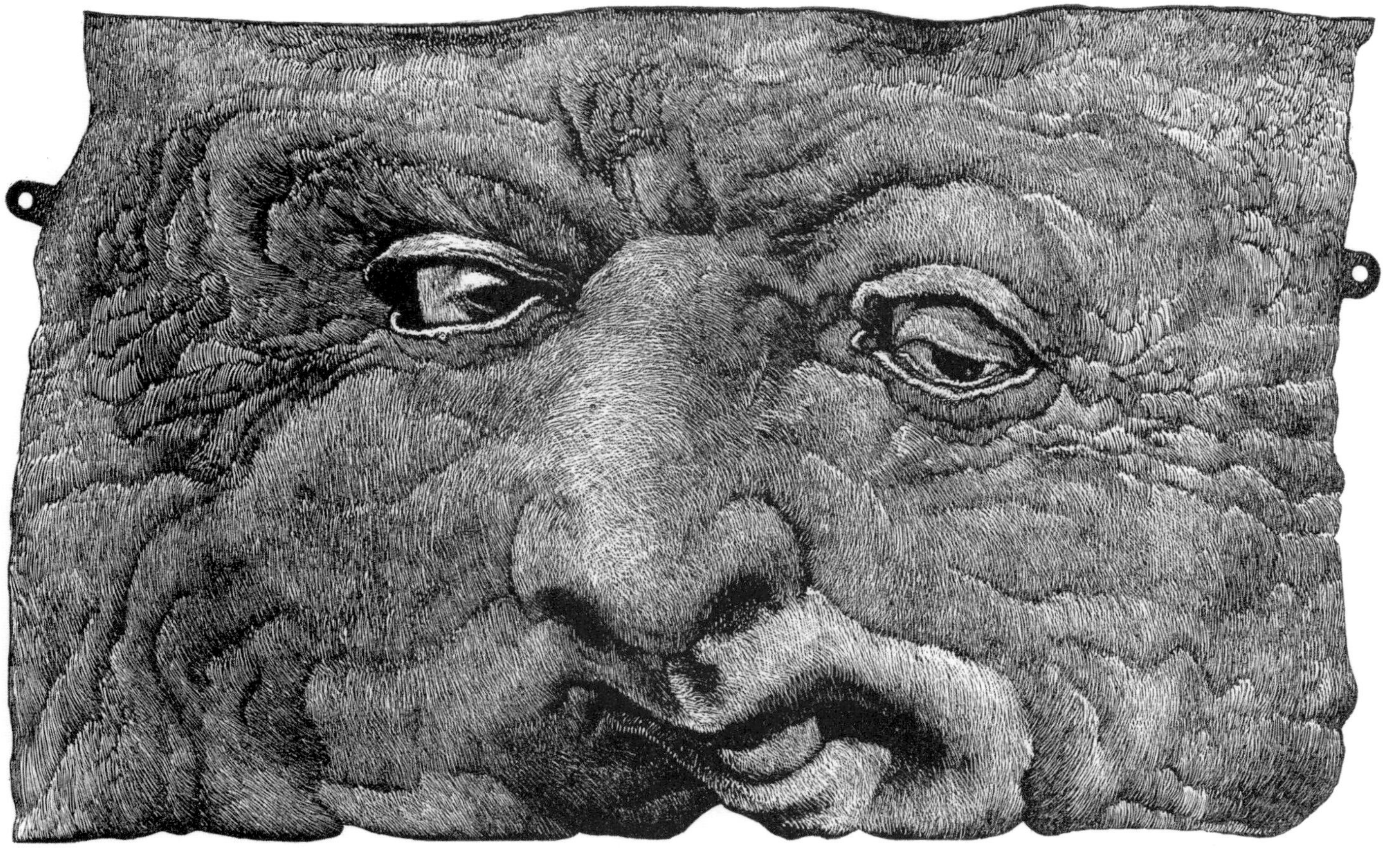

Annie Williams

Currently, my etchings are still-life compositions. I work entirely in aquatint from a sketch or watercolour, with no framework of etched line. I make a simple pencil tracing of my design and transfer it by laying it drawing side down on the grounded plate, covering it with damped blotting paper and running it through the press. If the transferred outlines are rather faint I go over them gently with a soft pencil. This gives me sufficient guidance for the stopping-out, in which my development of the image is rather like painting a watercolour in reverse. That is, I begin by stopping out the areas that in the finished print are to be highlights (whilst in watercolour I begin by painting the darkest colours). Then, after a brief immersion in the acid, I rinse and dry the plate and stop out the areas that are to be palest in tone, and so on, until after several successive stoppings-out I arrive at the darkest tones.

I work on zinc, giving the plate seven or eight bites in nitric acid diluted with water in the ratio of 1 part acid to 10 parts water. Precautions should, of course, always be taken when handling acids or alkalis (see glossary entries 'nitric acid' and 'ferric chloride'). I start with four to eight seconds, and each successive bite is for double the duration of the previous one. To help me to work on the plate in reverse, I use a mirror held at a convenient angle by a simple wooden stand, with my original design placed on the table in front of it.

When I haven't got access to a proper aquatint box I've used a cardboard box 15-inch cube, carefully sealed at all edges and with a separate wooden board inside forming a base. I cut a letterbox slot in one side, just above the baseboard, and having put a small mound of resin dust into the box I temporarily tape up the slot and give the box a good roll and shake, before quickly inserting the plate on an open-mesh rack with a handle – a

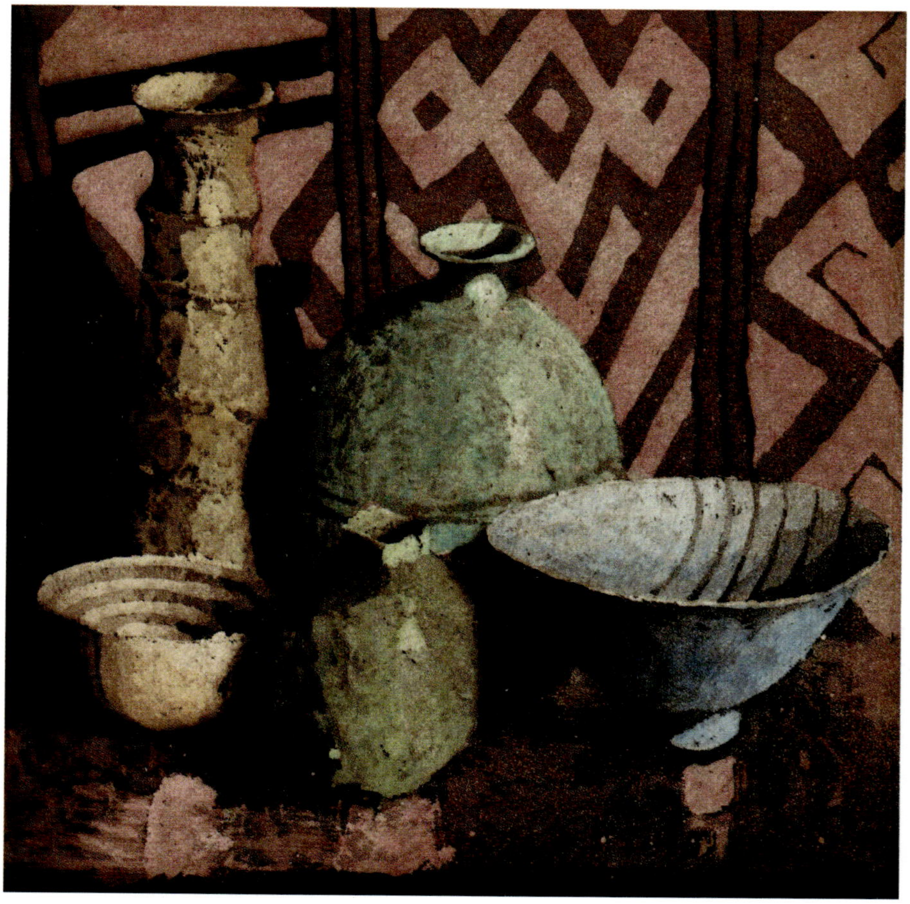

Zig-Zag, 2003. Aquatint and wash, 15 x 15 cm (6 x 6 in.)

frying-pan splash guard. The swirling dust inside settles onto the plate to produce an even covering which is melted over heat to form the ground. As an alternative to the box I sometimes sprinkle the resin through a muslin bag to get a grainier ground. **Aquatint resin should be used with great care, ideally in a specially designated room. My improvised method takes place in a well-ventilated space, even outdoors if weather permits; and I always wear a mask.**

I have very rarely completed a plate in one go, often repeating the biting several times and equally often having to lighten areas that have overbitten. I will sometimes open-bite these for a short time, but this can be quite tricky as you can lose everything and end up with a slight ridge at the boundaries of the biting; this may need scraping or burnishing down. However, open bite works well if you get the timing right.

I print most of my plates in burnt or raw umber, sometimes with a little black added. I am attracted by old sepia photographs and think that my images printed simply in black look rather heavy-handed. I sometimes print in two colours of ink and then hand-colour the prints with watercolour afterwards, putting them under pressure between blotters to stop them buckling whilst they dry.

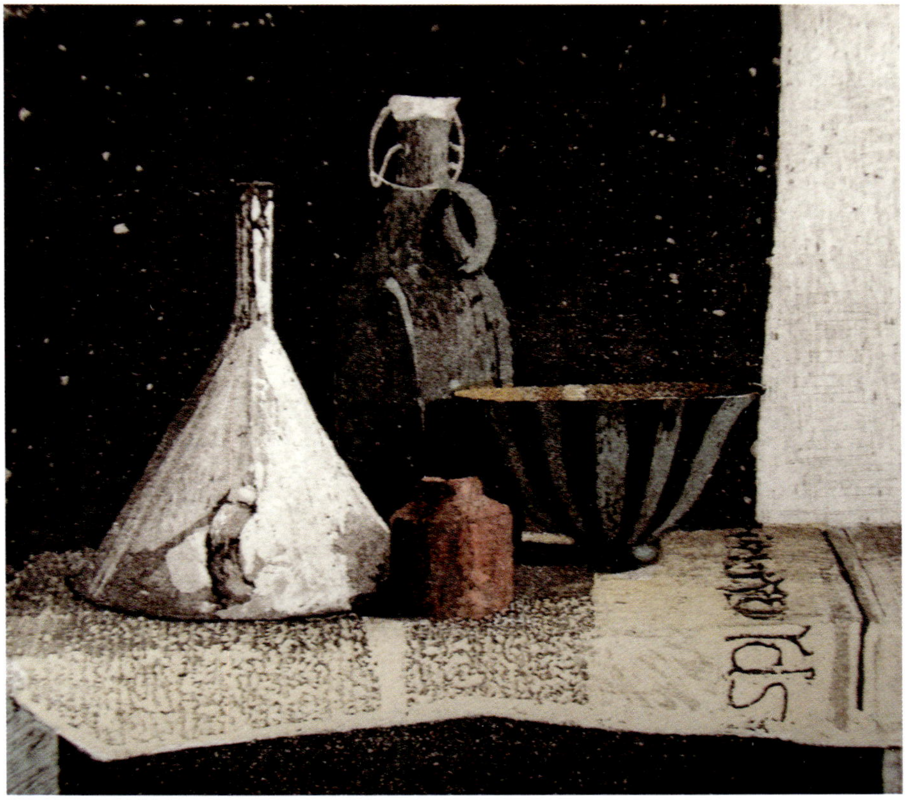

Vide Grenier, 2006. Aquatint and wash, 15 x 18 cm (6 x 7⅛ in.)

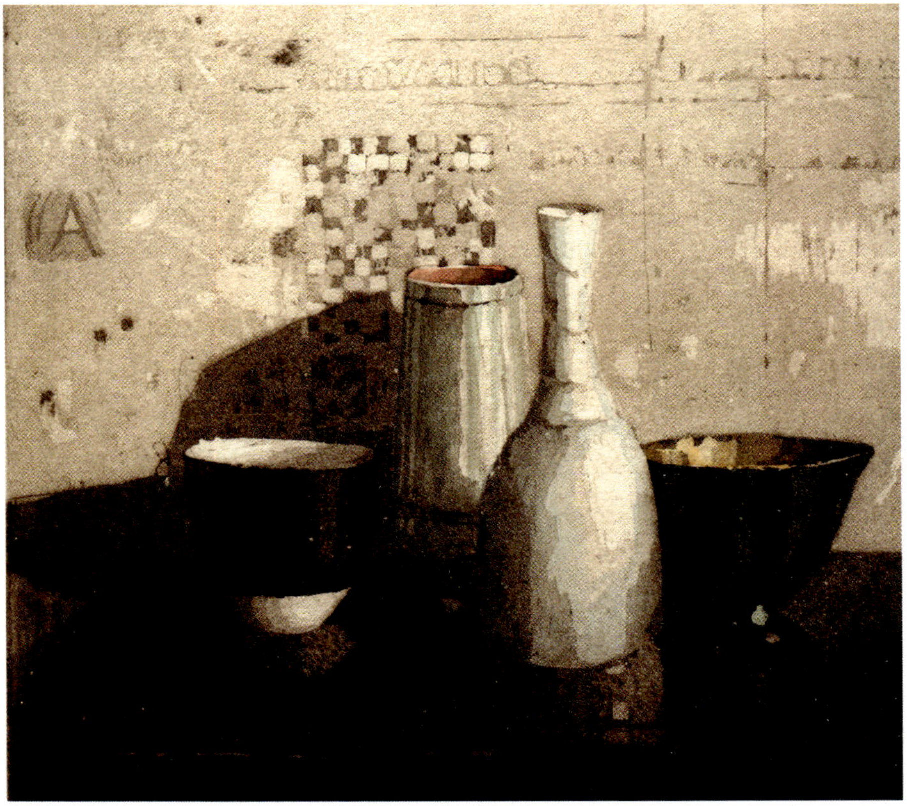

Black and White Still Life, 2005. Aquatint and wash, 15 x 18 cm (6 x 7⅛ in.)

Joseph Winkelman

I can only claim to command certain skills after thirty years of printmaking, acquired by trial and error, lessons learned that I shall never forget. As I started late and am largely self-taught, I have developed working methods that I continue to follow according to the same experimental approach.

When etching my first zinc plates during evenings at the Philadelphia Print Club in 1967, my obvious lack of basic drawing and painting skills were an obstacle. Three years at Oxford University's Ruskin School of Fine Art provided these, but the certificate course there had no facilities for more than minimal instruction in lithography and simple linocutting. After I qualified in 1971, I set up in a studio with a small, salvaged, Columbian press to start practising relief printmaking; an early manual by Michael Rothenstein was my guide. In the summer of 1974, I attended a Ruskin School print workshop for instruction in intaglio from Chris Orr and Tom Piper, which spurred me into acquiring a Rochat copperplate press to continue exploration, using as pilots the iconic texts of E.S. Lumsden, Anthony Gross, S.W. Hayter and John Buckland Wright.

To demonstrate my evolved working method, I cite the example of how the aquatint *Approaching St Kilda* was made. My fascination with the natural and built environment continually prompts me to exploit the qualities of the print media to convey, in a work of art, the grandeur of beautiful moments such as those witnessed in unusual light and strange weather conditions. Inspired by chance situations, I try to capture their essence in drawings, as a starting point to aid memory when making a matrix. In sketches, I gather information for a design and consider a variety of compositions. Anticipating the need for certain details, I make photographic records with a simple camera and, where possible, return to draw more closely and to look again.

I summarise the image in about six graded tones by marking numbers on the sketch to represent arithmetically progressive amounts of the number of minutes required by the plate in the acid, and thus increasing depths of bite. The drawing shown here served as a broad composition to be recreated as an aquatint matrix. I use the mirror image of the drawing to get the reversed profile of the distant islands and general shapes of clouds backwards on the plate so that they will print the right way round, stopping out discrete areas in descending order of tone with varnish painted on the aquatint ground, laid over the copperplate, working from light to dark. The sunburst and the lightest reflections on the sea I stop out first (as those areas are not to be etched at all) and I proceed to the next darker tone, a one-minute etch, and so on.

Such an aquatint image takes me more than a month's concentrated effort to make, stopping out the areas for different bites over several days, etching them for brief minutes only, immediately dousing the plate in water to cease the etching, drying it, then proceeding similarly to the next darker tonal area, until the entire range of etches is complete. On removing the varnish and resin ground to ink the plate and pull a proof, I consider scraping and burnishing certain areas of the aquatint matrix to adjust tonalities, an important part of balancing the final design.

What totally absorbs me is the unique form of expression that the art of printmaking affords, by means of the simple technology of rending metal or wood, then printing it with ink on paper, using heavy steel presses to produce delicate imagery of profound expressiveness; it is an all-consuming activity whose singular power of visual communication has no parallel. A democratic art form, its egalitarianism appeals to me; the artist's energies go into the creation of a printing matrix so as to pull an edition of multiple original prints for a wide audience, rather than producing a solitary work.

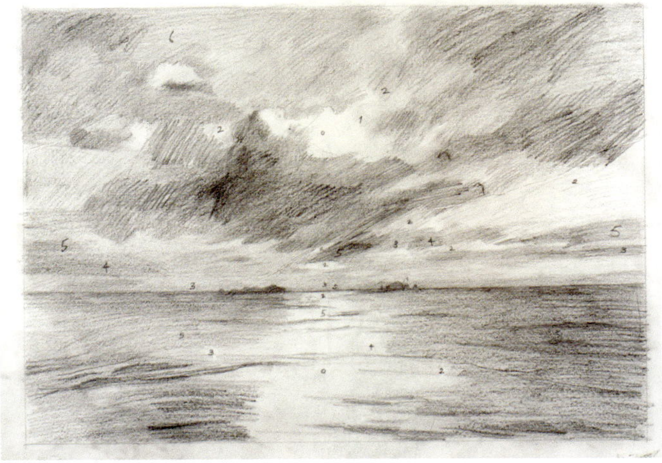

Approaching St Kilda, 2002. Sketch for aquatint, 39 x 54 cm (15⅜ x 21¼ in.)

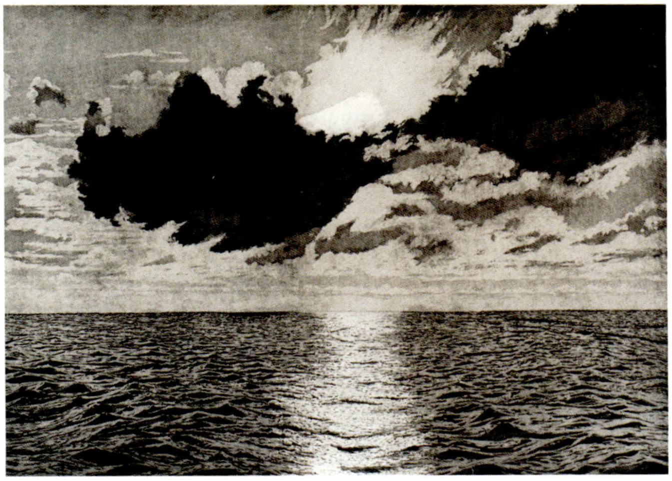

Approaching St Kilda (first state), 2002. Aquatint, 38 x 54 cm (15 x 21¼ in.)

Approaching St Kilda (fourth state), 2002. Aquatint, 38 x 54 cm (15 x 21¼ in.)

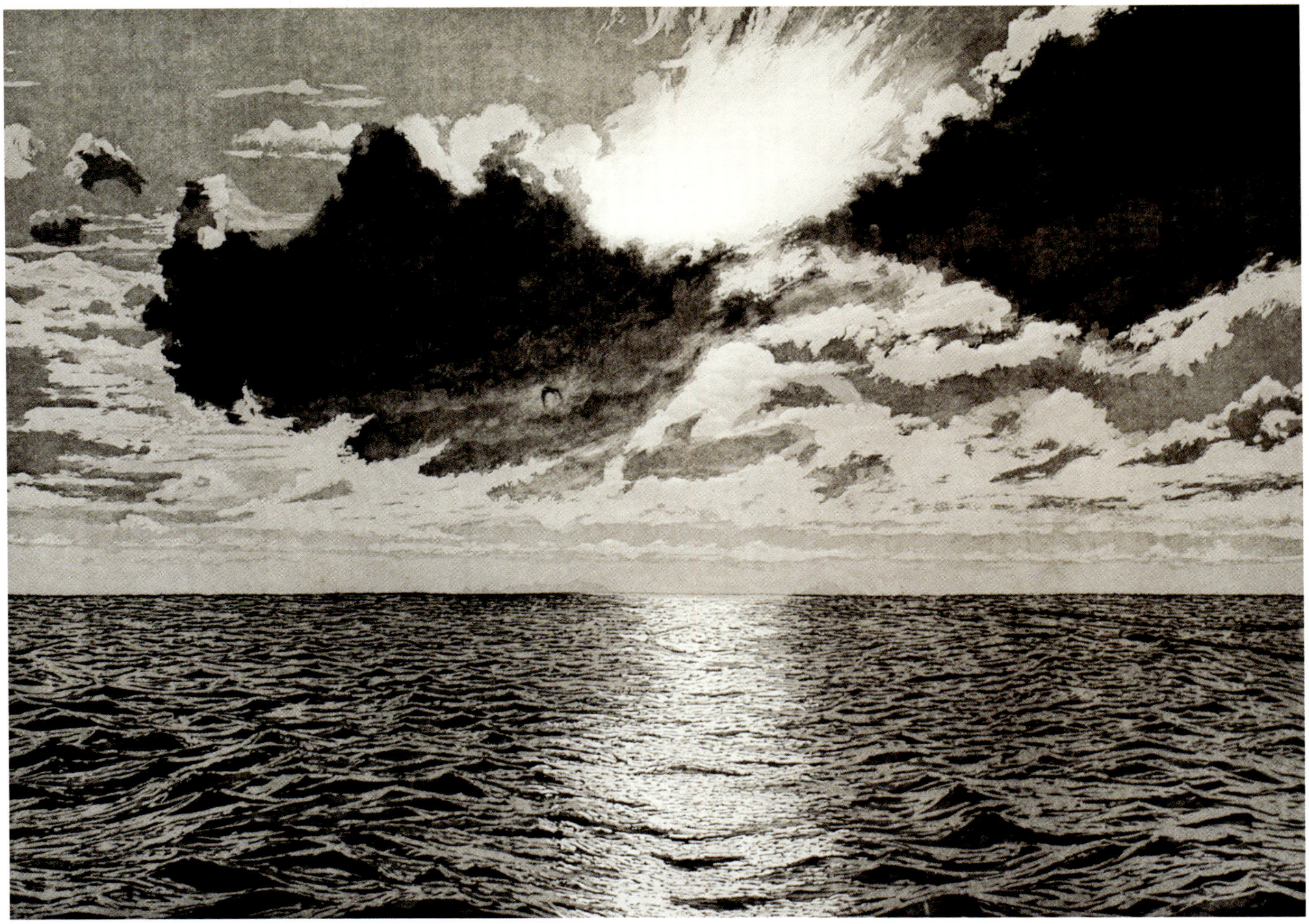

Contributors to Printmakers' Secrets

Abbreviations

AOI: Association of Illustrators
ARCA: Associate of the Royal College of Art
ARE: Associate of the Royal Society of Painter-Printmakers
ATC: Art Teacher's Certificate
Dip.AD: Diploma in Art and Design
FRBS: Fellow of the Royal Society of British Sculptors
FRSA: Fellow of the Royal Society of Arts
H.Dip.AD: Higher Diploma in Art and Design
HDFA: Higher Diploma in Fine Art (Slade School, London)
NDD: National Diploma in Design
NEAC: New English Art Club
PGCE: Postgraduate Certificate in Education
PRE: President, Royal Society of Painter-Printmakers
RA: Royal Academician
RBA: Royal Society of British Artists
RBSA: Royal Birmingham Society of Artists
RCA: Royal College of Art
RE: Royal Society of Painter-Printmakers
RI: Royal Institute of Painters in Watercolour
RP: Royal Society of Portrait Painters
RWA: Royal West of England Academy
RWS: Royal Watercolour Society
SWE: Society of Wood Engravers

Oranmore Castle, Afternoon, Norman Ackroyd, 1999. Etching, sugar-lift aquatint, 32 x 38 cm (12⅝ x 15 in.)

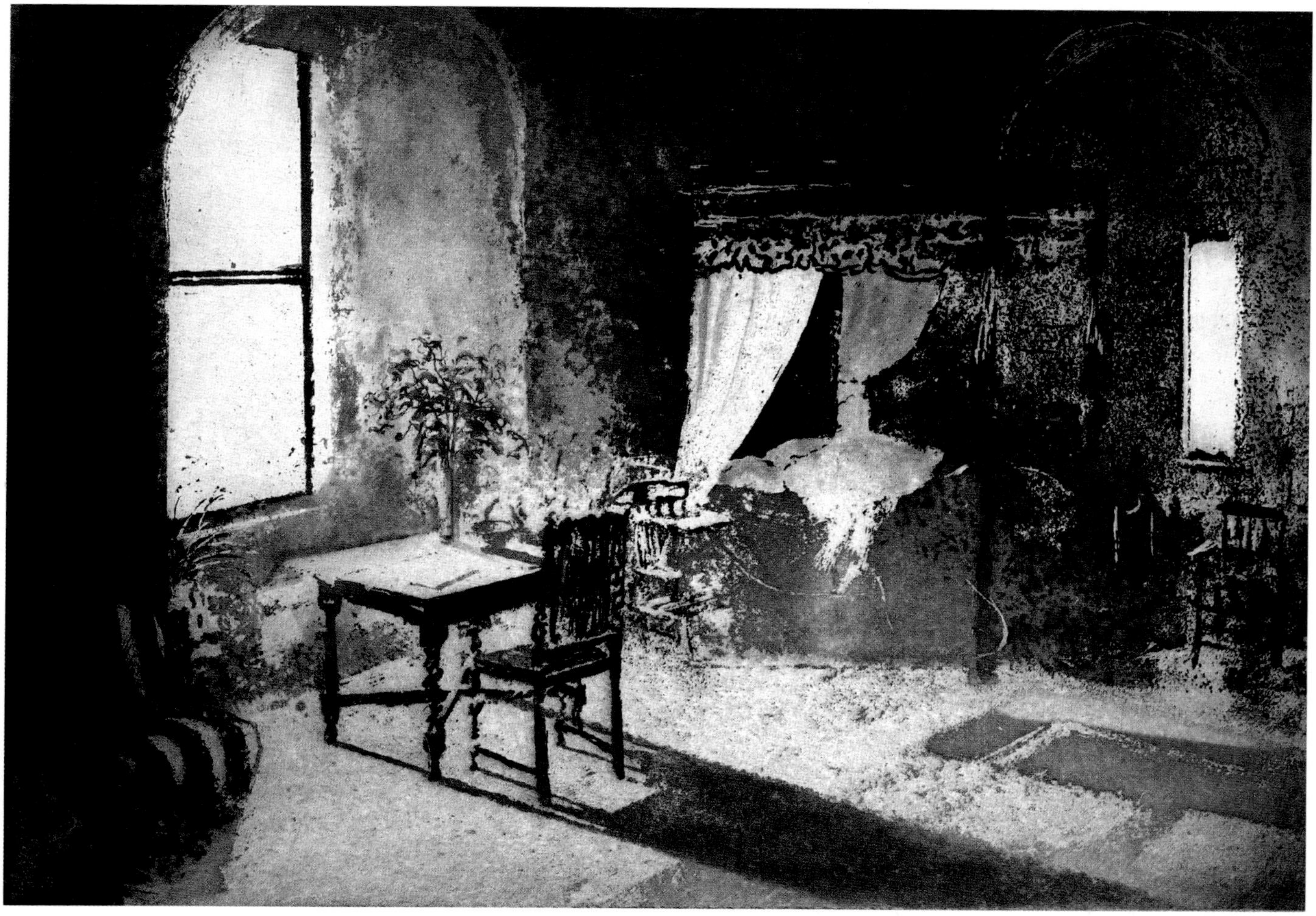

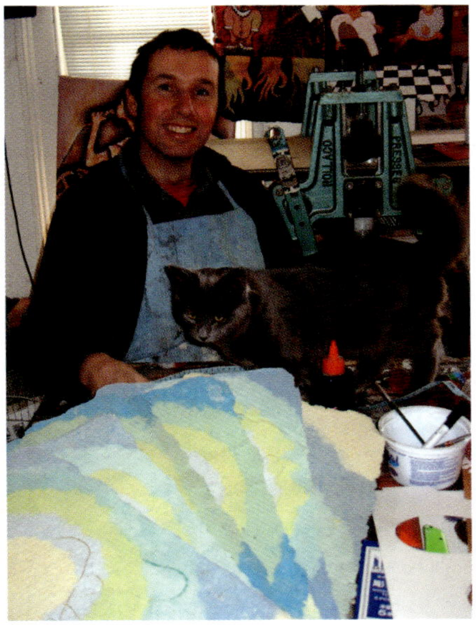

Jim Anderson at work

Ackroyd, Norman CBE RA RE Fellow of the Royal College of Art
www.normanackroyd.com

Adair, Hilary RE
Professional Qualifications: NDD (Painting), ATC.
www.hilaryadair.co.uk

Anderson, Jim RE
Professional qualifications: SAS (Special Advanced printmaking course), Central St Martins School of Art, London.
www.jimpanzee.co.uk

Antoniou, Andrew RE
Professional qualifications: BA Fine Art & MA Printmaking, Central School Of Art, London.
Membership of professional bodies: Australian Print Council.
Post(s): Lecturer in Printmaking, Australian National University; Lecturer in Drawing, Art Gallery, New South Wales Arts Society; Director of AntPress Print Studios, Mollymook, Australia.
www.andrewantoniou.com.au

Atkinson, Ted RE FRBS
Professional qualifications: Trained as a sculptor at Liverpool College of Art and at the Slade School and as a printmaker at Central St Martins, London.
Post(s): Previously Head of Sculpture Department at Exeter and Coventry Colleges of Art.
e mail: extex@btinternet.com

Bartlett, Adrian RE
e mail: ajb.Bartlett@virgin.net

Bawden, Richard RE RWS NEAC
Professional qualifications: ARCA.
e mail: h.r_bawden@btopenworld.com

Beale, James RE RWA
Professional qualifications: BA(Hons) and H.Dip.AD (Chelsea School of Art).
Post(s): Head of Printmaking and Ph.D. Supervisor, University of Gloucestershire.
e mail: jamesbeale@hotmail.com

Blighton, Jeremy ARE
Professional development: 25 years as Master Printer, Thomas Ross & Sons, Black Star Press and London Contemporary Art.
www.banksidegallery.com

Brodholt, Gail RE
Professional qualifications: BA Hons Fine Art (Painting).
www.gailbrodholt.com

Bryce, John ARE SWE
Membership of professional bodies: Guild of Aviation Artists and Wapping Group of Artists.
e mail: scorperjohn@aol.com

Button, Corinna RE
Professional qualifications: BA Hons Fine Art (Painting), Leeds; Postgraduate Advanced Printmaking, Croydon.
www.corinnabutton.com

Carpanini, David PPRE RWS RWA NEAC Hon.RBSA Hon.RWS
Professional qualifications: Dip.AD, MA (RCA), ATC.
Post(s): Formerly Professor of Art at the University of Wolverhampton.
www.banksidegallery.com

December, Gail Brodholt, Linocut, 10 x 19 cm (4 x 7½ in.)

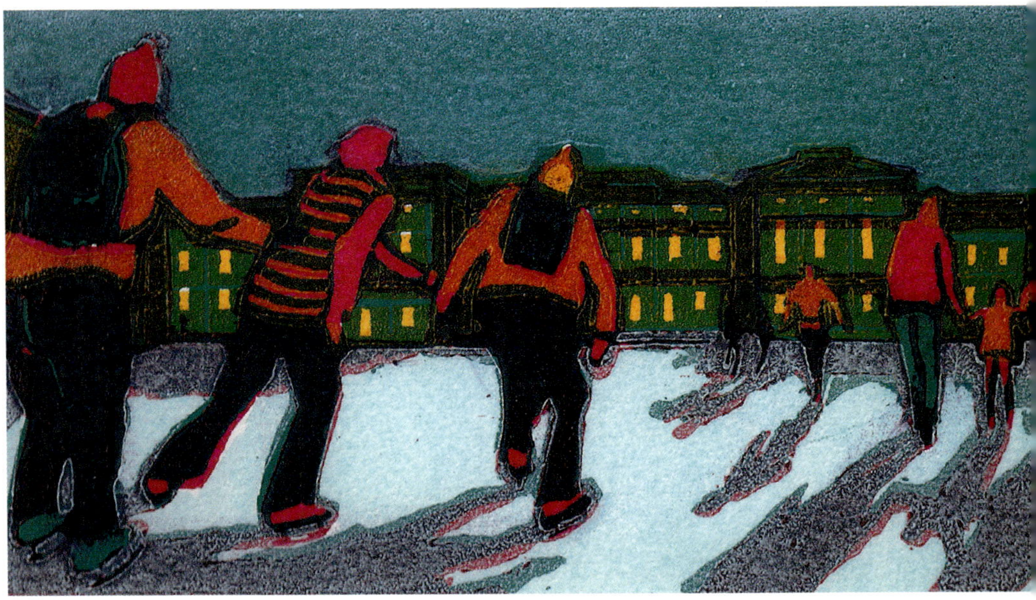

Cooper, Eileen RA RE
Professional qualifications: Dip.AD Goldsmiths, MA (RCA).
Post(s): Head of Printmaking, Royal Academy Schools.
www.artfirst.co.uk

Croft, Paul RE
Professional qualifications: TMP (Tamarind Master Printer).
Membership of professional bodies: Aberystwyth Printmakers.
Post(s): Lecturer in Printmaking, School of Art, Aberystwyth.
www.paulcroft.org

Dalby, Claire RE RWS SWE
www.banksidegallery.com

Desmet, Anne RE RWA SWE
Professional qualifications: BA & MA Fine Art, Oxon; Postgraduate Diploma in Printmaking, Central School of Art & Design, London; Prix de Rome Scholar.
Post(s): Editor of *Printmaking Today* magazine (1998–present).
www.annedesmet.com

Dicker, Kate ARE SWE
Professional qualifications: BA (Hons) Graphic Art, Camberwell College of Art, London; MA Fine Art (Printmaking), Winchester School of Art.
Post(s): Visiting Lecturer at Portsmouth University, School of Art, Design & Media.
www.katedicker.com

Downing, Holly RE
Professional qualifications: BA in Fine Art, University of California, Santa Cruz; postgraduate studies in printmaking, Royal College of Art, London; MA in Fine Art, Goddard College, Vermont.
Membership of professional bodies: Los Angeles Printmaking Society, California; Boston Printmaker, Massachusetts; Washington Printmakers, Washington, DC.
Post(s): Visiting art instructor at many institutions in the US and the UK, including the former Brighton Polytechnic.
www.hollydowning.com

Duffin, John RE
Professional qualifications: BA Fine Art, Goldsmiths College, London; MA Printmaking, Central St Martins, London.
Post(s): Associate Lecturer, University of the Arts London.
www.johnduffin.co.uk

Ferry, David ARE FRSA
Professional qualifications: BA(Hons) Painting and Printmaking; HDFA (Slade) Printmaking; Advanced Postgraduate Diploma in Printmaking, Camberwell School of Art and Crafts.
Post(s): Head of Printmaking, Cardiff School of Art and Design, University of Wales Institute, Cardiff. Visiting Professor, Long Island University, New York.
e mail: dferry@uwic.ac.uk

Feijoo, Fernando ARE
Professional qualifications: MA Fine Art (Printmaking), Winchester School of Art; BA Illustration, Kent Institute of Art & Design.
Post(s): Lecturer in Printmaking at Colchester Institute, and Head of Art Department at Bellerbys College, Cambridge.
www.fernandofeijoo.com

Frankland, Trevor PPRWS RE RBA Hon.RI
Professional qualifications: NDD, Royal Academy Schools Postgraduate Certificate.
Membership of professional bodies: Art Workers' Guild and The London Group.
Post(s): Associate Senior Lecturer, Middlesex University.
www.trevorfrankland.co.uk

Dream Landscape No.1, Peter Green, Woodcut and Stencil, 2007, 23 x 28 cm (9 x 11 in.)

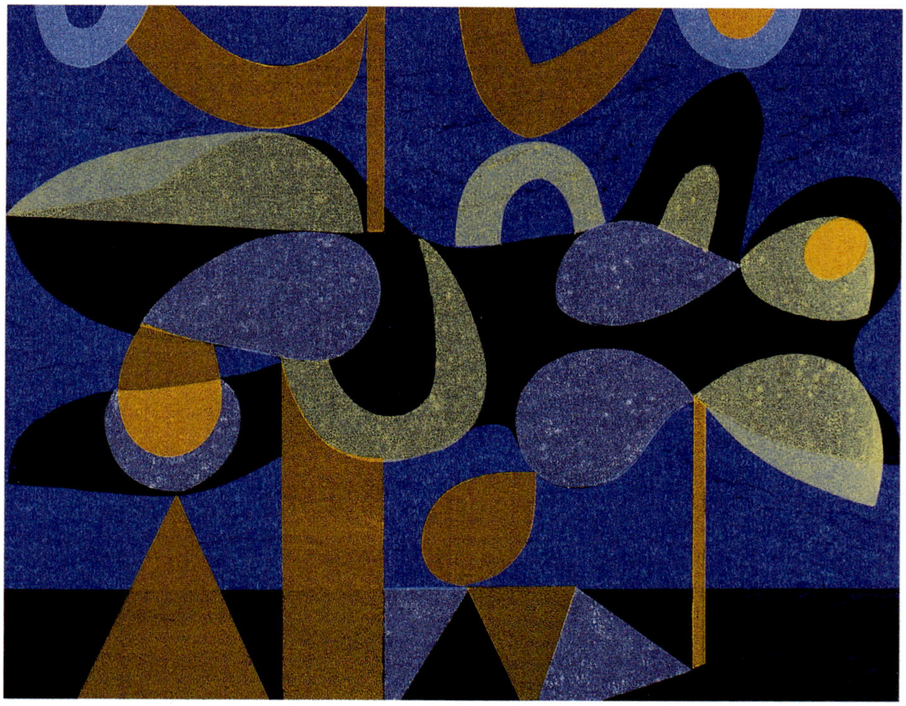

Freeth, Peter RA RE
Professional qualifications: University of London Slade Diploma in Fine Art; Prix de Rome scholar.
e mail: mariolina@talktalk.net

Gracia, Carmen RE
Membership of professional bodies: Greenwich Printmakers.
e mail: carmengracia@btinternet.com

Green, Peter OBE RE
Professional qualifications: NDD; ATD, University of London.
Post(s): Senior Lecturer, Hornsey College of Art and Head of Postgraduate Art, Teacher Training Department; Dean of the Faculty of Art and Design, Middlesex Polytechnic; Professor of Art and Design, Middlesex University; Emeritus Professor, Middlesex University.
e mail: plgreenart@waitrose.com

Hanscomb, Brian RE
Professional development: Journeyman letterpress copperplate engraver.
www.brianhanscomb.co.uk

Hanselaar, Marcelle RE
Professional qualifications: B.Tech Printmaking, Kensington & Chelsea College, London.
Membership of professional bodies: The London Group.
www.marcellehanselaar.com

Harris, Roger RE
Professional qualifications: NDD.
Post(s): Formerly Creative Director, Fisher, Ling & Benyon professional design group.
www.banksidegallery.com

Hartill, Brenda RE
Professional qualifications: Dip.FA (Hons), Elam School of Fine Arts, Auckland University, New Zealand.

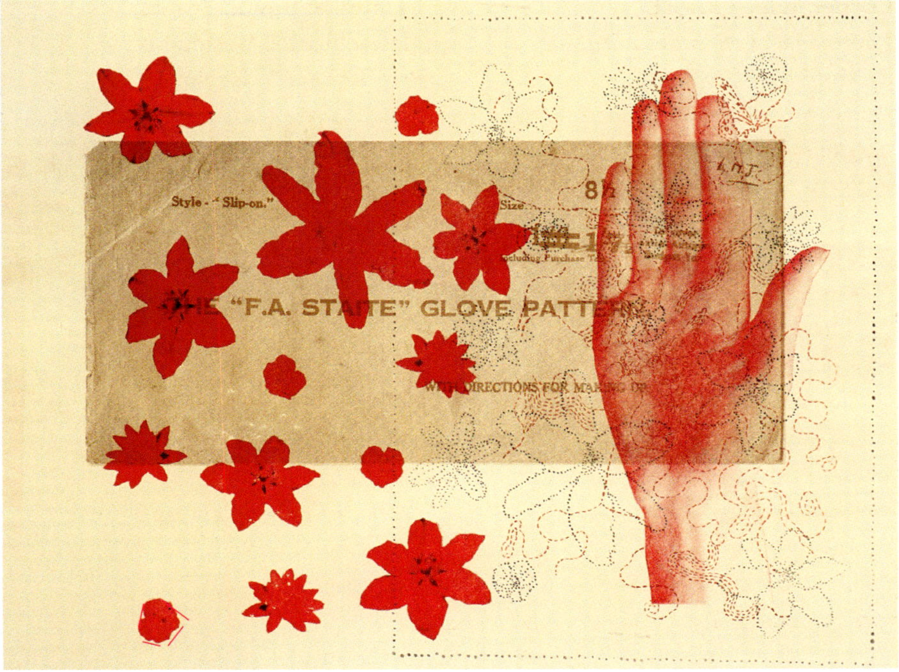

Palm, Carole Hensher, Lithograph, 57 x 79 cm ($22\frac{5}{8}$ x $31\frac{1}{8}$ in.)

www.brendahartill.com

Hawdon, Paul RE
Professional qualifications: BA (Hons) Fine Art; Postgraduate Diploma, Royal Academy Schools; Prix de Rome scholar, Printmaking.
www.paulhawdon.com

Hensher, Carole RE
Professional qualifications: BA (Hons) Fine Art, University of East London; MA Printmaking, Camberwell College of Art.
Membership of professional bodies: Greenwich Printmakers and Southbank Printmakers.
www.hensher.co.uk/carole

Jackson, H.J. RE SWE
www.norwichprintfair.co.uk

Jeffs, Howard RE
Professional qualifications: BA Fine Art, MA Printmaking.
Post(s): Senior Lecturer in Photography and Printmaking, Department of Visual Arts, Goldsmiths College (retired 2003).
e mail: howardjeffs@gmail.com

Kiely, Frank ARE
Professional qualifications: NDD, Galway, Ireland; BA Fine Art (Printmaking), National College of Art and Design, Dublin; MA Fine Art (Printmaking), Royal College of Art, London.
Membership of professional bodies: East London Printmakers, Hackney, London; Black Church Print Studio, Dublin.
Post(s): Visiting lecturer, Dun Laoghaire Institute of Art, Design & Technology, Ireland.
www.frankkiely.com

Klein, Anita PPRE
Professional qualifications: BA Fine Art, Slade School, University of London; Higher Diploma in Printmaking, Slade School.
www.anitaklein.com

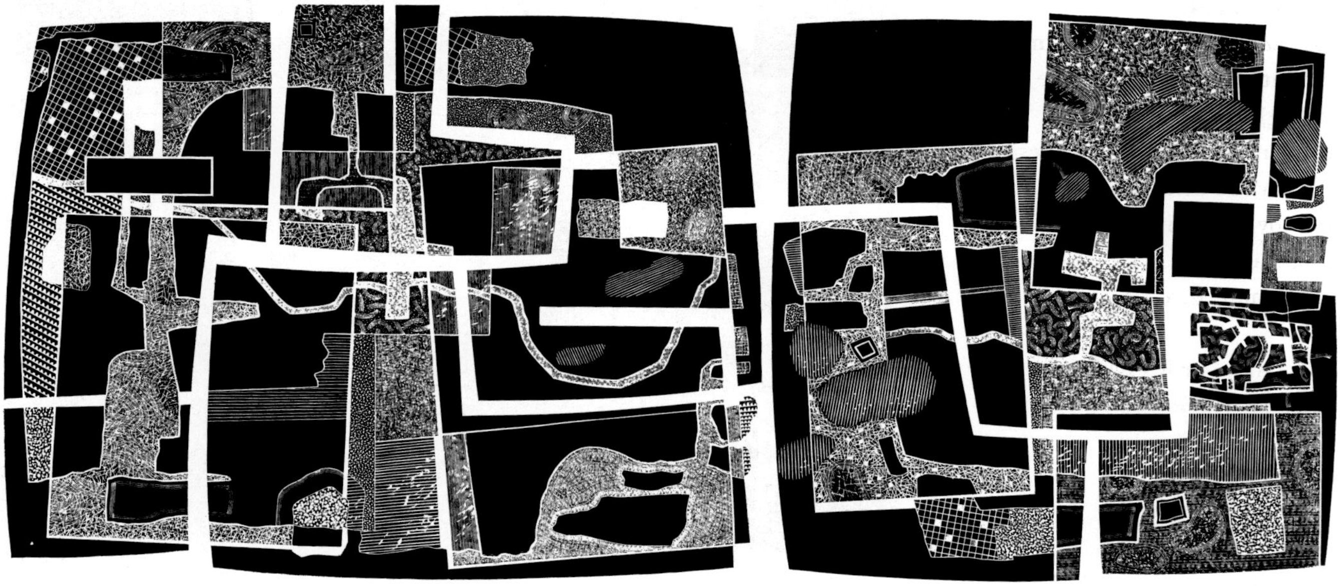

Montpelier, Peter Lawrence, 2007. Wood engraving, 15 x 36 cm (6 x 14 in.)

Lawrence, Peter RE SWE
Professional qualifications: Dip.AD (Illustration).
Post(s): Chairman of the Society of Wood Engravers.
e mail: pete@odi-design.co.uk

Leach, Ursula RE
Professional qualifications: BA(Hons) Fine Art.
www.axisartists.org.uk

LeBas, Ann RE NEAC
Professional qualifications: City and Guilds of London Art School Certificate of Merit in Drawing, Painting and Engraving (Drawing & Engraving Prize Winner).
Membership of professional bodies: New English Art Club, The Art Workers Guild, Somerset Guild of Craftsmen.
www.banksidegallery.com

Lodge, Jean RE
Post(s): Formerly Head of Printmaking, Ruskin School, University of Oxford.
tel (Paris): 00331 45405762

Loudon, Irvine RE Doctor of Medicine (Oxon)
Membership of professional bodies: Oxford Art Society; Oxford Printmakers Co-operative.
e mail: irvine.loudon@green.ox.ac.uk

Marinkov, Sasa RE
Professional qualifications: BA (Hons) Fine Art, Leeds University; PGCE, University of London; Advanced Diploma in Printmaking, Central School of Art and Design, London.
Post(s): Lecturer and Teacher of Art and Design and Art History, Middlesex Polytechnic, Richmond upon Thames College and workshops in galleries and museums in London.
www.sasamarinkov.co.uk

Martina, Toni RE
Professional qualifications: BA (Hons) Fine Art and Postgraduate study, Central School of Art and Design, London; Prix de Rome scholar.
Post(s): Tutor, Central St Martins College of Art & Design; Tutor, British Museum.
e mail: t.martina@btinternet.com

Middleton, Michael RE
Professional qualifications: Dip.AD (first-class honours), Sheffield; Higher Diploma in Art, Chelsea School of Art.
Post(s): Head of Printmaking, Colchester School of Art.
e mail: mike.middleton@btinternet.com

Midgley, Julia RE
Professional qualifications: Dip.AD.
Membership of professional bodies: Association of Illustrators; Cheshire Artists' Network; Manchester Academy of Fine Arts (past Vice-President).
Post(s): Reader in Documentary Drawing, Liverpool School of Art & Design, John Moores University.
www.juliamidgley.co.uk

Mumberson, Stephen RE
Professional qualifications: MA (RCA) Printmaking.
Membership of professional bodies: Printmakers Council.
Post(s): Reader in Fine Art (Printmaking), Middlesex University.
e mail: s.mumberson@mdx.ac.uk

Muñoz, Pilar ARE
Professional qualifications: MA in Fine Art (Printmaking), BA in Fine Art (Painting), Seville, Spain.
Post(s): One-year scholarship residency at the Curwen Print Study Centre, funded by the University of Salamanca.
www.pilarmunoz.co.uk

Orr, Christopher RA RE
Professional qualifications: MA (RCA)
Post(s): Professor of Printmaking, Royal College of Art.
www.chrisorr-ra.com

Paynter, Hilary PRE SWE
Professional qualifications: NDD ATC MA MSc.
Membership of professional bodies: SWE (Past President).
e mail: hilarypaynter@yahoo.com

Petterson, Melvyn RE NEAC
Professional qualifications: Postgraduate qualification (with distinction) in Printmaking, Camberwell School of Art.
www.melvynpetterson.com

Phillips, Tom CBE RA Hon.RE Hon.RP
www.tomphillips.co.uk

Pittaway, Neil RE RWS
Professional qualifications: BA Hons Fine Art (Painting), University of Gloucestershire; MA (Printmaking), University of Bradford; Diploma in Fine Art, Royal Academy Schools; PGCE, University of Huddersfield.
www.njpittaway.co.uk

Poole, Bryan RE
Professional qualifications: BA (Hons).
www.etchart.co.uk

Ridgwell, Martin ARE
Professional qualifications: MA in Printmaking, Camberwell School of Art.
Membership of professional bodies: Greenwich Printmakers' Association.
www.martinridgwell.com

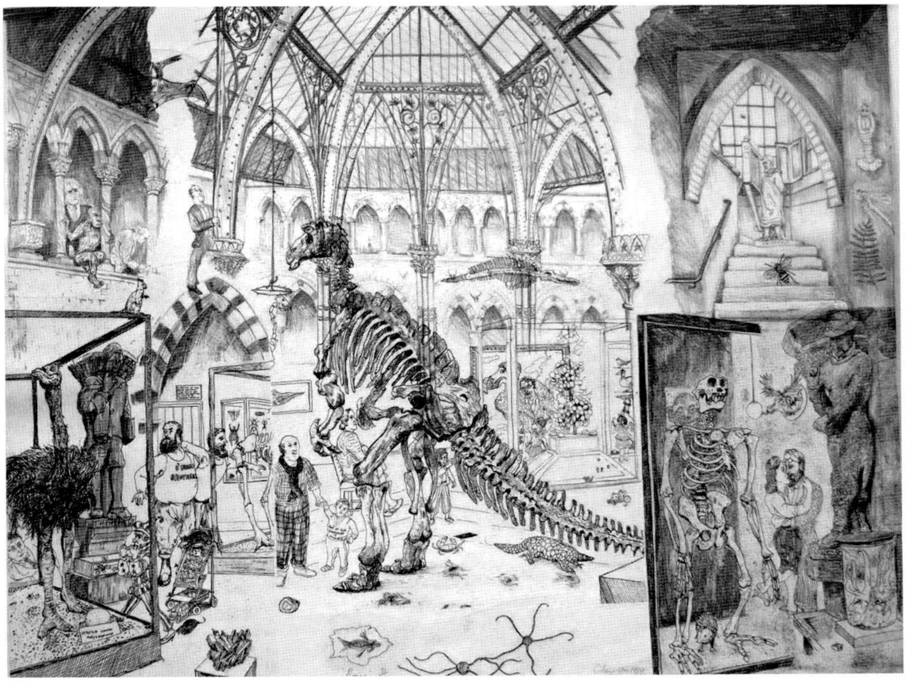

Bones, Chris Orr, 1988, Stone lithography and counterproof etching, 56 x 73 cm (22 x 30 in.)

Shiomi, Nana RE
Professional qualifications: MA (RCA).
Membership of professional bodies: Japan Artists' Association, Inc.
Post(s): Visiting Lectureships: National College of Art & Design, Dublin; Tama Art University, Tokyo; Royal College of Art, London; University of East London.
www.nanashiomi.com

Sloss, Sheila RE
Professional qualifications: BA in Fine Art (Painting and Printmaking) and postgraduate study (Printmaking).
Membership of professional bodies: Printmakers Council.
Post(s): Lecturer, London College of Communication, University of the Arts, London.
e mail: segulem@tiscali.co.uk

Sykes, Sandy RE
Professional qualifications: MA, ATD.
Membership of professional bodies: Printmakers Council.
Post(s): Senior Lecturer in Fine Art, University of Leeds and Visiting Lecturer at many other universities in Britain.
www.sandysykes.co.uk

Till, Tobias ARE
Professional qualifications: Postgraduate Diploma, Royal Academy Schools.
www.tobias-till.co.uk

Todd, James RE SWE
Professional qualifications: BA, MA, MFA, University of Great Falls, Montana, USA.
Membership of professional bodies: American Association of University Professors; Wood Engravers' Network (US); German Academic Exchange Service.
Post(s): Professor and Lecturer, Social History of Art; Chairman, Department

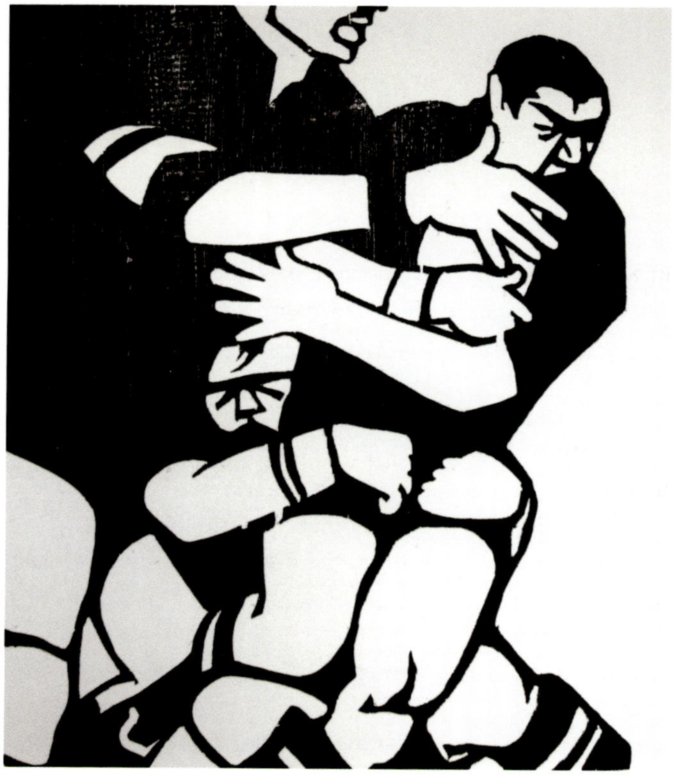

Tackle, Carol Walklin, Woodcut, 25 x 20 cm (9⅞ x 7⅞ in.)

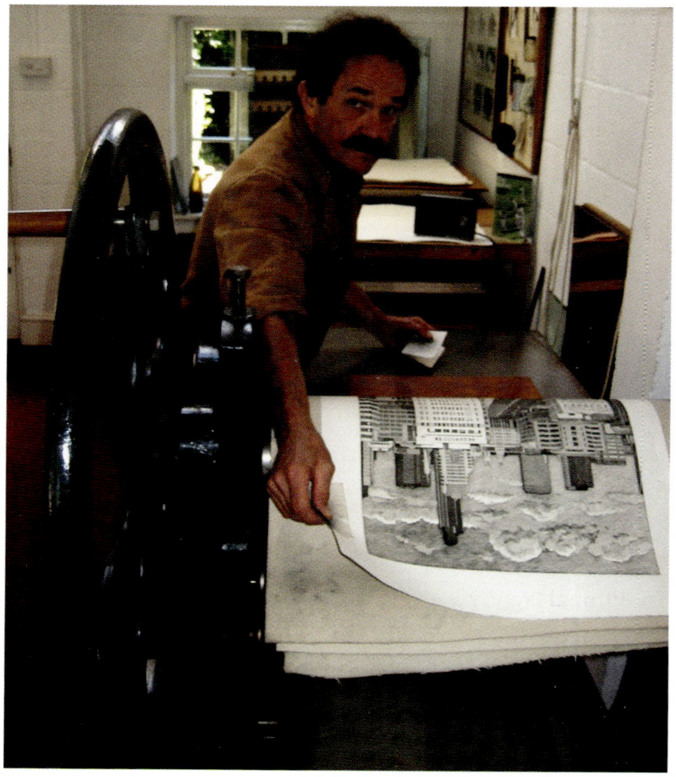

Joseph Winkelman at work

of Art; Head of Printmaking Program; and, since 2000, Emeritus Professor of Art and Humanities, all posts at the University of Montana, Missoula.
e mail: masuria@mtwi.net

Tout, Ann ARE SWE
Professional qualifications: ATD.
e mail: ann@anntout.com

Unwin, Bren Carolyn ARE
Professional qualifications: BA (Hons) Fine Art; MA (Research) Fine Art; PhD, University of Hertfordshire.
Membership of professional bodies: Newlyn Society of Artists.
Post(s): Visiting Research Fellow, University of Hertfordshire.
www.brenunwin.com

Walklin, Carol RE
Professional qualifications: Teachers' Certificate; MA Graphic Design, Royal College of Art, London
Post(s): Art and Textiles Tutor, Stockwell College of Education, Bromley; Print Workshop Tutor, West Dean College, Chichester, Sussex.
e mail: colinwalklin@btinternet.com

Westergard, Jim RE SWE
Professional qualifications: BFA & MFA (Drawing/Printmaking) Utah State University, USA.
Membership of professional bodies: Wood Engravers' Network; Fine Press Book Association; Boston (Massachusetts) Printmakers.
Post(s): Assistant Professor of Printmaking, Metropolitan State College, Denver, Colorado, USA; Assistant Professor of Drawing at Northern Illinois University, DeKalb, Illinois, USA; Instructor of Drawing & Printmaking at Red Deer College (retired), Red Deer, Alberta, Canada.
e mail: jimwest@telusplanet.net

Williams, Annie RE RWS
Professional qualifications: City & Guilds of London Diploma in Fine Art.
e mail: annie@baylissnet.freeserve.co.uk

Winkelman, Joseph PPRE Hon. RWS
Professional qualifications: BA, University of the South, Sewanee, Tennessee, USA; Certificate in Fine Art, University of Oxford.
Membership of professional bodies: Honorary Member, Printmakers Council of Great Britain; Honorary Member, Oxford Art Society.
Post(s): Artist in Residence (2004), St John's College, Oxford.
www.winkelman.co.uk

Glossary

A la poupée
A method, originally French, of working different colours into the pits and crevices of an intaglio plate with twists of muslin (dollies) and achieving a full-colour print in a single impression.

Adire
Traditional Nigerian textile printing using metal stencils through which starch paste is pushed onto the cloth. When this dries, the cloth is dyed with indigo and the paste is removed.

Adobe Photoshop
Computer software developed by the company Adobe Systems.

Analogue
In the context of computer-generated prints, 'analogue' describes a way of adding painted or drawn marks with the intervention of the human hand rather than via a software program.

Albion press
A cast-iron platen press originally produced in 1822 for typography and type-high woodblock illustrations. Versions are still used by artists for printing linocuts and woodcuts.

Aquatint
A means of adding tonal areas to an intaglio print by sprinkling and melting resin dust or asphaltum on the plate and allowing a mordant to attack the unprotected metal between the tiny melted globules to create a network of crevices which will hold ink. Aquatint need not, of course, be used in conjunction with etched line.

Atelier 17
The celebrated Paris studio founded by Stanley William Hayter in 1927. Artists from all over the world, including Picasso, Max Ernst and Joseph Hecht, gathered there to experiment with new printmaking possibilities. The work of the Atelier is best summed up in Hayter's own book, *New Ways of Gravure*, Oxford University Press, 1966.

Baren
A Japanese burnishing tool for printing relief blocks by hand. An enormous amount of time and care goes into the making of a genuine hand-made baren. See Salter, R., *Japanese Woodblock Printing*, A&C Black, 2001.

Bon à tirer
Literally, 'OK to print': the traditional French term marked by an artist in pencil on the margin of a proof to instruct the master printer to proceed with the edition.

Bitmap
This is computer terminology meaning simply a map of bits (i.e. of binary digits, the smallest unit of digital data).

Blankets
The layers of fine-quality felt used in a rolling press (see below) to provide

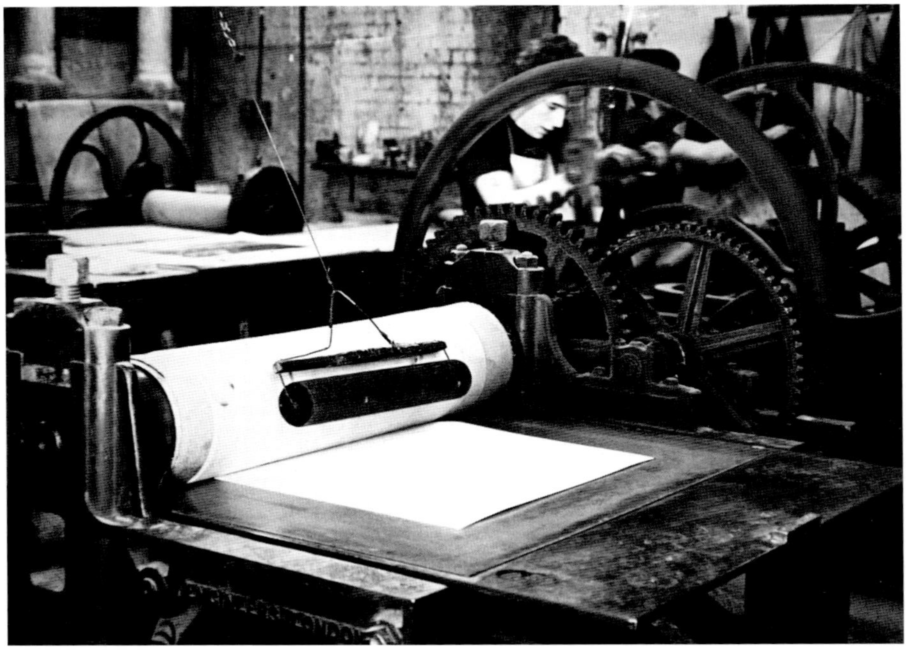

A rolling press at Thomas Ross & Sons (now Thomas Ross Ltd, Binfield, Berks.). The damp paper is in position and the blankets are held back over the upper roller by a smaller wooden one to prevent the blankets flapping down prematurely during the turning of the flywheel.

the resilience that presses the damp paper into the inked crevices of a metal plate to produce an intaglio print. Three to five blankets are usually used; the finely woven ones next to the paper are termed 'frontings', the springy one next to the roller is called the 'swanskin'.

Block
A printing surface of wood, plywood, lino or any other suitable material of moderate thickness (as opposed to a plate, which is usually of thin metal).

Boxwood
The traditional material widely used for wood engraving; the dense endgrain provides an ideal surface for accurate engraving in any direction. New blocks of excellent quality are made by Chris Daunt, 1 Monkridge Gardens, Gateshead, NE11 9XE.

Burin
Any one of a range of steel tools of differing cross section for engraving copper or steel plates.

Burnisher
A steel tool used for removing scratches or reducing the effect of unduly heavy passages in an etched or engraved plate; often used in conjunction with a scraper, a steel tool of triangular cross section with sharpened edges.

Carborundum
Silicon carbide, used in grit form with a glue to provide a tooth for ink on a printing surface.

Channels
In computer terminology this refers to the major combinations of colours that form computer-generated images. These combinations are either RGB (red, green, blue) or CMYK (cyan, magenta, yellow, black). The latter was the classic four-colour separation used in machine colour printing well before the advent of digital technology.

Chine collé
A tissue paper, usually coloured. Used as an element in intaglio and relief prints.

CMYK
Cyan, magenta, yellow and black (the 'K' standing for 'keyline'). (See also Channels, above.)

Collage
An image made by or supplemented by glued or pasted elements; a process famously given prominence by Picasso, Braque and others a century ago. The term may also be applied to computer-generated layers.

Collagraph
A print made from a low-relief surface (such as a collage) with, for example, glued-down sand, grit, found objects, fragments and materials of different textures.

Counterproof
An impression taken from any inked surface and transferred whilst still wet to any other surface (usually paper), blank or otherwise.

Defiling
This refers to tampering with or changing with creative intent the images in an existing published book with aid of a computer.

Diffusion dither
A Photoshop term (see Adobe Photoshop, above). In computer-generated images, diffusion dither creates little patterns of speckles between areas of colour so that the gradations from one to another are much smoother.

Drypoint
A method of intaglio engraving in which the plate's surface is scored with a sharp tool (also termed a drypoint). This tool incises lines and in doing so raises a crest or burr of displaced metal which, with the trench from which it is scored, retains ink when the plate is wiped and results in a soft, velvety, printed effect.

Encaustics
Wax-based pigments.

Epoxy resin
A filler for car bodywork repairs but useful, too, for disguising unwanted incisions in a lino block.

Gamboge
A natural pigment once generally used in the production of a rich, deep-yellow watercolour; these days substitutes are more frequently used.

Graver
An engraving tool, also called a burin.

Gum arabic
A product of the acacia tree, used in various lithographic processes and as a binder in some water-based paints.

Hand-wiping
The final stage in preparing an etched plate for the press. After wiping the inked plate with a pad of scrim it is usual to finish by wiping the palm of the hand on a block of whiting (chalk) and skimming the residual ink from the plate's surface. This is often done selectively, deliberately leaving a veil of tone on parts of the image and polishing highlights with a lightly chalked fingertip.

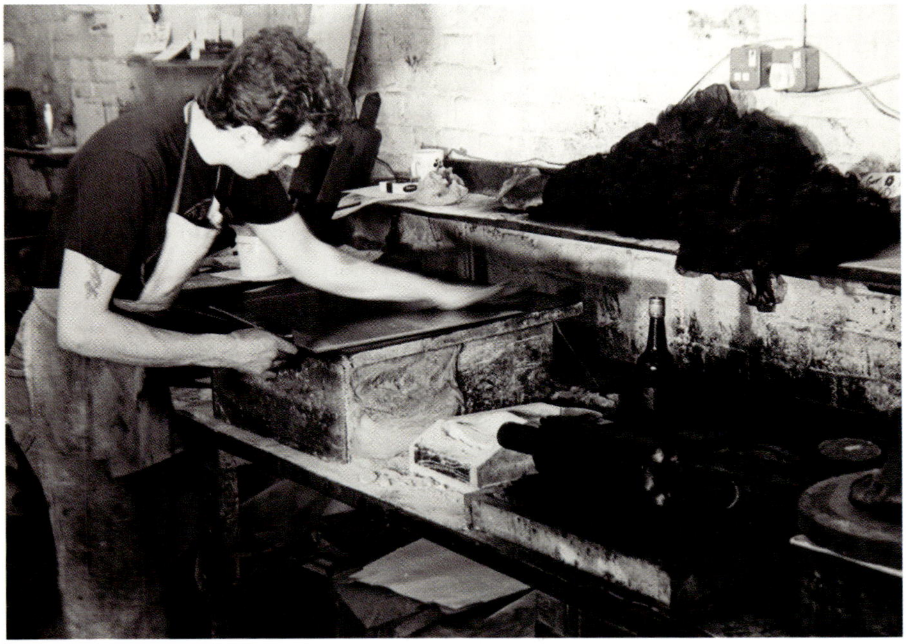

The hand-wipe. The block of whiting is in the box on the printer's right. Thomas Ross and Sons, 1983

Hiragana
One of four alphabets used by the Japanese, this one some 109 phonetic characters.

Hotplate
A heated metal surface for warming an etching plate in preparation for laying a wax ground and sometimes before or after the application of stiff ink in order to ease subsequent wiping.

Kanji
One of the four alphabets used by the Japanese, this one borrowed from the Chinese and consisting of ideographic characters, each representing a concept rather than a sound.

Katakana
A more modern version of Hiragana (see above), again with some 109 phonetic characters.

Layering
A digital printmaking term referring to the overlaying of image planes.

Lithography
A process first discovered by Aloys Senefelder in 1798, it depends on the incompatibility of grease and water. An image is made with a greasy pigment on the surface of a slab of limestone (now largely supplanted by lighter materials). When the stone is wetted, water shrinks from the image, which can then be rolled with a greasy ink. This is repelled by the wetted parts of the stone, allowing the image to be precisely reproduced.

Lowering
Subtly shaving parts of the surface of a wood-engraving block so that those areas will print slightly less strongly in the interests of creating special compositional effects.

Make ready
Pasting thin layers of paper to the reverse of a woodblock or, if using a press, to corresponding places on a tympan to even out or strengthen the pressure.

Matrix
Any surface prepared for printing.

Mezzotint
An intaglio process in which the first step is systematically to texture a copperplate with a toothed tool (a rocker), making thousands of small pits and crests of displaced metal. If when inked and wiped a print were to be taken from this surface, an intense, velvety black would be the result. The image emerges from this darkness, as

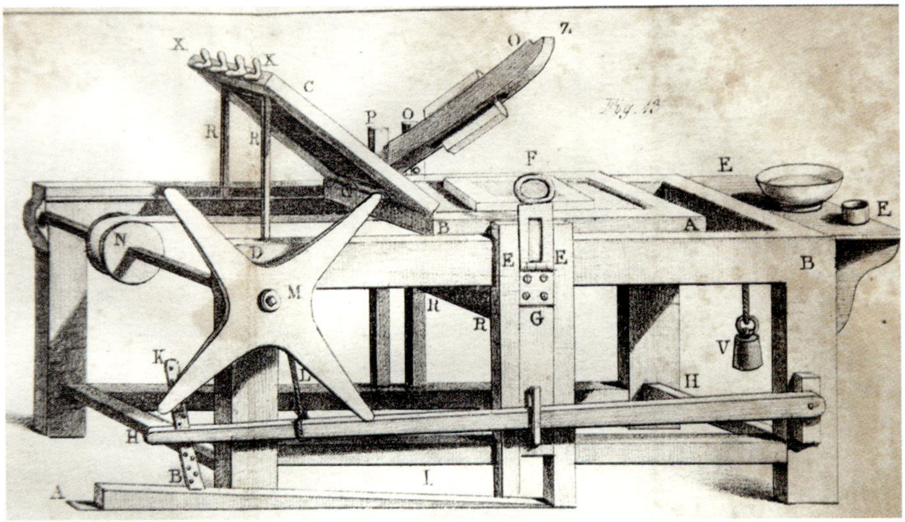

An early wooden lithography press illustrated in the 3rd edition of Brégeaut's *Manual of Lithography*, London, 1832

it were, when areas of the plate are scraped and burnished to create the required range of tones, those most completely smoothed holding practically no ink and thus representing highlights in the eventual print.

Monoprint
An impression taken from a block, plate or any other matrix which differs uniquely from any other print from that same matrix.

Monotype
A single impression, not exactly repeatable. Edgar Degas (1834–1917) was one of the earliest and most inventive exponents, painting with diluted printing ink or working into areas of rolled ink on unetched copper plates, sometimes taking successive, increasingly faint impressions which often became the basis for his pastels.

Mordant
Any acid or alkaline solution which will etch metal. The commonest are nitric acid and ferric chloride.

Newcastle Underground Mural
This was unveiled in 2004. Hilary Paynter's specially commissioned suite of wood engravings is enlarged to 2 x 22 m (6 x 72 ft) and printed on vitreous enamel panels installed in Newcastle's Central Station.

Open bite
Etching wide expanses of a plate to a shallow depth so that when the plate is wiped ink will lodge in the stepped edges, whilst the bitten area will be wiped practically clean.

Photopolymer plates
Light-sensitive plates used in lithography.

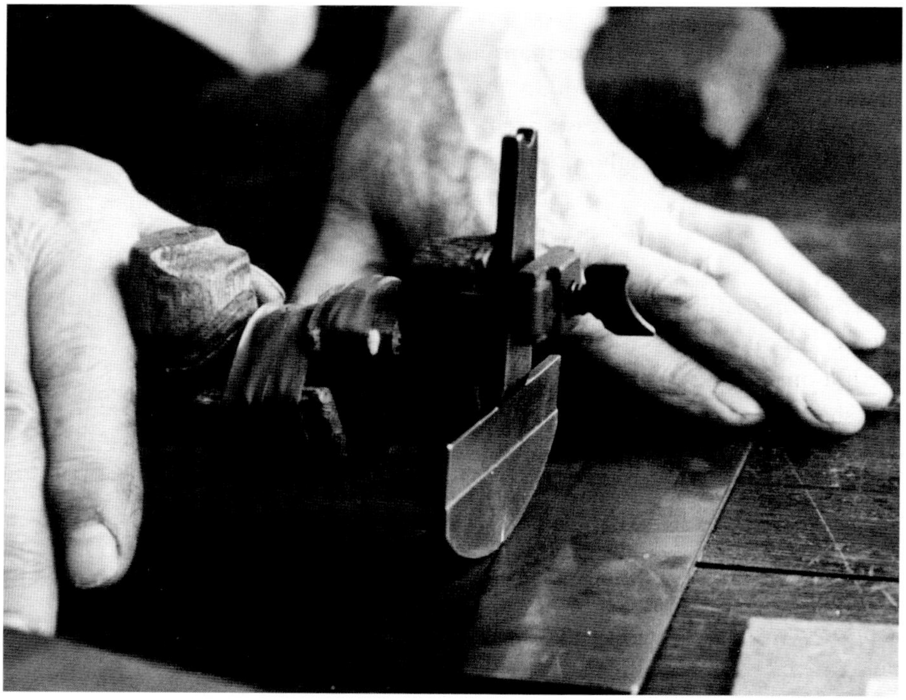

The hands of Lawrence Josset (1910–95) rocking a plate. To facilitate the action, the rocking tool is fixed to the end of a 4-foot pole, the other end of which rests on a support. Photograph: the author

Photrak
Trade name of a light-sensitive emulsion for coating etching plates prior to exposure to a light source and the subsequent etching process.

Plate
A thin sheet of metal, board, plastic or any other material suitable as a printing matrix. See also Board, above.

Plate tone
A subtle film of ink left on the surface of an intaglio plate as a deliberate enrichment of the image. A skilled printer can enhance a print immeasurably by using this device.

PVA
Polyvinyl acetate adhesive and sealant.

Reduction method
A method of making relief, screen or lithographic prints by printing the whole edition in the first colour, then cleaning the matrix, removing parts, printing a second colour on the first and proceeding in this way, colour by colour, until the full range has been printed. Sometimes referred to as the elimination method.

Resingrave
The trade name of a substitute for wood in the making of wood engravings.

Retroussage
A method of enriching an intaglio print by gently dragging the tip of a pad of soft muslin across the inked crevices of a plate to soften the printed lines.

Rocker
A chisel-like tool with a gently curved, toothed blade, used with a rocking action to texture the surface of a plate: the first stage in making a mezzotint.

Rolling press

This and 'cylinder press' are perhaps rather less misleading terms for an etching press, since such presses are used for all forms of intaglio printing, not etching alone.

Scorper

An engraving tool made from a rod of square-section steel, or of one with the bottom surface rounded, ground and sharpened to an oblique cutting edge. Used for broad incisions or for clearing larger areas in wood engraving.

Screenprint

A print made by supporting a stencil on a fine mesh stretched over a frame. The stencil may take the form of cut paper, adherent film or any ink-resistant pigment. It can also be created photographically.

Scrim

Sometimes called tarlatan or wiping canvas, this is a textile of open weave, stiffened with size and used in a pad to wipe ink from the surface of an intaglio or collagraph matrix, an action which simultaneously works the ink into the crevices.

Smoked hard ground

A thin layer of hard wax (as opposed to soft, see below) applied to an etching plate and blackened with the smoke from a bundle of tapers so that subsequent drawing with a needle (or etching point) may more easily be seen.

Scraper

The basic tool of a mezzotint engraver. (See also Burnisher, above.)

Soft ground

This is a wax which, when rolled in a thin coat on an etching plate, is soft enough for textured surfaces to be pressed into it and lifted away, to leave an accurate trace in exposed metal which may then be bitten. A drawing may be made on greaseproof paper laid onto such a ground; this, too, lifts away the wax to leave its trace, allowing a mordant to attack the metal so that an intaglio print may be made.

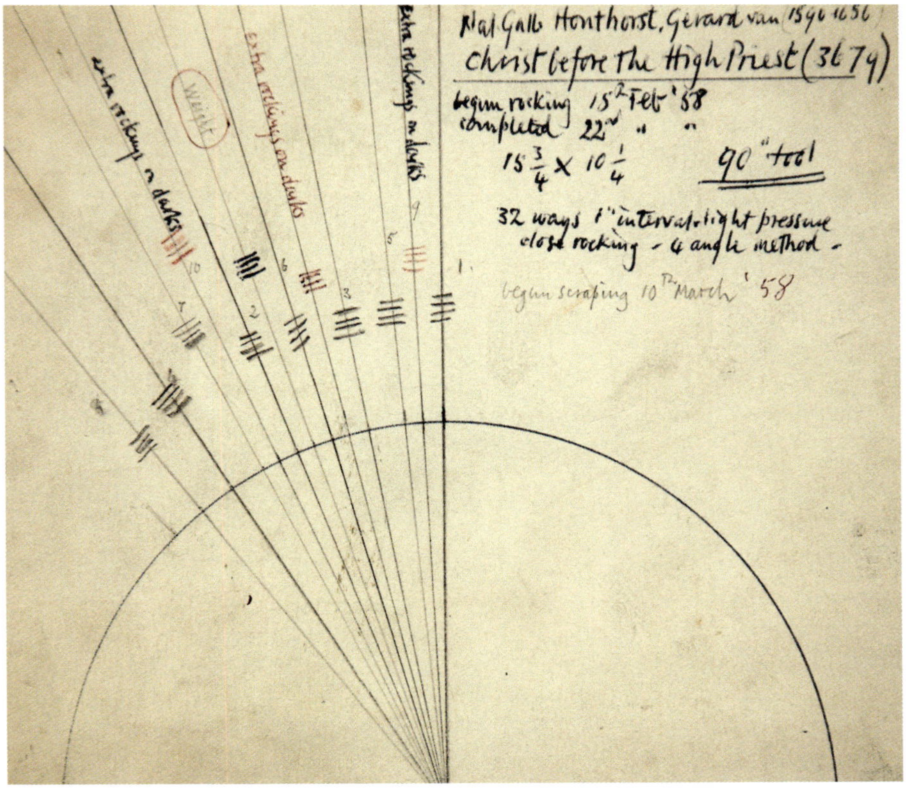

Lawrence Josset's diagram for keeping track of the directions, or 'ways' (in this case 32) in which his mezzotint plate is to be rocked. Collection: the author

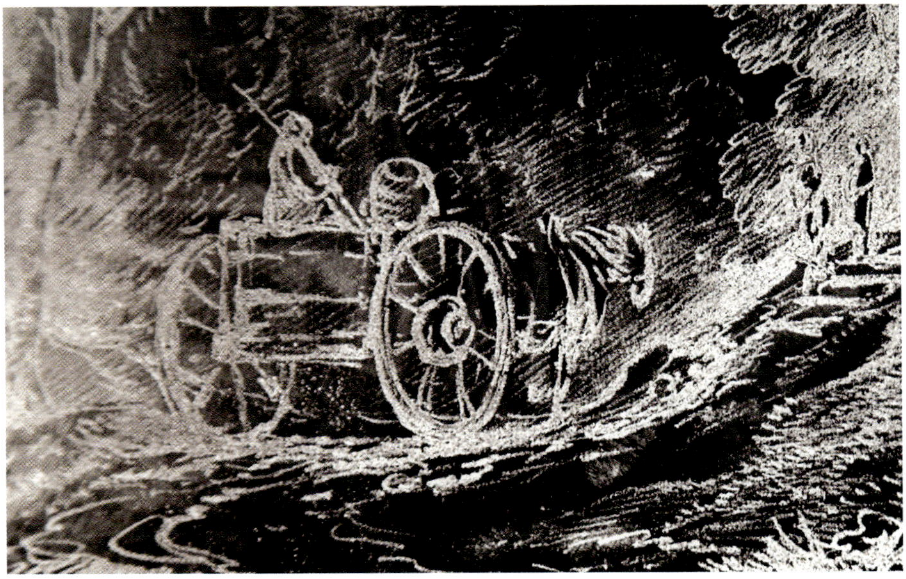

Detail of a copper plate etched in soft ground by Thomas Gainsborough (1727–88). Chalk in the crevices makes clear the crayon-like effect of the line. Collection: Tate Britain

Spitsticker
A wood-engraving tool of elliptical cross section, ideally suited to engraving curved lines.

Steel facing
Electroplating copper with, strictly speaking, iron. The process was first perfected in the early 19th century to protect etched and engraved plates from wear during printing. Drypoints, aquatints and mezzotints are especially prone to premature wear if not faced.

Stipple engraving
A method consisting of making clusters of small pits with a steel point, either directly into copper or through a wax ground for subsequent biting.

Stopping out
Protecting with mordant-resisting varnish those parts of an intaglio plate that have been judged sufficiently bitten. This allows progressive biting: lines that must remain delicate being stopped out early; those to be strong left unprotected longest.

Tiling
Computer terminology: literally, tiling a surface with images or with one large image produced in many sections.

Tint tool
A steel tool used in wood engraving to produce fine parallel lines which, when printed, give the impression of continuous tone.

Tusche
An ink emulsion used in lithography.

Touching proofs
Disguising small blemishes in otherwise perfect impressions.

Tympan
A device attached to a lithography or relief-printing press to protect the paper as it lies on the stone, plate or block during printing. In lithography it takes the form of a frame bearing a thin sheet of brass; in relief printing the frame usually carries sheets of strong paper or sailcloth. The tympan is particularly important in the case of a lithography hand press, in which it intervenes between the paper and the scraper bar, which provides the pressure.

Viscosity method
S.W. Hayter devised and propagated a method of colour printing intaglio plates by using inks of different viscosity and rollers of different degrees of hardness to enable a range of colours each to be applied to the varying shallow levels of a plate so that only a single passage through the rolling press was needed to produce the fully chromatic print.

A.D.

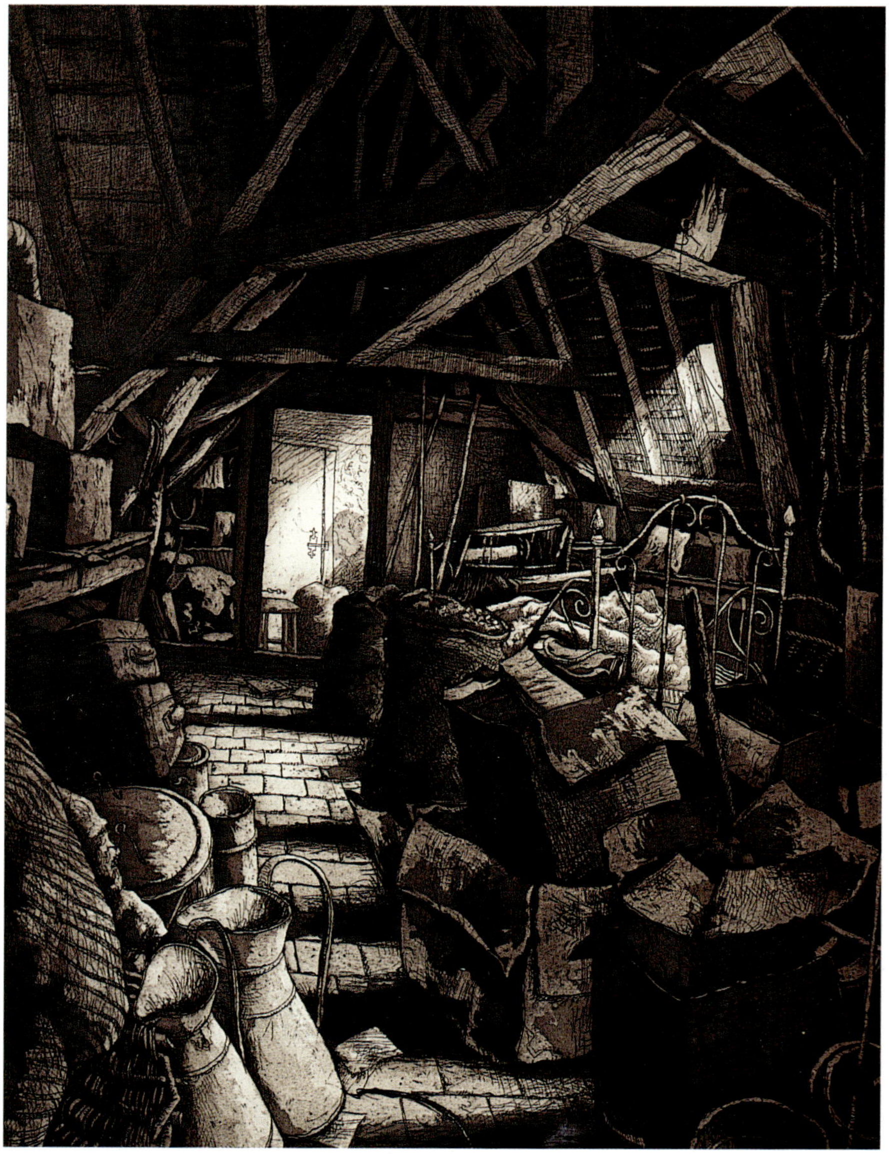

Into the Attic, Anthony Dyson, 2004. Etching and aquatint, 40 x 30 cm (15 ¾ x 11 ¾ in.)

Index